Home Gardening Wisdom

Home Gardening Wisdom

Dick and Jan Raymond

GARDEN WAY ✿ PUBLISHING
CHARLOTTE, VERMONT 05445

Illustrations by Elayne Sears and Lynn Severance

Printed in the United States
First Printing, March 1982

This material was originally published in 1978 by *Gardens for All, Inc.*

Library of Congress Cataloging in Publication Data

Raymond, Dick.
  Home gardening wisdom.

  Includes index.
  1. Vegetable gardening.   2. Vegetables.   3. Cookery
(Vegetables)   I. Raymond, Jan.   II. Title.   III. Title:
Home gardening wisdom.
SB321.R34   635   82-3050
ISBN 0-88266-265-1   AACR2

Contents

v

CHAPTER 1

Corn

Corn is authentically American. A member of the grass family, it was first domesticated from a wild grain by Aztec and Mayan Indians several thousand years ago in Mexico and Central America. The first corn was a loose-podded variety that looked like the seed head at the top of wheat stalks. The kernels were very small, each one covered by a hull. The Central and South American people came to depend so heavily on corn — maize, as they called it — they devised some of the earliest calendars just to keep track of their corn planting and harvesting schedules.

Eventually, corn's popularity spread to North America. By the time the first European settlers arrived on this continent, corn was the chief food crop of the native Indians. The colonists quickly learned how to grow corn, and they enthusiastically adopted the new staple. In fact, much of the early fighting that took place between the settlers and the Indians was over corn fields. The stakes were high: losing a corn field meant losing your food supply. Winning a cleared field gave you a head start in preparing for the long winter.

Back then, people raised what's now called field corn. Some corn was eaten fresh, but most of the harvest was cooked in fried cakes, breads and puddings, dried for winter storage or ground into cornmeal and corn flour. Field corn was also used for livestock feed as it is today. Sweet corn varieties weren't developed until the 1700's. Although many travelers took corn seed back to Europe, it never really caught on as a major food crop the way it did here.

Over the years, cross pollination during cultivation caused genetic changes which transformed corn into the shape and size we now know. Today, corn is still more popular in this country than anywhere else in the world. There are thousands of strains of corn, with more than 200 varieties of sweet corn alone.

Varieties

All the varieties can be divided into a few basic groups: field corn, sweet corn, popcorn and ornamental corn. Much of the corn grown in America's "Corn Belt" is field corn that is either made into corn meal or flour, used as silage for beef and dairy cattle, or processed for use in industrial products.

There are many varieties of field corn; some are favorites of gardeners and farmers who eat them as "roastin' ears." These can be "dent" corn or "flint" corn that can also be dried and ground for homemade meal. Flint corn has a hard-shelled kernel, and it does well in the cooler climates of New England and Canada. Dent corn is also somewhat hard-shelled, but the top of the kernel forms a characteristic dented shape when the ears are mature.

Popcorn is another hard-shelled variety that is grown both commercially and in home gardens. It contains extremely hard starch that expands when heated until the kernel pops.

Kernel texture, shape and flavor are often governed by the starch and sugar content, and this differs with each variety. These variations are exactly what make our favorite garden corn varieties the soft-shelled, moist and sweet-tasting ones; that's why they're known as sweet corn.

Whether you're raising field corn, popcorn or sweet corn, it all grows basically the same way. Once the seed or kernel is planted in an inch or two of soil, it germinates in five to twelve days, depending on the variety and the temperature. Corn won't germinate if the soil temperature is below 50° F. It germinates fastest in soil that's 68° to 86°F.

After the seed sprouts, it sends down a taproot and starts to develop its first leaves. These leaves resemble blades of grass when they first come up.

As it grows, corn develops a thick, fibrous stalk and many flat, pointed leaves. The stalk can grow as tall as fifteen feet, depending on the climate and variety. The roots of each plant grow down three to five feet and extend about a foot or so to each side of the stalk. Some of the roots develop above the ground. These are called "prop roots," and they serve as natural supports for the tall stalks.

When the stalk reaches about two-thirds its full height, its reproductive process starts. The plant first develops straw-colored tassels near the top. These are the "male" flowers of the plant. About three days after corn tassels, the silks or stigma of the "female" flowers appear lower on the stalk. These long, thread-like silks develop from the newly formed ears of corn. Each silk corresponds to a single kernel within the ear, and each kernel must be pollinated in order to have a completely filled ear. The tassels contain pollen that falls down and is carried to the silks by the wind. The tassels produce much more pollen than will ever be needed, and the silks flutter about in the wind to catch drifting pollen. The surface of each silk has tiny hair-like receptors to hold the pollen once it lands. It then travels down the silk to the kernel area,

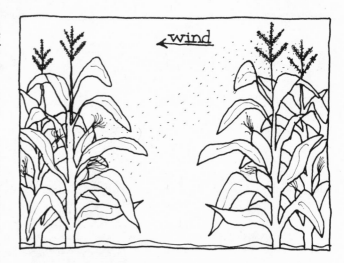

where fertilization occurs. Although it's possible for a corn plant to fertilize itself, the pollen usually travels to the silks of neighboring plants. To ensure complete fertilization, it's best to plant corn in several short rows or blocks rather than long, narrow rows.

Even with nature's added insurance, pollination can be hampered by weather and soil conditions. That's why some ears may be completely filled while others may not.

Each corn plant generally produces one or two ears, except for special multi-eared varieties. Once pollination takes place, the kernels begin to develop on each cob. It usually takes about three weeks from silking for the first ears to be ready to harvest. The weather plays a big part here. The kernels develop fastest in hot weather if there's plenty of water. If it's too cool or too dry, the harvest will be delayed.

The next stages of corn's growth determine the flavor and texture of the kernel. Here you have a great deal of control, since it's often just the timing of the harvest that counts.

Newly formed corn kernels are full of liquid or "milk." The milk stage doesn't last long in most varieties, since the plant's natural goal is to convert that sweet liquid into starch. (If the seed were allowed to continue its life cycle, the starch would be stored and used later as food to sustain the new plant.)

However, the milk stage is the peak harvest time for sweet corn, and gardeners who can successfully judge their corn's growing progress are well rewarded.

If corn is not harvested during the milk stage, the starch-making process goes ahead, and the inside of each corn kernel becomes more solid, losing its sweet taste. This is called the "dough" stage.

The final stage of kernel development occurs if we leave the stalks unharvested or if we dry them for winter storage. Sweet corn seeds become wrinkled and transparent as the natural starches eventually lose their water content.

PLANNING

Choosing Varieties

If you've never grown corn before, check with a local farm or garden store, a neighbor who raises corn, or your Cooperative Extension Service Agent before you buy seeds. They can tell you what varieties do particularly well in your area, as well as some of the disease, pest or weather problems you may encounter.

When asking for advice, keep in mind that gardeners are often emotionally attached to their favorites. For instance, I always plant **Silver Queen** corn, even though I have to wait nearly all summer long to harvest the first, creamy white ears. That waiting is part of what makes **Silver Queen** special, and the long-awaited fall harvest is one of life's fine pleasures. I know you'll find other folks who feel the same about **Country Gentleman, Trucker's Favorite** or **Stay Sweet.**

Sweet corn varieties are usually grouped according to the length of their growing season. You can really extend your harvest by planting more than one variety at the same time.

Common Sense & Cross Pollination

You may come upon words of caution in a seed catalogue or have another gardener tell you to isolate certain types of corn to avoid cross-pollination. It's true that corn's dependence on the wind for pollination means you sometimes have to watch out for accidental mixing of different varieties, but in most home gardens this is a minor problem, if it's a problem at all.

The technical explanation for the way corn changes when it's pollinated by another variety has to do with "recessive" and "dominant" genes plus a number of other factors. Luckily, you don't have to be a plant breeder to understand how to keep your garden corn from having an unwanted mix-up. You can just use common sense.

When one type of corn tassels—letting its pollen loose—that pollen can land on the silks of any corn in the immediate area. If only one variety of corn is silking, which is the case in most gardens—different varieties planted in one garden usually have different flowering and growing seasons—crossing cannot take place.

If two similar varieties cross, the difference in the resulting ears may be unnoticeable. However, because

of their genetic make-up, some types of corn suffer if they cross with a stronger or "dominant" variety.

There are three instances where this can be a concern in the home garden. First, yellow corn is dominant over white. If a yellow and a white variety cross, the white corn could end up with some yellow kernels. Because it's dominant, yellow corn wouldn't be affected by the cross.

Second, both popcorn and field corn have genes that are dominant over sweet corn. If a cross takes place with either popcorn or field corn and sweet corn, the sweet corn is likely to be tough and starchy. Again, because they're dominant, popcorn or field corn wouldn't be affected by the cross.

Third, many of the genes for extra-sweet flavor are recessive, so they're affected by any corn that crosses with them. That's why the seed companies advise isolating these varieties.

Isolating just means preventing an unwanted cross, and you have a choice of ways to do this. All you have to do is prevent the condition needed for cross-pollination. Simply plan to keep different varieties of corn that enter the tassel and silk stage at the same time far enough apart so that their pollens will not mix.

One way to isolate corn is to choose varieties with different length growing seasons if you want to plant them at the same time. You can also stagger plantings of varieties that have a similar number of days to maturity. Allow at least ten days between plantings, and your crops shouldn't cross.

Another trick is to plant the dominant corn on the prevailing *downwind* side of any variety that will suffer if they cross. If you're not sure in which direction the prevailing winds blow in your area, check with your local weather service.

If you have the room, you can isolate corn by planting varieties far enough apart so their pollens have no chance of crossing. The recommendations vary from 100 feet to 600 feet, depending on whom you ask. Naturally, the farther apart the better, but it seems that about 200 feet works fine unless you have generally very strong winds.

Some gardeners have told me that planting a "fence" of two rows of tall sunflowers between corn varieties is enough to prevent cross pollination. I'm sure that in many cases it would be, since the odds are generally in your favor when it comes to accidental crossing.

Old Favorites

An open-pollinated corn variety is a non-hybrid or a strain that has grown for many generations without plant breeders' modifications. There are only a few of these varieties that are easy to get today — **Country Gentleman, Golden Bantam, Trucker's Favorite** — but the seed companies continue to grow them to be sure there will always be seed available.

Since open-pollinated corn grows just like its parent plants, you can save the seed from one year to the next with good results. In fact, during the Depression, when we didn't have money to buy sweet corn seed each year, we kept the seed from the best ears of our **Country Gentleman** corn to plant the next season.

If you want to save the seeds of an open-pollinated variety, isolate the crop from other varieties, so there won't be an accidental mixing of pollens to affect the next generation.

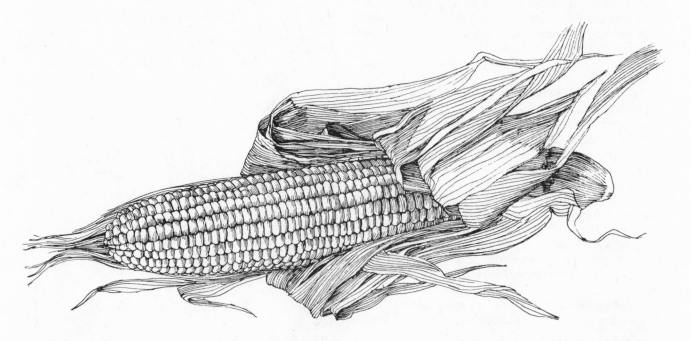

CORN VARIETIES

Variety—All hybrids unless indicated by (o)	Days to Maturity	Color	Length of ear	Comments
Polar Vee	53	Y	6-6½"	Does well in cool climates.
Earlivee (BW)	55	Y	7"	Dependable early producer.
Spancross	58	Y	7"	I heartily recommend this dependable, early variety.
Golden Midget	60	Y	4"	Space-saving plant for small gardens or tub planting.
Black Mexican (o)	62	W	7"	Open-pollinated, very hardy corn; ears are white in edible stage and turn blue-black when mature.
Early Sunglow	62	Y	7"	Early vigor in cool temperatures.
Silver Sweet	65	W	6"	Bright purple husks.
Sugar and Gold	67	Y & W	6-6½"	Tender, sweet ears produced on short plants. Ideal if you have a short growing season.
Early Extra Sweet	70	Y	7-9"	Isolate or stagger other corn plantings for best production. Holds sweetness up to 48 hours after harvest.
Butter and Sugar	73	Y & W	8"	Successive plantings every two weeks yield a steady crop of delicious ears; dependable producer.
Gurney's Mini-Max	77	Y	8½-9"	New variety designed to produce large ears on short plants.
Golden Bantam (o)	80	Y	5½-6½"	Open-pollinated variety; ears mature over a two to three week period.
Hybrid Truckers Favorite	75	W	9"	Large ears; good for eating fresh, roasting or freezing.
Quicksilver	75	W	7-7½"	Early white variety bred for its similarity to Silver Queen.
Seneca Chief (BW)	83	Y	8½-9'	Smooth, tight husks are resistant to insect attacks.
Reid's Yellow Dent (o)	85	Y	9"	Well adapted to southern soil and weather conditions. Good roasting variety.
Iochief	85	Y	9-10"	Strong stalks are wind and drought resistant; heavy yielder.
Illini X-tra Sweet	85	Y	8"	Needs warm soil for germination. Stays quite sweet up to 48 hours after harvest. Freezes well.
Golden Cross Bantam (BW)	85	Y	7½-8"	Good all purpose variety for main crop. Large kernels, good flavor.
Mainliner EH	88	Y	8-9"	A late, extra-sweet variety whose kernels retain their sugar content for a long time after harvest. It does *not* have to be isolated from other sweet corn.
Candystick	90	Y	9"	Slender ear especially good for freezing on the cob.
Bi-Queen (BW, SB)	92	Y & W	8½"	Disease resistance makes this two-colored variety good for southern gardens.
Silver Queen (BW)	92	W	8-9"	My favorite! Sweet, slender ears; good for freezing. Resists disease and drought well.
Country Gentleman (o)	92	W	7-8"	Open-pollinated variety. Irregular kernel arrangement. Good for cream-style corn.
White Cloud Popcorn	95	W	5"	Tall, sturdy plants with high yield of early, hulless, pearl-white kernels. Good flavor.
Popcorn-Purdue 410	105	W	5"	Heavy yielder; large cream-colored kernels have good popping action.
Strawberry Ornamental Popcorn	105	Red	2"	Small, strawberry-shaped cobs; double purpose—good for popping or decoration.
Rainbow Ornamental	110	Multi	8-9"	Colorful, festive, decorative corn for fall arrangements. Good roadside stand item.
Tennessee Red Cob	100	W	9"	Southern favorite for roasting. Large, deep-grained ears set on red cobs.

Key

Color

Y = Yellow
W = White

Disease Resistance

(BW) = Stewart's Bacterial Wilt
(SB) = Southern and Northern leaf blight
(o) = open pollinated

GETTING STARTED

Soil and Site

Corn likes soil that is rich and has good drainage. Ideal soil for corn is sandy loam that stays moist, without being too wet.

The fastest way to improve less-than-perfect soil is to add plenty of organic matter (leaves, compost, grass clippings and crop residues). If your soil is too sandy, organic matter will help it retain nutrients and moisture, which are vital to corn. If you have heavy clay soil, organic matter will wedge between the soil's tightly compacted particles to loosen it and improve its drainage.

Corn has the same needs as most vegetables when it comes to soil pH (acidity or alkalinity). The best range for all vegetables is between 5.8 and 6.8 on the scale that measures pH. This measurement indicates that soil is slightly acidic, since the scale runs from 0 to 14, with 7 marking the neutral point. Anything below 7 is acid; anything above is considered alkaline. Contact your local Extension Service to have your soil tested every few years to be sure the pH is at an acceptable level. To raise or lower your soil's pH, you add lime or sulphur, and specific amounts are usually recommended in the test results.

As you're planning your garden, whether on paper or in your head, arrange the corn so it will be in at least four side-by-side rows, to ensure good pollination. Be sure it gets full sun, away from trees that might shade it.

Since corn is tall, it can shade shorter crops, so plant it on the north or east side of the garden.

If you're growing corn for the first time, you may need to enlarge your existing garden.

All you need to "sod bust" or turn a patch of lawn or an overgrown garden into a productive seedbed is a spade or tiller. Although it's best to break new ground the fall before you want to plant, you can create a new garden in the spring with fairly good results.

If you spade an area by hand, dig in to a depth of eight to ten inches and turn each spadeful of soil bottom-side up. This helps to keep grass from resprouting. Keep working the soil by chopping and stirring it, breaking up the clumps to make it loose and friable.

A tiller will also turn over sod to create a loose, friable seedbed. Till the soil back and forth until the seedbed is worked eight to ten inches deep.

If you've grown corn before in the same garden, change the place where you plant it or "rotate" it every year. This can be tricky if you don't have lots of garden space, but when you rotate corn, you prevent disease and pest problems from recurring. You also keep your garden's natural fertility in balance by moving heavy feeders, like corn, around. If your garden is too small for yearly rotation, rotate it at least every second or third season. If you run into a bad insect or disease problem one year, rotation the following season is a must.

Timing

Corn is a warm weather vegetable that grows best during the long, sunny days of summer.

Because I love the challenge of growing warm season crops earlier than is supposed to be possible here in Vermont, I've discovered some ways to gamble successfully and have very early corn. However, I plant my main crops of mid-season and late corn "by the book" — two weeks before the last expected frost date.

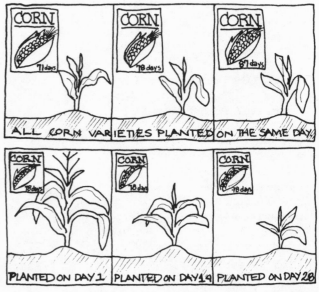

Once the ground is warm enough to plant, to extend the harvest a few weeks stagger your corn plantings. This also prevents accidental cross-pollination of certain varieties.

Time your plantings by checking the days to maturity and counting back from the date you want to begin harvesting. One thing to remember is that the harvest time may vary slightly if the weather is very cool or very warm during the growing season.

Fertilizer - A Fish Story?

Many of us have heard that colonists learned from the Indians to plant each corn kernel on top of a dead fish. This is no "fish story." Decaying fish contain nitrogen, which corn needs for good growth. The Indians and colonists may not have known why it worked, but liked the results so continued to do it.

Because of the need for a steady supply of nitrogen throughout the growing season, corn is called a "heavy feeder." It's only logical that a plant that can grow over six feet tall and produce hundreds of seeds needs lots of food. It's not so much the *amount* of food that matters as the *steady diet* while it's growing. In fact, at planting time, corn needs about the same amount of fertilizer as most other garden vegetables. During the growing season, however, you give corn additional feedings by sidedressing the crop.

There's quite a selection of fertilizers available today, and you should use whichever seems best for your garden and you.

Going along with the notion behind the dead fish of early American times, you can use an organic fertilizer such as well-rotted compost, aged or dehydrated animal manures or concentrated animal or plant extracts, such as blood meal or alfalfa meal. These materials may be available at little or no cost to gardeners in some areas. In other areas they may be pre-packaged and sold at garden stores and the prices can be high. An advantage of these fertilizers is their ability to condition the soil as well as to feed plants. They also provide nutrients over an extended period of time, which helps corn. On the other hand, because their nutrient content may not be known, it's hard to judge exactly how much of some of these materials to use for best corn production.

Many gardeners use a balanced commercial fertilizer such as 10-10-10. The numbers indicate the percentages of nitrogen, phosphorus and potassium (N-P-K), and they're always listed in the same order on the label of each bag of fertilizer. Since corn does best with high amounts of nitrogen, pay special attention to the first number when selecting a commercial fertilizer. It should be equal to or higher than the other two elements listed. Chemical fertilizers are fairly inexpensive, and it's easy to use them in accurately measured amounts.

To achieve the best of both worlds, try combining equal parts of an organic fertilizer such as dehydrated chicken manure or compost and 10-10-10.

You can apply fertilizer at planting time by "broadcasting" or sprinkling fertilizer evenly over a patch of soil, or "band" the fertilizer in the row where your seeds will be planted. Broadcasting makes sense if you want to fertilize a large area in a short time, since you just sprinkle it on and work it into the top three to four inches of soil. It also guarantees fertilizer being available to every seed, although in smaller amounts than if you applied it in a band.

If you broadcast fertilizer, use about four to five pounds per 100 square feet of soil, or a 12-quart pail per 1,000 square feet. Use about four times as much if you are broadcasting bulky organic matter.

Even though broadcasting fertilizer works well, I usually fertilize in bands to make the most efficient use of the plant food. To do this, sprinkle about one to two cups of balanced commercial fertilizer down each ten feet of row. Again, use about four times as much if you're using organic material which has less concentrated amounts of the three key elements. Cover all fertilizer with an inch or two of soil before planting.

Because corn is such an important crop in this country, there have been many studies to determine how to make the best use of fertilizers. As home gardeners, we can benefit from the results of this research.

It's been proven that the best place for fertilizer at planting time is in bands to the side and slightly below the seed. With this placement, the seed can't be burned by the nitrogen in the fertilizer, and the fertilizer is readily available in the soil by the time the taproot starts downward and sideroots start to grow.

Over the years, at corn planting time I have experimented with where I placed the fertilizer — including using none at all. The differences in the harvest don't seem that striking to me, but careful fertilizer placement makes sense if you're trying to make the best use of it.

PLANTING

Once the seedbed is well-worked and fertilized, you're ready to plant. There are two traditional ways to plant corn: three to five seeds grouped together in small circles or "hills" or spaced evenly down straight rows, one behind the other.

I prefer to plant corn in rows. It takes less time, there's usually less thinning needed, and I think it's easier to cultivate rows during the season.

To plant in rows, stake each row the length you want and stretch a string along the ground to mark the planting line. Use the edge of a hoe or the end of its handle to draw a shallow furrow, one to two inches deep, along one side of the string. A handy way to fertilize the row at this time is to draw a second shallow furrow down the other side of the string. Sprinkle a band of fertilizer in this furrow. When it's time to cover the seeds, one pass with a hoe will cover the fertilizer at the same time.

To plant, just drop seeds into the planting furrow, spacing them eight to ten inches apart. Firm the seeds into the soil with the back of a hoe to keep the seeds in place. This allows good contact with the soil, which is important for germination.

Next, cover the seeds with one to one and one-half inches of soil. You can draw the hoe along the string to flatten the ridge of soil created by making the furrow. This automatically brings the planting furrow and the fertilizer furrow to ground level, covering the seeds and fertilizer with the right amount of soil. You can also cover corn seeds by raking one to one and one-half inches of soil over them, using soil from the edges of the furrow.

Firm the soil one more time after covering.

For cultivation leave 24 to 36 inches between the rows, and plant at least four rows for the best pollination. If you intend to weed and cultivate the corn rows with hand tools, you don't need as much room between the rows as you do if you plan to cultivate by machine.

To plant in hills, stake out the rows the same as you would for rows, but don't make the straight-line planting furrow. Instead, every 18 to 24 inches use your hoe to draw a circular planting furrow, about six inches in diameter. Place a small handful of fertilizer to the side of the seeds and cover it. Plant three to five seeds in each circle. Firm the seeds, cover with one to one and a half inches of soil and firm again.

If all the seeds in each hill come up, you'll have to thin out all but the two or three strongest or they'll be too crowded. Since I don't like to thin corn, I don't like to plant in hills. However, there are plenty of gardeners who do. Try planting both ways and decide for yourself.

A Note on Treated Seed

Treated seed is protected with a light coating of a fungicide such as captan or maneb that protects the seed and seedling from "damping-off." Damping-off is caused by fungi that can rot seeds and kill newly emerging seedlings.

Some seed treatments also contain an insecticide such as diazinon which wards off wireworms and root maggots that can invade a young corn crop. If the seed has been treated, it will say so on the seed packet, and the seed surface will be noticeably powdery. The powder is often pink or white.

If you can't find treated seed, you can purchase small amounts of captan or maneb and treat your own seeds before planting. A little captan goes a long way — you only need one-quarter to one-half teaspoon for eight ounces of seed. Place the fungicide right in the seed packet and shake the seeds to coat them.

If you prefer not to use treated seed, check what you're getting before you buy. Some seed companies will send treated seed unless you request otherwise.

Planting Variations

Over the years, I've tried planting corn many different ways. Here are some variations on the basic planting methods you may want to try.

Double rows: Corn can handle a little crowding, so I often plant it in double rows to save space. Double rows are simply two regular rows planted about eight to ten inches apart. The only difference is that double rows need a little more fertilizer.

Double rows are easy to irrigate, especially if you use soaker hoses or drip irrigation for an even water supply. Double rows also increase the chances for good pollination, since the rows are close together. You save space because you can fit four rows into the space of two.

It's a snap to keep the weeds down in double rows, since one swipe down the middle with a narrow hoe or hand weeding takes care of two rows at once. Once the plants have grown some, their leaves will shade the soil between the rows discouraging many weeds.

To plant double rows, stake two planting lines, side by side, about ten inches apart. Stagger plant the seeds ten to twelve inches apart in each of the two rows. Hill planting won't work very well in double rows because the plants will be too crowded.

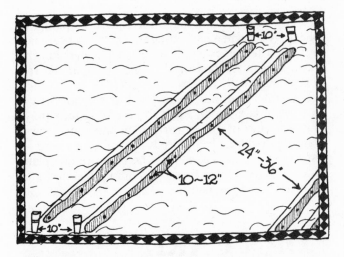

Walkways need to be 24 to 36 inches wide between each set of double rows, just as with single rows.

Furrows: Plant corn in four to six-inch furrows, firming the seeds and covering them with one to one and one-half inches of soil. In a furrow you can plant either in rows or hills. Once the seedlings emerge, I fill in the furrow with another two inches of soil, being careful not to cover up the plants. As the corn grows, hill the soil around the stems by adding another inch or two of soil every week.

Adding soil keeps out weeds and gives added support to the stalks. I find this early soil support anchors the plants and helps them stay upright, even in high winds. By keeping weeds down, corn can grow tall and healthy without competition for food and water. Because the roots are deeper than corn planted on level ground, furrow-planted corn often needs less watering.

Presprouting: Use presprouting to test the germination rate of seed that's over a year old. You can also presprout to have completely germinated early corn.

To sprout seeds or to test germination, fold four paper towels into one. Moisten them and sprinkle the seeds onto the moist towel mat. Even though you're sprouting the seeds indoors, it's a good idea to use treated seed to protect them when they're planted outside.

If you want to presprout all your seeds for planting, sprinkle about 25 to 30 seeds on each paper towel mat, using as many mats as you need.

Roll each mat jelly-roll fashion, being careful the seeds remain evenly spaced. Next, roll each paper towel cylinder into a damp facecloth.

Put the roll-ups in a plastic bag. Don't seal the bag, since air needs to circulate for germination. Place the "seed sprouter" in a warm spot for four to six days. As soon as the seeds germinate, take them out and plant them. Plant sprouted seeds just as you would unsprouted.

If you're just testing germination, you need to use only ten seeds. If seven seeds sprout, you'll have about 70 percent germination for that batch of seeds.

If you sprout seeds to test germination and the results show a rate less than 100 percent, you'll need to plant enough extra seeds to make up the difference. For instance, if the germination rate is 75 percent, plant 33 percent more for a full row or hill.

Transplanting: Although I prefer to plant corn outdoors the traditional "seed into soil" way, some gardeners like to start corn indoors and transplant the young seedlings. The benefits of transplanting are getting an early start and knowing that each of your seeds will produce a corn plant. It can also save space in small gardens because you don't have to take more room to plant extra seed to ensure a good stand. If you plant extra-sweet varieties which often have problems germinating, transplanting can avoid some of them.

If you want to try transplanting corn, sow the seeds in individual peat pots or one-inch cubes of sod. Homegrown sod cubes are handy, readily available seed-starters. Plant the seeds on the root side with the grassy side facing downward.

Start seeds four to five weeks before the average last frost date in your area. Give the seedlings plenty of light and regular doses of food and water. When they're established, harden them off for about a week before you want to plant. To harden them off, place them outdoors protected from sun and wind for increasingly long periods of time. In a few days, they can be left out all night, and they're ready for planting in a week to ten days. Plant each seedling in well-worked soil.

Raised Beds: A raised bed is mounded up garden soil, and some of the best corn I've harvested is from

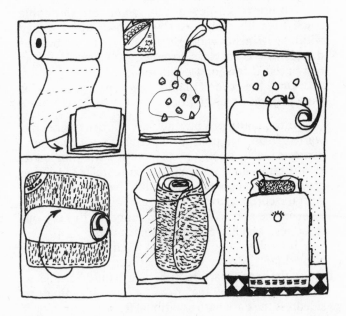

beds raised six to eight inches. Since corn does best in soil that has good drainage, raised beds can provide quite a boost for corn in less than ideal soil. For instance, a patch of land that takes forever to dry in the spring or one that stays wet after each rain is the last place to grow corn. Raised beds with loose soil can counteract those problems. It will dry faster after rain and be ready to plant earlier in the spring.

You can make raised beds anytime the soil is workable. For earlier corn planting in the spring, make them the preceding fall. If you make them in the early spring, the crop will still be able to take advantage of the added soil warmth. Raised beds keep the soil five to ten degrees warmer.

To make a raised bed, work the soil well first. Stake the first row the length and width you want. Then, use a hoe or rake to pull three to four inches of loose soil from the far walkway. Don't walk on the walkway until after you've drawn soil from it. If you do, the earth will pack down making it more difficult. You're actually lowering the walkways at the same time you're raising the bed. If you take three to four inches of soil from the walkway and add it to the bed, the difference will be a six to eight-inch raised bed.

Rake the tops of the beds to smooth them out, then plant as usual. Don't walk on them.

To use raised beds wisely, plant corn in double rows. I usually plant two rows on beds that are rake width or 16 inches wide. By placing two raised beds of double-row corn close together, you have the four rows needed for good pollination.

Once the corn is planted, care for it just as if it were planted on level ground.

Interplanting: You can save garden space and ward off animal pests by interplanting pole beans, winter squash, pumpkins or gourds with your corn. Pole beans climb right up the corn stalks, and vine crops spread between the stalks. Neither interferes with the corn's growth. The dense foliage and prickly vines in the corn rows are also supposed to keep out raccoons, which are pests in some areas.

Interplant vine crop seeds when you plant your corn. Plant in rows or hills between the corn rows. Once the vines start to run, you won't be able to cultivate between the rows. When it's time to sidedress the corn with additional fertilizer, sprinkle it

carefully so it doesn't touch the squash or pumpkin foliage. Also, when harvesting the corn, take care not to step on the vines as this might damage or kill the sensitive plants. Harvest the vine crops in the fall when they're fully mature.

To interplant pole beans, wait until your corn is six to eight inches tall. Plant the beans on the sunny, southern side of the cornfield on the outer rows. Plant two or three beans seeds around every third or fourth corn stalk. Later, thin the beans to one plant for each stalk. Guide them to climb up the corn and harvest both crops as usual.

CORN CARE

Corn doesn't need any more attention than other garden vegetables, but it's a crop that can take up a fair amount of time if you plant a lot. Make it easier by combining tasks. For instance, when you sidedress, pull any weeds you see, or sidedress at the same time you hill the rows.

Weed Control

Like any plant, corn produces better if it doesn't have to compete with weeds. It's especially important to keep weeds out when corn plants are young. Once the stems and leaves are established, they can tolerate weeds better. Plus, the stems and leaves of larger corn plants shade the soil somewhat to block out weeds.

I weed my corn every few weeks, starting before I even plant a seed! Work the soil several times before planting. This not only conditions the soil, it stirs up and kills tiny weed seeds that are lurking near the surface. It also buries some seeds so deeply they never get a chance to sprout.

Once the corn is planted, scratch the surface of the planting bed every week or so with a weeding rake. I designed a tool that works well for this chore called the "In-Row Weeder." Its long, flexible tines break any crust that has formed on the soil surface while eliminating any weeds there. Because of its shape, you can use this weeder right over the tops of plants up to eight inches tall without damaging them.

When corn is tall enough to be hilled, you'll automatically get rid of weeds by covering them with soil as you hill.

Hilling

Hilling is pulling up soil to mound it around the base of a plant. When you hill a young corn plant, the added soil around its stem helps support it as it grows taller. This protects it from being blown over in a strong wind. To really anchor plants, it's a good idea to hill corn every two to three weeks until the plants start to tassel.

Hilling also covers and smothers any weeds around the base of your corn plants. You might say you're creating a "soil mulch" around your plants. If dryness is a problem, extra soil helps the corn roots retain moisture.

You can hill with a hoe by scooping a few inches of soil from the walkways into loose mounds on both sides of the corn. I usually hill my corn by machine, using a tiller with a special hilling attachment. This is not only faster and easier than using a hoe, it also does a uniform job.

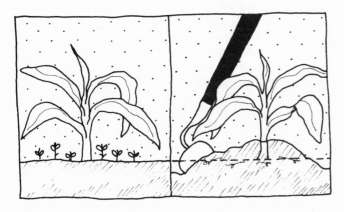

Sidedressing

The more you feed corn, the more it will feed you, so "sidedressing" is a must with corn. Sidedressing is a second dose of fertilizer that boosts growth.

You can use any high nitrogen fertilizer to sidedress corn, since nitrogen is the plant nutrient needed. I use a commercial fertilizer such as 10-10-10, but you can also use well-composted or dehydrated manure.

Sidedress corn twice: when it's knee high and when it tassels. To sidedress, sprinkle a thin line of fertilizer or manure about four inches from the plants on both sides of each row of corn. To sidedress hill-planted corn, simply sprinkle fertilizer around each hill, about four inches away from the corn stalks. It often helps to make a shallow furrow first for either rows or hills. The furrow serves as a guide and the indentation helps the fertilizer stay put.

If you sidedress shortly before it rains, you're lucky. Otherwise, you should water, so the fertilizer leaches into the soil where it can be taken up by the corn roots.

Water

Corn doesn't need more water than other vegetables. It just suffers more if the supply runs short. Since the plants are relatively tall and exposed to the wind and drying heat of summer, they often "transpire" or give off moisture faster than their roots can take it up.

Corn's need for water is most critical from the time it tassels until the ears are ready for harvest. At this time the plant is devoting all its energy to seed production holding nothing in reserve for a dry spell. During its growing season, corn needs at least an inch of water per week. If it has to go through a dry stretch, it may not produce well. Use a rain gauge to keep track of weekly rainfall. If your garden receives less than an inch of rain in a week, water.

When you water, water thoroughly. If you're using an overhead sprinkler, use your rain gauge to determine how long it takes to deliver an inch of water. Or, simply water until the soil feels moist three to five inches down, depending on your soil type. (Sandy soil absorbs water faster than clay.) One sign of too little water is the corn leaves curling or rolling. If you want healthy, sweet, well-filled ears, pay close attention to the weather at the tail end of the season and water if your corn needs it.

If you have the equipment, it's most efficient to water corn with a soaker hose or use furrow irrigation. A soaker hose is made of a material such as perforated canvas that lets water seep out slowly. If you water directly from a hose or bucket into a furrow, it accomplishes the same beneficial watering at the base of the plant. With these watering methods, less water is lost to evaporation than if you use an overhead sprinkler. The water doesn't end up on the leaves of tall corn plants, instead it's near the roots where it's really needed.

How to Have the Earliest Corn

I like to have corn that's "shoulder high by the Fourth of July," and you can easily beat that date if you live farther south. The advantage of early corn really pays off if you want to sell corn at a roadside stand. Choose an early variety; I like **Spancross, Early Sunglow** and **Sugar 'n Gold.** Plan to plant four to six weeks before the last frost date in your area. It's a good idea to use treated seed to prevent damping-off and other diseases.

The key to growing early corn is to plant in a garden spot where no organic matter, manures or fertilizers have been added recently and use *no* fertilizer at planting time. These materials can cause early-planted seed to rot in the soil or the seedlings to be too tender to survive cool temperatures.

Plant the seed about one and one-half to two inches deep—a little deeper than usual. If you want to, you can cover the rows with a plastic tunnel for extra heat or with chicken wire to protect the seeds from birds.

The seeds may take longer to come up than you'd expect. That's because they can't germinate in soil that's too cool. But after the first hot sunny spring day, you'll see them shoot up and take off.

When the seedlings are eight to ten inches high, give them their first dose of fertilizer. Sidedress with a balanced fertilizer and then water. Sidedress again when the plants are knee-high, and give a third nutrient boost when they tassel. Soon afterward you'll have the first local corn.

Under-Cover Corn

As a heat-loving plant, corn is easily set back during a cold spell, especially immediately after planting. Some gardeners like to protect their corn seeds and seedlings from cold weather by covering their rows or hills with plastic sheets or hot caps. This is one way to guarantee an early harvest of your early corn, but I find that it's more work than it's worth.

An easier solution for me against the threat of cold weather is to plant early corn deeper and use no fertilizer. If a corn seedling is zapped by cold weather, as long as the plant is less than 12 inches high, it will usually recover and start growing again. This is due to the location of corn's "growing point," the place where new growth begins.

Every vegetable plant has a growing point, and a frost-sensitive plant can be killed if its growing point is hit by a freeze. Luckily, in the first weeks of growth, corn's growing point lies below the soil surface, protected from frost. Although it eventually reaches the soil surface and grows above it, this doesn't happen until the corn plant is about a foot tall—about 21 days after planting, and that's quite a frost-beating edge. Naturally, if you fertilize, the plant will grow faster and be susceptible to frost that much sooner.

If you are planting early, relax for the first three weeks after planting. Mother Nature is providing the vital frost protection corn needs.

Mulch

Many gardeners mulch their corn to prevent weeds and to keep the soil moist. I don't recommend mulching, since you'd need quite a load of mulch material—hay, straw, leaves, peat moss, etc.—to take care of a good stand of corn. As long as you give corn a steady supply of food and water, it really doesn't require much other care.

Thinning

If you plant corn in hills or plant the rows too thickly, you'll have to thin out some plants to make sure the others have enough room to grow. Thin when the seedlings are about four inches tall.

The best time to thin is after a rain when the plants have dried but the soil is still moist. The plants pull easily from the soil without disturbing neighboring seedlings.

To thin, just pull up enough plants so those remaining in the row or hill will be ten inches apart. I crowd my corn a bit—about eight inches apart—and it does fine, but if you're just getting the hang of raising corn, give your plants more room.

HARVESTING

The prime harvest time for sweet corn passes quickly, so gardeners need to know how to judge when to pick to get the most from their crop.

Corn is ready to be picked as soon as the ears have completely filled out. This goes for sweet corn and "roastin' ears." You can tell when this happens by feeling the end of an ear. If it's rounded or blunt rather than pointed, the ears are ready. The silks also dry up when the ears are almost ready to be picked.

If you don't trust your judgment, you can pull back a bit of the husk and check to see if the ear looks well filled and the kernels are creamy yellow or white. Many gardening guides tell you to pierce a kernel with your thumbnail to test for ripeness. If the liquid inside is watery, that ear isn't quite ready. If the liquid is white or "milky," you're in business.

Although opening the husk is a fairly sure test, I don't like to do this because if you open an immature ear, it's susceptible to insect and bird attacks as it continues to ripen. I find that it takes only a little practice to become a good judge by feeling the ends of the ears.

If you have a choice, it's a good idea to harvest corn as close to the time you're going to eat or use it as possible. In fact, we often have the water boiling for corn-on-the-cob before we head out to harvest.

To harvest sweet corn, grab an ear and twist it down and off the stalk.

If you're interested in the sweetest corn possible, try to harvest each ear at its peak. Keep in mind that the natural conversion of sugar into starch isn't cut short when you harvest. It may even be speeded up. The moment you pick an ear of sweet corn, its sugars start to change into starches because the natural goal is to nourish seed for reproduction. In 24 hours, most varieties convert over half their sugar content.

The loss of sugar is much slower at lower temperatures, so refrigerate corn if you are not going to be able to eat it right away.

If you're not near a refrigerator and you have some harvested corn, keep the freshly picked ears in single layers, rather than stacking them. Corn tends to overheat inside its tight husks, so give each ear as much "breathing room" as possible. It also helps to cover the ears with a damp cloth.

Extra-sweet varieties have been developed so they take quite a long time to convert their natural sugar into starch, which makes them last longer on the stalk, and helps them retain their flavor for a few days once harvested. Many seed catalogues claim they are "twice as sweet at harvest time as ordinary hybrids, and four times sweeter after 48 hours." It's sweeter than ordinary corn would be after two days, because it doesn't convert its sugar to starch as rapidly.

Some people prefer corn that's less sweet, with more texture in each kernel. They take advantage of the natural conversion process and don't harvest it until it's somewhat "doughy" from the increased starch content. They may also wait a day or two to serve it after picking.

If you want to store corn over the winter or grind your own corn meal, give it time to harden completely. This means it has passed through its entire carbohydrate production cycle. It will then contain such heavy starch that it will be too hard to bite and it will keep for many months in storage.

Popcorn Pointers

The only way growing popcorn differs from growing sweet corn is at harvest time, and popcorn is actually easier to harvest. You don't have to worry about catching it at the peak of sweetness; you leave popcorn in the garden until the stalks and husks are brown and dry. Popcorn is picked like sweet corn, by twisting and snapping each ear from the stalk. You do this before the frost hits. To prepare popcorn for indoor curing, carefully strip away the dried husk from each ear. The kernels are partially dried or "cured," a necessity for long-term storage.

In addition to drying on the stalks, popcorn requires another four to six weeks of thorough drying in a warm, well-ventilated place. Corn can't pop unless there is the right amount of moisture inside the kernel. When it's heated, the moisture turns to steam, which causes the kernel to burst.

Place the ears in mesh bags or spread them out in an area where they'll have warm air circulating around them. We hang mesh bags full of popcorn ears in our carport where they can cure for about four weeks. After curing, I usually hang the bags of corn from the rafters of our root cellar. The corn can keep for years in the cool, dry, dark conditions there.

The kernels can be taken off the ears after a month of curing and stored in airtight jars.

Whether you're taking off the kernels before storage or just before popping, there's no real trick to it. Simply grasp the ear firmly in both hands and twist

until they drop out. Once the ear is started, the kernels drop off with very little pressure. Beware of the sharply pointed kernels if you're using your bare hands. After two or three ears, you may have a few nicks and scratches. If you want to remove the kernels from a lot of ears, it might be a good idea to wear gloves.

Popcorn doesn't take much garden space for a sizeable harvest. Each ear is loaded with tiny kernels come harvest time, and three or four rows about five feet long each should be plenty. Since many popcorn varieties produce one or two ears per plant, you may have enough by growing five or six plants.

When we harvested popcorn recently, we ended up with one and one-half cups of kernels from six ears. The ears were three to five inches long. From the six ears, we had over 20 cups of nice, white popped corn.

Pop home-grown popcorn just as you would store-bought. Heat a few tablespoons of oil in a deep pot or popcorn popper. Sprinkle enough kernels to cover the bottom and cover the pot. If you're using a popcorn popper, follow the manufacturer's instructions. If not, as soon as you hear the first kernel pop, shake the covered pot vigorously while the rest pops. Shaking prevents the kernels from burning, and the unpopped kernels stay on the bottom nearest the heat.

When the popping stops, remove the pot from the heat and take off the lid to let the steam escape. The popcorn is ready. Most folks like to add a generous sprinkling of salt and some melted butter, but it's also good plain.

DISEASES & PESTS

Most of the trouble gardeners have with corn can easily be controlled. Diseases aren't much of a problem, and insects can easily be kept in check. Birds and four-footed visitors who want to share your corn harvest can be kept out with any number of scare-off devices and fences. Prevention is 100 percent of the cure. Check regularly to catch trouble before it starts and you'll have healthy corn. Healthy vegetables can withstand nibbling or insect damage better than weakened ones. In many cases, a crop that's healthy will often be spared disease and insect attack altogether.

One of the most important steps you can take for disease-free corn is to clean up all the corn stalks as soon as the harvest is over. I like to till my healthy corn stalks into the soil as additional organic matter, but you may prefer to compost or simply discard yours. Dealing with them will prevent many diseases and insects from overwintering, which is crucial to the health of crops grown in future seasons.

Diseases
Here are the most common corn diseases, and the best preventions against them.

Stewart's bacterial wilt can affect sweet corn at any stage, but is most harmful to young plants. Causes dwarfing and wilting of the plant, and tassels often develop early and die without completing pollination. Leaves develop yellow-brown streaks and wavy edges. In young plants the leaves may dry out, and the stem eventually dies. Often characterized by a yellow slime on inner husks and in stem. The bacteria winters over in corn flea beetles. This disease is prevalent after a mild winter, when more disease-carrying flea beetles have survived. To prevent, clean up all crop residues, rotate corn each year, plant resistant varieties and control corn flea beetles.

Root Rot is caused by fungi in the soil and shows up as stunted plants or irregular plants with rotten roots. Can be caused by planting seed in cold, damp soil. To prevent, use treated seed and plant on raised beds if soil drainage is a problem.

Corn smut is caused by soil fungi. It is an unpleasant looking, but not disastrous condition that can strike corn anywhere. In the early stages, grayish-white, spongy growths called "galls" usually appear on the corn ear or tassel. As these galls ripen, they turn black and eventually burst open releasing powdery spores that spread the smut. The disease thrives in hot, dry weather and often infects weak or injured plants first. To prevent, rotate crop. As soon as you notice any galls, pick them and burn them before they blacken and burst. This will halt the smut's spread and is often all it takes to keep the disease in check from one season to the next.

Southern corn leaf blight - This disease reached epidemic proportions in 1970 and wiped out 15 percent of the total United States corn crop, for an estimated loss of one billion dollars. Caused by fungi, it is characterized by tan streaks or lesions on the leaves, may cause early seedling death, mold-covered kernels or rotted cobs. A similar disease, northern corn leaf blight, results in grayish-green or tan lesions on the leaves and reduced yields. The fungi over-

winter in infected seed and plant debris. Plant resistant varieties, using healthy, fungicide-treated seed. Rotate crops and remove or till under crop debris. If disease has been severe in your area, check with your local Extension Agent for a preventive fungicide program.

Insects
Here's a rundown of the insects that affect corn, along with the best control measures for the home gardener.

Corn earworm - One- to two-inch long worm, ranging from light green to purplish brown. This same insect attacks tomatoes and cotton, and also is known as the tomato fruitworm and cotton bollworm.

Moth lays eggs on corn plant and larva feeds first on the silk, then on the kernels at the tip of each ear. It can prevent pollination or open kernels to fungus invasion. To discourage, select varieties with tightly closed husks. It can be controlled somewhat by squirting mineral oil into each ear after silks have started to dry, using half a medicine dropper per ear. Plant and silks can also be sprayed with Dipel or Sevin. If earworm damage occurs, you can clip off the tip of the ear and any affected kernels. The rest of the ear should be fine to eat.

European corn borer - Inch-long tan or brown caterpillar with rows of dark brown spots and a dark brown head. The moths fly mostly at night and lay eggs on the undersides of corn leaves. The hatched larvae bore into corn stalks and ears to feed. Broken tassels, bent stalks and "sawdust" around corn are all signs of borer damage. If you catch it in time, you can often cut out the borer from the stalk with no permanent damage. Spray with carbaryl (Sevin) or diazinon at five-day intervals from the time you first spot borer activity or when the tassels begin appearing. Make at least two applications for best results. Be sure to till or spade under crop residues at the end of the season, so the borer has no place to winter.

Corn sap beetles - Small, black beetles whose maggot-like larvae eat into the kernels of roasting corn. Larvae are whitish, up to one-quarter inch long. To prevent, plant resistant varieties and clean up all crop residues. To control, spray plants with malathion six days after silks appear. Spray again in ten days.

Southern corn rootworms - Small, yellowish grubs, larvae of the spotted cucumber beetle. Weaken corn plants by feeding on roots, causing the stalks to blow over easily in wind or heavy rain. Adults lay eggs around roots of cornstalks in the fall. The eggs hatch in the spring. You can avoid damage from corn rootworms by tilling under cornstalks and rotating crops each year. Control spotted cucumber beetles with carbaryl (Sevin) or malathion.

Corn root aphid – Tiny, light-green insects that feed on corn roots, causing plants to be stunted and yellowed. These aphids overwinter in the nests of cornfield ants. The best way to control corn root aphids is to plow the garden in the fall, destroying ant nests.

Corn flea beetles – Small, black, jumping beetles, about one-sixteenth inch long, that chew corn foliage and transmit Stewart's bacterial wilt. Beetles abound during cool, wet periods and after mild winters. They hibernate in weeds and plant debris over the winter, so keep garden and surrounding areas clean. Many of the later, white corn varieties are resistant to wilt. To repel flea beetles, sprinkle plants and soil with a light dusting of wood ashes. To control flea beetles, spray plants with carbaryl (Sevin) or malathion.

Wireworm – Slender, yellowish or brown larvae of click beetles, one-half to one and one-half inches long, they resemble a jointed wire and damage corn plants by feeding on the roots. Most often present in newly worked sod. Rotate crops and till or spade garden thoroughly in the fall. Heavy infestations may require chemical soil treatment before planting, but do so only under the advice and supervision of your local Cooperative Extension Agent.

Seed corn maggots – Cream-colored, legless larvae about one-half inch long that bore into sprouting seeds and prevent further growth. When early corn is planted in cool, wet soil, the slower germination makes the seeds more susceptible to maggot attack. Use treated seed or plant in warm weather if maggots are a problem in your area.

start their tales of raccoon damage with the words, "The night before we were going to pick the first, ripe, sweet corn..."

When you lose ripening sweet corn to raccoon raiders, you swear they were on hand at planting time reading your seed packets, jotting down the days to harvest, and keeping track of the time back in the woods. Actually, the raccoons are attracted by the smell of the sweet corn tassels.

There are many old-time tricks to keep raccoons out of the corn patch, but only one rule: Put your defense in action *before* the raccoons can set one foot in your garden. Once a raccoon—or any other animal—has a taste of your sweet corn, it will be almost impossible to keep him (or her) out.

To protect sweet corn, I now use the ultimate defense: a three-foot chicken wire fence topped by an electrical wire. A few years ago, I was like many other gardeners, still trying to find the best, least expensive home defense.

Other things I've had good luck with—before the electric fence—included spreading moth crystals between corn rows at each edge of the garden. The raccoons don't like the taste of the crystals on their paws. I never had to use them down the entire row—just working the edges seemed to do the job. I used one or two boxes of crystals each season and sprinkled them lightly after each rain or cultivation. I don't recommend moth balls because children might think they are candy.

If you have tall grass around the garden, sprinkle it with a little kerosene. Raccoons don't like getting the oily substance on their fur. However, kerosene can be tricky because too much will kill the grass.

Some folks have successfully discouraged raccoons by keeping a portable radio playing in the cornfield all night. In my garden, this just provided the local raccoons with dinner music!

A careful observer might be able to find the paths that raccoons take to the garden. If so, you can

Uninvited Guests

One of the biggest challenges in growing corn is keeping it for yourself. From the day you plant to the day you are ready to harvest, it seems there's always some "critter" who'd just love to share in the bounty. Fortunately, most of the animals and birds that invade corn can be outwitted. Raccoons are smarter than we'd like them to be, but they, too, can be kept at bay.

Here are some of the best ways I know to keep corn free of uninvited guests. Some of these tricks can solve pest problems in other parts of your garden, too.

Raccoons are well-known for their expertly timed raids on the sweet corn patch. Many people

sprinkle a little creosote along them. Raccoons don't like getting this on them either, and it may discourage them altogether.

Another often-used deterrent is planting a crop such as pole beans, pumpkins or winter squash between the corn rows. Supposedly, raccoons don't like to tread on any vines or foliage covering the ground around corn stalks. The lush foliage of pole beans cuts down their ability to see, and this is also said to discourage their corn raids.

Some of the methods that keep raccoons out will also work for skunks, woodchucks, deer and squirrels. An electric fence is the best all-around pest barrier I know, except when it comes to squirrels. These agile creatures aren't put off by any fence, electric or not. One way to keep squirrels away is to sprinkle red pepper or Tabasco sauce on some ears on the outer rows of the corn. It won't affect the corn flavor when they're cooked, but any squirrel, skunk or raccoon who takes a nibble of the "hot" ears isn't likely to come back for seconds.

It seems there's an endless list of home remedies to try to keep the cornpatch free of four-footed pests: running barefoot around the corn rows to leave a strong human scent; tying your dog near the corn to guard it; placing a paper bag over each ear.... Since some of these methods work some of the time, try anything you think might work for you.

Birds – I have a love/hate relationship with the birds who visit my garden. The ones that eat damaging insects and save my vegetables I love. When birds go after the corn, I don't like them one bit!

Over the years, I've found some ways to keep birds away from the corn at each stage of the game. After planting, I cover each row with a long strip of chicken wire, bending it in an inverted U-shape about 10 inches high in the middle. The close mesh keeps out prying beaks, and by the time the seedlings touch the top of the wire, the birds are no longer interested. Then I remove the wire and store it until the following season.

For those of you who think a scarecrow might work, forget it. An ordinary scarecrow might be fun for the kids to put together, but it will only serve as a handy perch for most birds. However, there are other effective ways to scare birds away.

We've had fairly good results by putting a real-looking, life-size, plastic owl on a tall post near our corn. It keeps birds in check, and we've noticed fewer mice and rabbits in the neighborhood as well.

I've seen a dead crow hanging from a post as an "example" to scare its friends. I suppose it might work, but I've also heard tales of bears or other animals carrying off the dead crow, post and all!

If you can keep birds away from your newly planted corn, they shouldn't bother the crop again until the ears start to fill out. Then you need an effective bird-scarer or chaser. Rig up noisemakers or aluminum pie plates around the corn to frighten them. A cat or dog near the garden often does the trick.

One time-consuming, but sure-fire bird barrier is a paper bag tied around each ear of corn, but only after it's been pollinated. This also can ward off invading insects, but it's too much work for a large cornfield. If it rains, the bags break and need replacing; they can also blow off.

Sunflower Power

Whenever I picture the rows of corn at the back of our garden, I can't help but envision their taller, cheerful companions—sunflowers. These annual flowers add a burst of color to any garden. They're easy to grow and they're functional.

Because they grow so tall and have such sturdy stalks, sunflowers serve as a living fence and natural windbreak. You can use them as pole bean supports or let them become a "decoy" crop, attracting birds that might otherwise go after your corn. On the other hand, if you protect some of the large-seeded, flower heads from birds, you can harvest a good supply of sunflower seeds. Store the seeds unshelled for homegrown bird feed during the winter, or shell them for their delicious seed inside.

A popular sunflower variety is **Mammoth.** The ten to twelve-foot stalks have huge flower heads with thin-shelled, striped seeds and take about 80 days to mature. This is the variety that produces prize-winning giant flowers that draw so many "oohs" and "ahs" at the county fair. An earlier, shorter variety is **Sunbird Hybrid.** It matures in about 68 days, but still produces good-sized heads.

You can plant sunflowers as early as two weeks before the last frost date in the spring. They're hardy and can take a light freeze. For the earliest sunflowers, start the seeds indoors and transplant the seedlings near the last expected frost date.

You plant sunflowers like corn. Work some fertilizer or organic matter into the soil just before planting. Place seeds ten to twelve inches apart and cover them with about an inch of soil. Firm the soil. If you are planting more than one row, leave two to three feet between the rows.

The seedlings will show above ground in one to two weeks, depending on the weather. After that, be sure the plants get a steady supply of water, and they'll produce impressive flowers full of seeds. If you're after a gigantic flower to enter in the fair, sidedress your plant once or twice with about a tablespoon of nitrogen fertilizer or a large handful of compost when the plant's about knee-high and again when it's shoulder-high.

Many gardeners raise sunflowers because they look beautiful, but they save the seeds, too. As the seeds start to form, the flower heads bend with the weight. Tie a plastic mesh bag or a piece of cheesecloth loosely around each flower. The birds may peck out a few seeds around the edges, but they won't be able to reach most of the seeds.

Harvest the heads late in the fall before the first frost hits. The seeds will fully ripen and dry somewhat. Cut off the heads, leaving about two feet of stem attached.

Hang the heads in a dry, well-ventilated spot letting them dry thoroughly. When the heads are dry, you can remove the seeds easily by rubbing two heads together or by scraping the heads against a wire screen or an old washboard (if you have one left from the "good old days" before automatic washers). Or rub the flowers with a stiff brush. If the seeds are still moist on the ends, spread them out for another week to dry completely; otherwise they won't keep long in storage.

If you want to use the seeds later as bird food, simply store them in covered containers in a cool, dry place. The simplest way to feed the birds in the winter is to leave the seeds on the dried flowers. When cold weather hits, hang a head outside for a natural, homegrown birdfeeder.

However, if you want to enjoy the seeds yourself, get out some elbow grease. As far as I know, no one has come up with a totally effective sunflower seed sheller—except the birds, of course. We've had some success using a grain mill set for coarse grinding to crack the seeds for shelling.

We like to roast sunflower seeds after shelling them. Spread the seeds on an oiled cookie sheet and roast for 15 to 20 minutes at 300°F. It's faster to put them under the broiler for a few minutes. They're tasty sprinkled with salt. Store roasted or unroasted seeds in airtight containers. They can keep for months.

Garden to Kitchen

Corn on the Cob

Biting into fresh corn on the cob slathered with butter is one of life's true pleasures as far as I'm concerned. Growing your own sweet corn allows you the simple luxury of savoring the unbeatable, indescribable flavor of eating it minutes after it's picked.

Here's a rundown on the various ways to prepare this summertime favorite. With all these methods, the crucial factor is freshness. Have the water boiling before you pick your corn. With most corn varieties, a few minutes can make a big difference. For the best flavor, corn on the cob should be served immediately after it's cooked.

Different cooks feel they know the *best* way to cook corn on the cob. I've included most of the favorites. Cooking methods and times vary according to taste, so try them all and use whichever you prefer.

Boiling — Remove the husks and silks from freshly picked ears of corn. Drop ears one at a time into enough boiling water to cover. Boil covered five to ten minutes (more mature ears need longer boiling time). Remove ears with tongs and serve.

Steaming — Husk corn and place it in a perforated steamer over rapidly boiling water. Cover and steam 8 to 15 minutes, depending on the corn's maturity.

Roast or grilled — Corn is a natural for roasting, since its husk is a ready-made steam cooker. Preheat oven to 475°F or have your grill good and hot. Remove the outer layer of husk, and turn down the inner layer. Remove silks and dip corn, husk and all, in water. Drain. Pull husk back around ear and place on rack in hot oven or over hot coals 20 to 25 minutes, turning frequently. Remove husk and serve.

Microwave — Peel down husks and remove silks. Brush ears with melted butter and pull up husks. Fasten with string or rubber bands. Place in microwave oven, allowing at least one inch between ears. Cook four minutes at full power and turn ears over. Cook four minutes more on full power. Let stand two to three minutes, then turn back the husks and serve. *(Recipe courtesy of Sharp Electronics Corporation.)*

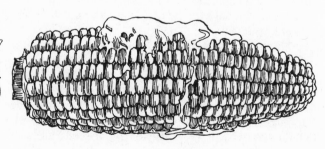

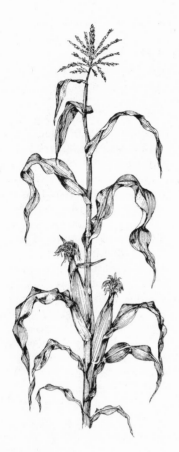

Roastin' Ears

Many southerners were raised on the rich, full flavor and chewy texture of white field corn picked early. I was able to get the directions for cooking this Southern specialty from Darryl Riggins, a friend in Georgia. It came with a note saying, "This is just how my daddy and grandaddy ate it."

"For best thickening action, use a variety such as *Trucker's Favorite, Tennessee Red Cob,* or *Hickory King.* Harvest just like sweet corn — when the ears are plump and milky, then shuck the ears and remove the silks.

"Cut down the cob, slicing half way or less through the kernels. Take your knife and scrape the cob to force all the milk out.

"Pour your treasure into an iron skillet, add a knob of butter, salt, pepper, and milk. Cover and cook over low heat 10 to 15 minutes, or until mixture starts thickening. Add more milk to keep the consistency right (about like applesauce).

"Serve with cube steak, biscuits and gravy, fried okra and sliced tomato."

Keeping the Corn Harvest

We eat corn on the cob almost every day during the fresh corn season, but I always freeze or can enough corn to last through the winter.

For the best tasting results, use only freshly picked corn. I pick just what my daughter and I are able to can or freeze within two to three hours — about two to three bushels. Because corn loses its flavor and its sweetness quickly, you have to work fast during processing.

Freezing

Whole kernel — Husk and wash ears. Scald four minutes in boiling water. Plunge quickly into ice water to cool. Leave in water about four minutes and then drain. Cut kernels from cob at about two-thirds their depth. Pack in freezer containers. Seal, label and freeze.

Cream style — Best way to use mature, starchy ears. Husk, wash, scald and cool ears as for whole kernel corn. Cut kernels from cob at about half their depth. Scrape the cob with the back of the knife to remove juice and meat of the kernels. Pack in freezer containers, leaving 1/4-inch headspace. Seal, label and freeze.

Corn on the cob — Husk and wash ears. Scald small ears (1 1/2 inches or smaller in diameter) six minutes; medium ears (1 1/2 to 2 inches across) eight minutes; ears larger than two inches in diameter ten minutes. Cool quickly in ice water for same amount of time as scalding. Drain. Pack in freezer containers or wrap ears individually in moisture and vapor-proof film and place in plastic freezer bags. Seal, label and freeze.

To cook frozen corn on the cob with the freshest taste, place it unthawed in cool water. Bring the water to a boil and cook for five to ten minutes, depending on the size of the ears.

Canning

Whole kernel corn:

Hot pack — Husk, remove silks and wash corn. Cut whole corn off cob; *do not* scrape cob. Measure corn. To each quart of cut corn, add 2 cups boiling water and heat in a large kettle until boiling.

Pack boiling hot corn in hot jars leaving one inch headspace and cover with hot liquid, again leaving one inch headspace. Add 1/2 tsp salt to pints, 1 tsp salt to quarts. Adjust lids; process in pressure canner at 10 pounds pressure. Pints: 55 minutes, quarts: 1 hour, 25 minutes.

Cold or raw pack — Husk and cut corn as for hot pack. Pack corn *loosely* in hot jars, leaving one inch headspace. Add 1/2 tsp salt to each quart, if desired. Cover with boiling water, leaving one inch headspace. Adjust lids; process at 10 pounds pressure. Pints: 55 minutes; quarts: 1 hour, 25 minutes.

Cream style corn:

Hot pack — Husk, remove silks and wash corn. Cut kernels off cob at 2/3 of their thickness. To make the cream, scrape the cob but do not cut it. Measure corn and add one pint boiling water to each pint. Heat to boiling, then pack immediately into hot *pint* jars only, leaving one inch headspace. Adjust caps, one inch headspace. Adjust caps, process 1 hour, 25 minutes at 10 pounds pressure.

Cold or raw pack — Husk, wash and scrape kernels as for hot pack. Pack corn loosely into hot pint jars, cover with boiling water, leaving one inch headspace. Adjust caps and process pints 1 hour, 35 minutes at 10 pounds pressure.

Drying Sweet Corn

This old-time method is a good, low-energy way to have sweet corn on hand all winter.

Use freshly picked sweet corn, and prepare it as you would for freezing. Husk the ears. Don't worry if the silks cling; they'll come off easily after drying. Blanch the cobs in boiling water two minutes. This "sets" the milk inside the kernel. Drain and cut kernels off the cob.

Spread the kernels on trays for drying. Dry for two to three days in the sun, bringing the trays indoors at night. They can also be dried in an oven or dehydrator set at 120°F for 12 to 18 hours. Stir the kernels occasionally and keep them separated. Corn is dry when it's shriveled and hard. Shake off the dried silks and store the dried kernels in airtight containers. They should keep indefinitely.

To cook: Cover 1 cup dried corn with 2 cups boiling water and simmer, covered, 50 minutes or until corn is plump and tender. One cup yields about two cups cooked corn.

Corn for Grinding

More and more gardeners are becoming interested in growing corn for grinding. You can actually dry and grind any late-season variety: field, flint, sweet, even popcorn can be ground into cornmeal or flour. However, because of its hard starch, flint corn grinds beautifully, so it's preferred by most folks. No matter what variety you choose, leave the ears on the stalk until after the first fall frost to give the kernels a chance to mature and harden completely. Gardeners who live in areas with relatively snowless winters like to leave the corn standing in the field all winter. Although you can dry corn this way, it's better to harvest the crop and dry it away from hungry birds. Wet winter weather can also lead to mold.

Harvest the ears, remove the husks and place the ears in mesh bags. Or braid or tie the husks together. Then hang the corn in a cool, dry place for several months to dry.

You can leave the kernels on the cobs until you're ready to grind them, or shell the dry kernels and store them in airtight containers in a dry place.

Use a hand-cranked or electric grain mill to grind corn. Grind it as you need it, so it will have the fullest flavor and nutrition. Depending on how coarsely you grind the kernels, you can enjoy cracked corn for a delicious hot cereal or finer cornmeal for breads and hot cakes. Ground corn will be yellow or white according to the variety grown. Corn flour is made by stone grinding the kernels to a fine powder; this flour can be used in baking. The thickening agent, cornstarch is made commercially by a special wet-milling process that removes the hull before grinding.

Note on corn cobs: If you like to smoke meat or fish, dried corn cobs left from the corn you dry and grind work beautifully and impart a wonderful flavor. Chop or shred the cobs for the best results. Cobs left over from sweet corn roasts won't work because the cobs have to mature and dry thoroughly.

Cornmeal Collection

There is an endless array of bread and cakes made with cornmeal. They can be made from your own ground meal or from store bought.

Here's an explanation of some old-fashioned favorites for those who may not be familiar with some of the names.

Spoon bread — A soft corn bread made with sweet milk, eaten like pudding with a spoon.

Spider bread — Basic cornbread baked in an iron skillet, or "spider" as the three-legged kind was known in Colonial times.

Hush puppies — Finger-shaped fried corn patties. One explanation of the unusual name is that they were often served at fish fries, and the fishermen would keep hungry dogs from pestering them by tossing a fried cake or two out and yelling, "Hush, puppy!"

Gems — Cornmeal muffins baked in shallow pans known as gem pans.

Cornmeal mush — A cooked mixture of cornmeal and salted water or milk, served as cereal or chilled to be sliced and fried. Often eaten at every meal, this was sometimes called hasty pudding by homesick English settlers as a reminder of well-loved porridge. In Italy, the dish is called *polenta,* and served with cheese, onion and spices as a sidedish at the evening meal.

Corn pone — Finger-shaped baked cornbread, named for the Indian word for baked, *apan.*

Dodgers — Bitesize, baked cornmeal pancakes, dropped from a spoon or your hand onto greased baking sheets. A tradition at the Kentucky Derby.

Crackles — Paper-thin, tortilla-like rounds baked on ungreased sheets until crisp.

Fritters — Fried or sautéed cornmeal batter, often containing fruit or meat.

Hominy — This is simply dried corn that has had the hull and germ removed by soaking it in water. Grits are made by coarsely grinding dried corn or hominy. Both hominy and grits are used very much like cornmeal in cereal, bread or fried cake recipes.

FAVORITE RECIPES

Many of the recipes in this book call for whole kernel corn cut from the cob. Although it would be ideal if you could make them each with garden-fresh corn, the season for fresh corn passes too quickly to make that possible. Luckily, corn freezes and cans beautifully, so you can preserve a good share of the harvest and serve it up year-round.

Fresh Cornbread

There's nothing quite like steaming hot cornbread served with butter and jam! This recipe is best made with garden fresh corn, but frozen or canned works fine.

```
1     cup corn kernels
1     cup cornmeal
1/2   cup flour
4     tsp baking powder
1/4   cup sugar
1/2   tsp salt
1/2   cup milk
1     egg
1/4   cup vegetable oil or bacon drippings
```

Combine dry ingredients. Add corn, milk, egg and oil and mix well. Pour into greased skillet or 9-inch baking pan. Bake at 450°F for 20 to 25 minutes or until golden brown. Serves 8.

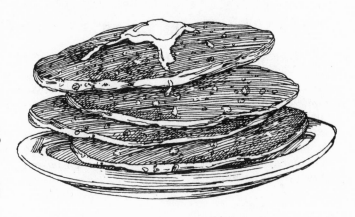

Corn Pancakes

```
1 1/4   cups flour
    1   tsp baking powder
  1/2   tsp salt
    2   eggs, beaten
    1   cup milk
    2   Tb salad oil
    2   cups whole kernel corn
        honey or maple syrup
```

Sift dry ingredients together. Combine eggs, milk and oil. Combine with dry ingredients and add corn. Spoon batter onto preheated, lightly greased griddle or frying pan. Serve with honey or maple syrup. Makes 12 medium pancakes.

As You Like It Cornbread

Depending on the peppers you use, this cheesy bread can be mild or quite spicy.

```
    3   eggs, slightly beaten
1 1/2   cups fresh or frozen corn
    1   red sweet bell pepper, 1 anaheim chili pepper, or 1 small
        jalapeno pepper, chopped
    2   cups buttermilk
1 1/2   cups grated Cheddar cheese
  1/4   cup chopped onion
1 1/2   tsp salt
    3   Tb sugar
    2   tsp baking powder
    1   tsp baking soda
2 1/2   cups cornmeal
```

In large bowl, combine eggs, corn, pepper, buttermilk, 1 cup grated cheese (holding 1/2 cup for topping), and onion. Combine salt, sugar, baking powder, baking soda and corn meal. Add dry mixture to liquid and mix thoroughly. Pour batter into greased 9 x 13 baking pan, bake at 450°F for 30 to 40 minutes. Remove from oven, sprinkle 1/2 cup grated cheese on top and place under broiler for two minutes or until lightly browned.

Anadama Bread

Tradition has it that this bread got its name from a man who had to bake his own bread when his wife, Anna, was away. He wasn't happy as he stirred his concoction of cupboard leftovers and cursed under his breath, "Anna, damn her!" Despite all his protests, however, he invented a moist, slightly sweet cornmeal yeast bread that's easy and requires no kneading. This "accidental" recipe has been passed down for generations.

2	cups milk
1	cup cornmeal
3	Tb butter or margarine
1/2	cup molasses
1/2	cup warm water
2	Tb dry yeast
1	Tb honey
2	tsp salt
5 1/2	cups white flour

In sauce pan bring milk to boil. Remove from heat and stir in cornmeal. Add butter and molasses and mix well. Cool until lukewarm.

In a large mixing bowl, dissolve yeast in warm water. Add honey and stir until bubbly. Add cornmeal mixture, salt and 2 1/2 cups of flour. Beat five minutes.

Gradually add 2 1/2 to 3 cups more flour. Beat with large spoon until mixture is very stiff and it holds up firmly in center of bowl. Cover with damp towel. Let rise until double in bulk, about 1 hour.

Deflate with spoon. Divide in two parts and place in greased loaf pans. Push into corners of pans.

Bake in 350°F pre-heated oven for 45 to 50 minutes. Cool on a rack. Makes two loaves.

Fresh Corn Fritters

1	cup vegetable oil
2	cups whole kernel or cream style corn, cut from cob
2	eggs, separated
2	Tb minced onion
1/4	cup sifted flour
1/2	tsp salt
1/2	tsp baking powder
	pepper to taste

Heat oil to 375°F, in a skillet or fryer. In a bowl combine corn, egg yolks and onion. Mix well. Add sifted flour, salt, baking powder and pepper. Beat egg whites until stiff; fold into corn mixture. Drop mixture by teaspoonfuls into hot oil. Cook until golden brown, turning once. Drain on paper towels. Serve hot. Makes about 2 dozen.

Corn Pudding

2	cups whole kernel corn
2	eggs, well beaten
2	cups milk or 1 c milk and 1 c cream
2	Tb melted margarine or butter
2	Tb flour
1	Tb sugar
	salt and pepper to taste

Stir corn, eggs and milk together. In another bowl blend flour and margarine or butter. Combine the two mixtures and add sugar, salt and pepper. Mix well.

Pour into a greased, 2-quart casserole and place casserole in a pan of hot water. Bake in 350°F, preheated oven for 45 minutes or until the pudding is firm. Serves 4 to 6.

Corn Chowder

Dick likes to make this quick, hot and hearty chowder at camp.

1/2	lb bacon, diced
1	medium onion, chopped
1/4	cup celery, chopped (optional)
2	Tb flour
2	cups whole kernel corn
2	cups diced potatoes, cooked
4	cups milk
	salt and pepper to taste

Sauté bacon, onion and celery until tender. Remove from heat, drain off all but 2 tablespoons bacon grease. Stir in flour. In a large saucepan, heat corn, potatoes and milk. Add sautéed bacon, onion salt and pepper. Heat to boiling, stirring constantly. Serve hot. Each serving can be sprinkled with chopped parsley, paprika or both.
Serves 6.

Succotash

Our family likes this traditional country dish best when it's made with Vermont cranberry shell beans.

2	cups whole kernel corn
2	cups cooked shell beans, lima or kidney
2	Tb margarine
1 1/2	cups milk or 3/4 cup light cream and 3/4 cup milk
	salt and pepper to taste.

Combine all ingredients, heat and stir until hot. Be careful not to boil or scorch. Serves 4 to 6.

Chopped sweet red and green pepper (1/2 cup combined) can be cooked with the beans and corn to make the dish more colorful and tastier.

Corn Husk Tamales

Traditional tamales use corn husks lined with cornmeal mush as wrappers. The filling can be ground beef, chicken, chili, corn, or cheese with a variety of seasonings. Steaming is the traditional and best way to cook tamales.

Carefully remove the husks from 12 to 20 ears of corn, saving the largest leaves for the wrappers. Soak these leaves 5 minutes in hot water to soften them. Drain.

To form each tamale, slightly overlap 3 or 4 large leaves and place 3 tablespoons of your favorite filling in the center. Fold leaves over filling with the short ends tucked in to form an envelope. Tie tamales around with white string. For extra corn flavor, line the bottom element of your steamer with leftover corn husks. Cover with 1 1/2 inches boiling water. Place tamales upright in upper part of steamer, cover and steam over low heat one hour.

Cut strings, cool tamales slightly and serve either with or without husks.

Skillet Corn Relish

This hearty side dish is an all-round favorite at our house; it's as easy to make as it is delicious.

     4 Tb margarine
     3 medium onions, sliced
     1 medium green pepper, cut in 1/2 inch strips
     1 clove garlic, crushed
     2 cups fresh or canned whole kernel corn
     2 large tomatoes, peeled and chopped or 2 cups canned tomatoes, cut up
   1/2 tsp chili powder
        salt and pepper to taste
   1/2 cup stuffed olives, thinly sliced (optional)

Sauté onions, pepper and garlic in margarine until tender, about 5 minutes.

Stir in corn, tomatoes, chili powder, salt and pepper. Cover and simmer about 15 minutes.

Stir in olives and heat thoroughly. Serves 6.

Shepherd's Pie

This traditional meat pie is a great way to use leftover meat and potatoes for an economical one-dish supper.

     1 lb ground lamb (or beef, venison or pork)
     1 clove garlic, minced
     1 medium onion, chopped
   1/4 cup green pepper, chopped
     2 Tb flour
     2 cups water
        salt and pepper to taste
     2 cups cooked whole kernel corn
     4 cups mashed potatoes
     1 Tb parsley

Brown meat, garlic, onion and green pepper in skillet for about 10 minutes over low to medium heat. Mix flour, salt and pepper into meat. Stir in water and cook until it bubbles. Simmer about one minute until mixture thickens.

Pour meat mixture into a 3-quart casserole. Layer corn on top of meat.

Spread mashed potatoes on top and sprinkle with parsley flakes.

Bake uncovered at 350°F for 30 minutes or until potatoes are browned. Serves 6.

Corn and Zucchini Soufflé

     1 cup whole kernel corn
     2 cups zucchini, washed and grated (if zucchini is small, do not peel)
     5 Tb margarine or butter
   1/4 cup chopped green onion
     3 Tb flour
   1/2 tsp salt
   1/8 tsp pepper
   1/4 tsp nutmeg
     1 cup milk
     4 eggs separated
   1/2 cup shredded Swiss cheese

Sauté corn and zucchini in only 2 Tb margarine for 5 minutes. Stir in onion and set aside.

Heat 3 Tb margarine in a large saucepan. Blend in flour, salt, pepper and nutmeg. Cook until smooth and bubbly. Add milk gradually. Stir and cook over medium-low heat until mixture thickens. Cook 1 minute. Remove from heat. Beat egg yolks into a bowl, then gradually stir into hot mixture. Add sautéed corn and zucchini mixture; stir in shredded cheese.

Beat egg whites until stiff. Blend one-third of the egg whites into milk mixture. Carefully fold in the remaining eggs until no white streaks remain.

Pour into greased, flour dusted, 2 quart soufflé dish or casserole. Bake at 350°F 50 to 60 minutes, or until puffy and golden brown on top. Serves 6.

Pickled Corn Relish

Like other pickled vegetables, this relish tastes best six weeks after canning, when the flavors have blended.

```
    8     cups corn (16 to 20 ears)
    3     cups cabbage, finely chopped
    2     large onions, chopped
    2     large sweet green peppers, chopped
    2     large sweet red peppers, chopped
1 1/4     cup sugar
    2     Tb flour
    1     Tb salt
    2     tsp turmeric
    2     tsp celery seed
    4     cups vinegar
    2     cups water
```

Blanch corn 5 minutes. Cool. Cut from cob into a large skillet. Add remaining ingredients and simmer for 20 minutes. Pack boiling hot into hot, clean Mason jars leaving 1/4 inch headspace.

Run a rubber spatula down around the inside of each jar to remove air bubbles. Put lids on jars, rubber side down, and screw band on firmly, so it's "fingertight."

Fill a canner or other large kettle half-full with hot water and place filled jars in a rack on the bottom so they don't touch. Add hot water, if needed, to cover jars with at least an inch or two of water. Cover and turn up heat. Start timing when water reaches a rolling boil; process for 15 minutes in the boiling water bath.

Use tongs or jar lifter to remove jars. Place upright for twelve hours. Store sealed jars in a cool, dry, dark place for at least six weeks before serving. Makes about 6 pints.

Corn and Cabbage Surprise

This is simple, but it always gets rave reviews. The cabbage all but disappears during the cooking, leaving only a delicate hint of cabbage flavor.

```
    6     slices bacon, diced
  3/4     cup water
  1/4     cup green pepper, finely chopped
    2     cups whole kernel corn
    2     cups finely shredded cabbage
    1     tsp sugar
          salt and pepper to taste
```

Fry bacon in a skillet until crisp. Add water, green pepper, corn and cabbage. Cover and cook over low heat until cabbage is tender, about 5 minutes. Add sugar, salt and pepper and mix lightly. Serve hot. Serves 6.

Yankee Rarebit

We like this with whole kernel corn; but for a smoother sauce, chop corn in food processor or blender.

```
    2     cups whole kernel corn
  1/4     cup margarine
  1/4     cup flour
          salt and pepper to taste
  1/4     tsp dry mustard
1 1/2     cups milk
  3/4     cup shredded sharp Cheddar cheese
    8     slices toast or crackers
```

Melt margarine in skillet. Blend in flour, salt, pepper and dry mustard. Add milk and corn. Stir constantly over low heat until thickened. Add cheese and heat until melted, stirring occasionally. Serve on toast or crackers. Serves 6 to 8.

Optional: For an early spring treat, place cooked asparagus on the toast before topping with the rarebit.

Mexican Blintzes

Here's an easy dessert-type tamale filling.

```
18-20     ears tender sweet corn
  1/2     cup sour cream
    1     cup plain yogurt
  1/2     tsp salt
  1/4     cup sugar
  1/4     cup chopped almonds
  1/2     cup raisins
          Dash cinnamon
```

Wash ears of corn and scrape kernels from the cobs. Combine with all remaining ingredients except cinnamon to make filling.

Spoon filling onto corn husk wrappers, sprinkling each with a dash of cinnamon. Fold over, tie and steam. Serves 4.

CHAPTER 2

Tomatoes

If you're just starting a small backyard or community garden, I suggest you try growing 6 to 10 tomato plants, perhaps 2 or 3 different varieties. If you choose varieties that mature at different times, you can stretch your harvest over many weeks. It's a good insurance policy, too, because a calamity which strikes one variety may leave the others alone.

By growing different varieties, you'll also have plenty of tomato notes to share with other tomato growers. Whenever gardeners meet anywhere, you can be sure of one thing: they'll want to know your secrets of growing tomatoes and, hopefully, they'll share some of theirs, too. I think we all shop for information that will help us get bigger, better-tasting, earlier tomatoes with fewer problems.

On the following page are some of the more popular tomato varieties available today. There are many more, of course, and plenty of them would probably do well in your garden. There's a variety well-suited to just about every purpose: eating fresh, making tomato paste, canning and for growing in pots and other small containers.

When selecting a tomato variety, keep in mind what you're going to be doing with them — the length of your season, past experiences, the growing conditions of your area and what you like in a tomato. For example, if you have a short growing season, don't rely totally on tomatoes that need a lengthy season to produce a harvest. And if gardeners in your area have had a problem with harmful diseases like verticillium or fusarium wilts, you may want to shop for disease-resistant varieties.

Each year I try a few tomato varieties I've never grown before — perhaps a recently introduced variety, such as **Floramerica**, or a regional favorite recommended by someone I've met traveling. I love to see how they grow in my garden. But the steady performers for me year after year are **Pixie** tomatoes, which I transplant into the garden quite early; **Early Girl, Better Boy, Big Girl** and **Rutgers**. For my soil and weather conditions — and my taste, too — these are the best.

ON YOUR WAY

To grow tomatoes most gardeners transplant young nursery or home-started tomato seedlings when all danger of frost is past and the soil has warmed up. If you buy your plants, you may not get a wide choice of varieties. So if you have some special varieties you hope to grow or want to choose from an almost endless list of varieties, you may want to grow your own tomato seedlings.

To start your own plants you need to get going anywhere from 6 to 10 weeks before the average last frost date in your area.

It's easy to grow strong, healthy transplants. Here's all you need:

Tomato seeds

Seed-starting trays or "flats" or other containers: tin cans, paper cups, boxes, peat pots, milk cartons, etc. Be sure there are holes in the bottom for drainage.

Adequate light for the seedlings (either

Seeds, seeds, seeds

Early Season (50-65 days from transplanting)

Variety	Resistance	Growth Pattern	Comments
Burpee's Big Early		Ind	Early-ripening; rugged hybrid
*Early Girl (HY)	V	Ind	4-6 oz. tomatoes; stake or cage
Fireball		Det	4 oz. fruits; sets in cool weather
New Yorker	V	Det	Widely recommended; 6 oz. fruits
*Pixie (HY)		Det	Very early; sets fruit in cool weather
Spring Giant	VF	Det	High yields; large fruits
Springset	VF	Det	Widely adapted; short harvest
Starfire		Det	6 oz. fruits
Sweet 100 (HY)		Ind	Stake or cage; many 1oz. fruits

Midseason (65-75 days)

Variety	Resistance	Growth Pattern	Comments
Avalanche (HY)	F	Ind	Very crack resistant
*Better Boy (HY)	VFN	Ind	Widely recommended and adapted, but susceptible to blossom end rot
Bonny Best		Ind	Old-time favorite in South
Burpee's Big Boy (HY)		Ind	Very popular; large 12 oz. fruits. Long producer
*Burpee's Big Girl (HY)	VF	Ind	Like Big Boy, but has resistance
Burpee's VF (HY)	VF	Ind	Widely recommended; resistant to cracking and catfacing
Campbell 1327	VF	Det	Sets fruit in adverse conditions
Floradel	VF	Ind	Stake or cage. Crack resistant
Floramerica (HY)	VF	Det	Compact growth. Tolerant to many diseases
Heinz 1350	VF	Det	Productive canning tomato
Jet Star (HY)	VF	Ind	Widely recommended; 8 oz. fruits
Manapal	F	Ind	Bred for humid conditions. Good Southern variety
Marglobe	F	Det	Old favorite. Smooth, firm 6 oz. fruits
Moreton Hybrid	VF	Ind	6-8 oz. fruits; Northeast favorite
*Rutgers	F	Ind	Large, 6-8 oz. fruits
Super Sioux		Semi-det	Widely adapted; sets fruit in high temp
*Supersonic (HY)	VF	Semi-det	Widely recommended

Late season (80-90 days)

Variety	Resistance	Growth Pattern	Comments
Manalucie	F	Ind	Grows well in adverse conditions, Widely recommended in South
Oxheart		Ind	Heart-shaped tomatoes up to 2 lbs
Ramapo (HY)	VF	Ind	Sets well in adverse conditions. Resistant to cracking, blossom end rot
Wonder Boy (HY)	VF	Ind	Heavy producer of 8 oz. tomatoes

Beefsteak Varieties (large tomatoes; 80-90 days)

Variety	Resistance	Growth Pattern	Comments
Beefmaster (HY)	VFN	Det	Hefty fruits; up to 2 lbs.
Pink Ponderosa		Ind	Meaty, firm tomatoes. Cage plants to protect from sunscald

Yellow Orange Varieties (80-85 days)

Variety	Resistance	Growth Pattern	Comments
Golden Boy (HY)		Ind	Somewhat lower acid tomato
Jubilee		Ind	
Sunray	F	Ind	

Paste Varieties

Variety	Resistance	Growth Pattern	Comments
Roma	VF	Det	Widely recommended
San Marzano		Ind	Quite popular canner

Cherry and Container Varieties

Variety	Resistance	Growth Pattern	Comments
Burgess Early Salad (HY)	F	Det	Plant grows only 8 inches tall, but good producer
Patio Hybrid		Det	2-inch tomatoes
*Pixie Hybrid	VFN	Det	Great early variety for garden or sunny window. Fruits larger than cherry types
Small Fry (HY)		Det	Heavy producer of small fruits. Plant in garden or 5-gallon container
Tiny Tim		Det	3/4-inch fruits. Great for pots, windowsills

Key To Chart

V = resistance to verticillium wilt

F = resistance to fusarium wilt

N = resistance to nematodes and root-knot problems

Det = Bush or determinate type of growth. Terminal leader or main stem develops a flower bud at the top of its growth.

Ind = tall growing or indeterminate type of growth, good for staking, caging or trellising. Terminal leader does not develop a flower bud, allowing continued vegetative growth.

HY = hybrid variety

*My favorites

sunlight or fluorescent lights). Regular fluorescent lights will work, but the special grow lights now available are better for plants.

Pasteurized soil, potting mix or soil formula.

A Note on Soil: The soil mixes available at most garden stores are very good. They are pasteurized, that is, free of weeds and fungi which can cause young seedlings to collapse and die — a problem called "damping off."

If you're thinking about using garden soil to start your plants, you should pasteurize it first. You can do this by baking the soil in a shallow pan in the oven at 200° for an hour or two. This kind of baking doesn't do anything for your appetite, however — it can really smell. Instead I sometimes make my own soil mix by combining equal parts of sand, vermiculite or perlite, and peat moss.

Step-By-Step Growing

Here are the 10 basic steps to starting seeds:

1. **Moisten the soil mix,** put it in your container and level it out. The soil should be moist, not wet.

2. **Sprinkle the seeds** on top of the soil. I like to plant tomato seeds fairly thickly — spacing them about 1/4 inch apart.

3. **Firm the seeds** into the soil with a small piece of wood or other flat object. (I like a small, wooden shingle.) Then put a thin layer — about 1/4 inch — of moist soil mix over the seeds and level it, then firm it again. This brings the seed into good contact with moist soil, which is important for germination.

4. **Place the container inside a plastic bag** or cover it tightly with a sheet of plastic. This will retain moisture, which is important. (As soon as the seedlings start to show, take the bag off.)

5. **Put a few sheets of newspaper on top** of the plastic for insulation to help maintain an even temperature — another help for germination.

6. **Put the flat in a warm spot** — about 65 to 70° — where the temperature is even. I don't recommend windowsills, because they get very hot during the day and at night they're the coldest place in the house. Tomato seeds — and all seeds for that matter — need an even temperature for germination.

(Note: If you start tomatoes in individual containers such as peat pots, put 2 or 3 seeds in each, firm them into a good soil mix, cover with a thin layer of soil mix and firm again. Slip the pots inside a plastic bag until the seeds sprout. Thin, later, leaving only the strongest plant.)

7. **The seedlings will start to show in a few days** — check them each day so that once they're

up, you can remove the plastic before they grow too much.

8. **Remove the covering** and put the seedlings in a sunny window or under fluorescent grow lights. If you use lights, set the plants an inch or two below the tubes, and maintain that distance as the plants grow. If you put them too far away from the lights, the plants will stretch toward them and develop thin, weak stems. To grow well, plants must have darkness as well as light, so make sure the lights are off at least 8 hours a day.

9. **Keep the soil moist, but not wet.** When you water the plants, do it gently so you don't wash any of them out. Try to use room temperature water, if possible. Misting is very good for plants, too.

10. **Don't worry about fertilizing the seedlings right away.** Wait a week or so — or even until after the first repotting if you prefer. Then mix a small amount of a balanced, water-soluble fertilizer in with the plants' water once a week.

The First Repotting — A Must!

When the seedlings are 3 or 4 inches tall and show their second pair of leaves, it's time to take them out of the crowded flats and put them in roomier, deeper containers.

Since any part of the tomato stem covered with soil will develop more roots (and a large root system is important for transplants), one of the basic rules about transplanting tomatoes is that you should always use a **deeper container** and set the plants lower then they were before.

I try to get as much of the stem buried as possible. I pick off all but the top two leaves or so and set the plant in the soil right up to those upper leaves.

For this first repotting, I use deep plastic dishpans or similar containers and poke some drainage holes in the bottoms. I also put a thin layer of small stones at the bottom to help drainage. Again, I use a sterile soil mix. If you want to, you can mix a teaspoon or so of plant food or balanced fertilizer, such as 5-10-10, in with each gallon of soil.

Water the tomatoes well before you start to repot. The wet soil will stick to the roots and protect them from being exposed to light and air, which can kill them.

Spoon the seedlings out of the flat with a small utensil. If you have to hold the plants by the stems, do it gently. Too much pressure will injure the plant.

Pinch off the lower leaves of the seedling. In the new container, make a deep hole and set the seedling in right up to the top leaves.

Firm the soil around the seedling. Leave 2 or 3 inches between plants.

Water them gently but don't over water.

Fertilize once a week. The ratio is about a teaspoon of complete fertilizer for each gallon of water.

Moving Time Again

Before the tomatoes can be transplanted successfully in the garden, the seedlings need to develop enough roots and top growth. To be sure they have strong roots, I transplant many of my tomatoes a second time. Here's why: As I've mentioned, roots will form all along the buried stem of the tomato, so by transplanting deeply a second time, I further encourage the plants to increase the size of their root systems.

I wait until the plants in the dishpans are up 6 to 10 inches and transplant each one into a tall, half-gallon milk carton. I pick off all the lower leaves again and put the plants in as deeply as possible, so that just a small amount of the stem and the top leaves rest right at the surface.

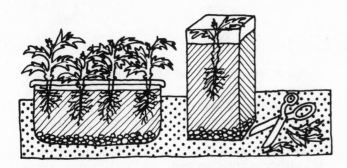

If you do this, somebody might holler, "Whoa! You're making a big plant small." Don't worry. You're encouraging the stem to thicken and to produce more roots — nothing could be better for a tomato transplant! Plus, we're leading up to a unique way to plant tomatoes! (See page 32.)

Extra Early Plants

Since I putter around the house a lot before the gardening season is under way, I start some tomato seedlings even earlier than the recommended 6 to 8 weeks before planting time, especially seeds of my favorite early variety, Pixie. I plant around Vermont Town Meeting Day, which is always the first Tuesday in March — and that's about 10 to 12 weeks before our last average frost.

I repot these tomatoes twice over the course of their long stay indoors to develop the biggest root system I can. Even repotting them deeply, they can be pretty good-sized when it's time to plant them outdoors.

In fact, the root system is often so well developed that when I transplant them in the garden I can place them in the ground straight up and at the same depth they were growing.

I start early and grow the plants indoors for such a long time because I want to get a real big jump on the season and be the first on the road with garden-fresh, red-ripe tomatoes. It takes some work but I get a kick out of having homegrown tomatoes weeks before the neighbors.

Indoor Care

Many gardeners often have a problem with "leggy" seedlings. This condition is caused by: too much fertilizer, growing them in a room that's too warm, placing them too far away from a sunny window or placing them too far away from fluorescent lights. (With lights, position the plant only an inch or two away from the tubes — that will keep them from stretching.)

Transplanting leggy seedlings deeply will help eliminate the problem. The stems of the plants will thicken, growing out a bit instead of up.

A Note on Shopping For Transplants

When you buy tomato transplants at a garden store, supermarket or roadside stand, take the time to pick out the best plants. Look for plants with thick stems — the thicker the better — and with large root systems, best indicated by a dark green plant in a deep container. The tall transplants are not necessarily the best ones. And don't pick any plant with blossoms. Unless it's in a deep pot, it won't have a strong enough root system to support fruit yet.

Be wary of plants with blemishes or poor color. Also, check the undersides of the leaves for aphids or tiny white flies. These are little pests that you don't want to bring near your garden. They multiply very rapidly and cause a lot of problems.

"Hardening Off" Transplants

Tomato plants — no matter if they're bought in a store or home-grown — must be toughened up or hardened off before you plant them in the garden. After all, they have been indoors for 6 to 8 weeks, and they're quite tender. They will get sunburned or windburned if they are transplanted before they're accustomed to the out-

doors. The extra time and care you devote to readying your plants for their new outdoor home will really pay off.

It takes about 10 days or so to harden tomato plants. I recommend even a little more time if you're going to get a jump on the season and put the plants out before the average last frost date.

The process of hardening a plant involves reducing the temperature of its environment by moving it outside, holding back water, and keeping it out of bright sunlight. The plant won't grow too much during this special period; in fact, it is storing food to use when it needs it — at transplanting time.

It pays to stop watering the plants a couple of days before the hardening process begins. The stems and leaves will lose a little water, but that starts to toughen them up and actually protects them. And outside they probably won't need as much water anyway because there is usually more moisture in the air outside than inside the house. Also, don't fertilize them during this time, as that will cause new, too-tender growth.

On the first day of the hardening process, take the plants outside for a few hours — and place them where they'll be protected from direct sunlight and wind. Each day lengthen the time outside a little, and gradually expose them to more sunshine and breeze. After a few days, leave them out all day and night. But if there is a chance of a frost, don't risk it — bring them indoors.

If you harden the plants well, you won't have to take the trouble at planting time to protect the seedlings from sun and wind with all sorts of contraptions such as hot caps, milk cartons, etc. You'll have done the job already.

GARDEN PREPARATION

Where you plant your tomatoes in the garden is important. Tomatoes need at least 6 to 8 hours of sun a day to produce well — and full sun is best, especially in cooler, more northern climates. They also like to keep their roots fairly dry and warm. So a sunny, well-drained part of your garden is the best spot for them.

Tomatoes like their soil pH around 6.0 to 6.5. Briefly, pH is a measure of soil acidity or alkalinity. On the pH scale, 7.0 is neutral; so the 6.0 to 6.5 range, which tomatoes prefer, is slightly on the acid side. (By the way, that's the range at which most vegetables grow best.)

If your soil pH is too low or too acid, you'll have to add lime to the soil to bring the pH back in the proper range. Gardeners in Western states often have high pH or alkaline soils; some of them need to add sulfur to lower the pH. Lime and sulfur can be added to the soil any time of the year when the ground isn't frozen. Get recommendations from the Extension Service on how much to apply based on your soil test report.

Better Soil

No matter what kind of soil you have in your garden, you can shape it into a great home for your tomatoes with just a little work.

In troublesome, light, sandy soils which drain too rapidly or in heavy, clay soils which take forever to drain and warm up in the spring, you can either spot-improve the soil where your tomato plants will grow, or you can work on a garden-wide basis.

Either way, it boils down to working plenty of organic matter into the soil, such as leaves, compost, grass clippings, garden residues or easy-to-grow cover crops — buckwheat, cowpeas, or annual rye grass.

Organic matter will feed the millions of microscopic soil organisms who live and work in your soil. This active soil life breaks down organic matter into nutrient-rich-humus — in effect, making fertilizer for your vegetable crops.

In problem soil, such as extremely sandy soil which drains and dries out too quickly, organic matter builds up the water-holding capacity of the soil. With a lot of organic matter in it, the soil can act more like a sponge, holding moisture. This is vitally important for tomatoes, because they really depend on a continuous supply of moisture all season long.

But tomatoes don't want to sit in puddles; organic matter really improves heavy soils that stay wet. The particles of organic matter, when worked into the soil, wedge themselves in between the tight particles of clay, so that air and water circulate better.

If your tomato crop has been only so-so the past few years, work extra organic matter into the soil where your plants will be. You will see a big difference in the harvest.

It's also important to work the soil before transplanting time until it's loose to a depth of about 6 to 8 inches. You can do the work with a garden tiller or with a shovel. The tomato roots will be able to expand quickly in the loose seedbed and you'll also uproot and kill many weeds by working the soil.

Fertilizer

It's very important to work some fertilizer into the soil at transplanting time, so that your transplants can get off to a good start.

After the soil has been well tilled and is loose, I make a trench or furrow about 6 to 8 inches deep down what will be my row of tomatoes. At the bottom of the furrow I first put a thin band of commercial fertilizer, such as 5-10-10. (Incidentally, the numbers 5-10-10 refer to the percentages, by weight, of nitrogen (N), phosphorus (P) and potassium (K) in the bag of fertilizer. They'll always be listed in that order, too: N-P-K.)

Another method I have used successfully is to put down a deeper band of organic fertilizer. I use dried chicken manure, but you can use any dehydrated animal manure, as well as additional organic matter including compost or rotted leaves — whatever is on hand.

Then — no matter which method I have chosen — I cover all this fertilizer with 2 or 3 inches of soil. I don't want the roots or stems of any transplants to come in direct contact with the fertilizer. If the plants come in direct contact with fresh fertilizer, the salts in the fertilizer can draw moisture from the roots which is harmful. If the fertilizers are deep underneath the plant, then the roots will grow to it and absorb the nutrients gradually.

After covering the fertilizer, it's just a matter of transplanting the tomatoes into the furrow which is now 3 or 4 inches deep.

TRANSPLANTING

You're the Boss

As a gardener, you must realize that each season some things are simply out of your control — rainfall and sunshine, for example. But at a very important time in the life of your tomatoes — transplanting time — you're the boss.

Make no mistake about it — transplanting is a major step. If you do it carefully and use a little extra time and care, you can look forward to a crop that will be on time — or even ahead of everybody else's — healthy and prolific.

Mistakes, such as rushing your plants into the ground before they are properly hardened, or roughing up the tomato roots when you're handling them, can really set the crop back.

So let's look at some of the general guidelines for transplanting tomatoes — and a couple of transplanting methods, step by step, so you can decide which is the best way for you to transplant tomatoes.

Transplant tomatoes (and other crops, too) on a cloudy day or in the late afternoon or evening if you can. Bright sun can harm newly planted transplants.

Soak the transplants with water in their flats an hour before transplanting. This will help keep the soil around the roots and protect them, and the root mass will be easier to handle.

Have everything ready before taking the plants out of the flats. Have the soil prepared, the fertilizer applied in the furrow or in the holes, all tools at hand, etc.

Don't put too much fertilizer under the plants. One of the big mistakes people make is to toss too much fertilizer in the hole before they put their tomatoes in. Excessive fertilizer shocks and burns the plant. It's better to hold off and give them extra nourishment later when they are established.

Protect against cutworms. Before putting the tomato plant in the ground, wrap a newspaper collar around the stem to protect the plant against cutworms. These ground-level pests can chew completely through the thin tomato stem. The collar should span from an inch or two above the soil surface to an inch below — the cutworm's territory.

The newspaper collars are easy to put on and last long enough for the stems to thicken enough to discourage the cutworms. Tight collars of plastic can restrict the stem growth, so I never use them.

Cup the roots in one hand when you take a transplant out of its container. To protect roots from needless exposure, work quickly. A smooth and speedy transition from flat to soil means less of a shock to the plant.

Keep transplants watered. They need water in the beginning to help them get over the shock of being transplanted, to encourage new root growth and to replace the moisture they give off or "transpire" because of heat or drying winds.

Trouble-Free Transplanting

If you talk to as many gardeners as I do, you quickly get the notion there are as many methods, tips and tricks to the art of transplanting as there are ways of baking a cake.

But despite all the variations — which give tomato growers so much to talk about — there are just a couple of basic ways to transplant.

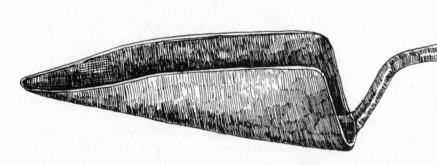

Trench Planting

In trench planting, you simply pinch off all the lower leaves of the tomato plant and lay the whole plant in a shallow trench *horizontally*. Then cover the stem with 2 or 3 inches of soil and bring just the top cluster of leaves above the surface.

There are several advantages to this system. For one thing, additional roots will form all along the buried stem, so the plant can take up more water and nutrients and get off to a quicker start.

Also, setting the roots only a few inches from the surface helps them to warm up quickly — and the heat-loving tomato plants love that. When the rays of the sun hit the soil early in the morning, the roots start to feel the heat. That wouldn't happen if they were set deep in a hole. The extra heat the shallow roots receive helps to lengthen the growing day and speed up the first harvest.

The buried main stem will also enlarge, so it can handle the job of transporting nutrients to all the tomatoes, branches and leaves throughout the season.

Though you might think only northern gardeners with short seasons would be interested in

trench planting, it's practical in the South, too. Because it gets too hot in the middle of the summer in some parts of the South for tomatoes to do well, gardeners try to plant early so they can harvest before summer heat slows up production. And trench planting also helps their tomatoes get a quicker start than if they were planted vertically in deep, cool spring soil.

When you trench plant tomatoes, the first blossoms and tomatoes will develop near the cluster of leaves you brought above the ground at planting time. I consider these first tomatoes that form close to the ground a bonus harvest. With other transplanting methods, the first tomatoes will develop 8 to 10 inches up the stem. So encouraging clusters of fruit to form down near the ground will give you more tomatoes by the time the plant reaches the top of the stake or the end of its growth pattern.

How to Trench Plant

When the trench is dug, fertilizer added and covered, and everything else is ready, I carefully take a tomato plant out of the flat, or tear off the milk carton, cup my hand around the roots, pinch off the lower leaves of the plant, and leave just the top cluster of leaves.

I wrap my newspaper cutworm collar around the top of the stem and lay the plant down in the trench horizontally, quickly covering the roots and entire length of stem up to the leaves with 2 or 3 inches of soil, and firm it down.

Don't try to bend the top of the plant up — just push a little pillow of soil underneath to support it. Mother Nature will see that it grows up in the right direction.

Give the area a good soaking after the seedlings are planted.

When I trench plant tomatoes, I space the plants so the top clusters of leaves showing above the surface are 16 to 20 inches apart. You can put them closer if you're going to stake them ... 12 to 15 inches apart if you want. Between the rows I leave about 3 feet of space, so I can cultivate and later get around the plants to prune and harvest.

If I'm going to stake these trench-planted tomatoes, I do it right away because I know where the long stem is under ground. I put the stakes on the east side of the plants because the prevailing winds in my area are from the west. When the wind is strong, the plant will be held against the stake. Otherwise, if the wind pushes the plant against the string or cloth tie, the plant might cut or snap.

I don't put any mulch down around the plants at this time because mulch insulates the

soil from the sun and keeps it cool. Tomatoes want heat! If I mulch with hay or straw or other organic materials, I wait 4 or 5 weeks until the soil is warm.

Straight Up-and-Down Transplanting

With this method you prepare a hole for each of your tomato plants and set them in vertically. You can plant them to the same level they were growing in the flat, or pinch off some of the lower leaves and plant them deeply, which is what I prefer to do. Roots will form along any part of the stem that is buried, and the extra roots will give you a stronger plant.

The main advantage of this deep, vertical planting comes when the weather gets hot and dry. Because the roots are set in and grow more deeply than if trench planted, they will be closer to moisture deep in the soil, which is very important for southern and southwestern gardeners.

When you prepare each hole, add some organic matter at the bottom. This will increase the moisture-holding ability of the soil and also allow the roots to expand easily. When you put fertilizer in the hole, be sure to mix it with some soil

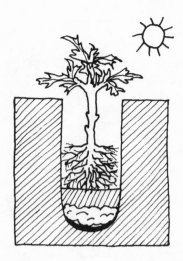

and cover it with 2 or 3 inches of additional soil before setting in the plant.

Raised Beds

If you have hard-to-work problem soil — for instance, if it stays quite wet in the spring and takes a long time to dry out, or if it packs hard after a rain — you can plant tomatoes (and other crops) on raised beds.

At the back end of my garden, the soil stays wet much longer than everywhere else. So I raise wide-row beds with my garden tiller. The soil that I plant on is about 6 inches above the walkway. I simply transplant the tomatoes in these beds as I would in other sections of my garden.

The raised soil drains very well, so I can get my tomatoes in the ground on schedule. When it rains, excess water doesn't sit on the beds and pack the soil down — it runs off. If water just sits on the surface for a long time, the plants' roots can't get any oxygen. Raised bed gardening really helps gardeners with heavy clay soils.

STAKING, CAGING AND TRELLISING

It's often said that tomatoes will grow like weeds — they'll keep sending out new stems and branching out all over the place. Every time you turn around the plants are bigger and bushier.

Well, to keep them from gobbling up too much garden space and to insure cleaner, healthier tomatoes, many gardeners support their plants, train them to grow a certain way and regularly pinch off unwanted growth. Stakes, trellises and cages are the most popular supports these days.

To Stake or Not to Stake

In my travels I've noticed that most gardeners stake tomatoes, so let's first look at the pros and cons of staking.

Advantages of Staking:

Saves space. You can grow more plants in a given area.

Keeps vines and tomatoes off the ground. Fruit is cleaner with less rotting.

Earlier harvest. The pruning that staked tomatoes require forces more of the plant's energy into ripening fruit.

Each tomato is larger than if not staked. The required pruning puts more energy into fewer tomatoes.

Easier to pick tomatoes and to work around the plants.

Insect and disease control is easier, too.

Disadvantages of Staking:

Takes time and effort to stake, train and prune the plants.

Tomatoes are more open to cracking, blossom end rot, and sunscald problems because they are pruned and more exposed.

The total yield of staked plants is often a little lower than similar plants that are not staked. You have to prune off side shoots and branches to support the plant with a stake and that actually reduces the total leaf surface of the plant. Since the leaf surface is the site of the plant's food manufacturing operation, less leaf surface means a smaller total food supply, and that affects total yield.

Staked plants usually need mulching material such as hay or leaves to cover the soil near them. The mulch helps retain moisture in the soil. Staked plants actually need more water than unstaked tomatoes because they are held up and exposed to the sun and drying winds.

Not all tomato plants need staking. A tomato with what we call a "determinate" growth habit stops growing at a certain height — usually when it's fairly short. It stops growing taller because the main stem develops a flower bud at the top and produces fruit. Most of the determinate varieties are early types, and they are bushy plants with short, stout stems that support them pretty well.

For example, the Pixie tomatoes that I put in my garden very early each year are determinate plants. I don't stake them; sometimes I will use a low cage to keep some of the lower branches off the ground, but even that's not necessary.

Some other determinate varieties are Spring Set, New Yorker, Spring Giant and Fireball.

Tomatoes with an "indeterminate" growth pattern will just grow and grow if you feed them well and let them take off. You may see a photograph in the newspaper during the summer of a tomato plant being trained up the side of a house. The plant may be anywhere from 6 to 15 or 20 feet high. That's a well-fed indeterminate plant, for sure!

Many of the seed catalogs mention whether plants are determinate or indeterminate, which helps you plan your garden better. Some seed packets say whether the variety is good for staking or not. If you're buying transplants and you're not sure which kind of plant you've selected and whether it needs support or not, by all means ask the sales person or grower!

How to Stake

As I mentioned earlier, when you support a tomato, try to put the support on the prevailing downwind side of the plant, so that the plant will be against the support when the wind is blowing hard.

Six to eight-foot stakes are good for most tomatoes. Many garden stores sell tomato stakes just 4 or 5 feet high, and they work well, too. I know an ice hockey coach who collects broken hockey sticks from his players during the winter and uses them in the tomato patch in the summer. Put the stakes in right after you've put the plants in the ground.

Drive the stakes about one foot deep in the soil, about 5 to 6 inches away from the plant. Of course, you don't put the stake on the root side of tomatoes you've trench planted. As the plant grows, tie a strip of cloth, a cord or *coated* wire tightly to the stake and loosely around the stem of the plant. Leave at least an inch or two of slack. Add ties as needed as the plant grows up the stake.

Supporting Tomatoes with Cages

One of the simplest ways to support plants is with cages — tall cylinders of wire mesh. Cages have more advantages than just being easy to use.

Advantages of Caging:

Less time removing suckers, pruning branches or training the plants up the cage. Most of the time you leave the plant alone.

The plants grow naturally and support themselves as they get big and the branches start resting on the mesh.

Caged tomato plants develop enough foliage to provide plenty of shade for ripening the fruit.

The shaded soil underneath the plant retains more moisture.

The shade protects tomatoes from sunscald.

Even moisture in the soil reduces blossom end rot and cracking problems. That's especially important for central and southern gardeners with brilliant sunshine and hot, dry weather.

Disadvantages of Caging:

If left untended, the plants will put on excessive foliage, but an occasional pruning can easily remedy the situation.

Cages cost money.

How to Cage

Garden stores sell tomato cages, but you can easily make your own. They should be strong, at least 5 feet tall (to handle most varieties) with holes big enough to get your hand in to bring out nice, big tomatoes! Otherwise, it looks a little odd heading out to pick tomatoes with a pair of wire cutters!

Concrete reinforcing wire is often regarded as the ideal cage material, but I don't think it is. It's hard for many people to find, it's somewhat expensive and it's ugly in the garden because it rusts quickly. You can paint cages with rust-resistant paint, of course, but I don't think the extra work or expense is worth it.

For caged tomatoes, I prefer a sturdy galvanized wire mesh that you can use for years. The cages can be from 12 to 30 inches in diameter. You need about 3 feet of material for every 1 foot diameter of cage. A friend of mine in Texas reports that 1-foot diameter cages work well for him with most tomatoes. I like a cage diameter of 24 or 30 inches, especially for my main crop tomatoes like **Better Boy** and **Big Boy**. Because

they grow luxuriantly and get heavy with tomatoes, they need the extra room and support.

I like to fasten the cages on two sides to short stakes I drive into the ground. Then I know the cages won't ever topple.

Fencing only a foot or two high can be used to hold up the shorter, earlier varieties such as **New Yorker, Pixie** and others. Though it's not necessary to keep these plants up, you will probably get more rot-free tomatoes by using short cages.

Extra Mileage from Cages

Here's an easy way to give your caged tomato transplants a boost early in the season. (With a couple of twists, you can adapt the following suggestions to plants you're growing with other supports or even if you're leaving them unstaked.)

When you put the tomato plants in the ground, set the cages over them immediately and secure the cages with small stakes or push them firmly into the ground if you can.

Then make a tight circle of 1-foot-high black felt roofing paper (or dark plastic) around the outside of the cage at ground level. Staple the overlapping ends of the paper together.

The black paper will gather heat for the tomato plants — they appreciate it early in the season — and it will also protect the plants from bruising winds.

If you don't use cages, rig up some kind of support system for the black paper — maybe using cut coat hangers — so that the paper stands straight around the plants. Keep it about 8 to 10 inches away from the plants.

Researchers recently studied this method of aiding caged plants in Texas and saw yield increases of 25 to 50 percent over unprotected plants of the same variety.

It's pretty easy to find the inexpensive roofing paper. Most lumber and building stores have it. You can probably get some free from scrap piles at construction sites.

Trellising

Trellising can be creative and attractive, but it can also be a lot of work.

Advantages of Trellising:
Trellises require little space, and tomatoes can be planted closer together.
Fruit ripens earlier.

Disadvantages of Trellising:
Necessary to build support system, using slats of wood, wire-mesh fencing, pipes or poles and wire.
More time necessary for pruning and training — at least some time required each week.
Fewer tomatoes because of pruning.
Greater sunscald susceptibility because of less shade from leafy growth.

How to Trellis

My favorite trellising system is one using 4-foot stakes placed 5 feet apart down the row with 3 wires running horizontally between them — a foot above one another.

As the tomatoes start to grow, I simply train them so their branches interweave around and through the wires. I train 2 or 3 main stems per plant, and keep all other side shoots picked off. These shoots that spring up right above the crotch where the branches grow from the main stem are called "slips" or "suckers." I also tie some of the stems to the wires.

When the tallest branch grows beyond the top wire, I cut it off. This stops the branch from getting any higher. If it grows too far over the upper wire, it will break off anyway. If you don't control its growth, the plant may expend all its energy and use up all its nutrients getting taller and growing new shoots and not producing fruit.

When this happens — whether with trellis, staked or caged tomatoes — the quality and size

of the fruit suffers. Try to get your plants to concentrate more on producing fruit than on growing larger and leafier.

A Word on Free-Growing Tomatoes

Now that you've heard all about staking, caging and trellising, here are some things to think about if you plan to let your tomato plants sprawl.

Advantages of Free-Growing:
No doubt about it, this method saves work. No stakes or supports to set up, no training the plants, and much less pruning to do.
A bigger tomato crop is possible because the plants bush out quite a bit, develop plenty of leaf surface and extra tomatoes will form on the well-developed side stems.

Disadvantages of Free-Growing:
You'll probably need a light mulch to keep the tomatoes from resting on the ground where they're prone to rot or nibbles from insects and animals. Mulch, though, tends to attract insect and rodent pests. But since the plant shades the ground well and keeps it moist, you don't need a whole lot of mulch to conserve moisture.
You need room for these plants to grow. Figure at least 1 square yard for each tomato plant.

PRUNING

Never Give a Sucker an Even Break!

In my garden, all the tomato plants get some pruning, whether they're staked, trellised, caged or sprawling. Left unpruned, a tomato plant will produce a surprising number of them. So I prune all my tomato plants. Staked and trellised plants need the most pruning, and they need it on a regular basis.

Basically, pruning means pinching off the shoots or suckers that grow out from the stem right above a leaf branch. If you let a sucker grow, it simply becomes another big stem with its own blossoms, fruits — and even its own suckers! With staked or trellised tomatoes, pinch off these suckers and just keep the energy of the plant directed at one (sometimes 2 or 3) main stems.

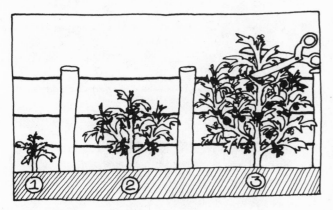

Pinch off most suckers to direct growing energy to main stems.

Tomato plants really grow fast when the weather warms up, and new suckers form all the time, so you should go on 'sucker patrol' at least twice a week during the heavy growing season.

If you live in a very hot, sunny area, you can let some of the suckers put out a couple of leaves and them pinch out the tip to stop its growth. The sucker provides a little more foliage to help the plant manufacture food and also to help shade tomatoes from the sun.

Pruning Unstaked Plants

When I go into the garden and look over my tomato plants, I sometimes think I'm just looking at a series of suckers growing.

With sprawling plants, I pinch off some suckers and here and there a branch or two that doesn't have blossoms or tomatoes. I try to keep the plants from getting too much foliage.

Pruning these low-growing plants improves ventilation, which is important in preventing disease. Pruning branches late in the season opens the plant up to more sunlight. Then on cooler days the plants are a little warmer, which is good for ripening tomatoes.

In hot parts of the country, don't over-prune. Tomatoes need protection from the bright sun or they may get sunburned. Tomatoes ripen better if they are shaded some.

Pruning Tops of Plants

You can pinch off the tip of the main stem above the top blossom to keep a flourishing plant from growing any higher. I do this when a plant is outgrowing its support, or toward the end of the season when I know taller plants won't help me much. At that point, I'd rather see the plant put its energy into ripening the tomatoes already on the vine.

Pruning Roots

Root-pruning is a special trick I use to speed up the ripening of early tomatoes. It simply involves cutting some of the roots of a plant when it has 3 or 4 clusters of tomatoes on it. By cutting the roots, you put quite a bit of stress on the plant, and when they're under stress, plants tend to mature more quickly. It's as if the plant were worried that it might not have time to complete its life cycle, so it rushes to mature some fruit and seed. The plant won't die if you root-prune it correctly; the growth process is simply inter-

rupted. But after a little rest, the plant is ready to start producing again.

To root-prune trench-planted tomatoes, I take a long kitchen knife and make a cut down along just one side of the buried main stem. I cut only on one side of the stem, 1 to 2 inches away from it, and I go down 8 to 10 inches.

If the tomatoes were planted vertically, I cut halfway around the plant, 1 or 2 inches from the stem, 8 to 10 inches deep. If a knife doesn't work well for you, try a spade or a shovel.

Some years ago when my family and I had a one-acre market garden, I root-pruned some plants to hurry our first harvest along. The early tomato not only brought the earliest dollar — it was the best advertising we could ever do.

TOMATO T.L.C.

Mulching

Mulch is simply a covering over the soil that keeps moisture in, blocks weeds and protects low-growing tomatoes from resting on the ground and developing rot. For many growers, mulching is vital.

There's some extra benefit using organic mulches, such as grass clippings, wood chips, sawdust, hay or leaves, because these materials — unlike the plastic, aluminum and other synthetic mulches — decompose and provide food for all the millions of micro-organisms that live in the soil. They feed on the organic mulches, break them down and thereby provide nutrients your plants will be able to use in the future.

Mulches can raise or lower soil temperature, too. In the North, sheets of thin black plastic are often put down at planting time to warm up the soil, so the heat-loving tomatoes can get off to a good start.

As soon as the sun starts hitting that plastic in the morning, the plants receive extra heat. I have to chuckle a little bit, though, at folks who lay down black plastic a week or two before they've got their seeds in the ground to try to heat the soil for their transplants. I hate to tell them the plastic does not insulate, so the soil cools off each night. They are just about starting over every morning.

I don't like to use black plastic in my garden. It's not cheap and can be a bother to lay down each spring and take up each fall. I hate to use a mulch that the earthworms and soil life can't dine on, and I think black plastic detracts from the natural beauty of a garden.

If you use a woody material as a mulch, such as bark, sawdust or woodchips, I recommend you add some nitrogen fertilizer to the soil. Otherwise the soil micro-organisms, which use nitrogen to break down the mulch, will rob the nitrogen your plants need. Some commercial wood mulch is pretreated with nitrogen.

In the South and Southwest, gardeners use thick mulches of hay, straw or pine needles to protect tomato roots from too much heat in the hot summer months, as well as to help retain moisture in the soil. Some gardeners also pile soil up 5 or 6 inches around the stems of their plants to insulate the roots some more and promote some extra root growth. This technique is called 'hilling.'

Using black plastic sheeting is good in the South and Southwest only early in the season when the plants appreciate a little extra heat. If used in summer months, though, the roots would literally cook. It'd be too hot for the plant to grow. If you use black plastic you can cover it with a heavy organic mulch that will help keep the soil temperature down when the weather heats up.

Some gardeners in hot areas use a commercially available mulch with an aluminum foil surface that reflects the sun and keeps the soil cool. Of course, it also keeps weeds down and conserves moisture.

Mulching Pointers

Many people make a big mistake by putting heavy mulches around their tomatoes too early in the season. Wait 4 or 5 weeks until the ground has really warmed up — especially in the North. With hay or any heavy mulch you are insulating the soil, so early in the season mulch keeps the soil cool, and that's no good. You delay the harvest a few weeks if you do this.

If you're going to use black plastic, put it down at planting time when the soil is moist. (The 3-foot-wide plastic is probably best.) Secure it firmly around all the edges. The better contact the plastic makes with the soil, the more heat and moisture you trap. Then, to put in a transplant, simply punch or cut a hole or a slit in the plastic. Additional small holes here and there to let rain water soak through are a good idea, too.

Staked and trellised plants usually need mulch to save moisture. Growing up in the air and exposed to sun and winds, they transpire more heavily than unstaked plants. It takes extra effort to provide them with an ample and even supply of moisture, but in rain or water-scarce climates, it's worth it.

Sidedressing

Tomatoes need quite a big food supply over the season — they are what we call "heavy feeders." This is no surprise when you look at all the work they're doing: extending the stem, putting out more branches, leaves and blossoms; developing, nurturing and ripening all those fruits! To do all this work they need a steady diet of water and nutrients.

So in most gardens, we have to sidedress tomatoes. That simply means placing fertilizer around the plants to give them extra nourishment through the season. One or two sidedressings is fine for most gardens.

Many kinds of fertilizers can give tomatoes the extra nutrients they need. I prefer a complete fertilizer (5-10-10 or 10-10-10), or an organic fertilizer such as dried manure, bonemeal or cottonseed meal. I don't like to see gardeners using the high-nitrogen fertilizers such as urea or ammonium sulfate because it's so very easy to use too much. When you overfertilize, you get tall, dark green plants with few tomatoes.

The first time to sidedress is when the first tomatoes have just formed — maybe when they are the size of golf balls. About a pound (2 cupfuls) of 5-10-10 should be enough for all the plants

in a 30-foot row (about 20 plants). I put a small handful of the fertilizer in a one-inch-deep circular furrow around each plant. I make a furrow 3 or 4 inches away from the stem, usually right under the leaf drip line of the plant. I'm careful not to get any of this fertilizer on the leaves or stem because it will burn them. Then I cover the fertilizer with 1 to 2 inches of soil. The next rain or watering will start carrying the nutrients down into the root zone of the plants.

You don't have to worry about getting organic fertilizers like well-dried manures or bonemeal on the leaves. These fertilizers won't burn the leaves and so are quite easy and safe to use.

Weeds

Weeds are usually no problem around tomatoes in the home garden. As the plants are starting to grow, they are far enough apart for you to get close to do any weeding necessary. If you let some plants grow freely, you'll soon see that, with their dense foliage, they shade out weeds very well and smother them. A good mulch around staked or trellised plants will keep down weeds, so they won't rob the plants of water and nutrients.

Watering

Tomatoes like an even supply of water through the season — and if their water supply gets turned off and on all the time they'll develop problems. I can't emphasize the need for an even water supply enough.

Like most other vegetables in the garden, tomatoes need at least 1 inch of rain or irrigation water per week for steady growth. In the hotter, dryer parts of the country, their needs go up to 2 inches of water per week during the summer months.

If you're curious about what an inch of water measures out to . . . . well, it's about 60 gallons for each 100 square feet of garden. So if you ever have to water by the bucket brigade, that's something to bear in mind.

I heard of a clever way of watering tomatoes from a friend in Texas. He cuts the tops from some gallon-size cans, punches holes in the bottoms, and sets them in the ground with only about 1 inch of the can showing above the surface. He uses two cans near each tomato plant and fills them two or three times per week — or more often if he needs to. When the plants start fruiting, he adds one or two teaspoons of a complete fertilizer, such as 5-10-10, in each can once a week for his sidedressing. I tried it, and it works fine.

You can develop your own way of watering as long as you follow these watering guidelines:

Water thoroughly to encourage the tomato roots to seek water and nutrients deep in the soil. With an extensive, deep root system the plants hold up better in dry spells. When watering, soak the soil to a depth of 6 to 8 inches at least. A thorough soaking every 4 or 5 days on light, sandy soils and every 7 to 10 days on heavy soils is a good general guide for irrigating tomatoes if you don't get enough rain.

Water only when your plants need it. Tomatoes like moisture, but overwatering is harmful. You not only waste water, but you can prevent the roots from getting air. If your plants look wilted on a hot summer afternoon, that's normal. They'll usually perk up overnight. If plants are wilted in the morning, don't wait — water them!

Water early in the day to cut down on evaporation losses and also to give your plants plenty of time to dry out. Wet foliage overnight may help trigger some diseases. With furrow irrigation, drip irrigation, or soaker hoses, which all deliver water right at the soil surface and not on the leaves, you can water most anytime. Try to avoid watering at midday though, because that's when evaporation losses are highest.

Use a good mulch to help retain moisture in the soil. Mulches reduce the fluctuation of soil moisture and that helps the crop enormously. But, remember, don't apply mulch until after the transplants have been going for 4 to 5 weeks.

COMMON TOMATO PROBLEMS

Blossom end rot. This rot shows first on the bottom of the tomato — it appears as a large, dry, brown or black sunken area. It affects both green and ripe tomatoes and is caused by a fluctuating moisture supply that results in a lack of calcium in the plant.

Staked and pruned plants are more likely to suffer from it than unstaked tomatoes. It's also most likely to appear on the earliest fruits of the season.

The rot often starts as the plants are putting on some quick growth when suddenly they get hit by a hot, dry spell. They suffer moisture stress, and this brings on the problem.

It's sad to see blossom rot erupt in a tomato

row because you can't help the tomato once it's started. Concentrating on keeping the water supply even through the season and mulching will help.

One on-the-spot measure for gardeners facing a blossom end rot crisis: apply calcium right away to the leaves and fruits. You get the calcium in the form of calcium chloride — sold as de-icing salt at hardware stores. Mix 2 tablespoons to a gallon of water and spray 2 or 3 times a week. This will help some.

Cracking. Tomatoes can start to crack during warm, rainy periods — especially if this weather comes after a dry spell. The tomatoes simply expand too fast. Some varieties are resistant to cracking. Again, the best way to avoid the problem is to keep the moisture supply as steady as possible throughout the season.

Catfacing. This is another kind of cracking or scarring. Tomatoes develop unusual swelling and streaks of scar tissue. It is not a disease. It's caused by abnormal development of the pistil of the tomato flower at blossom time. Cool weather is believed to cause the flower problems.

Blossom drop. Some years many of the early season blossoms will simply fall off. It's caused by cool night temperatures (below 55°F). Some varieties such as **Pixie** will keep their blossoms and set fruit in cool weather, but most varieties won't. Some blossom drop will also occur when night temperatures get above 75° in the summer.

This is partly the reason it's difficult to get a summer-long crop of tomatoes in the hot sections of the South.

Curling of leaves. Curling or "leaf roll" is very common, but it does not harm production. It's often most noticeable when the plants are about a foot tall. As the vines become bushy, the new leaves tend to hide the older leaves which may be curled. Too much pruning may promote curling, too.

Sunscald. This occurs when green or ripening tomatoes get too much exposure to the hot sun. At first, a yellowish-white patch appears on the side of the tomato facing the sun. The area gets larger as the fruit ripens and becomes grayish-white. Some varieties develop a lot of foliage and so are good in hot, sunny areas of the country. To guard against sunscald, be careful not to over-prune plants and remove all their shade, or grow them in cages where they'll develop lots of protective foliage.

Although these common problems make tomatoes look ugly, they're okay to eat fresh. Just cut away the affected part and enjoy the rest.

Diseases

Early blight is one of the most common and most harmful diseases. It is caused by a fungus and appears first as a simple brown spot, surrounded by yellow, that spreads outward like a target. First the lower leaves are affected and then they wither. Higher leaves are hit, too, and the crop can be badly damaged. To help keep early blight in check, mulch to reduce splashing, use a good all-purpose tomato dust, and make sure the plants have good ventilation by not crowding them.

There are also chemical fungicide sprays, such as Maneb or Zineb, which can be effective against early blight. You have to use them regularly. Be sure you read the label and follow all directions carefully.

Late blight is a serious disease in areas east of the Mississippi and more pronounced in cool, moist weather. Leaves develop large, brown spots and wither. Spots on tomatoes turn brown and harden.

Use of a standard tomato dust throughout the season helps combat this problem.

Leaf spot is a fungus disease that can hurt production. It's often a problem in the Southeastern states and some Northern areas that have warm, moist weather. The leaves start showing small spots with light centers. They may turn yellow and drop off. The fungus that causes the disease lives on old tomato vines, in the soil and on perennial weeds. Rotating crops is important to keep this disease in check. Spraying with a fungicide, such as Maneb or Zineb, may be effective, too. Also, keeping your garden free of perennial weeds will help.

Insects

Let's run down some of the more common tomato insect problems gardeners have to deal with from time to time:

Cutworms: If you've seen cutworms, you know these gray, brown or black critters curl up tight when disturbed. They're about 1 or 1 1/2 inches long, hide in the soil during the day and come out at night to feed on young plants. They chew tomato transplants right off at the soil surface.

No need to spray in the home garden for these. Simply put on a newspaper collar around the tender stem at transplanting time, spanning at least 1 inch above to 1 inch below ground. (See page 31.)

Flea beetles: These small, tiny black or brown insects jump all over and eat small holes in the leaves, most often early in the season. Spray or dust with Sevin or rotenone to control them.

Blister beetles and **Colorado Potato Beetles:** They feed on tomato foliage, too, and may also be controlled with rotenone, Sevin or an all-purpose dust or spray especially for tomatoes.

Aphids can bother tomato plants all season long. They suck the sap from the plants and weaken them, and, indirectly, spread disease. Spray with malathion.

Hornworms: These huge, green, caterpillar-like worms with thornlike horns at their back end eat both leaves and tomatoes. They work fast, too. Hand-picking these creatures is the best bet in the home garden because you usually discover them at harvest time when it's unwise to spray. Sevin or the natural spray 'bacillus thuringensius' (available as 'Dipel' or 'Thuricide') is effective. Wait at least one day before harvesting if you spray with Sevin. And wash sprayed fruit well before eating or processing. No waiting time necessary for Dipel.

Tomato fruitworm: Here's a season-long pest which eats tomatoes big and small. Control worms with Sevin as soon as you notice them.

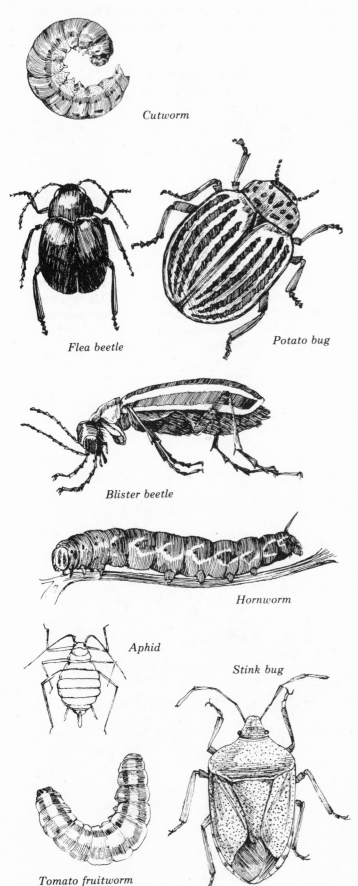

Cutworm

Flea beetle

Potato bug

Blister beetle

Hornworm

Aphid

Stink bug

Tomato fruitworm

Stink Bugs: Sucking insects, they are mostly a Southern problem. Like aphids, they suck sap from the plant. To control, keep weeds in check in the garden and spray with Sevin or Malathion.

If you use chemical sprays be very careful about following the directions exactly. Read the directions 3 times: before you make a purchase, so you know what you are getting; before you use it, to ensure that you are using it correctly; and after you have used it, so that you store it properly and out of risk to people and pets.

Notes on Disease Prevention

The way we look forward to our tomato harvest each year, I can't imagine not taking every precaution to prevent disease problems that could reduce our yield. I recommend these steps:

Rotate the crop each year to avoid soil-borne diseases. Some serious diseases can live in the soil for several seasons. We like to wait three years, if possible, before planting tomatoes where we had them before. I never plant tomatoes where I grew potatoes or eggplants the previous season, since some diseases attack all these vegetables and live in the soil from year to year.

Plant resistant varieties. Many are resistant to Verticillium wilt and Fusarium wilt — two troublesome diseases for which there is no cure. Fusarium is characterized by yellowing of the leaves, wilting and early death of the plant. Verticillium has the same symptoms but seldom kills tomato plants; plant growth will slow down, plants will lose leaves, and tomatoes may be sunburned.

Some seed companies list resistance to these diseases by putting F (Fusarium) or V (Verticullium) after the variety name. 'N' stands for resistance to nematodes, the tiny worms that plague many Southern gardens and cause stunting of the plants and poor crops.

Don't let anyone smoke in the garden since they can infect tomato plants with tobacco mosaic virus, a serious disease which can really cut down on the harvest. If you smoke, wash your hands with soap and water before handling tomato plants.

Use an all-purpose tomato dust to give your crop protection. It contains ingredients mixed together which give your tomatoes protection against early and late blight. Use it regularly and follow the directions on the label very carefully.

Pull up and get rid of any diseased plants.

Help is available if you need it. Remember that your local Extension Service can help you identify diseases and recommend remedies. Many

offices publish pamphlets with pictures and descriptions of tomato plant problems you may encounter.

Tomatoes in Crocks, Pots and Baskets

Tomatoes will surprise you! They can stand mighty close quarters and still deliver. So if you have a hanging planter or a bushel basket and a sunny spot somewhere, you can grow your own!

Some points to keep in mind:

Sun. Container tomatoes, like those in the garden, need at least 6 to 8 hours of sunshine a day to produce a worthwhile harvest. If you grow them indoors, put them where they'll get maximum sunshine . . . moving the container from window to window if you must.

Soil. For hanging planters and small pots, regular potting soil is good. With larger containers, you may want to invest in a bag of soil mix such as Jiffy Mix or Pro Mix. They'll retain moisture very well, which is important for tomatoes. Garden soil is okay, but mix in peat moss or some other soil mix, so that it will hold water and not pack down too much.

Containers. Almost anything will do. You can have a great crop from a plant in a 5-gallon can or pot, a small hanging planter . . . or even a bushel basket or larger container.

At our place, we line our bushel baskets with plastic trash bags to keep the dirt in, retain moisture and keep them warm. We put an inch of stones at the bottom of the bags and poke through some drainage holes. We put three tomato plants in each basket and use short stakes to support them. They look beautiful on our deck!

Varieties. Cherry tomatoes and other small varieties are the ones to grow in containers. If you're going to try container growing for the first time, I'd recommend a cherry patio type such as

Sweet 100, **Tiny Tim** or my favorite, **Pixie**. They'll be easier to stake and support and they'll produce very early.

Water. Container tomatoes need watering often because the plant roots obviously can't reach for extra moisture as garden tomatoes do. In the heat of the summer when the plants are big, we water them daily.

Fertilizer. Give the plants some fertilizer every week or so. Mix a small amount of plant food or balanced fertilizer into their water. Tomatoes like regular feedings of small amounts of fertilizer rather than infrequent, large doses.

Planting. Pinch off the lower leaves of the seedlings and set them in the baskets, pots or hanging planters vertically as deep as you can. For fall pot plantings, take 6 or 8-inch suckers or "slips" from tomato plants in the garden (smaller varieties preferred), set them in a deep pot, and water heavily for a day or two. When you bring these pots or baskets indoors and give them a sunny home, you can extend the tomato harvest for many weeks.

Pollination. When the plants have flowered, give them a little shake in the middle of the day to help pollination along.

Care. Whether they're on the back porch or in the house, tomatoes need protection from diseases just like garden plants.

HARVESTING

One of the great joys of gardening is reaching for the first red-ripe tomato on the vine and biting into it. There's a flavor, juiciness and pleasure you'll never get from a supermarket tomato. I consider it a modern luxury to pick a plump, vine-ripened tomato — especially one you've grown yourself. Because tomatoes ripen from the inside out, when the outer skin is firm and red, you know you've got a beautiful ripe one.

The red color of tomatoes won't form when the temperatures are above 86°F. So if you live where the summers get quite hot, leaving tomatoes on the vine may give them a yellowish-orange look. It's probably better to pick them in the pink stage and let them ripen indoors in cooler temperatures.

Tomatoes don't need light to ripen, so don't put them on a sunny windowsill. The sun will burn and redden them before they can ripen naturally from the inside out. Put them in a place out of direct sunlight — even in a dark cupboard — where the temperature is around 65 or 70°F.

Frost-Time Harvest

Tomatoes will succumb to the lightest frost, but don't panic when the weatherman predicts the first frost and your tomato vines are still loaded with green fruit. If it's going to be a light frost, you can protect the plants overnight by covering them with old sheets, plastic, burlap bags or big boxes. I think it's worth the effort because in my experience the second frost is often 2 or 3 weeks after the first one.

If a heavy freeze is on its way, go out and pick all the tomatoes. Green tomatoes that have reached about three-fourths of their full size will eventually ripen, and smaller, immature green ones can be pickled.

THE GREAT TOMATO RACE

To have the first ripe tomato in your neighborhood:

Select an early variety — such as **Pixie, Stokes Alaska** or other tomato known to set fruit well in cool weather.

Plant the seeds yourself indoors 10 to 12 weeks or more before the average last spring frost date.

Repot the seedlings into a deep container when they are 3 or 4 inches high, picking off all the lower leaves and putting the plant in up to the leaves. Repot a second time when the plants are 8 to 10 inches high, again pinching off all the lower leaves and setting the plants as deep in tall milk cartons or pots as you can.

Harden off the plants well — at least for 10 days. You should try to get the plants in the ground two or three weeks before the average last frost date, so plan your hardening period accordingly.

Choose a sunny section of the garden for your tomatoes. Till or spade the soil there deeply, mixing in a generous amount of fertilizer, compost or manure. If possible, transplant on a cloudy day. In sunny weather, try to wait until late afternoon or evening.

If you transplant according to the trench method, the roots will be near the surface. If you set the plant in the ground vertically, keep the roots close to the surface by not planting them deeper than before, so they can warm up. Soak the area after transplanting. Don't use any mulch except black plastic.

Use some kind of heat-gathering technique — such as hotcaps or circling the plants with black felt roofing paper or with an old tire. The more heat you draw to the plant, the sooner the harvest.

It's vital to use windbreaks and frost protection devices such as hot caps, paper bags or bushel baskets.

Spray flower clusters twice a week with "blossom set," a hormone spray which helps fruit setting.

Sidedress the plants with a balanced fertilizer when the plant has blossomed.

Be sure the plants get enough water and watch out for signs of insect or disease damage.

Root prune a couple of tomato plants when they have formed 3 or 4 clusters of tomatoes. This will hasten ripening.

Before harvesting your first vine-ripened tomato — weeks before your neighbors — ask them over to witness the event and collect your bets right on the spot!

Some people like to pull up the whole tomato plant and hang it upside down in a dark basement room and let the tomatoes ripen gradually. You just have to check them regularly to keep a very ripe tomato from falling onto the floor — splaat!

At our place we put all the tomatoes that need ripening on a shelf and cover them with sheets of newspaper. Some people wrap up each tomato individually but that's too much work — especially when you want to check for ripe tomatoes. You have to open each one! Instead, we just lift up the flat newspaper cover, take a peek and take all the ripe tomatoes and remove any that may have started to rot. The newspaper covering helps trap a natural, ethylene gas that tomatoes give off which hastens ripening.

Fall Tomatoes

In the Southern and Southwestern states you can grow an abundant crop of fall tomatoes. Though my home garden is way up north, I try to grow late tomatoes, too.

The big question is "Where do I buy young tomato plants in the middle of the summer?" It's very hard to find them for sale.

An easy way to solve the problem is to cut small suckers from spring-planted tomatoes and let them grow to full-sized plants. Earlier I told you to pinch out most of the suckers on your tomato plants, but if you want some plants for the fall, allow some suckers to grow 4 or 5 inches and produce a bud. Then in mid- or late summer, cut the suckers from the plant, remove the lower leaves up to the bud and set them in a jar of water for an hour or two. This will start the rooting process. Then plant them in pots or directly in the garden. Firm the soil around the suckers and water them heavily for two or three days.

You can also simply lop off the top foot or so of a healthy plant and set it in water and plant it later.

These plants will do just as well as any you could raise from scratch or buy at a garden store. They'll give you a nice fall crop, too.

Garden to Kitchen

Tomatoes are wonderful!

They taste best fresh from the garden with the warmth of the sun still in them, but we also love them with a little salt or sliced with just a sprinkling of oil, salt and pepper on top. Homegrown tomatoes go great in salads, broiled, baked, fried, with eggs or cheese, as relish, in stews, stuffed — fantastic both summer and winter.

Cherry tomatoes are great as appetizers; Italian plum tomatoes are especially good for sauces and cooking. Beef-steak tomatoes — the really, nice, big, fat, firm ones — are terrific for slicing or stuffing. And the "garden variety" tomatoes are excellent broiled, served plain, in salads or canned whole or stewed.

Tomatoes come in such pretty colors, too —

luscious golds and yellows, but for us nothing beats a beautiful, red one.

Until the beginning of this century, in many areas of this country, people didn't eat tomatoes because they thought they were poisonous. I learned that the green leaves really are toxic, and that the plant is related to other noxious plants — deadly nightshade, belladonna and tobacco — but we know that the fruit of the tomato plant makes for fine eating!

Because tomatoes are used in so many recipes, it was difficult for me to decide which to share with you. The recipes here are our favorites, and more especially ones that I think are difficult or impossible to find elsewhere. Some have been made up by me or my family or friends. I have carefully copied these from well-used cards in my own recipe file. Others I have collected from various cookbooks and magazines over the years, making changes as I went along. I hope you like them.

CANNING TOMATOES

Just looking at my jars of tomatoes gives me a nice, satisfied feeling, but the real benefit comes in the eating. In the winter when the stores carry only mealy, dry, flavorless, pale pink things they call tomatoes, I love turning to my own storehouse of homegrown and home-canned ones for a real taste treat.

Canning is an efficient way to preserve tomatoes, and it's easy to do right. I heartily recommend giving it a try if you've never canned before. Here are ten easy steps to follow:

Boiling Water Bath Canning

1. **For safety, it is always important to use careful canning techniques.** Because tomatoes contain sufficient acid, they may be canned safely in a boiling water bath rather than in a pressure canner as required for all other vegetables. If you are canning tomato sauce that contains meat or other vegetables, use the pressure canning method.

Because instructions accompanying canners sometimes vary, I urge you to follow the instructions that came with yours.

2. **Assemble all utensils:** Canner with rack, Mason jars, lids, tongs or jar lifter, timer, cooling racks, wide-mouth funnel, slotted spoon, nonmetallic spatula.

Use only Mason jars for home canning; they are made by a number of manufacturers. These jars are safe for canning because the glass is heat-tempered, and they can seal perfectly. If you have saved other jars, use them for jellies or jams with paraffin seals.

Never re-use dome lids for canning. The rubber compound loses its ability to seal perfectly after one use. Metal screw bands and Mason jars may be re-used.

3. **Examine and clean all equipment.** Check all bands for rust, dents or nicks and the jars for chips or cracks. Recycle them or use them in the workshop or elsewhere if they are not perfect.

Wash all equipment in hot, soapy water. Rinse in clear, hot water. Keep jars and screw tops hot. Keep dome lids in simmering water until ready to use.

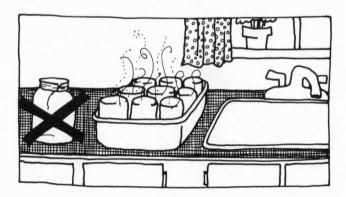

4. **Prepare freshest, cleanest produce possible. One bushel of tomatoes will yield about 18 quarts of tomatoes; 3 pounds of tomatoes will produce one quart.** Of course, if you cook them down for sauce, paste or juice, the yield varies.

Wash tomatoes well.

To peel them, put them in boiling water for 30 seconds until the skins split. Put them in cold water briefly. Then, using a paring knife, the skins will slip off easily.

Remove the stems and any green spots from the tomatoes, and do not use any tomatoes that

are over-ripe or unhealthy. One bad tomato is like one bad apple — it can spoil the whole batch. So, be careful when you select your tomatoes.

Tomatoes don't always have to be peeled. If they are going to be used in smooth sauce or in juice, there's no need to peel them. When they are sieved or strained, the skins will be eliminated.

5. **Cold pack or hot pack.** Fill only the number of jars your canner can hold at one time. If you are canning whole tomatoes, use cold (or raw) pack, because the tomatoes will keep their shape better. If you want a denser pack, cook them first. Sauce, juice and relishes are packed partially cooked (hot pack).

Cold pack: Pack clean, cored tomatoes firmly in jars. Depending on size, pack the tomatoes whole or quartered. Squeeze as many tomatoes as you can into the jar, pressing down as you fill them, so the juice is released and covers the tomatoes. To retain the shape of whole tomatoes, add extra tomato juice rather than squeezing down so hard, but still pack them firmly. Salt, 1/2 tsp per pint, may be added. Leave 1/2-inch headspace. Release all air bubbles from jar by running spatula down around inside of jar. Wipe jar top and threads clean with damp cloth. Put lid, rubber side down, on jar and screw band on firmly.

Hot pack: Tomato juice, stewed tomatoes, cooked sauce and chutneys, chili sauce, ketchup and relishes are all packed hot in hot jars.

Tomato juice: Cut washed, cored and unpeeled tomatoes into quarters and cook slowly in large, heavy aluminum, stainless or enamel pot until the tomatoes are soft. Press them through food mill or strainer. Salt, sugar and spices may be added. (We like pure tomato juice with salt, 1 tsp per quart.) After straining, reheat juice until it is almost boiling. Pour it hot into hot jars, leaving 1/4 inch headspace. Wipe jar tops and threads clean. Put lid, rubber side down, on jar and screw band on firmly.

Tomato sauce: Use whatever recipe you like; favorite is on page 51. Because sauce is cooked down and a lot of water has evaporated from the tomatoes, sauce requires proportionately less shelf space and fewer jars than the same number of canned, whole tomatoes. Pack hot in hot jars, leaving 1/2-inch headspace. Wipe jar top and threads clean with damp cloth. Put lid, rubber side down, on jar and screw band on firmly.

Tomato paste: Try the recipe on page 51. It's good, but all tomato pastes take so many tomatoes and such a lot of time to cook down, that I'm not sure they're worth the energy consumption for home processing.

6. **Process in water-bath canner.** Fill the canner half full with hot — not boiling — water. Place rack in bottom. Put filled jars in canner, so that they do not touch each other or the side of the pot. Add hot water, if necessary, so that the jars are covered with at least 1 to 2 inches of water. Cover. Start timing when water reaches rolling boil.

Canning Time

	Headspace	Jar Size	Boiling Time
Paste	1/4 inch	half pint/pint	45 minutes
Plain puree	1/4 inch	half pint/pint	30 minutes
Seasoned puree	1/4 inch	half pint/pint	45 minutes
Whole tomatoes			
Cold pack	1/2 inch	pint	35 minutes
	1/2 inch	quart	45 minutes
Hot pack	1/2 inch	pint	10 minutes
	1/2 inch	quart	15 minutes
Juice	1/4 inch	pint	10 minutes
	1/4 inch	quart	15 minutes
Ketchup	1/4 inch	pint	15 minutes

Do not skimp on processing time. This is very important to ensure that all bacteria are killed. Altitude lowers the temperature at which water boils, so increase processing time 2 minutes for each 1,000 feet above sea level.

7. **Complete the processing.** Using tongs or jar lifter, remove the jars and put them upright on a rack or thick towel in a draft-free area, allowing enough room between jars so that air may circulate freely.

Do not tighten the metal rims, because you may break the seals.

8. **After twelve hours of cooling, test the seals.** There are three tests recommended for checking the seals on dome lids:

1. As the tomatoes cool and the vacuum forms, the lid pulls down into the jar and makes a kerplunking sound.

2. The lid will be concave or dished and should stay that way as long as the vacuum is present — you can feel it.

3. Push the center of the lid down with your thumb. If it makes a clicking sound, the seal is *not* complete.

If you find some jars with incomplete seals, put the jars in the refrigerator and eat the food soon. The food is perfectly good, but it won't last in storage. It's best to eat it right away, but you can also freeze it. Some glass canning jars are okay in the freezer, and others are not. If you do decide to freeze the tomatoes, just make sure you have a freezer container that's suitable. You can also reprocess the tomatoes, but they lose a lot of flavor and texture.

9. **Wipe the jars with a clean, damp cloth, label clearly and store.** The outer rims should be removed. It is important that the storage area is dry, because moisture may affect the lid and seal on the jars. A cool, dry, dark place is best.

10. **Before serving, reheat canned tomatoes.** It is recommended that you simmer stewed tomatoes or sauce for 10 to 15 minutes — without tasting — to make sure any bacteria are killed. If the tomatoes smell "off" or if the color or appearance doesn't look right, don't taste them. Throw them out so that even pets or wild animals can't get at them. Rule of thumb: When in doubt, throw it out!

If you follow these easy steps, you can have lots of good eating!

FREEZING TOMATOES

Whether it's practical for you to freeze tomatoes or tomato sauce depends on the size of your freezer and what else you need to store in it. Because tomatoes can so well, you may want to save your freezer space for other things.

Freezing sauce is handy, especially if you have just a pint or two left over from a whole canning batch or if you want to add meat to part of a batch of tomato sauce and don't want to drag out the pressure canner. Just put the sauce in containers, leaving 1/2-inch headspace and put it in the freezer.

In the summer when tomatoes are ripe, you may not have much time. To make time, a friend of mine simply stews her cored tomatoes after washing them. She cooks them down slowly, adding just a little sugar. Then she freezes the plain, cooked-down tomatoes in pint containers. In the winter she has a freezer full of garden tomatoes ready for sauces and stews with a minimum of hassle.

Yes, you can freeze whole tomatoes! Whole tomatoes, which have been scalded for 30 seconds in boiling water — just enough time to loosen their skins — may be frozen raw and whole. This is especially handy if you have an over supply, but select especially meaty ones for freezing whole, because otherwise they break down and are fairly mushy when thawed.

Place the tomatoes, whole or sliced, on a greased cookie sheet and place it in the freezer. After 24 hours, when the tomatoes are frozen solid, place them in containers.

FAVORITE RECIPES

Tomato Sauce

A few batches of this sauce should last a family of four all winter and spring. I use this sauce for spaghetti, lasagna, veal and eggplant parmesan, goulash, stews, soups and many, many casseroles. We like it mixed with different vegetables, such as zucchini, eggplant and snap beans — a whole lot of ways!

　1 peck (12 to 15 pounds) fresh tomatoes
　2 cups chopped onions
　1 cup chopped green peppers
　1 cup chopped celery
　2 Tb brown sugar
　2 cloves garlic, finely minced
　1 Tb parsley, minced
　1 Tb basil
　1 Tb oregano
　1 1/2 Tb plain (non-iodized) salt
　1/2 tsp pepper

Wash ripe tomatoes well, and if you want to peel them, dip in boiling water briefly until skins split. Rinse in cold water. Remove cores and green spots. To reduce cooking time, chop tomatoes. Put in large, heavy kettle. (The largest heavy pot I own is my pressure canner. It can hold 7 quart jars without touching, so it can easily hold a peck of tomatoes.) It's important to use a heavy pan, so that the tomatoes do not stick or scorch.

Simmer tomatoes 2 hours, stirring frequently. Add remaining ingredients and using asbestos mat simmer overnight or until the sauce has cooked down by half. If you want a smooth sauce or if you haven't peeled the tomatoes, you may sieve the sauce or run it through a blender or food processor. Pour hot sauce into hot jars, leaving 1/4-inch headspace. Adjust lids. Process 45 minutes in boiling water bath. Makes 8 pints.

Below are just some of the easy and interesting ways this basic sauce can be changed to create really different tastes. The proportions are based on one quart of sauce. These ingredients are added when preparing the sauce for a meal — not prior to canning. Some of the additions — if canned — would lengthen the processing time drastically.

Prior to serving, if the sauce is too thick, add beef consomme, stock, or red or white wine to thin it to the consistency you like.

Three slices of bacon, sauteed and crumbled; 1/2 lb of browned, lean ground beef, 1/2 to 1 lb sliced, sauteed mushrooms, 1/4 cup grated cheese (cheddar, Parmesan or whatever you have on hand).

One-quarter cup browned, minced lean ham; 1 cup browned, chopped beef, 1 strip of lemon peel, pinch of nutmeg, 1 cup of beef stock, 1/2 cup dry white wine. Before serving, remove lemon peel and add 1/4 cup of whipping cream.

Half-pound browned sausage, 1/2 lb browned ground beef, 4 or 5 crushed mint leaves.

Half-pound ground, browned lamb, 3 bay leaves, 1/2 cup dry white or red wine.

Tiny meatballs made of 1 cup soft breadcrumbs, 1 Tb milk, 1/2 lb ground beef, parsley, 1 egg. I brown them well under the broiler or in a skillet before adding them to the basic sauce.

One ounce boned anchovies; small can of tuna; 6 large, pitted, chopped, black olives; 3/4 cup diced mozzarella cheese.

Small pinches of saffron, coriander, fennel and basil, 1-inch piece of dried orange peel.

Tomato Paste

　6 quarts Italian tomatoes
　1 Tb salt
　1 large celery stalk with leaves, cut up
　3/4 cup chopped onion
　2 cloves garlic
　1 sweet red pepper

In a heavy, enamel, stainless or aluminum pot, cook tomatoes until soft. When soft, put through food mill, fine sieve or food processor and reheat. Put onions, celery, garlic, salt and pepper in blender or food processor and liquefy. Add to tomatoes. Simmer using an asbestos mat. It is most important to prevent scorching — stirring frequently helps. After several hours the pulp will be reduced to a thick paste. Pack hot in hot, half-pint jars, leaving 1/4-inch headspace. Release air bubbles, adjust lids and water bath process 45 minutes.

To make handy pasteballs you can spread the paste on moist plates to a depth of 1/2 inch. You may then dry it in the sun or in a warm oven. When it's dry enough, roll the paste into balls and dip them in olive oil. They can then be stored in an airtight jar in the refrigerator.

Fresh Sliced Tomatoes with . . .

... a sprinkling of oil, fresh chopped basil, salt and pepper
... raw spinach, onions and anchovies
... cucumbers, dill, oil and vinegar
... a sprinkling of oil, a dash of vinegar, chopped onions and oregano
... mayonnaise
... in a sandwich with lettuce, bacon and cheese
... sour cream and chives (my favorite!)
... sugar — white, powdered or sifted brown

Fried Tomatoes

"It's wonderful! It has a gravy, and it's really scrumptious!" That's the recommendation I received along with this mother-to-daughter-to-me recipe, and I agree.

Core and slice tomatoes; they can be either green or red. Dip the slices in flour to which some salt and sugar have been added. Brown slices on both sides in butter or bacon fat (bacon fat is better) until crisp. Turn just once. When brown on both sides, put the slices in a casserole in a warm oven. Some of the browning flour will remain in the skillet, and that's okay. Just add more butter or fat as needed for browning more slices.

When all the slices are done, add milk gradually to the pan stirring constantly over a moderate heat to make gravy. Season as needed. Pour hot sauce over tomatoes and serve promptly. If you don't, the tomatoes will get soggy.

Gazpacho (or Salad Soup)

2 cloves garlic
2 slices white bread
1 sliced cucumber
1/2 green pepper
1/2 cup water
1/4 cup olive oil
2 lbs ripe tomatoes
1/4 cup minced onion
1/4 cup chopped pimiento
1 tsp salt
black pepper
2 Tb wine vinegar
2 to 3 cups clear vegetable stock or chicken bouillon
1/2 cup fresh chopped mixed herbs, such as chives, parsley basil or tarragon

Crush garlic in bowl and add bread broken into bits, along with cucumber, green pepper, water and olive oil. (Don't balk at the bread. It gives the soup a great consistency, and after you blend it, you won't know it's there.) Allow this mixture to marinate for several hours. Then add cut up tomatoes, onions, pimiento and salt and pepper. Blend in blender or food processor. Chill thoroughly.

Before serving, mix in vinegar, cold stock and herbs. Serves 6 to 8.

For added texture, flavor or color, you may garnish with additional chopped green pepper, cucumber, celery, watercress, garlic croutons, bean sprouts or lime slices.

No-Pot Tomatoes

In the summer when we grill hamburgers, steak or chicken outdoors, I often serve these, because it means no pots to wash. I love No-Pot-Suppers!

Per serving:
1 tomato
1/2 onion
1/2 tsp olive oil or butter
pinch of basil, tarragon and oregano
sprinkle of garlic salt
salt and pepper

Wash, core and cut each tomato into 8 chunks. Peel the onions, chop them roughly and add to tomatoes. Add butter or oil, salt, pepper and herbs. Wrap the mixture in foil and seal the edges well. (You may even want to wrap it in two layers.) Tuck the package down in the coals or place it on the grill. Depending on the heat of the fire, allow 15 to 30 minutes, enough time for the onions to get tender.

Sensational Tomato Quiche

 1 partially baked, 8-inch pie crust
 2 Tb olive oil
 1/2 cup chopped onion
 1/2 cup chopped green pepper
 1 clove garlic, minced
 2 lbs firm, red, ripe tomatoes
 1/2 tsp each basil, oregano, salt
 3 Tb tomato paste
 3 Tb chopped parsley
 1/8 tsp pepper
 1 egg plus 3 egg yolks
 12 pitted black olives
 8 anchovies (optional)
 1/3 cup grated Parmesan cheese

Preheat oven to 350°. Saute onions, green pepper and garlic in 2 Tb oil in heavy skillet. Add chopped, seeded, peeled tomatoes, herbs, and parsley. Cover and cook over low heat for 5 minutes. for 5 minutes.

Remove cover and raise heat so liquid evaporates. Do not let it scorch. Remove from heat.

Put eggs, anchovies and tomato paste in bowl and mix well. Combine with tomato mixture and pour into pie crust. Top with olives and grated cheese. Bake until firm and golden, about 30 minutes. 30 minutes.

Serves 4 for lunch. Wonderful just with a green salad. Or cut it into a lot of small pieces for excellent hot or cold hors d'oeuvres.

Quick Chicken Cacciatore

 4 Tb butter
 4 Tb olive oil
 1 frying chicken, cut up
 1 qt tomatoes (fresh or stewed) or tomato sauce
 2 cloves garlic, minced
 1 medium onion
   salt and pepper to taste
 1/2 tsp basil
 1/2 tsp oregano
 1/2 cup dry white or red wine

In a large, heavy pot, sauté the onion and garlic in butter and oil, and add the chicken to brown. Add remaining ingredients and simmer, covered, for 30 minutes or until juices run clear from chicken. Serve with buttered broad noodles and a green salad. Serves 4 to 6.

Scalloped Tomatoes

 6 cups tomatoes, peeled and cut up, fresh or canned
 1/4 cup margarine
 1/4 cup chopped onions
 1/4 cup chopped green pepper
   salt and pepper to taste
 1 Tb sugar
 1 1/2 cups toasted bread cubes

Cook onions and green peppers in margarine until tender. In a 2-quart casserole, mix all ingredients together, except for 1/2 cup bread cubes. Sprinkle top with remaining bread cubes and bake in pre-heated 350° oven for 30 minutes. Serves 6. For even better taste, top with grated cheese and put under broiler until bubbly brown.

Baked/Broiled Tomatoes

These are an easy, delicious addition for brunch, lunch or supper that make guests think you've gone to a lot of trouble.

Per serving
 1 tomato
 1/2 slice of bacon
 1/2 ounce grated cheese
   bread crumbs
   pat of butter
   pinches of basil, oregano
   salt and pepper

Wash tomatoes and core. Cut in half crosswise and sprinkle with salt and pepper, herbs and top with cheese, bacon, bread crumbs and butter. Put on oiled baking pan and bake in preheated 400° oven 15 minutes or until tomatoes are tender but not soft. Put under broiler for a minute to brown.

Sort-of Spanish Rice

 1/4 cup chopped onion
 3 Tb chopped green pepper
 2 Tb oil
 1 cup raw rice
 2 cups stewed tomatoes
 2 tsp sugar
 1/2 cup grated Parmesan cheese
 4 pork chops or 3/4 lb hot sausage

Sauté onions, green peppers and rice in oil until rice is translucent. Add sugar and tomatoes to skillet. Top with pork chops and cheese. Bake covered, in 350° oven for about one hour. Serves 4. Served with a green salad, it's a one-pot supper even kids can prepare.

Stuffed Tomatoes

6 firm, red tomatoes, 3 to 4 inches in diameter
1/2 lb sausage meat or lean, chopped beef
    olive oil
2 cups rice, cooked
1 medium onion, finely chopped
1 clove garlic, minced
1 tsp fresh basil, finely chopped
4 Tb Parmesan cheese
1 tsp fresh parsley, finely chopped
    salt and pepper to taste

Cut tops off unpeeled, washed tomatoes. Save the tops. Squeeze or scoop out the seeds of the tomatoes and reserve the juice. Sprinkle insides with salt and invert to drain.

Brown meat, drain fat and set aside. Sauté onion and garlic in olive oil in heavy skillet over medium heat. Combine onion, meat rice, herbs, cheese and reserved tomato juice.

Stuff shells with mixture. Place tomatoes on oiled, shallow baking pan and bake in preheated 350° oven for 30 minutes or until tomatoes are soft but still firm. May be served hot or cold.

Raw tomatoes can also be filled with various cold salads, such as seafood, egg, potato or rice.

Tomato Jam

1 lb tomatoes, red, green or yellow
1 lb sugar
2 ounces ginger root or preserved ginger
1 4-inch cinnamon stick
    grated rind of 1 lemon or orange

Peel, core and slice tomatoes. Cover with sugar and let stand for 12 hours. Strain off the juice and boil it until the syrup falls from the spoon in heavy drops. Add the tomatoes, rind and spices. Cook until jam thickens and then put in hot, sterile jars. May be sealed with paraffin.

Spicy Tomato Relish

We serve this with meats instead of store-bought ketchup. It's our favorite tomato relish.

20 tomatoes, peeled and chopped
1 1/2 cups onions, chopped
1 cup green peppers, chopped
1 1/4 cup sugar, white or brown
2 tsp celery seed
2 tsp plain (non-iodized) salt
3/4 tsp each cinnamon, cloves, ginger, allspice
1 cup vinegar

Mix all ingredients in a large, heavy kettle. Bring to boil and then simmer until as thick as desired. Stir to prevent sticking. Pour, boiling hot, into hot jars. Leave 1/4-inch headspace and adjust lids. Process 35 minutes in boiling water bath. Makes about 8 pints.

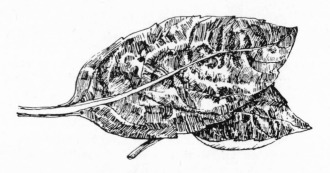

Tomato Bread

This unusual, reddish bread is wonderful as a base for melted cheese sandwiches and mini-pizzas.

2 cups tomato juice
2 Tb butter
3 Tb sugar
1 tsp salt
1/2 tsp each basil, oregano
1/4 cup ketchup
1/4 cup grated cheese
1 pkg active dry yeast
1/4 cup warm water (110° to 115°F)
7 cups sifted, all purpose flour

Heat tomato juice and butter together until the butter is melted. Add sugar, salt, herbs, ketchup and cheese, and let mixture cool to lukewarm. Sprinkle yeast on warm water and stir to dissolve. Add tomato mixture and 3 cups of flour to yeast. Beat with electric mixer at medium speed, scraping the bowl occasionally. Mix for 2 minutes or beat by hand until smooth.

Gradually mix in enough remaining flour to make soft dough that leaves the side of the bowl. Turn onto lightly floured board and knead for 8 to 10 minutes, when dough will be elastic and smooth. Place in lightly greased bowl; turn dough over so top is greased.

Cover and let rise in warm place until doubled — 1 to 1 1/2 hours. Punch down and divide in half. Cover and let rest 10 minutes. Shape into loaves and place in greased, 9 x 5 x 3″ loaf pans. Cover and let rise until almost doubled, about 1 hour.

Bake in hot oven (375°F) about 25 minutes or until done. Makes 2 loaves.

Pottsfield Pickle

Why this recipe has such a strange name, I don't know. It was given to me by a friend who came from Maine; she got it from a relative who lived in the South. Somewhere in that geographic maze, I suspect one could find the origin. Anyway, it's a very good way to use leftover tomatoes — both red and green — at the end of the season.

    3 pts green tomatoes
    3 pts firm, red tomatoes
    3 large onions
    3 red, sweet peppers
    3 bunches of celery (or less)
    1/2 cup salt (non-iodized)
    1 tsp cinnamon
    1 tsp cloves
    1/2 cup white mustard seed
    3 pt vinegar (or less)
    4 cups sugar

Cut up all the vegetables; add salt. Let the mixture sit for 6 hours or overnight. Drain and rinse. Add remaining ingredients; cook until tender. It will be juicy. Pour in hot, sterile jars, leaving 1/4-inch headspace. Adjust lids and process for 35 minutes in boiling water bath. Makes 6 to 8 pints.

Tomato Apple Chutney

    20 medium, ripe tomatoes
     8 apples
     3 large onions
     2 large, sweet red or green peppers
     1 hot red pepper
     1 cup seedless raisins
    2 1/2 cups brown sugar
     1 clove garlic, crushed
     2 tsp each ground ginger, cinnamon
     1 tsp salt
    3 1/2 cups vinegar

Scald tomatoes in boiling water, cool and peel. Pare apples. Peel onions. Core peppers. Chop all roughly. Combine all ingredients and simmer in heavy, covered kettle for about 2 hours or until mixture is thick. Stir frequently to prevent sticking. Pour boiling hot into hot, sterile jars. Leave 1/4-inch headspace. Process 10 minutes in boiling water bath.

Our Special Green Tomato Mince Meat

Dick usually lands a buck during hunting season, so I use venison in this recipe, but beef is also good.

    3 lbs venison or lean beef
    2 qts finely chopped green tomatoes
    4 lbs tart apples, cored and chopped
    3 cups white sugar
    3 cups brown sugar
    2 lbs raisins
    1 Tb salt
    1 cup vinegar
    2 Tb cinnamon
    2 tsp cloves
    2 tsp nutmeg

After stewing the meat until tender in a little water in a Dutch oven, chop it finely. Mix all other ingredients together with meat and cook thoroughly for 1 hour.

To preserve it, the mince meat must either be pressure canned or frozen. If pressure canning carefully follow the instructions accompanying your pressure canner.

Before serving the mincemeat — plain or as filling in pies and tarts — you can add brandy to it.

CHAPTER 3

Peppers, Okra and Eggplant

Peppers make the garden brighter for gardeners everywhere. The glistening greens of the leaves and the ripening peppers, the true scarlets and yellows from pale to pow of different varieties, all mark the rows where peppers are growing. I truly enjoy walking through the garden where the peppers are growing to feast my eyes on the rich colors. And I try to plant them in a spot where they can be easily seen and appreciated by our visitors. Peppers look so good growing that they make everything around them look better, healthier and tastier.

Besides their appearance, there's another reward from peppers. They're delicious. Sweet bell peppers go well with just about anything and are wonderful eaten right out of the garden, while the hotter varieties spice up many recipes. Some pepper varieties add color as well as flavor: a pimiento pepper strip in stuffed olives and stuffed eggs with a dusting of paprika on the top. (Paprika is made from peppers.) Stuffed peppers, pickled peppers, fried peppers — peppers fit in, deliciously, everywhere.

In spite of the same name, our table pepper and the sweet and hot peppers we grow are not related. The black and white pepper we use are the seeds of a plant, *Piper nigrum,* while our garden peppers belong to the species *Capsicum. Capsicum annuum,* one group of the Capsicum species, accounts for most of the varieties grown in this country. The exception is the Tabasco pepper which belongs to another species.

If you cut open a pepper crosswise near the stem, you'll notice thin walls that divide the pepper into sections. These sections are called the "lobes" or "cells." Most seed companies describe a well-shaped sweet bell pepper as being "blocky." The blocky shape comes from the division of the pepper into lobes, and a good blocky pepper will have three or four lobes. The shape of blocky peppers make them great for stuffing, pepper rings and general all-round use.

Pepper Groups

Seed companies break the peppers we grow down into two categories: hot and sweet. The "hot" include: Cayenne, Celestial and Large Cherry. Included in the "sweet" category are: Bell, Banana, Pimiento and Sweet Cherry.

Bell — These peppers are characterized by large, block-shaped fruits that have three or four lobes. They are about three inches wide, four inches long, and they taper slightly. Starting off as dark green to yellow-green, most turn red when fully ripe, although some turn yellow. They are often harvested and used when green. There are around 200 varieties in the Bell Group. **California** and **Yolo Wonder** belong to this group.

Pimiento — These peppers are sweet and have very thick walls. The fruit is conical, two to three inches wide, three to four inches long and slightly pointed. Pimientos are red when ripe, and they're most commonly used at this stage. Popular varieties include **Bighart, Truhart, Perfection** and **Pimiento.**

Cherry — These peppers are cherry or globe-shaped with three cells. They grow on long, upright stems, usually above the leaves of the plant. They are usually orange to deep red when harvested and may be sweet or hot, large or small. Varieties include **Bird's Eye**, **Red Cherry Small** and **Red Cherry Large**.

Cayenne — These are hot chile peppers. The fruit are slim, pointed and slightly curved, ranging in length from two to eight inches. Most of the fruit are green, ripening to red. They can be used in either the green or the red stage. Examples are **Anaheim**, **Cayenne**, **Serrano** and **Jalapeno** varieties.

Celestial — These very hot, cone-shaped peppers grow upright above the leaves of the plant. They're three-quarters of an inch to two inches long, have three cells and may or may not change color from yellowish to red or purplish to light orange-red. Different colored fruit can appear on the same plant at the time, which makes the plant very attractive. They're ornamental and grow best in containers. They're a wonderful patio plant. Popular varieties include **Floral Gem**, **Fresno Chile** and **Celestial**.

Tabasco — These one-inch to three-inch long fruits are slim, tapered and *very* hot. They are attractive ornamental plants as well as having fruit that can be harvested. The most popular pepper of this group is **Tabasco.** They're grown commercially for making Tabasco Sauce. Others are **Japanese Cluster, Coral Gem, Chili Piquin, Small Red Chili** and very small **Cayenne**.

Chile, Chili, Cayenne, Jalapeno — By Any Name, It's HOT!

Names for hot peppers can get confusing. Some people call them chili peppers, some call them cayennes or jalapeno, and folks like me just call them hot peppers. What are they really called? Is each of these names a separate category?

The confusion started in Mexico. "Chile" means pepper. To specify which type of pepper, Mexicans would add the word for the particular type after the name *chile*. Therefore, *chile dulce* would be sweet pepper, *chile jalapeno* would be the jalapeno pepper, and so on. When *chile* found its way into this country, different meanings were given to it in various parts of the country, and it even acquired a new spelling. In the Southwest and West, *chile* is used to refer to the Anaheim pepper. In other parts of the South and Southeast and still other sections of the country, *chile* refers to any type of hot pepper. In still other parts of the U.S., *chili* is the word for hot pepper. Some folks refer to all hot peppers as *cayennes* or *jalapenos*. And all over the country we have the dishes chile and chili con carne which are pepper based. Cayenne and Jalapeno are only two types of hot peppers; there are Anaheims, Serranos and numerous others. *Chile* and *chili* are not varieties of peppers, but only words used to describe that the pep-

per is hot. So whether you say *chile* or *chili, cayenne* or *jalapeno,* and whether the word describes just an Anaheim pepper or all hot peppers, watch out! That pepper is HOT!

What Makes Peppers Hot?

Everyone has a theory on where the "hotness" is in peppers. Some say it's in the seeds, some say the skin, some say the inside walls, and some folks say that you can bite off about one-eighth of an inch from the bottom of a hot pepper without tasting any hotness at all.

Capsaicin, a substance present in most peppers, causes the hotness. Of course, it's present in much greater quantities in hot peppers, which makes them taste hotter than bell or sweet peppers. Capsaicin is so strong to the human taste bud that even a dilution of one part per million can be detected.

Where is the capsaicin? It's found in tiny blister-like sacs between the lining and the inner wall of the pepper. If you cut a pepper in half lengthwise, you will see the inside partitions that divide each pepper into lobes and surround the seed cavity. The clear membrane that covers these partitions also covers the blister-like capsaicin sacs. These sacs are easily broken if a pepper is handled at all roughly, releasing the capsaicin throughout the inside of the pepper and spreading the hotness.

If the capsaicin sacs have broken and spread the fire, that bottom eighth of an inch will be just as hot as the rest of the pepper.

Can Anything Take the Hotness Out?

Hot pepper seeds cause a burning sensation if they come into contact with your eyes or mouth, so always remove the stem and seed core when preparing them. You should wear rubber gloves when working with the extra hot varieties because the seeds and skins can burn your hands.

I don't know of anything that can take the fire out of a canned, pickled or store-bought chile pepper. But if you grow your own and want to eat some fresh out of the garden, there is a way to take out some of the hotness.

Roll a fresh chile pepper between your hands, or roll it on the table as if you were rolling dough. This dislodges the seeds and breaks the capsaicin sacs. After rolling it for a while, take a razor blade or sharp knife and cut the pepper from near the stem end down to the bottom. Cut only through the wall of the pepper; don't cut the pepper into pieces. Repeat this cut in two other places. You now have a pepper that is in three sections, held together by the stem end. Holding it by the stem, dunk the pepper in a glass of water. After about 30 seconds to a minute of dunking, the pepper should be ready to eat. The water will wash out the seeds and a lot of the capsaicin. If the pepper is still too hot for your taste, dip it into a fresh glass of water for another minute or so. This will remove even more of the capsaicin.

In an Anaheim pepper, most of the capsaicin is contained near the stem end. Cutting off an inch of the pepper from the stem end makes for a milder tasting Anaheim.

OKRA

Okra shines in the garden. It's a member of the hibiscus family. You've probably seen pictures of Hawaiian girls with large hibiscus blossoms tucked behind their ears. Well, the blossoms on okra plants aren't quite as large and showy as those blossoms, but they are definitely one of the most beautiful blooms in the vegetable garden. They're ivory to creamy yellow in color with a deep reddish purple throat. They bloom only for a day. By sundown, the okra flower is wilted, whether or not it's been pollinated. If it is sunny and good bee-buzzing weather, you will see miniature okra pods underneath the wilted flowers. All the blooms on the okra plant won't be pollinated, but since they blossom for a long time, you should get a sizeable harvest.

Asia and Africa gave us okra. It grows wild in the upper Nile region and was used in northern Africa for centuries. In fact, okra is an African word. Trading ships brought this vegetable to this country,

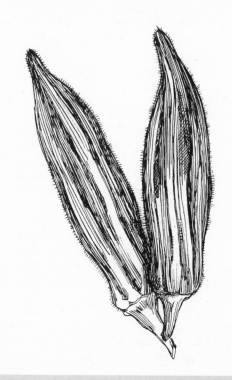

and it quickly found favor as a crop and as an ingredient in French and Creole cooking in Louisiana.

Okra is a tasty and important ingredient in many foods, especially Creole dishes. Many of us have enjoyed gumbo soup. Gumbo, from the French word "gombo," means okra and is a natural thickener for soups and stews. Okra is also often stewed with tomatoes, deep-fried, pickled, boiled or steamed and served with butter, as well as eaten raw, fresh from the garden. Some folks don't like the gummy quality okra has when it is boiled or steamed, and it seems to be more popular when combined with other vegetables, fried or pickled.

I've also heard of folks making coffee out of the dried, mature okra seeds. They let some pods ripen on the plant, collect the seeds when the ribs of the pods have opened, and roast and grind the seeds. Then they perk this "coffee," using more of the ground okra than they would regular ground coffee. Although I've never had a cup of okra java, the flavor is supposed to be similar to coffee without the bitterness. Still other people take advantage of the versatile okra by grinding the dried seeds and using them to make bread, usually in combination with another meal such as cornmeal.

Because it is easy to grow in hot climates, okra is one of those vegetables that's considered a "Southern" crop. It is true that the southern parts of our country have the long, hot growing seasons that okra needs to bear really well, but okra can be grown anywhere.

From seeds or house-started transplants, I can grow okra in my garden in Vermont where we can count on only four frost-free months a year. Because okra can't tolerate frost, yields in the North may not be as high as yields from plants grown further south. But Northern growers, who really like okra, can make up for that by simply growing a few extra plants.

EGGPLANT

Eggplant — the queen of the garden. Deep purple, almost purple-black in color with a glossy sheen and caps like crowns, they look like royalty. The taste is fit for royalty, too! Mouth-watering eggplant parmigiana, stuffed eggplant or a southern-style dish like french-fried eggplant is always a treat at our table.

Eggplant has been around a long time. It originally came from India and was known in Arabia, where sheiks and shahs thought very highly of it. It was introduced by Arabians to the people of Spain, who later brought it to this country, and both purple and white varieties were growing here by 1806.

One of the earliest references to eggplant is from a fifth-century Chinese book. It seems that the Chinese ladies considered it high fashion to stain their

teeth with a black dye made from eggplant. They then polished their teeth until they shone like metal. Sure glad that fashion has gone out of style!

But eggplant, as a food or fashion accessory, wasn't popular everywhere. In 15th and 16th-century Europe, eggplant were called "mad apples" because it was thought that eating them would make a person insane. Even when this fear started dying away, Europeans still wouldn't eat eggplant as they considered it poisonous. Eggplant is a member of the nightshade family, the same as tomatoes, potatoes, tobacco and belladonna. An eye drop substance, derived from belladonna (also called deadly nightshade), was used by fashionable ladies to make their eyes appear larger. Once in a while, someone would drink belladonna and die of the effects. No wonder, knowing eggplant and deadly nightshade were related, they shied away from eating eggplant. (Tomatoes, too, were taboo in certain areas.)

Eggplant, however, became as popular in Europe as it had been in the Middle East. In fact, it remains more popular in the Old World than it does here. There are more varieties under cultivation in Europe than there are in America, and Japan is now developing even more varieties.

The commercial production of eggplant in this country is mostly in Florida, with a small part of the summer crop grown in New Jersey. It's also grown commercially in many states including California, Ohio, Colorado, Michigan, Illinois, Missouri, New York and Texas. So you see eggplant is grown successfully almost everywhere. There's no reason you can't grow this pretty and tasty vegetable in your own home garden.

PICKING WHAT TO PLANT

Choosing varieties to plant is a most important step in planning your garden. Although we have our favorites, so many new types are being introduced every year that a good study of seed catalogs and packets before you choose is time well spent. There are many factors to consider: days to maturity, yield, size of plant, disease resistance. Below I've listed some of our favorite varieties of peppers, eggplant and okra, as well as some new varieties that we think are worth trying. I haven't indicated disease resistance on this list because some companies offer a disease-resistant type while the same variety from another seed company may not have that resistance. So check the description in the catalog or on the seed packet to choose resistant varieties. It's worth it.

It is important to know that the days to maturity noted on the seed packet or in the catalog for peppers and eggplant is the number of days from the time you set your plants out in the garden; days to maturity of okra is from seed. It takes from six to ten weeks to grow an eggplant or pepper seedling sturdy enough for transplanting.

One other point before you start selecting seeds — there are so many different varieties of hot and sweet peppers (especially the hot peppers), it would have been very easy to write a whole book on varieties alone! If you don't find what you are looking for on my list, check seed catalogs.

SEED VARIETIES

SWEET PEPPERS

Variety	Days To Maturity From Transplants	Description
California Wonder	75	Green when young, red when ripe. Large, blocky shape with thick walls. Good for stuffing. Harvest when green or red.
Yolo Wonder	72–75	Green, turning to red when ripe. Big, blocky, 3 to 4 lobes. Harvest when green or red.
Golden Calwonder	75	Medium green to yellow, yellow when ripe. Medium thick walls, 3 to 4 lobes. Harvest when green or yellow.
Bell Boy Hybrid	75	Medium long, most 4 lobed fruit. Green, maturing early to red. All America winner. May be harvested when green or red.
Sweet Banana	72	Long, tapered fruits. Green changing to yellow and orange, red when ripe. Okay to harvest when orange, yellow or red.
Hungarian Sweet Wax	65–70	Long, tapering fruit. Medium to thin walls; green to yellow, crimson when ripe. May be harvested as soon as fruit is large enough.
Sweet Cherry	78	Nearly round fruits about 1 to 1½ inches across. Red when ripe. Good for pickling whole. Best harvested when green or red.

HOT PEPPERS

Variety	Days To Maturity From Transplants	Description
Anaheim M	77	Long, tapering fruit. Green turning bright red when ripe. Medium-thick walls, mildly hot.
Hungarian Wax	65	Bright yellow turning red; 6 to 8 inches long. Fairly hot. Harvest when red.
Long Cayenne	70–75	Finger-shaped, wrinkled and twisted fruit. 5 inches long. Red when ripe and very hot. Harvest when red.

Variety	Days To Maturity From Transplant	Description
Jalapeno	65–75	Tapering, 3-inch fruits. Dark green maturing to red when ripe. Favorite for Mexican foods; very hot; ornamental. Harvest when red for storing.
Large Cherry	69	Slightly flattened globe fruits; 1½ inches across. Green turning red; hot. Harvest when red.

SWEET PIMIENTO PEPPERS

Variety	Days To Maturity From Transplants	Description
Truhart Pimiento	78	Heart-shaped; sweet; 3-inch fruits. Green maturing rapidly to red. Harvest when red.
Burpee's Early Pimiento	65	Heart-shaped; 3½ inches long; thick-walled fruits. Dark green turning bright red when ripe; smooth skin.
Pimiento Select	75	Small, smooth skin. Very mild. Green; red when ripe.

EGGPLANT

Black Beauty	73–80	Dark, purplish-black fruits; round to globe-shaped fruits. Blunt and broad at blossom end when developed.
Burpee Hybrid	70	Tall with medium-sized, oval to round fruit. Highly drought and disease resistant.
Dusky	63	Early maturing, oval fruits. Glossy, very dark purplish-black. Medium sized.
Ichiban	61–65	Early maturing, oriental-style fruits (slender and long). Slow to develop seeds. Soft, dark purple color. Heavy fruit set.
Black Bell	60–80	Round to oval fruits; deep purple-black. Prolific fruit set. Widely adapted.
Morden Midget	65	Medium-sized, deep purple fruits. Small bushy plants, excellent for small garden or container growing.

OKRA

Clemson Spineless	56	Dark green, slightly grooved pods. Pods are straight, pointed and spineless.
Louisiana Green Velvet	60	Light green, smooth, spineless pods. Tender.
White Velvet	60	Large, round white pods.
Spineless Green Velvet	58	Smooth, round, spineless pods, about ¾ inch in diameter.
Dwarf Green Long Pods	52–56	Ribbed, pointed fleshy pods. Dark green in color. Good for market or shipping.
Emerald	60	Dark green, round, spineless pods.
Red Okra	60	Rich red color, reddish tint to plant. Grooved pods. Turns green when cooked.
Park's Candelabra Branching	50–60	Base-branching habit, with 4 to 6 bearing spikes per plant. Requires less growing space per yield than standard varieties. Pods are slightly rounded; lightly ribbed.

Ornamental Peppers

Ornamental peppers are a true member of the Capsicum family like the peppers that are grown for food outdoors. Give them lots of sun and keep them evenly moist, and they'll produce many small cone-shaped peppers. These plants, which you can usually buy through a seed catalog, at a florist shop or even in a supermarket, are very pretty when the miniature peppers start to ripen. Often you'll have a plant splashed with green, yellow, red and orange all at the same time since each pepper ripens at its own pace.

These mini-peppers are edible, but they are hot! You can use them in cooking or for attractive and different hors d'oeuvres along with crackers and a dip. Just be careful not to confuse them with a plant called the Jerusalem or Christmas Cherry. Instead of the cone-shaped peppers, these plants have round fruit which is reddish-orange when ripe and they are *not* edible.

STARTING UP

Very few gardeners I know sow their pepper or eggplant seeds directly into the ground. Most prefer either to buy transplants or start their own indoors for outdoor planting when the weather and the ground has warmed enough.

Okra has a reputation for being hard to transplant and since it doesn't require a very long season, many gardeners will sow their okra seeds right in the ground at the proper time. But if you want to and are willing to take a little extra care of the long tap or main root that okra develops, you can successfully transplant this crop.

Starting from Seed Indoors

It's very easy to grow your own transplants, and growing your own gives you the freedom to pick your own varieties. It also lets you make sure the plants get the best care right from the very first seeds.

To grow some of your own transplants, all you need is:

1. Some sterilized soil or potting mix,
2. Suitable containers such as peat pots, flats, Jiffy 7's, milk cartons cut in half, or anything that will hold soil and provide proper drainage,
3. A place to put the seeds while they are germinating which will provide a warm, even temperature,
4. Plenty of sunshine or grow lights,
5. Seeds.

For good seed germination, make sure the container has holes for good drainage. If excess water can't drain, your seeds will rot.

All your efforts can be ruined by "damping off," a fungus disease that attacks the emerging seedlings, if you don't take steps to prevent it. The best preventive measures are to make sure your potting soil mix is sterile and that you don't over-water. Purchased soil and mixes are usually sterile. If you want to use your own garden soil, you can get rid of all the fungus organisms and weed seeds by baking the soil in a shallow pan (such as a cookie sheet), in a 200° oven for about an hour. Don't do this when you're hungry; the smell is enough to make you lose your appetite. And don't try to sterilize soil in a microwave oven. I talked to a few companies that manufacture these ovens, and they told me that it shouldn't be done because it may damage the oven. Another way to prevent damping off is to treat the seeds with captan, which can be bought at a garden supply store. Be sure to follow the directions on the package.

Okra Seeds — A Tough Nut to Crack

Okra seeds have a very tough outer covering that makes it harder for them to sprout. Here's a little trick I use to make them germinate faster: place your okra seeds in the freezer overnight. This makes the moisture in them expand and crack the outer covering. When you plant them the next day in the usual manner, they already have a good start toward germinating. Some gardening friends of mine soak the seeds for 24 hours. This, too, speeds germination by softening the outer covering. It takes a little longer than the freezer trick, but it also works well.

To start growing your transplants, fill the container with moistened, not wet, potting mix or soil. If you are using peat pots or Jiffy 7's, plant a few seeds in each. This ensures at least one good plant per pot. In flats, sprinkle the seed about one-fourth to one-half inch apart. Then firm them into the soil with a flat, rigid object. I usually use a small wooden shingle, but a kitchen spatula would work, too. Sprinkle some more of the potting mix over the seeds, covering them only to a depth of three to four times their own diameter. For pepper and eggplant seeds, I find about one-fourth inch of the moistened soil or mix is about right. Okra seeds are bigger and can take about an inch of covering. Firm the top of the soil again, so that the seeds come into good contact with the moistened soil to help germination.

Cover the flat or container with plastic wrap or put it in a plastic bag to help retain moisture. Then place the bundle in a spot, such as the top of the fridge, that is consistently warm but not hot. I cover the packages with a few sheets of newspaper, too, to help insulate them.

A sunny window is the worst place to put seeds that are trying to germinate. It's the hottest place during the day and usually the coldest spot at night. These temperature extremes don't help the seeds to germinate. The top of your refrigerator is a good spot because the temperature is warm and constant, not to mention that it gets the flats or containers out of your way. Light is not important to germinating eggplant, pepper or okra seeds. They don't need sunlight to sprout, just warmth and a bit of moisture.

Seedling Savvy

Start checking your seeds in a few days to see if they've sprouted. But be patient! Seeds don't usually sprout overnight, and okra may take longer than the peppers and eggplant. Making sure they receive consistent warmth will be the best thing you can do to help your seeds sprout.

Once the seeds have sprouted, they'll need light. Remove the plastic and put them in a sunny window or under fluorescent lights. If you are using lights, place the containers or flats a few inches below the tubes. As the plants grow, keep moving them so that the tops remain a few inches below the tubes. Too much distance between the plant and the lights will result in spindly, "leggy" plants. Plants need darkness too, so make sure the lights are turned off for at least eight hours a night.

If the nights are still cold and you have placed your plants in a window, move them away from the window during the night. Seedling leaves can be damaged if they come in contact with a very cold, frosty window, and the chill won't help tender, young plants, either.

Keep the soil moist but not wet. Water your seedlings gently and use room temperature water if possible.

Fertilizing your plants is not necessary for a while. They have enough nutrients in their seeds and are getting nourishment from the soil. Wait at least a week or two after they've sprouted to fertilize, or even until it's time to repot. Watch out for overfertilizing. Use a small amount of a water-soluble, balanced fertilizer once a week. This will encourage healthy, stocky growth.

Time to Repot

When your plants are three to four inches tall and start to crowd together in their containers, it's time to repot them into individual or bigger containers such as large peat pots or milk cartons. I like to use a plastic dishpan for repotting. Poke some holes in the bottom of the pan, and put a layer of stones or gravel in the bottom to help with drainage. Using sterilized potting mix, fill the dishpan almost to the rim. You can mix about a teaspoon of plant food or fertilizer in with each gallon of soil; 5-10-10 is a well-balanced fertilizer to use.

Water the young plants well before you transplant. The wet soil will stick to the tender roots protecting them during transplanting. Using a tablespoon or other small utensil, carefully lift the plants out of the flat one at a time.

Make a deep hole in the dishpan soil and set in the plant, about an inch deeper than it was in the flat.

Leave three to four inches between plants. Firm the soil around the plants and water gently. Fertilize them once a week using half the recommended dosage of water-soluble balanced fertilizer mixed with one gallon of water.

If you can't or don't want to start your own transplants, you can usually buy the varieties you want at a garden store or supermarket (see p. 60). Healthy pepper, eggplant and okra plants will be unblemished and have a nice, dark green color.

Watch out for tall spindly plants. Often, these plants didn't receive enough light when they were started. Blossoms on the plant are also a signal for "don't buy." A transplant's root system usually isn't strong enough to support flowers or fruit unless the plant is in a deep container. Also, check under leaves for aphids, white flies and other insects — you want to buy a transplant, not future trouble!

Take time to choose the best, healthiest transplants. These are the plants that you'll be depending on for food. A little extra time being choosy will pay off in a healthy garden and a better harvest.

Hardening Off Transplants

One of the most important steps in planting comes before your plants get near the garden. This is the process of hardening off. Your plants have spent their short lives in a warm, sunny, protected place and need to get used to the outdoors gradually before they can be planted safely in your garden. Even your store-bought transplants need to be hardened off.

About 10 days before you intend to plant, put your transplants outdoors in an area where they will be protected from the direct sunlight and wind. Leave them out for a few hours and then bring them back inside. Repeat this each day, gradually increasing the amount of time they are outside. After a week or so, leave the transplants out all day and all night. Of course, you should bring them indoors if there is any chance of a frost.

If you harden off your plants properly, they'll be strong and able to withstand full sun, breezes and all the challenges they'll meet in the garden.

Where to Plant

Sunshine is important for these heat-loving crops. When you plan your garden, put okra, eggplant and peppers where they will receive the maximum amount of direct sunlight. Also be sure to place them in a well-drained area.

Vegetables in a Flower Bed

If you're a flower gardener, you can still grow peppers, eggplant and okra. Where? In the flower bed! Okra can be grown as a background plant, eggplant and peppers in with your other flowering plants. Their greenery, pretty flowers and ripening fruit will complement your other plants and give you something to eat, besides.

I've seen gardeners who have a long stretch of flowers and then put some peppers and eggplant in between beds to provide some refreshing green between masses of color. Mighty pretty and mighty practical!

Another place you can grow eggplant and peppers is between shrubs, providing the shrubs don't shade the plants too much. I think that's a great idea. Maybe that's because I'd rather be picking peppers than pruning.

So look around your yard and see where you can put some okra, peppers or eggplant. I'll bet you'll find space you didn't think you had. Just be sure that you can pick your produce without damaging your other plants.

NO LAND?
GARDEN ANYWAY

We've talked to folks who would like to have a garden, but who don't have enough land, live in an apartment and have no land, or have some other problem that makes them think they can't garden. Sometimes these folks can find community gardening space in their city or town. But I always tell the ones who can't find space, to garden anyway — in containers. You can place containers on patios, porches, rooftops or other locations and have a fresh vegetable harvest no matter where you live. Growing in containers is not only easy and productive, it can be decorative as well.

Peppers and eggplant are good container gardening choices because of their relatively compact size and growing habits.

To get growing, buy some plants at your local garden store or start plants indoors as you would for transplanting into an outdoor garden (see p. 68). You'll also need some containers large enough to give the plants plenty of root room.

When your plants are ready for transplanting into a larger pot, harden them off as I've described earlier. It's easier to harden them off while they are still in their flats or small pots. This saves you the trouble of moving a large, heavy pot in and out every day.

When the transplants are properly hardened off, it's time to move them into their permanent containers. This container can be a large pot, a redwood tub, or even a bushel basket. No matter what type of container you choose, make sure it will hold about five gallons of potting mix per plant and that it has drainage holes. Some people who garden in containers like to have casters underneath their pots to make moving them easier. It's also a good idea if you have to move your potted plants around during the day to follow the sun.

You'll need some drainage material, such as stones, gravel or clay pot shards (small broken pieces), a good potting mix or sterilized garden soil (see p. 62), and a place to put your potted plant where it will get the most sunlight. Place an inch or so of the drainage material in the bottom of the container, then fill it with the potting mix or soil, packing the soil very lightly. The soil line should be about an inch below the rim of the pot. When this is done, follow the same rules outlined for transplanting outdoors (pg. 68).

More than likely, you won't have to worry about cutworm damage, so you can forget the cutworm collars. Instead of transplanting indoors and having to move a heavy pot outdoors, I find it easier to put the container where I want it to stay and transplant there.

Container Plant Care

Mother Nature takes care of outdoor container plants pretty much the same way she takes care of plants in the garden. But I've found that, since there is less soil available to the container plant than there is to the garden-grown plant, they tend to dry out a bit sooner. Check your containers to make sure that the soil is kept moist but not wet, especially if your containers are on a balcony with a roof which prevents rain from watering the plant.

Fertilizing is no problem. A liquid fertilizer should be applied weekly. Fish emulsion, purchased from your garden store, or a solution of one teaspoon of 5-10-10 to a gallon of water may be used to fertilize.

Even though your plants aren't out in the garden, they are still fair game for insects. Keep an eye on container plants for any signs of damage. If you find a pest, deal with it in the same way as those in the garden. Of course, if you are container gardening on an apartment balcony, a patio, or similar place, you'll have to be extra careful using an insecticide to make sure that none of the dust or solution gets on surrounding surfaces such as a barbecue grill or a child's toy. Some of the homemade remedies like a soapy water solution or a chile powder and water solution may be the better answer to your problems.

GARDEN PREP

Because they're heat-loving, okra, eggplant and peppers are probably among the last vegetables you'll plant in the spring. So if you plan to put them in the vegetable garden, the soil is probably completely prepared. But just in case, here are a few reminders about thorough soil preparation that you may find helpful.

Work the Soil

In order to have good root development, which is important for the growth of the plant, the soil needs to be loose to a depth of six to eight inches. I use a tiller to break up the soil to this depth, but it can also be done using a garden shovel. Breaking up the soil helps roots develop, and it also uproots any weeds that are beginning to sprout.

Add Some Organic Matter

All types of soil can benefit from the addition of organic matter. It helps a light, sandy soil hold moisture and nutrients better, and wedges between the soil particles of heavy, clay soils to help them drain better. Grass clippings, turned-under cover crops, leaves, compost, garden residues or whatever you add that can decompose (with the help of millions of tiny bacteria already present in the soil) turn into that key ingredient of all good garden soils — humus. You'll also be feeding that old gardener, the earthworm, who helps aerate your soil by digging his tunnels and helps build up your soil's richness by adding his leftovers, "castings."

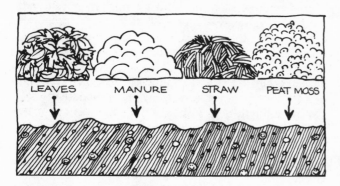

LEAVES   MANURE   STRAW   PEAT MOSS

Take a Soil Test

You can test your garden soil for pH level with the help of one of the soil test kits on the market today. Or your local County Extension Service Agent can probably do it for you for a small fee.

Peppers and eggplant need a soil pH of about 5.5 to 6.0 (slightly acid). Okra also likes this pH range, but is more tolerant of pH variations than eggplant and peppers.

Your soil test will tell you if your soil is too "sweet" or alkaline, or whether it is too acid. Add lime to an acid soil and sulfur to alkaline soil to bring the pH level into the proper range.

Fertilizer

Eggplant, peppers and okra are heavy feeders, but they are also picky eaters. They like small amounts of food all season long. Too much nitrogen will give you a beautiful foliage plant but won't give you much in the way of food. I've had as many as 21 peppers on a plant no higher than 12 inches. So before planting, I like to add some organic fertilizer such as dehydrated chicken manure, or any other type of animal manure. I also might work in about two to four pounds of a good fertilizer, such as 10-10-10, into each 100 square feet of soil. The numbers 10-10-10 refer to the percentages, by weight, of nitrogen (N), phosphorus (P) and potassium (K) in the bag of fertilizer. Work all this fertilizer into the soil, making sure it is covered. Be sure to cover it well as your plants are liable to suffer from a hot foot, or burned roots, if they come into contact with the fertilizer. Giving someone a hot foot in a vaudeville show may have been funny, but giving one to your plants can be a killer.

Match This!

If you've tried to grow peppers in the past and you've been disappointed with the results, try this trick. Since peppers like a pH that is a bit on the acid side (5.5 to 6.0), take a few matches from a matchbook and mix them with the soil and fertilizer in the bottom of the transplant hole. Then cover this mixture with two to three inches of soil. The roots of the transplants must not come into contact with the matches because the sulfur can damage them. The sulfur in the matches lowers the pH around the roots, and the peppers seem to love it.

A variation of this trick can be done by buying sulfur powder at the drugstore, mixing a pinch of it with the soil in the bottom of the hole and covering it before planting.

Try the match trick. It just might give you the largest pepper crop you've ever had.

Anyone for Raised Beds?

If your garden is too wet, either in certain sections or all over, make raised beds for your plants. Determine the width and length of the bed and walkways using stakes for guidelines. Use a hoe to pull the soil from the walkways up onto the bed until there is a four to eight inch difference between the height of the bed and the height of the walkway. After you've raised the soil and leveled off the bed, simply plant your transplants into the bed as you would in a conventional bed. The raised bed drains faster because excess water doesn't just sit there; it runs off. And having this water run off means your plants' roots will get the oxygen they need for good growth. An

added bonus of raised beds is that they warm up faster in the spring and stay warmer all day long. This is a real help for plants such as peppers, eggplant and okra.

A Pinch to Grow an Inch

When digging the holes for eggplant and pepper plants, give them the extra boost they need to get off to a good start by putting some fertilizer or compost in the bottom of the hole. Put a teaspoon of 5-10-10, mixed with some soil, into the bottom of the hole and then cover that mixture with one to two inches of soil. The fertilizer should not come into direct contact with the roots because it can injure them. If you are using compost, a handful in the bottom of the hole gives plants that extra boost for needed quick healthy root development.

Spacing

When you're ready to transplant peppers and eggplant, dig a hole for each plant about six to eight inches deep. Space two holes about 10 to 15 inches apart, then move down the row about 10 to 15 inches and dig another hole in that row between the first two holes. The rows have a diamond pattern with about 10 to 15 inches between each plant on all sides. You can get more produce from the space available by planting this way, but the peppers and eggplant are still far enough apart for good, thick foliage to develop. I've often heard folks say that, when the plants get bigger, the foliage of one eggplant needs to be touching the next one in order to fruit. This isn't true, but it is a good way to tell if you have spaced your plants properly. Good foliage is important to protect the fruit and help prevent sunscald. Pimiento peppers need a bit more growing room than bell peppers.

If you want to space your plants in single rows, set them one behind the other with about 10 to 15 inches between plants and about two feet between rows. Adjust the width of your rows depending on the way you cultivate your plants. If you cultivate with a hoe or other hand tool, your rows can be a bit closer together. One to two feet will give you enough room so you and the plants don't feel crowded. I cultivate with a tiller, and have to leave more room between the rows.

Okra is easily grown from seed started right in the garden. Just stake out the length of the row, then dig a shallow furrow with a hoe in the prepared seedbed. Drop a seed every three to four inches and then cover them with about one-half to one inch of soil. About 100 feet of row can be planted with one ounce of okra seed. After covering the seed, firm the soil with the back of the hoe, so that the seed makes good

WALKWAY   WALKWAY   ←PROPOSED→ RAISED BED

TOP OF RAISED BED READY FOR PLANTING!

WALKWAY   WALKWAY

6-8"

ORIGINAL SOIL LEVEL

◆ CROSS·SECTION OF A RAISED BED ◆

contact with the soil. Once you've finished planting, water the soil if it's dry. This will firm the soil around the seeds and also prevent them suffering from dehydration. Don't water before planting because you don't want to pack the soil down.

When the new okra plants are about three to four inches high, thin them to their proper spacing — 12 to 15 inches between plants.

TRANSPLANTING

On transplanting day, as I place each young plant in the prepared ground, I can almost taste the goodness of each of them. But it's important to keep your mind on the business at hand, because transplanting is a major step that can make or break your crop. However, it doesn't have to be traumatic to you or your plants if you have thoroughly prepared the soil, hardened off the plants well, and if you keep these few basic principles in mind.

Timing Is Everything — Peppers, eggplant and okra are heat-loving plants. While some vegetables can tolerate a frost, these three won't stand for it. It's important that all danger of frost is past before you set these plants out in the garden. But how can you do that and still make sure they have enough time to produce a good crop before fall's first frost? Well, here's a way that's simple and almost foolproof. Call your local County Extension Service or the National Weather Service and ask for the first and last average frost date in your area. Then look at the dates to maturity on the seed package or in your garden catalog, for varieties of pepper, eggplant and okra. (Remember, the dates to maturity for peppers and eggplant are from the time you set the transplants out into the garden, not from the time you first plant the seed indoors.) Choose varieties that will produce in the time you have available. You can also figure out if you have time for two plantings of these crops — some parts of the country do.

Transplant On A Cloudy Day — Bright sun can hurt newly planted seedlings, so always plan to transplant on an overcast day, in late afternoon or in the evening.

Early Planting — Generally, set out your plants the week after the last average frost date to be sure the tender young plants don't suffer from frost bite. To get a jump on the season, you can plant around the last average frost date (perhaps even two weeks before), depending on how warm the weather has been. When you plant early and frost is expected, protect your plants with hotcaps or cloches, either store-bought or homemade of newspaper or wax paper.

Another trick to keep Jack Frost at bay and in-

crease the heat around these plants is to make a ring of black roofing paper about five to six inches high and six to eight inches in diameter. Place it so the plant is in the center of the circle. The black paper absorbs and holds the sun's heat, increasing the temperature in the area around the plant. It really seems to help the growth of peppers, eggplant and okra.

Plants Need A Soak — If you water your plants well, about an hour before transplanting, the soil will stay firmly around the roots to protect them, and make them easier to handle while putting them in the ground. The soil should clump together without being muddy.

Head Off Cutworms — One of the simplest treatments to prevent cutworm damage can be done when you transplant. Simply take a strip of newspaper about two or three inches wide and wrap it around the stem of the plant. When you place the plant in its hole, make sure that the newspaper strip is below ground surface for a depth of about one inch and the rest is above ground. This prevents the dreaded cutworm from chewing through the stem of your tender, young plant.

Have Everything Ready — Like a pilot before take-off, I always run through a check list in my mind before I start to transplant. This prevents me from reaching for something that isn't there while the roots of the plant I've just taken from its pot start to dry out. Is it cloudy or late in the day? Is the soil fully prepared? Are the plants properly hardened off? Do I have a shovel or trowel, fertilizer or compost, newspaper cutworm collars and watering can at hand? Have I taken the phone off the hook, so as not to be disturbed during this brief but critical time? If not, I do whatever is necessary before I start.

Work Quickly — Even though you've hardened off your transplants, they still have tender roots. Getting them into the ground quickly will help prevent any damage to the roots and help minimize the shock.

GROWING

Watch Out for Weeds

Weeds will compete with plants for the same space, sun, water and nutrients. So make it a practice to go out there and cultivate. Regular cultivation keeps the weeds down and makes sure the plants get all the water and nutrients available.

It's important to remember that whether you cultivate with a hoe, tiller, iron garden rake or other weed-beating tool, cultivation should be shallow — not more than one inch below the surface of the soil. Weed seeds are usually close to the surface, and deep cultivation will only bring more of them up near the surface where they can germinate. If you cultivate too deeply, you may injure the roots of your plants.

The best time to weed is after a rain when the plants have dried off, but before the soil has dried out completely. Get those weeds before they get a good start, and they'll pull easily from loose, moist soil.

Too Many Blossoms?

Sometimes pepper plants will have lots of blossoms but not enough fruit due to a lack of magnesium.

To remedy this situation, buy some epsom salts at the drugstore and add about one tablespoon to an empty spray bottle. Then fill the bottle with luke-warm water, shake it up so the epsom salts dissolve and then spray the solution on the leaves and blossoms of your pepper plants. If you do this a couple of times during the blossom period, you should have plenty of peppers.

Weed Beater and More

A good way to beat weeds is to mulch your plants. A thick mulch stops weeds from germinating by preventing sunlight from coming through. Mulch also keeps moisture in the soil, so your plants won't dry out. Many Southern gardeners use thick mulches

of hay, straw or other materials to protect the roots of their eggplant and pepper plants from too much heat in the summer months. Mulch two to three weeks after planting to allow soil to warm up.

With respect to black plastic mulch, I don't use it in my garden. Not only is it too much bother to lay down each spring and remove each fall, but I've got leaves, grass clippings and other things readily available, so why buy black plastic? It doesn't feed the earthworms, and it doesn't help the soil. I also think it's expensive.

Watering — A Little Dab Won't Do

For healthy and rapid growth, your plants need about an inch of water per week. I keep a rain gauge in my garden to measure the amount of rainfalls. You

can buy a gauge in a garden supply store or from a seed and garden supply catalog, or you can make a simple one from a tin can with measurements scratched on the side.

Check the gauge often, and if Mother Nature hasn't supplied enough water, get out there and water. It's easiest to let your sprinkler do the work if you have a large garden, but if your garden is small, a hose or even a watering can will do the trick as long as you make sure the plants are getting one inch of water each week.

If you use a sprinkler, place tin cans in different parts of the garden. Check the amount of water that collects in them as you sprinkle, and keep track of the amount of time it takes for the water to collect. Move the sprinkler when the amount of water in the can getting the greatest amount measures an inch. When you move the sprinkler, overlap the areas being watered. This simply means moving the sprinkler so that part of the spray falls on the area you have just watered that received less than an inch. When an area has received a total of an inch, move the sprinkler, overlapping areas again. After you have watered and measured in this way a few times, you'll have a good idea how long your sprinkler needs to run in different areas of your garden so that the entire garden gets just the right amount of H_2O.

Eggplant, although it has the same need for water as peppers and okra, is a fairly drought-resistant plant.

Be careful not to overwater your okra. Not only does overwatering cut off the vital supply of oxygen to the roots of all your plants, it also causes okra to produce too much foliage and not enough okra pods.

Some Weather Words and Temperament Tips

As any good gardener knows, a lot of variables go into producing a good crop of any vegetable. Just like any other plants, peppers, eggplant and okra have their likes and dislikes as far as good growing conditions are concerned. I've found that one of their biggest "likes" is warmth and one of their "dislikes" is cool nights.

Peppers and eggplant are fussiest right around blossom time. They'll have a poor fruit set if temperatures at night are below 55° or above 75° while they are blossoming, and they'll also drop their blossoms if daytime temperatures are above 90°. These temperatures will also delay the fruit that does manage to set. Eggplant and peppers, too, can become stunted during cool weather and then not grow rapidly once warm weather returns. Rapid growth is necessary for quality fruit production. It's also interesting to know that large-fruited eggplant

are more demanding than small-fruited varieties. So, if you've had a difficult time in the past growing eggplant, settle for the more succulent, smaller varieties.

There is not much a gardener can do about hot weather, but covering plants with cardboard boxes at night may keep in the day's heat if you expect a cool night. Using the circle of black roofing paper that I mentioned earlier may also help if the weather turns cool.

Okra blossoms last only a day whether or not they're pollinated. Constant rainy weather when they're blooming can reduce yields since bees don't buzz around much when it's raining. Despite these preferences, healthy plants will produce enough blossoms to help them during a spell of bad weather and still produce fruit.

A Little Something on the Side

Peppers, eggplant and okra are fairly big eaters, but they don't like their nourishment all in one dose. Sidedress them a few times during the growing season. Sidedressing is working a small amount of fertilizer in the soil three inches from the plants' stems to provide them with a steady diet. It's very easy to do, and the reward is a good crop.

Use a fertilizer such as dried manure, cottonseed meal or a balanced commercial fertilizer such as 5-10-10. When you are selecting fertilizer for these crops, be sure that it doesn't contain too much nitrogen. The lush foliage nitrogen encourages is great for plants such as lettuce, but when other plants are putting their energy into making greenery, they're not making fruits. It's better to have the food on the table!

Peppers, eggplants and okra should get their first sidedressing around blossom time, usually a month after they have been put outside. Sidedress them again about a month later, after the first fruits have developed. This helps them keep producing by giving them a little extra boost after all that work.

To sidedress, just dig a trench around the plant about one inch deep and about three to four inches away from the stem around the drip line of the leaves. Put about a handful of manure or compost or two to three tablespoons of a balanced fertilizer in a band in the trench. Cover the fertilizer with soil. If the plants are in rows, dig a shallow trench, about one to three inches deep along either side of the row, again at the drip line of the leaves. Then sprinkle a band of balanced fertilizer in the trench, using about one-half cup per 10 feet of row, or a layer of manure about one inch deep along the length of the row. Cover that with soil, too.

No matter whether you use the circular-trench or row-trench method, be careful not to sprinkle any fertilizer on the plants as it will burn them. Next, water the soil to send the fertilizer down to the roots.

Be careful not to over-fertilize when you're side-dressing. That's probably the most common mistake that folks make with okra, peppers and eggplant. Once, after I had set about 18 bell pepper plants in

the garden, I chose a few of the plants to over-feed during the season. Each time I sidedressed, I gave those few the extra pinch of fertilizer many people are often tempted to give their plants. At the end of the season, those plants were taller, healthier-looking and beautifully lush, but each had only six peppers. My other plants had grown steadily but they weren't that tall. But what a crop — a few of them had more than 20 peppers each! So sidedress properly, and you should be rewarded with healthy plants and lots of produce.

WHAT'S BUGGING THEM?

Insect Control

Some folks prefer using homemade remedies for insect control as opposed to chemical remedies. These homemade bug chasers include a soapy water solution for aphids and a chile powder–and–water mixture for other pests. Or if you find small groups of insects starting to chew on your plants, you can often pick off the bugs before they've done any real harm. Keep your garden clean of debris, so that insects won't have a place to reproduce. If they've already laid their eggs, it doesn't matter if you've cleaned or not; lack of debris, though, helps against those pests that winter over.

Although I prefer to use home remedies, for some insect problems I need to rely on commercially available controls. Be extremely careful when using commercial insecticides. Things to keep in mind when controlling insects in the garden:

Some chemical products, including Sevin, are harmful to bees. If you use them, do so near evening after the bees are done gathering for the day. Decreased bee activity will reduce pollination in your garden.

Check the label on any commercial product to find out if there is a waiting period between use and harvest. Read the label three times: when you buy the product, when you use it, and when you carefully put it away.

Pay attention to the timing and the life cycle of the insect you're dealing with. If you catch the problem early — before the adults have laid eggs and hundreds or thousands of new insects emerge — you'll need less control and there'll be less damage to the crops.

Since pesticides come under a safety review on a regular basis, we recommend that you check with your County Extension Agent or Cooperative Extension Specialist (located at the land grant college in your state) about the latest commercially available

Drip Line

When rain or water falls onto a plant, it will drip off the leaves. The circle on the ground made by the rain dripping off the outermost leaves of the plant is called the drip line. The diameter of this drip line varies with the size of the plant: the bushier the plant, the bigger the drip line. You can also figure out the drip line by the shadow cast by a plant. When the sun is right above the plant, look at the shadow on the ground cast by the leaves. The outer rim of the shadow will be about the same as the drip line.

controls which are safe and effective for home garden use. The pesticide recommendations in this book are based on the most up-to-date information available, but the reader should be aware that they are subject to change because of safety reviews.

Insect Problems

Here in the North, we don't have too many problems with insects bothering our okra, peppers and eggplant. Southern gardeners, though, have more problems. Here's a run-down of the most common pests and what can be done for them.

Aphids — Small and of various colors, these sucking insects can drain the sap from peppers, eggplant and okra all season long. If you notice ants near your plants, look for aphids. The aphids give off a sweet substance called ''honeydew'' which attracts the ants. Aphids also spread plant diseases, so be sure to control them if they're a problem. To get rid of aphids, try spraying with a mild solution of soapy water or put out yellow pans of soapy water (aphids are attracted to yellow). If the infestation is severe, spray with malathion.

Colorado Potato Beetles — These pests will feed on the foliage of eggplant and peppers. The adults are yellow with black stripes down their backs; larvae are reddish with a black head. Hand pick adult beetles and larvae every time you see them. Crush egg masses under leaves. They can be controlled by spraying with Sevin, rotenone or an all-purpose tomato-potato dust.

Cutworms — These gray, brown or black worms chew tender transplants off at ground level. Cutworms are about one to one-and-a-half inches long and curl up tightly when disturbed. They hide in the soil and attack at night. You don't have to use anything to control them except newspaper cutworm collars at transplanting time (see p. 68).

Flea Beetles — These tiny black or brown bugs attack all three of these crops. They eat small holes in the leaves, usually early in the season and if not con-

trolled, can wipe out the foliage entirely, seriously injuring the plants. I recommend dusting with wood ashes or spraying with a garlic or hot pepper solution. Spraying with Sevin or rotenone will also control flea beetles.

Pepper Maggots — These insects infect peppers and can cause serious damage. The adults are yellow flies with brown bands on each wing. They lay their eggs within the peppers, and the maggots feed from the inside out. If you see any of the flies, spray with rotenone to control before they begin egg-laying.

Pepper Weevils — These black-snouted beetles are very common in the South. They're only about one-eighth of an inch long. But don't let their size fool you; they can cause a great deal of damage. The adults feed on the foliage and lay eggs in the buds of immature pepper pods. The eggs hatch, and the larvae eat through the buds or fruit, causing them to drop or to be misshapen. To make matters worse, there may be several generations a year. A Sevin dust or spray will help control them.

Tomato Fruitworm/Corn Earworm — This is another pest of all three of these vegetables. Nearly two inches long, it is yellowish, green or brown with lengthwise light and dark stripes. It bores into the pods or fruit, robbing you of good vegetables to put on your table. To control, hand pick or spray with Sevin as soon as you notice them or the small holes they've bored into the fruit or pods.

Disease Problems

Peppers, eggplant and okra are troubled by a few diseases, especially in the South. Since peppers and eggplant are related to tomatoes, they are susceptible to many tomato diseases as well as some of their own. There are some things a gardener can do to avoid them, though. As the old saying goes, ''An ounce of prevention is worth a pound of cure.'' Follow these practices in the garden to avoid plant diseases.

Keep a close watch for insects, especially aphids. Plants that are weakened by insects are more susceptible to disease. Insects can spread disease by carrying the disease organism on their bodies.

Weed your garden. Weeds can have blights and diseases which can spread to your healthy plants. Weeds will also harbor disease-carrying insects. Mow around the garden if weeds are plentiful.

Stay out of the garden when it is wet. Diseases spread more rapidly among wet plants. If you are working among wet plants, disease organisms may cling to your clothes and find a new home in a drop of water on another plant. You could easily infect any plants that you brush against. Water during the early

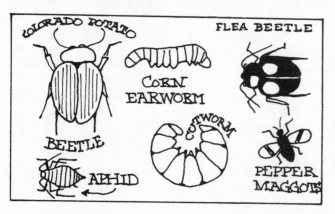

morning, so your plants have time to dry before nightfall. This helps check the spread of diseases.

Plant disease resistant varieties. Certain varieties of peppers, eggplant and okra are resistant to wilts and other diseases. These varieties will be noted in the seed catalog or on the packet as being resistant.

Rotate your crops. Since some diseases are soil-borne, crop rotation will greatly reduce the chance of a crop being stricken year after year. Try not to plant any member of the same plant family in a spot where a member of that family has grown during the previous three years. This really cuts down on disease spread.

Spade or till under crop residues. This clean-up work helps by not giving disease-carrying insects a place to spend the winter. Not only does it cut down on the insect population, but it greatly improves the soil by adding organic matter.

It is helpful to identify the diseases affecting your crop. By following the appropriate controls you may be able to avoid further problems.

There are some fungicides for controlling a few of the more serious diseases. But check with your Extension Service Agent before you do anything. He or she is the best person to contact to find out more about them.

HARVESTING

The most important thing about harvesting eggplant, peppers and okra is to start as soon as there's something to eat. Since it's the job of the plant to make seeds, too much of the plant's effort goes into ripening the fruit instead of producing new fruit if you don't harvest regularly and often. So make it a practice to go out every few days and pick what's ready to eat. Try to get the most out of each plant. After all, having good things to eat is one of the main reasons to garden.

You can harvest peppers when they are as small as golfballs. Most peppers, except for a few varieties like sweet banana peppers, are green when young.

EGGPLANT, PEPPER AND OKRA DISEASES

DISEASE	APPEARANCE ON LEAVES, STEMS, OR ROOTS	APPEARANCE ON FRUIT	SOURCE	CULTURAL CONTROL
Leaf Spots	Small, yellowish-green, or dark brown spots on leaves. Water soaked spots on old leaves.	Small, raised rough spots or rot spots. Fruit fails to set.	Seed- and soil-borne fungi.	Use disease-free seed. Rotate plantings.
Anthracnose	Very little effect.	Dark circular, sunken spots with black spores.	Seed. Soil. Infected plant debris.	Use disease-free seed. Do not cultivate when plants are wet. Rotate crops.
Mosaics	Green-yellow mottling of the leaf. Leaves become curved and irregular. Plant is usually stunted.	Yellow or wrinkled with dark spots. Small, bumpy and off-colored.	Aphids transmit the disease; humans may carry it from infected areas. Crop refuse.	Destroy infected plants Do not use tobacco while handling. Wash hands with soap and water before handling. Control insects which transmit the disease Use resistant varieties.
Blossom End Rot	No visible effect.	Big, black, sunken ring on base of pepper.	Lack of calcium. Dry spell following extra wet period.	Maintain pH between 6.0–6.8. Use soils with high water-holding capacity. Mulch. Regular waterings.
Root Knot Nematodes	Produce galls (knots) on okra & pepper roots.	Stunted plants.	Soil or seedling borne.	Rotate with grasses or legumes.
Wilts	Leaves wilt. Stunting and eventual death of plant.	Fruits are few, small and of poor quality.	Soil.	Rotate crops.

Don't be surprised if you see your bell peppers turning red; just about all of them do as they ripen. Harvest them by cutting through the stem of each fruit with a knife. You can have an almost continual harvest from your pepper plants by cutting often because this encourages the plant to keep blossoming, especially in the beginning of the summer. Later in the season, leave some green peppers on your plants to turn red. They are wonderful and colorful in pepper relish.

In the South pepper plants can be cut back after the first big harvest to encourage another crop. That's because peppers are really a perennial plant, although they are most often grown as an annual. If your season is long enough, cut the plant back to a few inches above the soil surface. The plant will grow back and give you a second, large harvest. Don't forget to sidedress, though, so the plant will have enough food to continue its work.

Eggplant tastes best when harvested young. If you cut into an eggplant and find an abundance of brown seeds, it's already too late for good eating. The fruit will be a dark, glossy purple when it's ready to harvest. The surface of the eggplant will turn dull and it will taste bitter as it gets older and past its prime. To harvest eggplant, cut through the stem above the green cap, or calyx, on the top. It's a tough stem, so have a sharp knife handy. The calyx also is a little prickly, so you may want to wear gloves to harvest eggplant. You can cut these plants back like peppers if your season is long enough for a second crop.

Gloves and a long-sleeved shirt are practically a must when you harvest okra. The pods and leaves are usually covered with little spines that you can hardly see. These spines can get under your skin and make your hands and arms itch for days.

Over-ripe okra is too tough to eat, and it grows so fast that you may have to harvest every day. A pod that is ready one day will have gone by the next. The best pods, which are not more than four inches long, should be cut with a knife or broken right below the cap on the bottom. Since only one pod grows beneath each leaf, break off the leaf after harvesting the pod. This helps you remember where you've already harvested and indicates where to start the next time.

These plants grow so tall in the South that I've seen people standing on ladders to harvest their okra! Okra doesn't get nearly that tall up here in the North. The tall stalks begin to look funny as the harvest progresses and the leaves are taken off from the bottom up. When the plants get too tall to harvest, a Southern gardener can cut the plant back about 12 to 18 inches above the ground. This is usually done in July or August. The plants will sprout again to make a second crop.

STRETCHING THE SEASON

The best way to get the most out of your garden is to extend the harvest. There are a few ways to do this. One of my favorites is to start harvesting as soon as there is something to eat. This tricks the plant into producing more. If your growing season is long enough, you can make successive plantings about a week or so apart at the beginning of the season. Because you'll be harvesting at intervals, this method can be a big plus if you don't have the time to do all your canning, freezing or pickling at once.

Another fun way to get a longer season from your peppers and eggplant is to bring your plants indoors. Bringing a few indoors when the outdoor gardening season is over gives you a double bonus for a while: more produce per plant and lush, green houseplants.

Before you attempt to bring your plants indoors, make sure they are healthy and you have a good indoor location for them. They'll need a sunny window or a grow light.

Up and In

Taking your plants from the garden requires the same care you took when you first transplanted them. The best time to do this is on a cloudy day or in the late afternoon. Have all your equipment ready beforehand. You'll need a garden spade, pots and soil.

The pots should be deep enough to provide room for good root growth and their diameter should be about 10 to 14 inches. (Small plants should go into

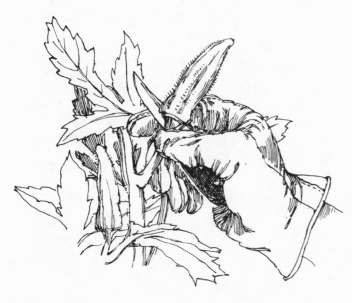

10-inch pots,while larger plants should be placed in 14-inch pots.) If you use old clay pots, scrub them well to remove all traces of dirt and fertilizer salts, that's the white powdery stuff that collects on the inside of clay pots. Clay pots should be soaked in water overnight before you repot to prevent the clay from absorbing the water you give the plants.

Any good brand of store-bought soil or sterilized garden soil can be used as a potting mix.

Put a few stones or pieces of a broken clay pot in the bottom of the pot for drainage. Add a few inches of moist, not wet, potting mix and then thump the pot on the ground a few times to settle the soil.

Two hours before you plan to dig up your plants, give them a good soak. Take your garden spade and dig around the drip line of the leaves of your plant. It's a good idea to dig deeper than you think necessary just to make sure you get the bulk of the roots. Dig straight down, not in towards the stem, to help avoid cutting the roots. When you've dug deep enough, lift the plant out of the ground with a spade, supporting the stem with your hand. Gently place the plant in the pot. Fill in the spaces with potting mix, packing it in lightly around the roots. After shaking the pot to settle the soil and eliminate any air pockets, fill in any remaining space up to about an inch below the pot rim with the potting mix. Soak the plant until the water comes out of the drainage holes. Now your plant is ready to bring indoors.

Indoor Care

Indoor care is just about the same as outdoor care, but this time you have to play Mother Nature. As I mentioned before, the eggplant and pepper plants will need a lot of light. They can be temperamental and may not produce if they don't like the conditions, so keep them away from drafts, radiators and heating ducts to avoid too cold or too hot a temperature.

Don't water them for a couple of days. This will give any broken roots a chance to heal and helps prevent root rot. After the first few days, keep them moist but not soaking wet.

Keep an eye out for insect pests, too. In the drier atmosphere of your house, peppers and eggplant are more apt to develop aphids, whiteflies and spider mites. If you see the leaves starting to turn a splotchy yellow, look at the underside of the leaves. Whitish dusty grains are whitefly eggs or spider mite eggs. If you find them on the bottom of the leaves, it's time to act. If the plants are small enough, tip them upside down under a gentle spray of water and wash away the eggs. A good houseplant insecticide should take care of the insect problems. To avoid the insects spreading, keep the infected plants away from the healthy ones.

If you use an insecticide, use it only where you have proper ventilation and away from children and animals. Wait for a week or two after spraying before harvesting, and wash the fruit before you eat it.

Since the eggplant and pepper plants inside don't have all the benefits of full sunshine, the fruit is not as large as fruit grown outdoors. The indoor fruits are usually one-third to one-half as large as the outdoor grown ones. But since nothing beats eating garden fresh vegetables, they're worth it.

After you've enjoyed your plants for a few months, they'll start to look peaked. Pick off the fruit and compost the plants. You've gotten your money's worth.

Bees Do It — But Only Outdoors

Bees provide pollination for your plants outside. Indoors, you're in charge. When your plants are in bloom, take a cotton swab or a fine paintbrush (the kind you might use for watercolor paints) and transfer the pollen from one flower to another. Just swirl the swab or brush lightly inside each flower, one after the other. I like to repeat this process again on the next day to make sure I catch the flowers when they're ready.

Not all of them will produce fruit. Where you have met with success, you will be able to see tiny fruits as the flowers wilt. Don't wait too long after the blossoms appear to pollinate, or they'll wilt before you have a chance. I find that I have good success if I do my "bee act" a day after the blossoms open.

Garden to Kitchen

FREEZING

Peppers

By freezing part of the summer's harvest, I really save money and add flavor to winter sauces and dishes. I often take just a few pieces of frozen peppers for a dish, and the remainder in the container stays nicely frozen.

Peppers are a snap to freeze because they don't have to be blanched. Choose firm, crisp, red or green, thick-walled peppers. Wash, cut out stem, and remove seeds. Cut peppers in halves, rings, in strips or dice. Pack into freezer containers leaving no headspace. Seal, label and freeze. Use unblanched frozen peppers just as you would fresh.

Peppers freeze perfectly well whole, but since they take up so much room in the freezer, I usually freeze halves for stuffing. If you want to fit more peppers into each freezer container, blanch them for a few minutes to make them limp. Blanch halves for three minutes, slices for two minutes. Cool in cold water, drain well. Pack in freezer containers, leaving 1/2-inch headspace for blanched peppers. Seal, label and freeze. Use scalded peppers in recipes that call for cooked peppers. You don't have to thaw them; just add to soups, casseroles or tomato sauce.

Eggplant

The most successful way to freeze eggplant is in precooked casseroles or Italian dishes. But if you have a large harvest or you want to freeze some slices to have on hand for frying, you can freeze it without too much trouble.

Pick eggplant when skins are a dark color all over. Prepare enough for one scalding at a time and work quickly, since eggplant discolors. Wash, peel and slice 1/2 inch thick or cut 1/2 to 1-inch cubes.

Scald 4 minutes in 1 gallon boiling water with 1/2 cup lemon juice or 4 1/2 tsp citric acid. Eggplant can also be dropped in 1 gallon cold water and 1/2 cup salt to prevent darkening. Cool, drain and place in freezer containers leaving 1/2-inch headspace. Slices may be separated by sheets of freezer paper then put into containers. Seal, label, date and freeze.

Okra

Use 2 to 3½-inch green pods. Wash, cut off stems but do not cut open pod. Blanch 3 minutes. Drain, and cool quickly in cold water. Drain and leave whole or slice. Pack in containers leaving 1/2-inch headspace. Seal, label, date and freeze.

CANNING

Canning isn't usually my first choice of a way to preserve these vegetables because freezing and pickling work so well. However, I do pressure can a few jars of eggplant to have for a quick dish of relish, eggplant patties or ratatouille. Canning peppers and okra is a good way to preserve them if you don't have a freezer.

Because peppers, eggplant and okra are low-acid vegetables, they must be canned under pressure unless you make them into relish or pickle them.

GENERAL COOKING TIPS

Peppers

Raw or cooked, sweet peppers are delicious. I serve them in salads, soups, stews, snacks, cut in rings as a garnish, in casseroles or stuffed and baked as a main dish. Since they're so easy to freeze, you can depend on a year-round supply from just one gardening season.

Red and green peppers are good sources of vitamin C, some vitamin A and small amounts of several beneficial minerals. Red peppers contain more vitamin A and C than green ones, and raw peppers are richer in vitamins than cooked ones.

Our favorite varieties are green and red bell peppers, sweet and banana, pimiento, cherry and jalapeno peppers. You don't even need exact recipes to get the most from any of these varieties. We sauté whole sweet banana peppers (stems, seeds and all) in a few tablespoons of butter or oil for a quick delicious side dish. Dick likes to put these between two pieces of bread for a "pepper sandwich." Sliced peppers and onions sautéed with home fried potatoes go great together for a quick, colorful, side dish. Or, add cooked chopped peppers to scrambled eggs for an instant western omlet. For shish kabob, thread raw peppers with uncooked meat, mushroom caps and cherry tomatoes on skewers and broil or barbecue. To roast peppers, brush them lightly with oil and bake or broil until browned.

Drying Peppers

In addition to canning and freezing peppers, you can grow your own "spice" peppers to dry for use all year long. Just plant the variety you want, let the fruit turn red on the plant and harvest.

We generally harvest the entire plant and dry our chili peppers by hanging the plants upside down in the carport in the late summer. We leave them there until the weather turns frosty, and then bring them indoors to use during the winter. We hang them from the ceiling of our root cellar, but dried peppers will keep fine right in your kitchen. They'll keep for two years or more in a dry place. You can dry peppers anywhere that's warm with good air circulation, and they dry just as well off the plants. We just find leaving them on the plant makes it easy to move them and hang them out of the way.

You can also string peppers with a needle on strong thread. Keep them in a cool, dry, dark place until they are totally dry, and then hang the plants or ropes of dried peppers where it's warm and dry.

Dried peppers are great for seasoning sauces or concocting a special supper.

Although we've never tried it, sweet peppers may also be dried in the same way as hot peppers.

The Spice Rack

Peppers are truly multi-purpose vegetables, since certain varieties are used to make seasonings and spices. Paprika, cayenne pepper, chili powder and Tabasco sauce are all made from pepper.

If you want to make your own spices, simply remove the stems and seeds from dried peppers. Grind the peppers to the consistency you want. Chili pepper flakes are a convenient size for seasoning sauces, chilies, stews and Mexican dishes. Store the ground peppers in airtight containers.

Be careful about the quantity of these hot peppers you use in recipes. A whole one is often too much!

If you're looking for another way to use hot peppers, try making a spicy vinegar. Combine twenty-four red chili peppers in a quart of distilled white vinegar and cover tightly. Shake the contents daily. After two weeks, strain the vinegar and place in a tightly corked jar. Use this homemade vinegar for your "house" French or Italian dressing. To make a milder vinegar, use fewer peppers. Add salt or other seasonings according to your taste.

You can also preserve long, thin, red chili peppers in sherry, for an unusual salad or hors d'oeuvres ingredient. Just pack the peppers into sterile jars, add the sherry, cover and store in a cool, dark place. The peppers will keep indefinitely. Add more sherry or peppers as needed to keep jars full.

Eggplant

Eggplant is both beautiful and versatile. The deep purple skin and bright green stem on this vegetable encloses the meaty pulp — a low-calorie, low-fat food that deserves more attention. The trouble is that it's fairly new to gardeners in this country, who sometimes avoid cooking it because they simply don't know more than one recipe. Finding new ways to serve eggplant is a lot like experimenting with summer squash; once you start, the possibilities really open up.

There's no need to peel eggplant; the skin is perfectly edible when cooked.

Many cooks prefer to remove the moisture from sliced eggplant before cooking so the dish isn't overly watery. There are a few ways to do this. You can pat and drain slices thoroughly between paper towels with fairly good results or salt slices liberally to draw out water and drain them on wire racks. Another method is to stack slices, cover them with a plate and place a heavy weight on to to squeeze out excess moisture.

Like so many light-fleshed vegetables, eggplant discolors when it's cut open. You can prevent this by sprinkling or rubbing the slices with lemon juice as soon as you cut them. Or dilute 3 tablespoons of lemon juice in a large bowl of water and place each eggplant slice in this "anti-darkening" solution until you're ready to cook it. It also helps to use stainless steel knives and non-corrosive cookware such as stainless steel, glass or enamel.

Eggplant can be steamed, sautéed, fried, baked or combined with many other foods in casseroles or vegetable medleys.

Okra

This southern specialty is a good source of vitamins A and C. It can be served alone or in soups or stews. Okra is delicious served with melted butter

and a squeeze of lemon or dipped in an egg batter and deep fried. Another name for okra is gumbo; that's why soups containing okra are often called gumbos. These thick and hearty soups usually include meat, fish, chicken and other vegetables. The okra, a natural thickening agent, is used instead of flour or other starch.

To cook, wash the pods well and cut off stem ends. Cut in 1/2 inch slices and cook in boiling salted water 10 to 15 minutes, or until just tender.

Okra will keep well for a few days in your refrigerator in a covered container, or you can easily freeze or can it.

FAVORITE RECIPES

Breakfast Peppers

A treat at any meal.

2   Tb margarine
2   large green or red peppers, cut in strips
1/2 cup cooked meat (ham, bacon, chicken or turkey)
2   tomatoes, peeled and chopped
1   small onion chopped
1/2 tsp salt
    pepper to taste

Sauté peppers and onions in margarine until tender. Add tomatoes, meat, salt and pepper. Cover and cook about 10 minutes.

Serve with scrambled eggs and horseradish sauce.

Mexican Omelet

Here's a hot and tangy quiche, without the crust. It's perfect for a Sunday brunch.

12   eggs
1/4 lb bacon
1/2 cup onion, diced
1   green pepper cored and diced
1/2 cup milk
1   tsp hot chili pepper, minced
     salt and pepper to taste
     dash curry powder
1/2 cup sharp Cheddar cheese, grated

Cook bacon until crisp. Drain bacon and pour off all but 2 Tb bacon fat. Sauté onion and green pepper in bacon fat until onion is translucent. Beat eggs in a large bowl. Stir in milk, chili pepper, salt, pepper and curry powder and pour into a greased oblong or round baking dish. Top with onions, peppers, crumbled bacon and cheese. Bake in 350°F oven 25 minutes or until eggs are set and the top is slightly brown. Serves 4 to 6.

peppers from paper bag, slip skins off peppers, core and remove seeds. Do this over a bowl to catch juices that run out of peppers. Still over the bowl, tear peppers into 1/2-inch strips. (Tearing is easier than using a knife to cut.) Reserve pepper liquid in bowl.

3. To help peppers keep their shape, layer strips in small freezer containers. Place one leaf of fresh basil in each container and pour reserved liquid over the top. Pimientos can be frozen at this point for year-round use.

4. To prepare for serving, thaw pimientos and cover with Italian marinade: olive oil to cover, one garlic clove cut in half, 1 tsp. oregano, salt and pepper to taste. Refrigerate marinated peppers for 1 to 2 hours to allow flavors to blend. They'll keep in the refrigerator for a few weeks.

These peppers are an important antipasto ingredient. They are also delicious in Italian grinders or served with tuna salad.

Pork Stuffed Pepper Wedges

    1   lb ground lean pork, cooked
    1/3 cup chopped celery
    1/4 cup chopped canned mushrooms
    1/4 cup chopped green onions
    4   large green or red peppers cut in quarters
        cooked green peas for garnish (optional)
    2   Tb soy sauce

Combine pork, celery, mushrooms and onions in a bowl, mix and add soy sauce.

Stuff pepper quarters. Garnish each pepper with a few peas. Steam or bake in 350°F oven for 15 minutes. Serve with soy sauce and rice. Serves 6 to 8.

Italian-Style Pimientos

This recipe is authentically Italian. It was given to me by our good friend, Vicki Spahn. She and her husband, Jack, own The Country Kitchen *in Ferrisburgh, a restaurant close to our home.*

The recipe is four easy steps. The marinade ingredients are largely a matter of personal taste. The secret is in roasting and skinning the peppers.

1. Preheat oven to 400°F. Wash 6 to 10 red pimiento peppers. Leave whole and place on an ungreased cookie sheet. Roast for 30 minutes, turning and browning each side until the pepper skins are charred.

2. Remove from oven and place peppers, cookie sheet and all, in a large paper bag to cool. This keeps the peppers from becoming soft. When cool, remove

Pickled Peppers

This is the way I pickle most of our peppers, and a peck of these are guaranteed to make Peter Piper smile. Dick likes to take these to camp for sharing during hunting season.

    8   quarts peppers

Pickling liquid:
    1/4 cup sugar
    2   cloves garlic (per jar)
    8   cups vinegar
    2   cups water

I use red, green, yellow banana, cherry and hot peppers. Hot peppers can be "cooled" to your taste by adding sweet peppers to them. For lively color, I like to mix red, green and yellow in some jars.

Wash peppers. (Remember to wear rubber gloves when washing and handling hot peppers to prevent your hands from burning.)

If using small whole peppers, cut two small slits in each pepper to allow for complete pickling. When using larger peppers, cut stems off, take out seeds and cut in fourths or eighths. I like to cut them in squares so they're the perfect "cracker" size for hors d'oeuvres.

Combine all ingredients in a kettle except garlic; simmer for 15 minutes.

Pack peppers and garlic into hot jars, leaving 1/4 inch headspace. For a little extra zip, add 1 whole hot pepper to each jar of sweet peppers. Heat pickling liquid to boiling, pour over peppers, leaving 1/4 inch headspace. Adjust caps. Process pints 10 minutes in boiling water bath.

Makes about 8 pints.

Green Pepper Jelly

This is delicious served with lamb or pork.

  7 medium green peppers, washed, seeded, cored and cut in pieces
1 1/2 cups vinegar
  3-6 cups sugar
  1/2 tsp salt
  2 hot red peppers, washed, cored, seeded and diced
  1 bottle liquid pectin

Put half the green peppers and half the vinegar in a blender and liquefy. Pour into large kettle. Place remaining peppers and vinegar in blender and liquefy. Add to kettle and stir in red peppers, sugar and salt.

Bring to a boil and add pectin. Boil until mixture thickens when dropped from spoon — about 20 minutes. Skim off foam. Pour into clean, hot canning jars or glasses.

If using canning jars, fill them quickly to within 1/8 inch of top. Wipe jar rim and threads with a clean, damp cloth. Put on hot lids and screw band on tightly. Invert jars for a few seconds so hot jelly will destroy any harmful organisms and create a vacuum seal. Cool, test to be sure a seal has formed and store.

If using jelly glasses, seal with a 1/8 inch layer of hot (not smoking) paraffin. Be sure paraffin touches all sides of the glass and prick any air bubbles to prevent holes from forming. When paraffin hardens, place lid on glasses. Store jars in a cool, dry place. Makes about 4 half pints.

Pepper Slaw

This slaw can take the place of a salad.

  3 sweet green peppers
  3 sweet red peppers
  3 large onions
  1 head cabbage
  1 Tb salt
1 1/2 cups sugar
  2 tsp celery seeds
  2 tsp mustard seeds
     vinegar

Wash, core peppers and remove seeds. Coarsely chop peppers, onions and cabbage. Add salt, mix and let stand in refrigerator overnight. Drain the liquid formed by mixture. Add sugar, spices and mix well. Cover with vinegar, bring to a boil, boil for 20 to 25 minutes. Cool and refrigerate. Makes about 7 cups.

This recipe can be *doubled* and *canned*. All you need to do after boiling for 15 to 30 minutes is pour into hot pint jars leaving 1/2 inch headspace; adjust lids.

Process in boiling water bath 5 minutes. Makes 7 pints.

Pepper Relish

This is a favorite hot dog relish. It's a must at any "weiner roast."

  8 cups (about 12) green sweet peppers
  8 cups red sweet peppers
  1 hot pepper
  3 cups onions
  1 cup sugar
  1 Tb salt
  1 Tb mixed pickling spices
  2 cups vinegar

Wash and drain vegetables. Remove core and seeds from peppers. Peel onions. Finely chop peppers and onions and place in large kettle. Cover with boiling water and let stand 5 minutes. Drain. Cover again with boiling water and let stand 10 minutes, drain.

Simmer vinegar, sugar, salt and spices (tied in a bag) 15 minutes. Add drained vegetables and simmer 10 minutes. Remove spice bag; bring relish to a boil and pour into hot jars leaving 1/4 inch headspace. Adjust lids. Process 10 minutes in boiling water bath. Makes about 6 half pints.

Stove-Top Eggplant Parmigiana

  1 eggplant cut into 1/4 inch slices
  1 cup fine bread crumbs
  1/2 cup milk
  1/2 tsp salt
  1/4 tsp pepper
     salad oil
  2 cups tomato sauce
  16 oz mozzarella cheese, shredded
  1/4 cup grated Parmesan cheese

Dip eggplant slices in milk, salt and pepper, then coat both sides with bread crumbs. Heat 2 Tb oil and cook eggplant slices in large skillet over medium heat until tender and browned on both sides. Add more oil as needed. When browned, remove slices to a plate.

When all eggplant slices are browned, pour 2/3 cup tomato sauce in bottom of pan; lay half of the eggplant slices on sauce. Sprinkle half of the mozzarella cheese over eggplant. Repeat with another layer of each. Heat over medium-high heat until boiling. Reduce heat to low and simmer 10 to 15 minutes until heated through. Sprinkle with Parmesan cheese and serve. Serves 4 to 6.

This recipe may also be layered in a casserole or baking dish and baked in a 350°F oven for 30 minutes.

Shrimp Stuffed Eggplant

2 eggplant (medium size)
1/2 cup green tail onions chopped
1/2 cup celery, chopped
2 4½ oz cans tiny shrimp, drained
2 cloves garlic, minced
2 Tb margarine, melted
6 slices bread
1 cup water
1/4 cup parsley flakes
1/2 tsp salt
1/8 tsp black pepper
1/8 tsp cayenne
2 eggs, beaten
1/4 cup grated Parmesan cheese
3 cups spaghetti sauce

Cook eggplant in boiling water for 15 minutes. Drain and let cool. Cut in half lengthwise. Scoop out pulp, leaving shells intact. Chop pulp and reserve.

Sauté onions, celery and garlic in margarine until tender. Soak bread in water and then drain and squeeze out water. Add bread, parsley, pulp, salt, pepper, cayenne and shrimp to onion mix. Stir. Cool slightly. Add eggs and mix well.

Place eggplant shells in a greased baking dish; fill each with shrimp mixture. Spoon sauce over each eggplant. Sprinkle with cheese. Bake at 400°F 20 to 25 minutes. To serve, cut each shell in half. Serves 8.

Eggplant and Rice Patties

2 cups peeled, cooked, mashed eggplant
1 1/2 cups cooked rice, cooled
2 eggs, slightly beaten
1 cup shredded Cheddar cheese
1 Tb grated onion
1/4 cup cornmeal or 2 Tb flour
1 tsp salt
2 drops Tabasco Sauce (use more if you like it hot)
1/2 cup salad oil

Combine all the ingredients except oil. Mix well. Form into patties. Place in skillet with oil, heated to 375°F. Cook until brown on both sides. Drain on paper towels. Makes about 18.

Deep Fried Eggplant

1 large eggplant, washed, peeled, cut in 1/2 inch strips
1 1/2 tsp salt
1 cup flour
2 eggs, slightly beaten
1 cup milk
1 Tb salad oil
hot oil (salad)

To prepare eggplant for frying, sprinkle eggplant with 1 tsp salt, cover with water and soak 1 hour. Drain, pat dry with paper towels.

In a mixing bowl, combine flour, 1/2 tsp salt, egg, milk and 1 Tb salad oil, beat until smooth.

Dip eggplant strips in batter and deep fry in oil until medium brown. Drain on paper towels. Serves 4 to 6.

Greek Moussaka

A delicious eggplant casserole.

2 large eggplants
  olive oil
2 cloves garlic, minced
2 onions, chopped
1 lb ground lamb (or ground beef)
2 Tb tomato paste
1/2 cup red wine
1/4 cup chopped parsley
1/2 tsp oregano
1 tsp cinnamon
1 tsp sugar
  salt and pepper to taste
1/2 cup fine bread crumbs
1/4 cup butter or margarine
2 cups milk
2 eggs slightly beaten
1/8 tsp grated nutmeg
1/2 cup grated Parmesan cheese

Slice unpeeled eggplants in 1/4 inch rounds and in a large skillet sauté a few slices at a time, lightly, in olive oil. Set aside.

Add more olive oil to skillet if needed and sauté the garlic, onion and ground lamb until the lamb is browned. Stir in tomato paste, wine, parsley, oregano, cinnamon, sugar, salt and pepper and simmer until the liquid has nearly evaporated. Stir in bread crumbs.

Place a layer of eggplant slices in the bottom of a deep casserole dish. Spread with a layer of meat sauce. Alternate layers until ingredients are all used, ending with a layer of eggplant.

In a saucepan, melt margarine. Add milk and nutmeg and heat 2 to 3 minutes. Remove from heat, add eggs and mix well. Pour custard mixture over casserole, allowing it to penetrate sides and lower layers. Sprinkle cheese on top and bake 35 to 40 minutes in 350°F oven. Serves 4 to 6.

Ratatouille

This classic French dish may be difficult to pronounce, but it's easy to make and it's one of our very favorite garden recipes. Feel free to use more or less of each ingredient — the amounts don't have to be precise for a delicious result.

1/3 cup olive oil
1 medium onion, chopped fine
2 cloves garlic, peeled and crushed
1 large eggplant, peeled and cubed
2 medium zucchini, sliced in 1/2 inch pieces (don't peel)
1-2 medium peppers, cut in strips
6 ripe, medium size tomatoes, quartered (or 2 cups canned tomatoes)
   basil
   salt and pepper

In large skillet or saucepan, sauté onion and garlic in oil until onion is transparent. Stir in remaining vegetables; add basil, salt and pepper to taste. Simmer covered over low heat 30 minutes. Uncover and simmer 15 minutes more, or until liquid is reduced and mixture is slightly thickened. Serve this as a hot or cold side dish. Serves 6 to 8.

Eggplant Dip

This is a garden-fresh dip that goes well with raw vegetables or crackers.

1 eggplant
1/4 cup chopped onion
1 Tb chives or scallions, chopped
1/2 cup tomatoes, chopped
1/4 cup celery, chopped
1/4 cup red or green pepper, chopped
2 cloves garlic, minced
2 tsp lemon juice
1/4 cup sour cream or plain yogurt
1/2 cup mayonnaise
   Salt and pepper to taste.
Optional:
1 Tb horseradish sauce for added zip
   paprika as garnish

Place eggplant in a large kettle, cover with water and bring to a boil. Cook until soft, about 25 minutes. Dip in cold water to cool. Peel and chop into a bowl. Add all remaining ingredients. Mix well. If you prefer a finer texture, blend all ingredients in a blender or food processor until smooth. Chill at least two hours. Garnish with sprinkle of paprika before serving. Makes about 3 cups.

Eggplant – Spaghetti Bake

This is quick and simple, with no frying needed. For large gatherings, simply double the recipe and bake it in two pans.

1 large eggplant
1/2 cup bread crumbs
3/4 cup grated Parmesan cheese
1/4 cup mayonnaise
1 8 oz pkg. spaghetti
2 Tb margarine
1 lb ground beef
6 cups thick spaghetti sauce
8 oz mozzarella cheese

Preheat oven to 425°F. Combine crumbs and 1/4 cup of Parmesan cheese in a shallow dish. Wash and cut eggplant into 1/2 inch slices.

Spread mayonnaise sparingly on both sides of each eggplant slice. Dip slices in crumb mixture to coat both sides and place on ungreased cookie sheet. Bake in oven about 15 minutes until browned and tender. Remove from oven and lower oven temperature to 375°F.

Cook spaghetti according to directions on package. Drain and toss with margarine until spaghetti is coated. Cover spaghetti and keep warm. Crumble beef in a skillet and brown over low heat. Add spaghetti sauce and heat through.

Grease 13 × 9 inch baking dish. Pour one cup of sauce in the bottom of the pan, place spaghetti on top. Pour remaining sauce over spaghetti. Arrange slices of eggplant then top with strips of mozzarella cheese.

Bake 15 minutes or until heated through and cheese is melted. Serves 6 to 8.

Okra Fritters

2 cups okra sliced in 1/4 inch strips, cooked and drained
1 cup flour
2 tsp baking powder
1 tsp salt
1/8 tsp pepper
2 eggs, beaten
1 tsp onion, minced
1 Tb margarine, melted
1 cup milk
1/2 cup salad oil

Combine dry ingredients, stir in eggs, onion, margarine and milk. Fold okra into batter and mix lightly.

Drop batter by tablespoons into skillet or fryer with 375°F heated oil. Cook 2 minutes on each side or until lightly browned. Drain on paper towels. Makes 16 fritters.

Colorful Okra Dish

Fresh okra, corn off the cob and ripe tomatoes make this easy side dish delicious. Make it a surprise for your next company meal.

2 1/2 cups sliced okra
1 1/2 cups fresh corn cut off cob
4 large tomatoes chopped
1/4 cup chopped onion
1/4 cup margarine, melted
salt and pepper to taste

Wash and slice okra, rinse well under running water and drain.

Combine okra with remaining ingredients in large skillet, cover and simmer 15 minutes. Serves 6.

Okra Beef Supper

1 lb ground beef
3/4 cups onion chopped
1 garlic clove minced
4 cups canned tomatoes
1/2 cup uncooked rice
1/4 cup bread crumbs
1 tsp salt
1/8 tsp pepper
6 drops Tabasco Sauce
2 cups sliced okra

Brown ground beef, onion and garlic clove in skillet. Add tomatoes and simmer. Add remaining ingredients, except okra. Cover and simmer 20 minutes.

Stir in okra, cover and simmer again until rice is done (20 to 25 minutes). Stir occasionally. Serves 6 to 8.

North-South Gumbo

3 cups okra, sliced
1 cup celery, diced
1 green pepper, chopped
1 medium onion, chopped
6 strips bacon
2 cups corn
1 cup diced potatoes
6 large fresh tomatoes, chopped (or 4 cups canned tomatoes)
2 cups flaked cooked fish
2 tsp brown sugar
1/4 tsp paprika
4 cups water
salt and pepper to taste

Cut bacon in small pieces, place in skillet and sauté with okra, celery, green pepper and onion for 5 minutes.

Combine all ingredients in a large kettle and simmer for 1 hour. Serve hot. Serves 6.

Pickled Dill Okra

2 1/2 quarts young okra
3 celery leaves (for each pint)
1 clove garlic (for each pint)
1 large head dill and stem (for each pint)
3 cups water
1 1/2 cups white vinegar
1/4 cup salt

Scrub okra, pack whole pods in hot pint jars. In each jar place 3 celery leaves, 1 clove garlic peeled, and 1 head and stem of dill. Bring water, vinegar and salt to a boil. Pour the boiling liquid over the okra and seal jars. Process 5 minutes in hot water bath.

Let stand 4 weeks before eating for best pickle flavor. Makes 4 pints.

CHAPTER 4

Vine Crops

For a heat-loving plant, the cucumber certainly has all the connotations of coolness attached to it. Considering that it originated in the hot, dry climates of Asia and Africa, we can understand how its crisp, white flesh must have seemed refreshing. Sliced cucumbers are still recommended to soothe hot, tired eyelids and for skin irritations. And there's nothing like sliced cucumbers in a summer salad to beat the heat.

Today, there are many cucumber varieties — picklers, slicers, gherkins, white cucumbers, bush and midget cukes. The most interesting hybrid to come along in quite a while is the "burpless" cucumber, guaranteed not to cause "social embarassment."

The art of pickling and preserving cucumbers is centuries old. You can pickle or preserve any small cucumber. Picklers taste very good right off the vine, so feel free to experiment with different varieties, regardless of how you intend to eat them. Also, remember to plant some dill seed early in the spring, so you'll be all set for pickling when those first young cucumbers are ready.

Picklers — 53 to 60 days — Smallish, often warty, green, used for small sweet pickles or large dills. Can also be eaten fresh. My best pickler is **Wisconsin SMR 18.**

Slicers — 58 to 65 days — 5 to 8-inch cylindrical cucumbers, used for slicing and serving fresh, but they can be pickled. Skin can be solid colored or white-spined (striped). My favorite is **Marketmore 70.**

There are also the lemon, serpent, white, burpless and bush cucumbers available for you to try. Check for them in seed catalogs or at a garden store.

Squashes and Pumpkins — The All Americans

Each of the different varieties — summer squashes, winter squashes and pumpkins — has a different length growing season, which makes them easy to tell apart. Summer squashes — zucchini, patty pans and cocozelles — all take a relatively short time from planting until harvest. Winter squashes take longer to mature, and pumpkins require the longest growing season of all. Plant them all at the same time, and you can have different varieties ready to harvest from midsummer up to the first frost.

Sometimes there is confusion over what's a squash and what's really a pumpkin. When I refer to pumpkins, I mean only the round, orange vegetables raised for Halloween and used in making pies.

At our house, Thanksgiving just wouldn't be complete without a couple of winter squashes. Winter squashes originated in Central America, and they were North American Indian specialties long before the Pilgrims ever stepped off the Mayflower.

Even though you'll soon discover your own

favorite variety, I must tell you that my all-time favorite winter squash is **Blue Hubbard.** (Smaller families may like **Sweet Mama** — it looks and tastes like a small Hubbard.) I have yet to taste as flavorful a squash as this big, gnarly, bluish-gray vegetable. **Waltham Butternut** is another fine variety and **Table Queen** acorn squash does well in most gardens.

As for summer squash, I usually plant varieties that produce very early and are resistant to disease. I have good luck with Straightnecks; they ripen early, are prolific and disease-resistant. Most zucchini varieties available these days are dependable producers. Zucchini are green and straightneck are yellow. Cocozelle and patty pan are two other varieties of summer squash that are as interesting to look at as they are to eat.

With pumpkins, I prefer a small variety such as **Small Sugar** for pies, and **Big Max** for our jack-o'-lanterns.

Melons — The Essence of Summer

If anything says "summer" to me, it's a bright red, juicy wedge of chilled watermelon at a picnic on a hot, sunny afternoon. It makes me think of those carefree childhood summers when I used to spit out the seeds with real flair and marksmanship.

Maybe you have always considered melons as fruit, but they are also vegetables because they are members of the vine crop (cucurbit) family. But, because technically the word "fruit" means any ripe, seed-containing growth from a flowering plant, melons can be correctly referred to as either fruit or vegetable.

There is also some confusion about the terms cantaloupe and muskmelon. A cantaloupe is actually a small, hard-skinned melon which originated in Italy but isn't grown much in America. The general name "muskmelon" is more accurate for all the round, netted or smooth-skinned melons belonging to this particular species which includes cantaloupe. The confusion arises because the two have come to mean exactly the same thing in this country. Seed companies, grocers and local growers use the terms interchangeably.

How All Vine Crops Grow

Vine crop seeds and plants are extremely tender. They don't tolerate frosts at all, and they need both warm weather and sunshine from the day you plant until the day you harvest.

Once the seeds are planted, they'll sprout (germinate) in seven days to two weeks, depending on the variety. In order to do this, the seeds need moisture and warmth.

Soon after the seeds have germinated, they'll send up their first leaves. The vines will lengthen quickly from this point on, putting on new leaf growth the entire time.

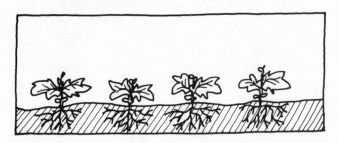

While the vines spread, the roots below develop an extensive but fairly shallow network in the top twelve inches of the soil. There is one strong taproot that grows as deep as two to three feet, but most of the food, moisture and air is delivered by the many branching offshoots just below the soil surface.

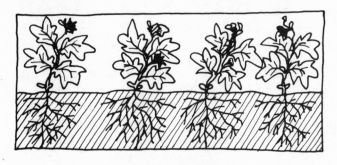

Tendrils will eventually form on the vines to anchor them. These tendrils can wind tightly around fences, trellises or even other vegetables for support.

Flower blossoms appear after about three weeks of this initial growth. The first blossoms that appear are usually male. They produce pollen.

About a week later, the fruit-producing female blossoms will bloom. You can tell the blossoms apart because the females have a tiny fruit at their base.

Once both the brightly colored male and female blossoms appear on the vine, bees and insects will transfer the pollen from the males to the females. Each flower lives for only half a day, and I understand there's only about one bee visitor for every hundred flowers. The odds may sound bad for pollination, but the only thing that would seriously hamper natural pollination of your vine crops is a long rainy or cold spell, when bees are not active.

The tiny fruits behind any pollinated female blossoms grow into the full-sized vegetables, and the plant continues to produce blossoms. The plant's natural goal is to produce seeds that will produce more plants, thus perpetuating the species. Once the seeds within each vegetable reach a certain size, the plant receives the word from Mother Nature to stop producing more female flowers for more fruit — the plant's job is done.

The Facts of Life

In my chats with gardeners all over the country, I've heard some pretty tall tales about the freak results of cross pollination between cucumbers and melons, pumpkins and squash. I can see that there are some old wives' tales that need clearing up.

First of all, the whole notion of mixed breeding of melons or squash only matters if you intend to save seed from one year for the next. Unlike corn, which can cross the first season, vine crops will *never* show the results of cross pollination the first season. It's what the bees were up to the previous year that can cause strange looking vegetables. That's why seed companies isolate vine crops very strictly — if two crops' blossoms mix this year, it will show up in the seed you buy for next year.

Sometimes, even with the most careful controls, the commercial seed that's available may have one or two "weirdo" seeds mixed in with it, and you may raise a strange-looking zucchini. But it isn't because of anything that happened in your own garden.

Now, if you do intend to save seeds from your pumpkins or squash to plant next year, you should understand that only some vine crops are able to cross with one another. I keep it straight with this formula: "Each species keeps to its own kind." Summer squash will cross with each other, but not with cucumbers. Cucumbers will inter-breed, but won't cross with anything else. Muskmelons will cross with each other, but not with watermelons.

Winter squash, summer squash and pumpkins are closely related, and they may cross among themselves. Gourds are species unto themselves, for the most part, but some will cross with summer squash. A botanical chart will tell you the species of the vine crops if you want to find out all the possible combinations. But it's really not worth worrying about — believe me!

If you want to grow two kinds of summer squash, say zucchini and cocozelle, and you plan to save the seed, plant them at least 100 feet apart to prevent the bees from traveling back and forth, mixing pollens. My advice is to stick with commercially grown, disease-resistant seed for your main yield, and only plant home-grown seeds for fun.

A point on hybrids — if you plant a hybrid, even a commercially-grown variety, don't save the seed. Hybrids don't reproduce themselves. Instead they revert back to the traits of their parent plants, usually inferior quality.

GETTING STARTED

Seed Know-How

When it's time for you to choose seeds, either at the garden center or from a seed catalog, check with a gardening neighbor or your local Cooperative Extension Service agent for advice on which varieties do best in your area. The seed companies have been busy developing strains that are resistant to such vine crop problems as mildews, mosaic, scab, anthracnose and leaf spot, and you should try to get disease-resistant varieties. These are indicated by capitalized initials on the seed packet or in the catalog. (SMR means scab and mosaic resistant, for example.)

It's also smart to start with treated seeds, those that have a powdery fungicide on them. This fungicide protects the seeds from rotting before they germinate and from damping off, where young seedlings just keel over and die. If you can't find treated seed, you can treat them yourself if you choose with an all-purpose seed protectant that's available in most garden stores. Be sure to follow the directions.

If you're interested in trying some seeds of the latest hybrids now available in the marketplace, great! But plant some of the old stand bys that you are sure will produce well in your area, in case the others aren't well-adapted. It's fun to see how a few white or all-female cucumbers fare in your garden, however don't depend entirely on these novelty varieties.

Garden Planning

It seems to be a law of nature that the sweetest, juiciest garden vegetables are the ones that require the most pampering. In order to be rewarded with fine melons, you have to treat the plants as if they're on vacation — lots of sun, water, food and warm weather. If you treat them royally, they feed you just as well in return.

Reserve a sunny, well-drained spot for your vine crops, preferably one with a slight slope to the south. Sunny means at least eight hours of full sun every day.

The amount of space you allow depends on how many plants you and your family want, and whether or not you plan to support the vines with trellises or fences. Naturally, I have no idea how much you like zucchini or acorn squash, but I must caution you to start off small if you've never grown vine crops before. Cucumbers and all summer squash are especially heavy yielders. My rule of thumb is one or two hills maximum for each person in the household, and that may still be too much. Of course, if you intend to preserve or store much of the harvest, plant more.

Grow more than one variety. A few that mature early and some later ones will extend the harvest and avoid a sudden overdose of ripe squash or cucumbers. You can stagger your plantings for continual harvests and to avoid losing an entire crop if weather or disease problems hit. Divide packets up with your friends — take a few seeds and pass them on. Believe me, you probably don't need to grow all the vine crop seeds contained in a packet.

Some varieties spread more than others. Keep this in mind as you plan your garden. If you plan to limit the space with supports, leave a walkway wide enough for you to cultivate by hand or machine. If you intend to let the vines run freely, beware . . . some need lots of room. One good place to plant vine crops is at the edge of the garden, so the vines can spread over the lawn rather than in among your other vegetables. I've seen squash and melons all tangled up in peas, potatoes and herbs — what a mess.

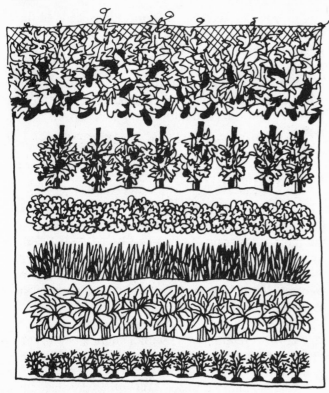

When to Plant

You must wait until all danger of frost is past unless you provide some protection for sensitive vine crops. These plants shouldn't go into the garden until after the average last frost date when the soil has really warmed up.

The average last frost date is fairly well known. Your local weather bureau can tell you when it's expected, or ask an experienced gardener in your area. The surprising thing is that it's always earlier than you think.

Prep Talk — Soil

Vine crops may be very particular when it comes to their place in the garden, but they are quite flexible when it comes to the soil itself. With a little help from you, they'll flourish in sandy soil, clay soil or just about anything in between.

It's up to you to till or spade the soil several times before planting day. The first time should be the deepest, to a depth of six to eight inches. Improve the texture of your soil by working in plenty of organic matter at that time. This can be old leaves, hay, grass clippings, compost or even organic kitchen garbage. The more organic matter you add to your soil, the more food you provide for the earthworms and soil organisms within it. They, in turn, break down the organic matter into humus, a nutrient-rich substance. Humus is the garden miracle worker — it will transform problem soils into productive soils.

If your soil is so sandy that it just doesn't hold moisture, humus binds the sandy particles together to create a more sponge-like texture.

On the other hand, if you're plagued by clay soil that either never dries out, or bakes as hard as concrete when it does dry, humus wedges itself between the clay particles. This allows air to circulate and water to seep down through the soil naturally, making the soil a fine growing medium.

By adding organic matter to the soil, and by loosening the top six to eight inches of soil, you make it easy for plant roots to expand and draw air, water and nutrients to the rest of the plant. Result? Healthy, delicious vegetables.

After the initial deep tilling or spading a week to two before planting, stir up the top two to three inches of soil every few days, using an iron garden rake, hoe, cultivating tool or tiller. Every time you disrupt a soil section, you bring hundreds of tiny weed seeds out into the open where they die. The more you work the soil, the less weeding you'll have to do later. This alone should inspire you to go out often for a soil-prep session.

Always work the soil one last time just before you plant, regardless of how often it's been worked previously. Your seeds are going to need fresh oxygen and loose soil around them to properly germinate and grow.

pH

Most vegetables grow best in soil that is slightly acid, and vine crops are no exception. You can measure your soil's acidity or alkalinity by determining its pH with a soil test. pH is measured on a scale of 0 to 14, with 7 indicating neutral. Any reading above 7 is considered alkaline or sweet, anything below is acid. The further the reading is from neutral 7, the greater the degree of acidity or alkalinity. A pH range of 6.0 to 6.8 — slightly on the acid side — is best for the home garden.

You should check your soil pH every couple of years. Do this by sending a soil sample to your local Cooperative Extension Service, if they do tests, or test your own soil using an inexpensive soil testing kit, which is available at most garden centers.

In most parts of the country, soils are slightly acidic, and so need lime. I spread a 10-quart bucket of lime over every 1,000 square feet of garden space, repeating this every three or four years on sandy soil, and every four to five years on clay soil.

If you have wood ashes, use about double the amount to get the same results. Remember, you can spread too many wood ashes on your garden.

Hearty Appetites — Fertilizer

I must say, vine crops are not exactly gourmets —their favorite food is compost or stable manure. But any balanced commercial fertilizer will also provide the nutrients needed for good production.

Planting day is the time to provide them with a hefty dose of food to start them growing quickly. It doesn't pay to broadcast the fertilizer widely, since the plants will be spaced at fairly good intervals and will only use what's directly around their roots. They'll make good use of the manure or fertilizer placed directly in the furrow or hole underneath where you will plant the seeds (or seedlings, if you use transplants).

As for amounts, it's difficult to give a specific measure for something as bulky as stable manure, but I find that a heaping shovelful for every five feet of row, or every hill, is fine. If you use a balanced commercial fertilizer, such as 5-10-10 or 10-10-10, use about a cup for every hill, or a cup or so for every five feet of row.

Cover all fertilizers with two to three inches of soil to keep the seeds from being burned by the nitrogen in these substances.

By the way, the numbers on the labels of balanced commercial fertilizer refer to the percentages

by weight of nitrogen (N), phosphorus (P) and potassium (K) contained in that particular mixture. They are always listed in the same order, N-P-K, for 5-10-10 or any other combination.

Radishes — Good Company Policy

Although I am generally skeptical of the benefits of companion planting, I am convinced that radishes are helpful in the garden. I plant radishes in with all my vine crops because they seem to repel many harmful cucumber beetles, black flea beetles and even annoying black flies. Whether it's their sharp odor or because they exude some chemical that insects dislike, radishes work.

Radishes also come up early to mark the row, so you won't disturb the germinating seeds when you cultivate around the hills or rows to keep down weeds.

You only need to sprinkle a few radish seeds in each planting spot — less than a pinch. Any spring radish (early maturing) will do.

Leave the radishes until they are huge — way beyond the eating stage. I don't pull mine from a row of cucumbers until I harvest the first small pickler from the vine. As you remove the radishes, you loosen the soil around the base of the cucumber plants, leaving good-sized cavities where the radish

roots were. These holes become ducts for air and water, keeping the vine roots better supplied.

Radishes seem to be most effective at warding off insects when vine crops are young. This is also when cucumber beetles can do the most damage, spreading disease that can knock out an entire young crop. By the time the radishes lose some of their potency, the vines are strong and well-established. The beetles that are repelled make it worth the small cost and extra seconds it takes to add some radish seeds to your cucumber or squash rows at planting time.

PLANTING

Hills and Drills — Simply Circles and Rows

Seed packets usually have planting instructions on the back, and you may be advised to plant vine crops in either hills or drills. These two terms have been used for years by gardeners and farmers to describe the planting arrangement of seeds, but it's much easier to picture these in terms of *circles* and *rows*.

When it comes to planting, a hill is not raised soil; it's a circle of four to eight seeds. A drill has nothing to do with your dentist; it's simply a row of seeds planted at regular intervals. I use the word *hill* to describe groups of seeds, but I prefer to use the word *row* for straight-line planting.

Contrary to the established tradition of planting vine crops in hills, I get terrific results by planting in rows, especially with the early maturing cucumbers and summer squash. These plants don't run as much as some of the others, and you can fit many more plants in the same garden space using rows. They're also spared a lot of potential insect damage, since they aren't vulnerably grouped together in hills.

Rows (Drills)

After preparing the soil and working it one last time on planting day, mark the row by stretching a string along the ground between two stakes.

Make a furrow beside the string, using either a hoe or a power furrower. The depth of the furrow depends on your fertilizer. If you use a concentrated, granular, commercial fertilizer, the furrow only has to be four to five inches deep. If you have bulkier organic matter such as manure or compost, just make a furrow that's four to six inches deep, spread two to three inches of manure in it, and top that with two to three inches of soil.

Drop a seed every six to eight inches in the row, depending on the variety.

Sprinkle a few radish seeds in, too.

Firm the seeds into the soil with the back of a hoe, creating good contact between seeds and soil; this is the key to good germination.

Cover the seeds with three-quarters to one inch of soil.

Firm again.

Hills (Circles, Groups)

Planting techniques similar to planting in rows are used for hills. Mark the planting area with a string, but instead of making a furrow, dig a four to eight-inch hole for each hill, depending on the bulk of the fertilizer.

Space the holes three to ten feet apart, depending on the vegetable.

Place either organic or balanced commercial fertilizer such as 5-10-10 in the hole and fill it back to ground level. Be sure it has at least a two-inch soil covering.

Plant six to eight seeds on the perimeter of a circle at each hill, allowing two to three inches between seeds. Drop each seed, add some radish seeds, firm, cover with soil and firm again, just as in rows.

Later you'll be thinning each hill down to the best four or five plants. The extra seeds just ensure a full hill, even if germination is poor.

Mounds

It's important for vine crops that the soil be dry and warm. If your soil stays very wet and you've had trouble raising healthy vine crops, try building the hills up three to five inches before planting.

These mounds aid the plant's germination and improve the growing environment because the soil warms up and dries out faster.

Vine Spacing

Generally, the longer the growing season, the more the vines will spread. So, you should allow more room for winter squash and melons than for summer squash and cucumbers.

Here are some guidelines for seed and row spacing. Sometimes I plant seeds closer together, just for the insurance of good germination. It's easy to thin if there are too many young plants in a row or a hill; it's harder to patch up an incomplete row.

	Seeds in Rows inches apart	Transplants inches apart	Rows or Hills feet apart
Cucumber	6 to 8	8 to 10	4 to 6
Summer Squash	8 to 10	10 to 12	4 to 6
Winter Squash	10 to 12	12 to 14	6 to 10
Pumpkins	10 to 12	12 to 14	6 to 10
Cantaloupe	6 to 8	8 to 10	4 to 6
Watermelon	6 to 8	10 to 12	6 to 8

To thin the rows or hills, allow the same spacing as for transplants. Sprouted seeds are spaced exactly like non-sprouted seeds.

BUYING TIME

Sprouting Tips

Melons are notoriously slow, undependable germinators. Here are a couple of tricks to give you germination insurance and a jump on the season. By the way, these work for all the vine crops.

Paper Towel Sprouting — Take four paper towels folded back into one and moisten them. Sprinkle about 12 seeds on the towel, about one-quarter to one-half inch apart.

Roll the towel up tightly like a jelly roll. Roll the paper towel inside a soaking wet hand towel. Place the entire seed roll in a plastic bag, twist-tie the opening and leave it in a warm spot at an even temperature — the top of the refrigerator is just right at our house. Just don't leave it on a windowsill because the temperature there fluctuates too much.

The seeds will sprout in four to five days. Sometimes all the seeds will sprout, sometimes only half or three-quarters. (You can also use this paper towel method to test the germination of any vegetable seeds. If you try to sprout ten seeds and only six

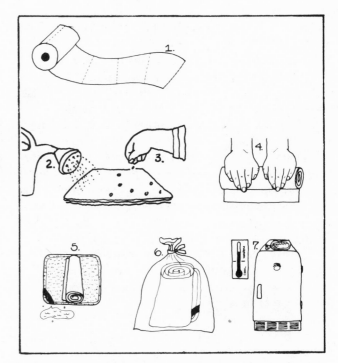

germinate, the germination rate for that variety is 60 percent. This is a help if you have seed left over from the last season, and you want to know if it's still good.)

By the time the seeds have sprouted, I have already prepared the soil. You must plant seeds as soon as they sprout or they'll die.

These sprouted seeds are planted in exactly the same way as regular seed. On planting day make the rows or hills and add fertilizer. Take the plastic bag out to the garden, unwrap and unroll it, and plant the seeds just as if they were un-sprouted. Don't forget to add some radish seeds. Cover the seeds and firm as usual.

Hot Caps — To gain two weeks on a short growing season, use inexpensive wax paper or plastic covers known as hot caps. They are designed to cover your seeds or seedlings, protect them from frost and bugs and gather heat for them as they grow. Presprout the seeds and place hot caps over the seeds after you plant. Sprout the seeds earlier, and the hot caps will allow you a week or two more growing time before the average last frost date.

When the danger of frost is past, remove the hot caps. The plants will be well up and on their way.

Transplanting — Yes or No?

The choice of starting vine crops indoors or right in the garden is totally up to you. However, there are both advantages and disadvantages to transplanting vine crops that you should consider before you make up your mind.

Transplanting does give you a head start of a month or more on the growing season, and it protects the seeds and seedlings from birds, insects, heavy rains, sudden cold weather and weeds.

On the other hand, starting seeds and transplanting seedlings is a time-consuming operation. It's also difficult to keep from injuring the sensitive roots when you transfer the plants into the garden.

Transplanting only makes sense as a time saver to get an early harvest. Even here in northern Vermont, I seldom start squash or melon seeds indoors. With only three summer months between spring and fall frosts, I can still produce bumper crops using hot caps and presprouting.

To start your own vine crop plants indoors, follow these basic steps:

Choose disease-resistant seed from a reputable seed company.

Assemble your seeds, soil mix and pots three to four weeks before the last frost date.

Use a separate planting container for each plant, rather than tubs or flats, so you won't disturb the roots during transplanting. You can use peat pots, pint milk cartons or paper cups as long as you punch a few holes in the bottom for drainage. I have the best luck with special pots that have sterilized, fertile soil mix already in them (Jiffy-7 pellets, grow cubes).

Moisten the soil thoroughly before planting the seeds.

Plant two seeds in each pot simply by pressing the seed into the soil **pointed end down** with your thumb and covering with one-half inch soil.

Group the individual pots together on a tray, board or rack, and slide the whole thing into a plastic bag to prevent drying. Top that with a few thicknesses of newspaper and place the pots in a warm spot that has an even temperature. Don't place it on a windowsill; the temperature changes there are too extreme.

When the seedlings first show, remove the plastic. Place the pots under grow lights (no more than five inches away) or in a sunny spot to give them eight to twelve hours of sun — no more — each day.

Choose the healthiest, hardiest seedling from each pot after a week or so. Pinch off the other; pulling it out will disturb the roots of the one you're keeping.

Water the seedlings whenever the soil is very dry to the touch.

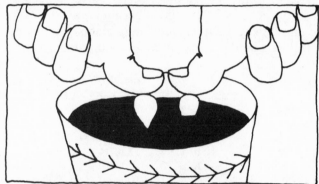

Hardening Off

You must gradually toughen young seedlings, or harden them off, so they won't get sunburned, windburned or chilled after you transplant them. This is accomplished by exposing them to the elements little by little until they're used to the outdoor conditions.

Allow at least a week to ten days to harden your seedlings. When you start the process, don't water them for two days before you first bring them outside. From then on, water only when they really need it.

At first, place the seedlings in a sheltered spot away from wind and out of direct sunlight. Increase their exposure every day until they can tolerate a full eight to twelve hours of sun. Then leave them out overnight, unless there's a danger of frost. After two or three nights outside, they're ready for the garden.

Wise Shopping

If you buy transplants rather than raise them yourself, look for stocky, dark green plants that aren't tall and spindly or leggy. The plants should be in individual containers. You must harden transplants, too.

Some peat pots or cardboard containers come with instructions telling you to plant the pots right along with the seedlings, that they will decompose in the soil. I find the plants recover much better if these organic pots are gently peeled off at transplanting time. The roots then have immediate access to the food and moisture in the soil at a time when it really counts.

Sod-Pots

Instead of planting in peat pots or other containers, you can use material from your own back yard — sod. Dig up a sod chunk six to eight inches square and two inches thick. Turn it upside down and cut it in two-inch cubes. Moisten the soil, and plant the seeds as you would in any container.

When the time comes to move the hardened seedlings into their permanent garden spot, prepare the furrows as usual, water the "sodlings" and place them in rows at the recommended intervals.

Transplanting

Once it's warm enough and your seedlings are well hardened, you're ready to transplant them to a sunny garden spot.

First, soak the plants thoroughly. Moist dirt sticks to the tender roots, protecting them from the elements and rough treatment.

Mark off the rows or hills in well-worked soil and make your holes or furrows. Always transplant seedlings into slightly deeper holes than their original containers.

Seedlings shouldn't be overfertilized at first because they may grow too quickly and be too tender to survive the transplant shock. Fertilize sparingly and give them extra fertilizer (sidedress) later, when the plants are hardier. Cover the fertilizer with two to three inches of soil.

When everything is ready, take one seedling and plant it. Tilt the pot and tap the bottom to loosen the root ball. The whole plant will slip out into your hand. If you use Jiffy 7's or peat pots, carefully tear the outer skin of the pot away from the roots, being careful not to harm them. If some of the pot sticks, leave it. You don't have to remove every last bit of peat, just enough so the roots aren't bound tightly on all sides.

Have some two-inch newspaper squares on hand to wrap around the stems to halt cutworms.

When transplanting, work quickly. Wrap a paper collar around the stem, so it spans one inch above to one inch below the soil surface, where it keeps cutworms from chewing on the tender stem. Set the plant into the ground, cover the roots and part of the stem with soil and firm the seedling into the soil to give the roots good contact with the soil.

Don't leave any of the seedling roots exposed to the air and light for more than a few seconds. If the phone rings when you're in the middle of this process, let it ring!

Water each plant thoroughly before going on to the next. Once the plants are in the ground, care for them just as you would plants started outdoors.

Trellising

Providing support for cucumbers and summer squash saves garden space. There are many kinds of homemade trellises, but let me just outline the ingredients for successful trellising:

The most sensible trellis is one that lasts, so keep this in mind before you start building.

You can make the support from wooden stakes and string, wooden slats nailed together to form a lattice, or chicken wire stretched between two posts. The vines climb easiest on criss-crossed materials the tendrils can grab and wind around.

Unless you're interested in picking cucumbers from a ladder, keep the top of the trellis within easy reach, no more than five feet high.

Install your trellis on or before planting day. If you try to pound stakes into the ground later, you're bound to injure some roots.

If you have a choice, put your trellis on the prevailing downwind side of the plants. They'll lean into it on a windy day rather than being pulled away and possibly being torn down.

Anchor the trellis solidly in the ground for the same reason.

Plant your seeds in rows on the prevailing upwind side of the trellis, and care for them just as you would free-sprawling plants.

When the plants are ready to run, guide them onto the supports. Wrap the tendrils or vines around the trellis to start them; they'll continue up on their own.

Stop the vines once they reach the top by picking off the fuzzy tufts on the ends. There's no sense allowing them to crawl down the other side. They'd just get tangled up in the rest of the plant and you could end up with lots of too-small cucumbers.

One trellis caution is that since the plants are off the ground, they require more water. They "transpire" or lose moisture more rapidly when they are exposed to warm air and drying winds, and you'll have to replenish the supply fairly frequently. Mulching helps to conserve moisture.

Babies' Bottoms

If you want to trellis any vegetables larger than cucumbers, you'll have to support each fruit, or the vines, tendrils and stems will break from the weight.

Make a sling by tying both ends of a long, wide strip of cloth to your trellis — discarded pantyhose is perfect. Gently lift each fruit into its cradle.

It looks like a playpen full of diapered babies' bottoms when you're all finished, but it does save space and keeps the produce clean. Be sure to pick off the ends to control the growth of the vines.

GROWING

Weed War

The most crucial time to control weeds is when the plants are young, before they start to run. Using a hoe, rake or cultivating tool, stir up the top one-quarter to one-half inch of soil around your plants at least once a week.

Stay shallow as you cultivate the soil. You won't injure the roots, and you'll expose the weed seeds just below the surface and get rid of them. You don't have to worry about deeper weed seeds; they are small and can only germinate if they're near the surface.

Once the vines start spreading, the broad leaves will shade out many weeds. You may have trouble picking your way through the network of vines, but do pull any tall weeds you see. You're bound to get weeds at the edges of the melon or squash patch where you've left room for the vines to travel. Rake or cultivate this area — one to two inches deep — once a week before the vines reach it and you'll diminish the weed problem.

Down with Fuzzies!

Once the vines take hold and start growing, you can expect to have lots of them sprawling over your garden — sometimes too many. This can be a problem, but there's a simple way to control it.

After the first fruits develop, pinch the fuzzy growth tips off the ends of the vines. These growth tips are the beginnings of the next leaf or vine extension. By keeping them picked, you interrupt the vine growth and prevent the vines from overrunning your garden.

You also cause the plant to direct its energy into ripening fruit rather than making longer vines. If you have a short growing season, or you're just impatient for that first melon or squash, picking the fuzzy vine ends can give you ripe fruit a week or so early. I also find it leads to better-quality cucumbers and summer squash, and it lets me head into winter with a well-stocked root cellar of winter squash.

Some gardeners have told me they control vine growth by simply lopping off sections of vines when they grow too long. I don't recommend this because cutting vines can open the stems to rotting or insect damage. Picking off only the ends does no damage.

New vines will shoot off in different directions once you start pruning the ends, but you can keep them in check with regular "de-fuzzing."

Mulching

One of the easiest weed controls of all, that also improves the growing environment (especially in the South), is mulch.

To mulch you simply cover the ground around your plants with a layer of protective material (straw, hay, grass clippings, newspapers, black plastic). This shades the ground, making it impossible for most weeds to grow. Mulching also conserves moisture in the soil and, except for a few kinds, such as roofing paper, or plastic, keeps the soil cool around the plants. This is especially important for Southern gardeners, whose plants suffer in the scorching midsummer heat.

If you mulch your vine crops, wait until the soil has really warmed up. Since my growing season is short, I want my vine crops to receive all the heat they can, so I generally don't use mulch on them.

For you folks who do want to use mulch, make sure it's three to four inches thick or it won't do its job effectively. As for newspapers, five or six thicknesses held down with stones will keep the garden weed-free. I don't recommend tilling colored newspapers back into the soil, since the ink may contain harmful elements.

Black Plastic

Black plastic is one mulch that keeps the soil warm, not cool, so it can really speed up vine crop growth in northern areas. Commercial growers use it with good results, and I know many gardeners who praise it.

The dark polyethylene or plastic surface absorbs the heat of the sun and warms the soil beneath it.

Black plastic blocks out light, preventing weeds from growing beneath it, and it also conserves moisture because it eliminates evaporation. Water condenses on the plastic and drips back into the soil, so you don't need to water as often.

Lay the plastic down before you plant, making sure the soil is fairly moist. Cover the edges with dirt and rocks to anchor them securely. Cut round holes or crosses in the plastic, so plants can come up through them and water can go down.

After trying black plastic on my garden, I find I don't like to use it for five reasons. Earthworms won't eat it. I can't till it back into the soil. It's fairly expensive. It's cumbersome to apply, and I also don't think it looks good. But some gardeners feel the results outweigh the disadvantages, and here again, the choice is yours.

Thinning

Young plants need room to develop a strong root structure and stem. If they are crowded, they will survive, but there may be too much competition.

If you plant six to eight seeds in each hill and they all come up, thin out all but the best four or five plants when they're a few inches high.

Plants in rows should be thinned to stand about eight to twelve inches apart, depending on the variety. There's no trick to thinning these vegetables — just pull up the smaller, least healthy-looking plants and leave the others.

I usually discard the thinnings, but sometimes I transplant them to fill in an especially spotty row. You really have to handle these seedlings with care — I use a big spoon or trowel to dig them and move them with lots of soil surrounding the root balls to protect them.

Sidedressing

Sidedressing is simply applying a small amount of balanced commercial or organic fertilizer to your plants once they are four to five weeks old. It's called sidedressing because you place food a few inches to the side of the plants, where it will gradually seep down to the roots. This boost helps the plants speed up and increase production of high quality fruit, and it's especially important for vine crops.

At one precise point in the plant's development, it seems to stand up very straight to a height of twelve inches or more. That's the time to sidedress. The next time you see it, it will have flopped over and the vines will start to run or sprawl along the ground as they grow. At that point, they put their energy into producing vines, blossoms and fruit, and they can really use the extra food.

If you are using balanced commercial fertilizer such as 10-10-10, make a shallow furrow down both sides of each row, or around each hill, about four to five inches away from the base of the plants.

Sprinkle the fertilizer evenly in the furrow — about one tablespoon for each two to three feet of row, and the same amount around each hill. Cover the fertilizer with an inch or so of soil.

If you sidedress with bulky organic matter, such as manure, make the furrow deeper and a few inches further from the plants. Spread the manure evenly in the furrow and cover it with an inch or two of soil.

Make it your golden rule to underfertilize if there's ever a doubt about how much to add. It's very easy to do your plants more harm than good with "one more handful just for good measure."

Water Wisdom

Vine crops are the camels of the garden! They contain up to 95 percent water at maturity, yet they don't require any more watering than other vegetables. What they do need is a steady supply of moisture — about an inch of water each week.

The steady water supply is very important for taste, because cucumbers and melons can become bitter or bland if they are put under stress from dryness or lack of soil nutrients. As I said earlier, planting them on top of organic matter is an easy way to keep them supplied with water, and mulching can help, too.

If you live in a fairly dry area, or if you experience a dry spell, you'll have to water. To make the most of your watering efforts, water when your plants need it, not just because you're in the habit of watering every seven days without fail. You can tell if your plants are thirsty by digging down into the soil. If the soil is dry four inches down, water. If you come upon moist soil around three inches, your plants are okay. Remember this even if the top of the soil is bone dry.

Another — and perhaps easier — way to tell if your plants need watering is if they look wilted before eleven o'clock in the morning. If your plants droop in the heat of the late afternoon sun, don't worry — that's normal.

How you water is just as important as when. Don't just sprinkle the soil surface to refresh the plants a little. Shallow watering promotes shallow, weak root growth and that's bad for the plants. You should water to a depth of six inches to do the most good.

You can water with an overhead sprinkler, a hose or by bucket brigade. However, a soaker hose is the most efficient watering device. It has tiny holes along it, and by laying it right next to the plants, the water seeps out to soak the soil thoroughly. You don't wet the foliage, and hardly any water is lost to evaporation.

You can install a homemade "automatic" water dispenser. Punch a few holes in the bottoms of large, wide-mouth cans or sawed-off plastic gallon jugs and bury these in the melon patch before planting. Plant seeds in hills around each can about four inches from it. Rain water will collect in the can and seep through the holes to the roots. Fill the cans when you water, and you'll make every drop go right to where it's needed.

Keep a careful eye on the weather and know your soil's water-holding capacity. With this knowledge, and by practicing good watering habits, you'll enjoy bigger, better harvests.

Beware the WET Garden!

One of the best pieces of advice I can give you for the disease-prone vine crops is to stay out of the garden when it's wet. After a rain, in the morning when there's a heavy dew or if you've just watered with a sprinkler, don't allow anyone in the garden. Diseases spread quickly if they can travel on beads of water from leaf to leaf or plant to plant, and even if you try not to touch the plants, you could transfer any number of plant bacteria without realizing it.

GOOD IDEAS DEPARTMENT

Tin Can Alley

For sweeter melons, ripened weeks before any threat of frost, put these tips into practice in your garden.

Sprout the seeds before you plant, or start seedlings.

Plant two weeks early under hot caps.

Start saving large tin cans. Coffee cans work well.

When the vines really start to take off, pick off the fuzzy vine ends to concentrate the plants' energy into producing flowers and fruit, rather than more vine.

When the melons start to form, bury the tin cans near them. The open ends should be placed downward, and the cans should be buried deep enough so they won't tip over.

When the melons are the size of baseballs, gently lift them onto the cans. The first sunlight of the day hits those cans and warms them, making the melons' day seem longer. The heat is transferred to the melons, and since they are sweetest if they ripen in hot weather, you'll have better-tasting melons.

The raised melons are kept out of the shade of their foliage and in full sun off the cool ground. They are also safer from insects and soil-borne bacteria.

Near the end of the summer, pick off all the little green melons you know don't have a chance of ripening before a frost. The remaining fruit will ripen faster and better.

These tricks give me an edge on the competition by giving me the earliest, best melons around.

The Champ

For some reason, vine crops — especially pumpkins and winter squash — seem to spark fierce and friendly competition among gardeners. The following tips should help you hold your own in the gardeners' game, "Top This!"

If you want to grow the biggest pumpkin on the block (or watermelon or squash), just follow these steps. But don't let any of the neighbors in on your growing secrets until harvest time.

Dig a hole and put in about a bushel of aged stable manure, or a pound of commercial fertilizer, or some combination of the two. Cover the fertilizer with about a five-inch layer of soil.

Select seeds that produce especially large fruit, For instance, **Big Max** is a favorite large pumpkin variety.

Plant three regular or presprouted seeds in the hill, adding a few radish seeds as well.

Cover the seeds with about an inch of soil and firm them into the soil.

When the seedlings have two or three leaves on them, select the healthiest plant and remove the other two.

When the vine blossoms and produces its first three small melons, squash or pumpkins, break off the vine's fuzzy end, so it won't grow any longer.

Pick off any new blossoms and fruit that appear, letting the plant feed only the original three.

When the fruit are about the size of your fist, again select the best-shaped one, and pick the other two. All the strength of that fertilizer will now go into just one fruit.

Roll the prize fruit over very gently once in a while. Changing its position helps it achieve a well-rounded shape with uniform color. Sidedress the plant a few times while the fruit grows. The pumpkin, squash or melon should grow to be a mammoth.

All this pampering and pruning is to produce one prize fruit. The plant's energy will all be directed into developing one single giant.

This is a great project for kids. They will tend "The Giant Pumpkin" faithfully, just knowing it may grow to weigh more than they do!

Kids' Corner

Cuke-in-a-bottle — Create a natural conversation piece. When a cucumber first forms on a vine, slip it into a small-necked bottle or jar. Soon it will expand inside the jar, nearly filling it. Cut the vine,

and bring the jar inside and put it on the kitchen table. The puzzled looks of friends are worth the small extra effort.

There are only two cautions about growing cukes in bottles. Be careful that the glass doesn't break in the garden by checking the size of the cucumber occasionally. And protect the bottle from the sun with a few sheets of newspaper; otherwise it will get too hot for the cuke.

Great Impressions — Have a child sign his name and the date with a ball point pen on any young melon, pumpkin or winter squash. The letters will expand right along with the vegetable. Even really young kids love watching their names grow in the garden. Or, as a surprise, you can write their names for them. Later, when they see their names and ask how they got there, just say the seeds must have had their names on them.

Jack-o'-Lantern Tips — Halloween pumpkins really are a crop you should grow if you like kids. Come Halloween, jack-o'-lanterns are expensive to buy — especially, if you feel as I do, that every kid deserves his own personal pumpkin on which he can carve his own grand design. A package or two of seeds will provide enough for the largest family and even enough for a few friends.

If you have a pumpkin carving party for kids — or even adults for that matter — here are a few things to keep in mind:

Even though pumpkins may be oddly shaped, as long as they sit well, they'll make great jack-o'-lanterns

The larger you cut the top, the easier it is to scoop out the goop and seeds from the inside. Save the seed for the birds or for yourself. Roasted, they make a great snack.

Black marking pens, plenty of newspapers, sharp knives and a good ghost story teller are all you need for a good carving session.

JUST FOR FUN!

Gourds — Ornamental and Unusual

There are two basic types of ornamental gourds. The first are brightly colored, having fanciful shapes. Their names often describe them — apples, bells, pears, turbans or eggs. You can grow them for table decorations, floral displays and autumn harvest baskets.

The second group of gourds are more functional, known as bottle or dipper-shaped gourds. They, too, are used for decorations, but they can also be used as ladles (as they have been used in primitive cultures) jugs, planters or even birdhouses.

In your garden, gourds are just like pumpkins, melons or squash, except they require a longer growing season — 140 to 150 days. Unless you live in an area that enjoys a long, hot summer, it's best to start the seeds indoors and transplant the seedlings after the last spring frost. Plant three or four seedlings in hills six to eight feet apart, and care for them as you would any vine crop. Seedlings in rows should be two feet apart.

The vines of gourds will spread up to 100 feet, so send them up a trellis or fence if you have one. This saves space, and it also gives you the best-shaped gourds. Also, a trellis draped with vines, blossoms, foliage and colorful gourds makes a beautiful outdoor display or natural screen.

Harvest gourds when they are fully mature — when the shells are brightly colored, the skins hard and the stems brown and dried. Don't use the fingernail test, because you'll ruin an unripe gourd if you break or dent the skin.

The larger, utensil-shaped gourds will tolerate light frosts, but small decorative ones will not. These should be harvested before the first frost. If they aren't quite ripe and an early frost is predicted, cover the plants for the night with a sheet or newspapers. They'll probably survive the first frost, and chances are good that the next one will be a few weeks off.

Cut the gourds off the vine when they're ripe, leaving a few inches of stem. Wash or wipe off any surface dirt and cure the gourds for a week or two, being careful not to bruise them or let them touch one another. Then wash them in a Clorox solution.

When they're completely dry, you can display the gourds just as they are, or you can wax, varnish or paint their shells. Cut the long, bottle-shaped or crook-necked gourds into a planter or birdhouse shape, and enjoy their appearance while they serve a useful purpose.

There are edible gourds, grown and eaten like summer squash, but I haven't sampled any yet.

Luffa, the Dishrag Gourd

Many specialty bath shops sell Luffa Sponges; these are usually grown commercially, but they are made from gourds you can grow at home. The seeds are available from companies that specialize in unusual vegetable varieties, and the plants require no more care than winter squash.

The plants grow quickly and will spread ten to fifteen feet. They need lots of water and sunshine, but if you live in a fairly temperate climate, you should be able to grow your own sponges with no problems.

Harvest the luffa gourds when they are mature. The sponge part of the luffa is its fibrous inner layer, so simply peel the skin away to expose it, and leave them to dry in the sun for a week or so. When the pulp has dried, you can shake out the seeds. Then you can bleach the coarse sponge in the sun or in a mild solution of peroxide and water, and voilà, your own home-grown skin scrubber.

In some countries, the young luffa fruits are delicacies, served steamed or stir-fried like pea pods.

PROBLEMS

Disease and Insect Rx

Doctors will tell you that the best way to fight disease is to prevent it. By making the effort to prevent problems, you won't have to worry as much about solving them.

How can you avoid trouble in the garden? First, buy disease-resistant seed varieties. Ask the Extension Agent in your area which diseases are likely to strike vine crops and look for seeds bred to resist those diseases. Also, use treated seed whenever possible to prevent rotting and damping off (a soil-borne disease that causes seedlings to fall over and die).

Keep your garden clean and weed-free during the growing season. This reduces the places for disease and insect populations to grow. Clean up all crop residues (vines, leaves, stalks and discarded fruit) as soon as you finish harvesting. Till or spade this organic debris into the soil or add it to your compost pile to keep any harmful organisms from living through the winter and attacking next year's garden.

Rotate your vegetables. Shift vine crops to different spots in the garden from one year to the next, and plant another vegetable family where those cucumbers or melons were. If you have a serious problem with any crop, don't plant it in the same place for two or three years.

Since so much of the damage that can be done to vine crops is spread by cucumber beetles, protect your plants from them. To keep beetles from landing on your vine crops, start plants under hot caps or cloches or spread a cheesecloth covering over the row. You'll be way ahead in the battle against disease.

You can also use sprays or dusts to ward off garden diseases and insects. By checking with the Extension Service you can be sure you are using the correct substance for your area and crop. Always read the instructions *twice* before applying any chemical sprays, following the directions carefully as you go. And once again when you put it away, so that you store it safely.

One final tip for a truly productive garden: test the pH of your soil every two years. The pH range should be between 6.0 and 6.8 for best vegetable production. Adding plenty of organic matter each year also helps enrich the soil.

If you have any questions about a plant problem, contact your local Cooperative Extension Agent. As the horticultural expert in your particular area, he or she can offer the most accurate diagnosis and solution.

Insects

Cucumber beetle — If you can control these striped or spotted pests in your garden, you may never have a diseased melon or cucumber crop. The most effective way to keep them in check is spraying: starting when the plants first break through the ground, spray with an effective pesticide. Be sure to treat the base of the plant, since beetles attack there. The beetles hatch four broods of eggs, so you have to repeat the spraying every five to seven days. Also respray or dust after a rain, and don't forget the undersides of the leaves. Again, follow instructions step-by-step and check with your County Agent if you have any questions.

Plant radishes along with vine crop seeds to repel cucumber beetles while the plants are young and vulnerable.

Aphids — These tiny, spidery-looking insects gather in colonies on the undersides of leaves. They can spread disease or destroy leaves and plants by feeding on them. Spraying with an effective pesticide is the best way to beat them.

Squash Vine Borer — The larvae of this insect bore into stems near the ground causing the plants to wilt and die. You can perform a home remedy when you see the signs of boring: cut out the vine borer and the part of the stem that was eaten, then quickly cover the remaining wounded stem with a mound of soil. The plant should recover and continue growing. You can also apply a pesticide in the same amount prescribed for cucumber beetles.

Cutworms — These small, round worms can do incredible damage to young seedlings or transplants. They chew through the base of the stem, causing the whole plant to topple over and die. The best way to control cutworms in transplants is to wrap the stem with a paper collar (newspaper strips are fine) one inch below to one inch above the ground. For plants started outdoors, you can either use spray or cutworm "baits." Both are sold in garden stores.

Squash Bug — This flat, brownish-gray bug attacks squash by sucking the juices from the leaves. It lives over the winter in trash and garden residues, so a thorough clean-up helps prevent an infestation the following year. If they do show up in the garden, you can lay boards on the ground near the plants where the bugs will gather at night. In the morning, you can lift the boards and destroy many bugs. You can also pick off any bugs or egg masses you see on the leaves (check the undersides, too). If you use an insecticide, be sure to spray on the top and bottom of the leaves — and follow directions carefully.

Diseases

Bacterial wilt — The leaves of the plant wilt, then the entire runner, including any fruit, wilts. The affected area of the plant dries up and dies; eventually the entire plant will be killed. The disease is totally dependent on its host, the cucumber beetle, to survive the winter and be deposited on the young plants, so control the beetle to control the wilt. Does not affect watermelons.

Fusarium wilt — Causes damping-off of seedlings, stem blight, and the vines may develop water-soaked streaks. Growth is stunted, leaves wilt, the vines decay and die. Only affects muskmelons and watermelons. Fusarium winters over from one season to the next on infected vines and builds up in the soil. Some seed is resistant to fusarium; that's indicated on seed packet by (F).

Downy-mildew — Shows up as irregularly shaped yellowish to brown spots on the tops of leaves; in moist weather, a purplish mildew may form on the underside of these spots. Leaves die as the spots grow larger. Affects cucumbers and muskmelons; thrives in wet weather.

Powdery mildew — Thrives in high humidity and warm weather. A gray-brown to white powder-like substance forms on the leaves and young stems. Foliage eventually dries up and dies. Fungus develops best in hot weather. Spray with an effective fungicide available at garden stores.

Anthracnose — Leaves will develop circular dark spots on them, vines may be streaked, fruit may blacken and drop off, leaves wither. Anthracnose thrives in humid, wet weather. The fungus winters over in seed and in refuse from diseased plants; will spread in splashing water. Affects cucumbers, muskmelons and watermelons.

Angular leaf spot — Water-soaked spots develop on leaves, turn tan and gray, then drop out leaving ragged holes. The spots on the fruit are rounded and may exude a thick oozing substance. The infection will go into the seed cavity, making the fruit inedible. The bacterium lives over the winter in seed and plant debris, and is spread during wet weather. Affects cucumbers, honeydew melons and zucchini squash.

Angular leaf spot can be confused with an insect — the stem borer, because the same symptoms occur. The stem borer gets inside the stem and cuts off the water supply. If he's present, just prune him out.

To test for angular leaf spot, cut a stem and rub the two cut ends together. Pull them apart slowly. If a thick, gelatinous strand forms between them, the plant suffers from angular leaf spot.

Buy good seed. Get rid of plant as soon as you notice disease.

Mosaic — Vines on virus-infected plants are stunted, leaves are mottled, dwarfed and sometimes oddly shaped. There's a different type of mosaic virus for each member of the vine crop family, referred to as cucumber mosaic virus (CMV), watermelon mosaic-2 (WM-2), and squash mosaic virus (SMV). Mosaic is carried by the cucumber beetle or by aphids if the virus has wintered over in perennial plants. It can also be spread by gardeners working in wet or moist garden conditions.

Scab — Dry, corky spots develop on cucumbers and muskmelons. You can tell scab from angular leaf spot because scab shows a dark olive-green velvety growth on the disease spots. Spots can cover young stems and leaves. Entire plant eventually dies. Disease thrives in foggy, cool weather and cool night temperatures.

If you notice a diseased vine or plant, cut it or pull it right away. The remaining plants or vines may be perfectly healthy, so you may keep the disease from spreading.

You can treat diseased plants with fungicides that you can learn more about from your local Extension Service. They can help positively identify the disease and its treatment. In many cases, planting disease-resistant varieties, cleaning up crop residues, rotating your crops, staying out of the garden when it's wet and keeping harmful bugs in check are your best and only preventions.

HARVEST TIME

Cukes and Summer Squash — You Deserve the Best

One of the wonderful things about having your own garden is that you have control over when you harvest your vegetables. You can pick them immediately before preparing them, ensuring that you have absolutely the freshest produce anywhere. But even better than that, you can also have the youngest. Most commercial growers don't pick tiny vegetables, knowing they'll get more for their money by waiting a few days. But the very best — especially cucumbers and summer squash — are the smallest. So it takes six zucchini to make a meal. So

what? There will be more — lots more — where they came from, so splurge. Treat yourself to the cream of the crop.

Be careful not to step on the vines when you harvest — you may kill the plants.

You may decide to let some cucumbers grow larger for pickles or a crop might just get ahead of your harvest efforts — zucchini always seems to take off overnight. If the fruits grow big enough, the plant will stop producing and go on to the next stage of reproduction. This is called "going by" or going to seed.

You can eat those larger vegetables, although they won't taste quite as good as younger ones. Cucumber skins toughen as they mature, and summer squash loses some of its flavor.

If your vacation time coincides with the first harvest and you'll be away from home, make a deal with neighbors. Ask them to keep the cucumbers or squashes picked, and let them keep all the produce. When you get back from your vacation trip, you'll be ready to reap your own harvest, your vines will still be producing and your neighbors will be well-stocked.

So, You're Overrun with Zucchini?

It's my feeling that we should practice ZPC — zucchini population control. If only one out of every three gardeners planted zucchini, there would still be plenty for everyone, with much less waste!

Most gardeners who plant zucchini end up with these long green vegetables coming out of their ears. I have some practical advice on this matter:

Give it away — to friends, neighbors, relatives, strangers (perfect or not). My neighbors parked a little red wagon on their lawn and filled it to overflowing with all the extra zucchini they had grown. "Absolutely Free — Help Yourself!" the sign on the wagon said. My neighbors enjoyed the reactions of the takers, and the takers enjoyed the zucchini — a good deal all round.

When you decide you've had enough zucchini, let one or two grow to be giants. The plant will stop producing. You can use the big ones in squash bread.

Melons

There is more than one way to judge a melon's ripeness, and most people learn from experience, which is the most dependable method for them.

Here are all the valid signs of ripeness I know for muskmelons and watermelons.

Muskmelons/Cantaloupes

Smell — I check ripeness by smelling for a strong, "musky" or perfumey scent around the stem end of the melon. That unmistakeable odor means ripeness every time.

Skin — When the skin color changes from green to yellow or tan and the netting becomes very pronounced, the melon is ripe.

Stem — The stems on melons will separate or slip from the fruit, with very little pressure as they start to ripen. A crack appears between the stem and the fruit, signaling their prime harvest time. When the stem finally separates completely, which is called full slip, the melon is very ripe and won't last long before turning all soft and mushy. Watch the slip signs and try to eat the ripest melons first to give yourself a steady supply of good ones.

Squeeze — Some people squeeze cantaloupes and assume a soft melon is ripe. This can be deceiving, since some harder melons may be ready to eat, too. So, save the squeezes and try other methods for melons.

Watermelons

Color — One of the signs of ripeness is the color of the spot where the watermelon rests on the ground. As the melon ripens, that "ground spot" turns from whitish to a deep, creamy yellow. Also, the shiny surface of the melon dulls somewhat when it's ripe.

Thumps — I love to watch folks at roadside stands with their ears pinned to watermelons as they thump away — it can be pretty comical. Unripe melons do make a sharp ringing sound when rapped and ripe ones sound muffled. But over-ripe melons make that same dead sound, so this isn't the most reliable test.

Curly-cues — Gardeners sometimes watch the watermelon stem to judge ripeness. When it turns brown and dries up like a curly pig's tail, the melon's ripe. But, some varieties may show this sign and not ripen for another week or so, so you could easily be disappointed.

However you judge your cantaloupes and watermelons for ripeness, if you cut into them and find juicy, deep orange or red flesh, you can be confident you know how to pick 'em!

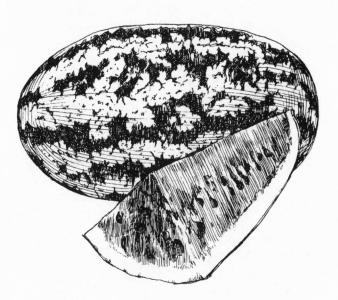

Winter Squash and Pumpkins — Thumbs Up!

First, you should know that you don't have to worry about these vegetables going by before harvest time. The seeds inside them won't grow large enough to trigger the plant's stop-production mechanism until there's plenty of fruit already on the vines. Wait until all vines die or until the first frost to harvest your winter squash and pumpkins.

The signs of ripeness are simple. If your thumbnail can't penetrate the vegetable skin, it's fully mature, long lasting and a good keeper in storage.

It may help to first check the vegetables for a deepening of their skin color before you stick your nail into them. If you test one and your thumbnail breaks the skin, use it first because it won't store very long.

Most of the winter squashes or pumpkins on each plant should be ripe about the same time. Those you intend to store harvest on a sunny day, after a few days of dry weather if possible.

Cut them off the vines leaving some stem on each. Roll them over and leave them outside for a few hours until the dirt and earthworms on the underside dry out and drop off.

Be careful not to bruise vegetables you want to store — they won't keep well, and they may spread fungus or rotting to other vegetables. Don't carry them by the stems; they won't support the weight.

You can wash winter squash and pumpkins with a bleach solution to kill bacteria on the skin. This helps them keep longer and better. Dilute a cup of Clorox in a gallon of water and sponge or dip the vegetables. Drip dry, and don't rinse them.

STORAGE

Winter Keep — Not for All

Back when winter keep, or common storage, was the only way to extend the harvest past the first killing frost, winter squashes were a household staple because of their good keeping qualities. They still keep best if stored properly in a cool, dry, dark spot, and you don't need any fancy rooms or equipment, either. Pumpkins also store well for months at a time.

The rest of the vine crops have to be preserved, pickled, canned or frozen if you want them to last, although some honeydew melons and large zucchinis will keep for awhile. One of the reasons I like melons and summer squash so much when they're in season is because they can really only be savored during the summer months.

Now that you know which vegetables you can store, select only the best of these for winter keeping. Any bumps, bruises, broken stems or rotting will only worsen and spread to other vegetables, so eat the less-than-perfect ones first.

Curing

Winter squashes and pumpkins must be cured to dry and harden their shells completely before being put into storage. Ideally, they should be aired out in a warm, well-ventilated place at a temperature

of 75° to 85°F for a week or two. It's usually too cool at harvest time to achieve the perfect temperature, but you can group the vegetables near your furnace, wood stove or on a sunny back porch where they can be sufficiently cured.

I cure my winter squashes right in the root cellar, running a small, portable fan directly on them round the clock for a week or so. Even though my root cellar is quite cool, the circulating air from the fan does the curing just fine.

Storing

After curing, I pile the vegetables two or three deep on shelves located halfway between the floor and ceiling of my root cellar — it's driest there.

My root cellar is fairly dry, but most cellars are too damp for storing vine crops. They keep best in a cool place (45° to 55°F) with low humidity.

In the past, folks stashed their winter squash and pumpkins under their beds. Unless your bedroom is unheated and your bed is high enough, this wouldn't be practical today. But any cool, dry, dark spot is fine — a spare room, closet floor, attic floor, basement rafters, or even in a large, cool kitchen cupboard.

Wherever you store them, check the produce regularly and take out any that are getting soft or look as if they're starting to rot. It's only natural that some will keep better than others.

By the time any of our winter squash gets soft spots, we've eaten quite a lot of our summer frozen vegetables, so there's room in the freezer for some additions.

If a squash has started to soften cook it plain, without butter or seasonings and freeze it in containers.

And don't worry about the soft spots. Just cut them out and eat the rest. It's perfectly good.

Garden to Kitchen

Winter Squash

You always cook winter squash (acorn, butternut, buttercup, Hubbard) before eating, either baked in their skins or peeled and steamed or boiled. Acorn squash is usually cut in half and baked; butternut can either be baked or peeled, cubed and steamed. Large Hubbard squash is most manageable if you cut it in sections and bake these in a buttered baking dish at 375° F for about one hour.

To steam winter squash, place pieces in a blancher, basket or colander over boiling water until tender, about 30 minutes. Scoop out cooked pulp and mash or purée in a blender or food mill. Use the cooked squash in recipes or freeze for later use. Pumpkin can be steamed or baked the same way.

You can flavor baked winter squash with spices and butter, honey, maple syrup or brown sugar. Served cooked squash as is, or combine it with other ingredients for pies, soups or cookies.

Other than root cellar storage, freezing is a good way to keep winter squash. I just fill freezer containers with precooked, cooled, mashed squash. Then I label the containers with the date and contents and freeze them. To freeze uncooked winter squash, peel and cube it, blanch it for three minutes, cool, drain, pack it in containers and freeze.

I have the best results when I freeze baked or steamed squash, rather than boiled. Because it's somewhat drier, it is the right consistency for casseroles, cookies or pies.

To reheat frozen winter squash, place it in the top of a double boiler over medium heat with water boiling in the lower pot, stirring occasionally until it's thoroughly heated. Or, place each pint of frozen squash in one-half cup boiling, salted water and simmer ten minutes, or until heated through.

A note on canning: Except for sealing pickles in a boiling water bath, I seldom can any summer squash, winter squash or pumpkins. These vegetables all require steam pressure canning, and canned squash tends to be mushy and flavorless when reheated. We have much better luck with freezing and root cellar storage.

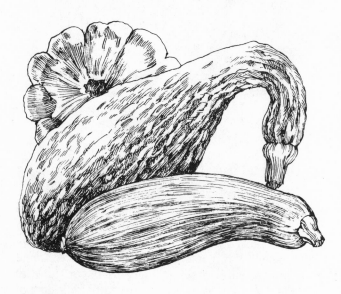

Summer Squash

To prepare summer squash (Yellow Straight-neck and Crookneck, Zucchini and Patty Pan), wash the whole vegetable, trim off the ends and cut into half-inch cubes or slices. Serve raw, unpeeled, thin slices in salads or with dips. Cook slices over steam or in a small amount of boiling water until just tender. Do not overcook. Three to five minutes should do it. Add butter, lemon juice, herbs or spices and serve hot.

If you want to store summer squash for any length of time, you'll have to freeze, can or dry it. However, it will stay fresh for several days in a plastic bag in the refrigerator.

For me, freezing is the best way to keep the surplus of our summer squash crop. I often peel, grate and freeze overgrown zucchini for use in breads and soups.

All fresh vegetables must be blanched or scalded prior to freezing to stop enzyme action and halt the ripening process. To do this, place sliced or cubed summer squash in a wire basket, then plunge the basket into a large kettle filled with rapidly boiling water for three minutes.

Then immediately cool the squash by plunging the basket into ice water, again for three minutes or when it feels cold when you squeeze it lightly between your fingers. Drain the squash well and pack in freezer containers with no salt or other seasonings. Seal the packages, label with contents and date, and freeze.

To prepare frozen summer squash at mealtime, place it in a small amount of rapidly boiling water, cover and boil for three to five minutes, or just until fork tender.

Pickling

You can pickle two ways. Either ferment vegetables in a brine for many weeks, or fresh-pack the produce in a vinegar solution in Mason jars, seal them using a boiling water bath, and let them ferment in the jars for four to six weeks.

I make nearly all my pickles using the fresh-pack method. It's quick and easy, and I can prepare just a few jars or a large batch of cucumbers when they're just ready for pickling. Whether you use a fresh-pack recipe or a pickling crock to ferment vegetables, your goal is tasty, crisp pickles that will keep indefinitely.

To ferment in a salt brine, use stone crocks or kegs, or clean, watertight, hardwood barrels that are lined with enamel, glass or paraffin. Although pickles will keep fairly well stored in such containers, for safety reasons we urge you to transfer fermented pickles to canning jars and process them for storage.

Use special pickling or dual-purpose cucumbers that grow no longer than two and one-half to four inches. Their small size and thin skins make them ideal for curing. Prepare the freshest, cleanest produce for pickling and try to use vegetables that are slightly underripe. Wash vegetables well, remove the end blossoms, then follow your favorite recipe.

Many people have asked me, "How do you get such crisp pickles?" The key to crispness is to use only fresh, just-harvested produce. Also, I always harvest cukes for pickling in the morning before the sun has heated them up. I think this plays a big part in their staying crisp. Even if you store vegetables in the refrigerator, you lose quality with each hour that passes after they've been picked. Also, work quickly once you start the pickling process, so the pickles will ferment uniformly.

The ingredients you use for the pickling brine are very important to ensure crisp, flavorful, evenly cured vegetables.

Salt — Use only pure, granulated salt with no non-caking material or iodine added. This is sold as pickling salt, barrel salt and kosher salt. Table salt and iodized salt contain materials that may interfere with fermentation, darken the pickles or cloud the pickle juice.

Vinegar — Use a 4 to 6 percent acidity cider or white vinegar. If the label doesn't have the acidity listed, don't use it for pickles or relishes. Never use less vinegar than the recipe specifies, since the amount of acidity is crucial to safe processing.

Water — Soft water is best for pickling. You can soften hard water by boiling it, skimming off the surface scum and letting it sit for 24 hours. Don't disturb the sediment at the bottom when you use this softened water.

Alum — It used to be essential for crispness, but if the proper ingredients are used, alum isn't needed. If you use alum, don't use it in excess — it can irritate the digestive system. I still use alum in some recipes, simply out of habit, I suppose.

Boiling Water Bath Canning

Note: This method is for pickles only! Summer and winter squash must be canned under pressure.

Once you have all your vegetables and pickling ingredients ready, use either the fresh-pack method or a salt-brine fermentation. Then follow these steps for the boiling water bath canning. If your canner instructions vary from these, follow the instructions that came with your canner.

Assemble all utensils: Canner with rack, Mason jars, lids, tongs or jar lifter, cooling racks and non-metallic spatula.

Use only Mason jars for home canning. They are made by a number of manufacturers and are safe because the glass is heat-tempered and can seal perfectly. If you have saved other jars, use them only for jellies or jams with paraffin seals.

Never re-use dome lids for canning. The rubber compound loses its ability to seal perfectly after one use. Metal screw bands and Mason jars may be re-used.

Examine and clean all equipment: Check all bands for rust, dents or nicks and the jars for chips or cracks. Don't use them for canning if they are not perfect.

Wash all equipment in hot, soapy water. Rinse in clear, hot water. Keep jars and screw tops hot. Keep dome lids in hot water until ready to use.

Follow recipe instructions for filling jars, always leaving one-quarter inch headspace for pickles.

Once jars are filled, release all air bubbles from jar by running a plastic or rubber spatula down around the inside of the jar. Wipe jar top and threads clean with damp cloth. Put lid on jar, rubber side down, and screw band on firmly, so it's "finger-tight."

Fill the canner half-full with hot water. Place the rack on bottom of canner. Only fill as many jars as the canner will hold in one batch. As each jar is filled, place it in the rack. The jars should not touch each other or the side of the canner.

Add hot water, if necessary, so the jars are covered with at least one to two inches of water. Cover and turn up heat under canner. Start timing when the water reaches a rolling boil. *Follow timing instructions for each recipe.*

To complete the processing, use jar lifter or tongs to remove the jars and put them upright on a rack or thick towel in a draft-free area, allowing enough room between jars, so air can circulate.

Do not tighten the metal rims, because you may break the seals.

After twelve hours of cooling, test the seals. There are three tests recommended for checking the seals on dome lids:

1. As the jar contents cool and the vacuum forms, the lid pulls down into the jar and makes a "kerplunking" sound.

2. The lid will be concave or dished and should stay that way as long as the vacuum is present — you can feel it.

3. Push down on the lid with your thumb. If it doesn't push down, the jar is sealed. If it makes a clicking sound, the seal isn't complete.

If you have some jars with incomplete seals, reprocess the contents, using a new lid and a clean jar. Or, if the contents have already been fermented, simply put the jars in the refrigerator and use the pickles soon.

Wipe the jars with a clean, damp cloth, label clearly and store. The outer rims should be removed, because moisture can build up under these and affect the lids and seals on the jars. Store jars in a cool, dry, dark place.

Don't open the jars for several weeks — this will allow the flavors of the herbs and spices to fully develop.

Before serving, check pickles or relishes for signs of spoilage, sliminess, softness, frothing or a foul odor. Don't eat any pickles you think are bad — don't even taste them. Throw them out if there's the slightest doubt as to whether they're good.

I could easily have filled this entire section with pickle recipies, but I am only giving you my five favorites. For more recipes and pickling ideas, I suggest two fine books: **All About Pickling,** Ortho Book Series, National Edition and the **Ball Blue Book,** a guide to home canning and freezing.

Dill Pickles

I start harvesting batches of tiny cukes for dill pickles when they are only two to three inches long. Even so, they grow so fast they tend to get ahead of me. We plant our dill early to be sure it's in bloom when pickling time arrives.

I put up a lot of these because our family, relatives and friends love them.

Per quart jar:
1   Tb salt
1   tsp mustard seed
1   small piece alum (size of a small grape)
2   heads fresh dill or 1 Tb dill weed
1   cup vinegar
2   cups water

Wash quart jars. In each jar put salt, mustard seed, alum and dill.

Sort the cucumbers according to size and put similar-sized cukes in each jar, so they pickle uniformly. Use only small cucumbers or spears. Fill to an inch from top of jar.

Measure vinegar and water for each filled jar and heat to boiling. Pour hot liquid into jars, leaving 1/4-inch headspace. Adjust lids and process 10 minutes in hot water bath.

Sunshine Pickles

The turmeric makes these pickles a bright, "sunshine" yellow.

4   quarts ripe cucumbers, cut in small chunks
4   large onions, sliced
1   Tb salt
1   Tb celery seed
1   Tb turmeric powder
4   cups sugar
2 1/2   cups vinegar
1/2   cup water

Select ripe cucumbers. Wash, peel, cut in half lengthwise, scoop out the seeds, then cut in chunks enough to make four quarts.

Cook all ingredients until cucumbers are fork tender. Put in jars, leaving 1/4-inch headspace, adjust lids and process in hot water bath 10 minutes.

Icicle Pickles

This pickle is a specialty of a friend at Gardens for All, Tommy Thompson. He gets rave reviews from anyone who samples these crunchy, sweet/sour pickles. Again, I recommend processing the crock-cured pickles in a boiling-water bath for long-term storage.

Fill one gallon crock with good quality, green, solid cucumber spears. Mix 1/2 pound of canning salt in enough boiling water to cover spears. Cover them with a weighted-down plate or lid.

Let stand one week. Drain thoroughly. Add two pieces of alum, each about the size of a grape, or 2 Tbs. powdered alum, to enough *boiling* water to cover the cukes. Let stand 24 hours and drain well.

Mix — 5   cups vinegar
       5   cups sugar
       1   small handful pickling spice
           (in mesh bag)

Bring to a boil and pour over pickles. Let stand 24 hours, then drain again, saving the syrup. Repeat this procedure once a day for four days, bringing the syrup to a boil each time.

On the fifth day, or anytime thereafter, put pickles in canning jars and add hot liquid to fill jars leaving 1/2-inch headspace. Seal and process in a boiling-water bath ten minutes.

Large batches are easy to make. Use a larger crock, proportionately more cucumbers and other ingredients. A little simple arithmetic — depending on the size of the crock — and you'll have it.

Watermelon Rind Pickles

This is a great way to use the rinds of watermelons after a summer picnic or family gathering. Enjoy the watermelon but save the rinds.

       8 cups watermelon rind
          (1 large watermelon)
     1/2 cup salt
       2 quarts water
       2 cups vinegar
          water to cover
       3 cups white or brown sugar
       1 lemon, sliced thin
       1 stick cinnamon
       1 tsp allspice
       1 tsp whole cloves

Remove skin and pink from rind. Cut rind into 1 inch cubes or chunks. Soak chunks overnight in brine mixture of 1/2 cup salt and 2 quarts water. Drain and rinse in fresh water. Drain again. Add more fresh water to cover, and simmer until tender. Make syrup of vinegar, brown sugar, lemon and spices. Simmer 5 minutes. Add rind and cook until clear. Pack rinds into hot jars and fill with syrup, leaving 1/2-inch headspace. Adjust lids and process in hot water bath for 10 minutes.

Gram Ma's Tongue Pickles

This sweet pickle recipe has been in my mother's family for generations. We call them tongue pickles because of their shape.

       5 lbs. ripe cucumbers
   1 1/2 lb. brown sugar
       1 tsp cinnamon
       1 tsp cloves
       1 tsp ginger
     1/2 tsp pepper
       1 tsp salt
       2 cups vinegar

Wash, peel, cut in half lengthwise, then cut cucumbers in two-inch slices. Place them in an enamel kettle or pot. Put spices in mesh bag or cheesecloth tied at the top. Add sugar and vinegar and spice bag to pot. Cook until transparent. Let sit overnight. Reheat, put pickles in jars, add liquid leaving 1/4-inch headspace, adjust lids and process in hot water bath 10 minutes.

Zucchini Relish

       4 cups chopped zucchini
       3 cups chopped carrots
       3 cups chopped onions
   1 1/2 cups green or red sweet peppers
     1/4 cup salt
       2 Tb salt
      2¼ cups white vinegar
       1 Tb celery seed
     3/4 tsp dry mustard

Mix all ingredients together in a large skillet. Cook for 15 minutes or until all vegetables are just tender but still crisp. Pack in hot, clean jars, leaving 1/4-inch headspace, adjust lids and process in hot water bath for 20 minutes. Makes 4 to 5 pints.

Et Cetera

Melons

I use melons cut in wedges, plain or with a squeeze of fresh lime and a mint leaf. For dessert, I top melon wedges with scoops of ice cream or sherbet, or serve sliced cheddar cheese alongside.

When the harvest is really overflowing, I scoop out the melons with a melon baller, serve plenty of fruit cocktails or compotes and freeze what we can't eat right away.

To freeze melon balls, slices or cubes, use only firm, ripe fruit. Cut melon in half, remove any seeds, and cut out fruit. Don't cut into any of the rind.

You can place melon directly in containers, label, date, and freeze. But to keep their shape, place melon pieces on a cookie sheet and place in freezer overnight (6-12 hours). Transfer frozen fruit to plastic freezer bags or containers. Seal, label and date. Return to freezer and use as needed. Melons if properly frozen will keep up to a year in your home freezer.

Canteloupes and watermelons really spruce up a summer meal when you scoop out the fruit and fill them with a cold combination salad. You can carve scalloped, pointed, fluted or zig-zagged edges. Be creative!

Summer Salad Ideas

Sliced cucumbers and summer squash combine easily with other vegetables, or stand alone with spices or as vegetable dippers. I never peel away the thin, brightly-colored skins when I serve these vegetables raw. Just wash them well using a vegetable brush. For a special party look, score the skin down the length of the cucumber or squash with a fork, then slice off rounds. They'll be evenly fluted — and so easily. Serve them with . . .

Bermuda onions, sliced
Cottage cheese
Flaked coconut
Green-top onions
Lettuce or other greens

Olives and pimientos
Sour cream
Tomatoes, quartered or sliced
Vinegar and oil
Yogurt

Oriental Marinade

1/4 cup soy sauce
4 Tb vinegar
1 Tb honey
4 Tb oil

Combine all ingredients. Toss with fresh vegetables to coat lightly. Chill. Good dressing for cucumbers.

Tangy Red Dip

2 cups mayonnaise
3 Tb catsup
2 Tb honey
1 tsp curry powder
8 drops Tabasco sauce
3 Tb grated onion

Mix all ingredients and chill. Super with sliced summer squash, and also good with other raw vegetables.

Sweet & Sour Lo-Cal Dressing

1/4 cup vinegar
    artificial sweetener, equivalent to 2 tsp sugar
1 tsp chopped dill weed
1/8 tsp pepper

Mix all ingredients. Chill, then pour over vegetables, especially good with chilled cucumber slices.

A Word About Herbs and Spices

Cucumbers and summer and winter squash readily accept the flavor of many herbs and spices. I used to be somewhat timid about combining different spices, but now I enjoy mixing and matching to come up with new recipes. I've rarely had unpleasant results. If you're trying new combinations, go easy at first — you can always add, but it's impossible to take some out.

Here are the herbs, spices and flavorings that go best with each vegetable in the vine crop family:

Cucumbers and Summer Squash

Basil	Cumin	Freshly ground pepper
Caraway seeds	Curry powder	Mint
Chives	Dill seed	Parsley
Coriander	Dill weed	Summer savory

Winter Squash and Pumpkins

Allspice	Ginger	Oregano
Anise	Honey	Parsley
Basil	Mace	Sage
Brown Sugar	Maple Sugar	Savory
Cinnamon	Marjoram	Thyme
Cloves	Nutmeg	Turmeric

Spaghetti Squash

This unusual squash is quickly becoming a favorite among home gardeners, adding a new dimension to Italian-style dishes. It grows just like any winter squash and should be harvested when it's fully ripe — when the rind turns completely yellow.

The crisp, spaghetti-like strands of this unusual squash can be used in all your recipes that call for macaroni, noodles or spaghetti.

To cook, wash the squash and bake it whole in the oven (350°) for about one hour — until the skin is fork tender or soft to the touch. You can also boil the whole squash for about 30 minutes, until tender. If the squash is very large, cut it in half using a sharp knife. Scoop out the seeds and cook only as much as you will use. Refrigerate the rest.

After the squash is cooked, cool it slightly. Split whole squash in half lengthwise and remove the seeds and membrane. Gently lift the meaty squash strands from the shell with a fork, or simply fluff up the strands and serve the squash right in the shell.

This is delicious simply with butter, pepper and salt. Or you can add parsley, grated cheese or your favorite spaghetti sauce. The strands of squash can be layered in a casserole with sauce and cheese and baked like lasagna. One medium squash serves four.

Ripe vegetable spaghetti will store just like winter squash, and two plants will yield enough fruit to feed four people all summer.

FAVORITE RECIPES

Winter Squash Soup

There's a wonderful restaurant in Middlebury, Vermont — The Bakery Lane Soup Bowl — and this is their recipe for Squash Soup. It's delicious.

2	lbs winter squash
1	cup water
1	tsp salt
1	cup chopped onion
1/2	small clove garlic, minced
2	Tb butter
2	cups milk
2	cups light cream
1/2	cup medium dry sherry
	salt & pepper to taste
	toasted sliced almonds

Peel, seed and dice squash. Combine with water and 1 tsp salt in saucepan. Bring to a boil and simmer, covered, until squash is very tender.

Meanwhile, sauté onion and garlic in butter until tender. Liquefy squash and onions with milk and cream in blender. Add sherry and salt and pepper to taste. Heat to serving temperature. Serve garnished with toasted almonds.

Variation: Depending on how rich she wants this soup, a friend varies the proportions of cream and milk. She also uses pumpkin sometimes instead of squash — two cups of pumpkin purée. This soup is very good for cozy, winter suppers with hot bread and a green salad. Makes about 10 cups.

French Fried Zucchini

Here's a nice change from potatoes that kids (and grown-ups) really go for, and it's so easy.

2	cups zucchini, cut in 1/2 inch julienne strips
	salt and pepper to taste
2	eggs, well beaten
1/2	cup flour
1/2	cup bread crumbs
	hot salad oil or shortening

Sprinkle squash slices with salt and pepper. Dip into egg, dredge in flour, then dredge in bread crumbs. Fry in deep fat until golden brown. Or fry in skillet in hot oil turning once. Drain on paper towels, serve hot. Serves 4.

Baked Stuffed Zucchini

This is a good way to use zucchini that have hidden under the leaves and become too big.

4	zucchini, 6″ long (or 2 large, 10-12″ zucchini)
1/2	cup soft bread crumbs
1	egg, beaten
1/2	cup grated cheese, cheddar or Parmesan
1/4	cup onion, chopped
1	clove garlic, minced
1	lb ground beef or hot sausage
1/2	tsp salt
1/8	tsp black pepper
2	Tb margarine or butter
3	Tb grated cheese

Wash zucchini and trim ends. Simmer in boiling, salted water until just tender — about 10 minutes. Cut in half lengthwise. Remove seeds and stringy center. Scoop out squash and combine it with bread crumbs, egg and cheese. Drain zucchini shells upside down on paper towel.

Sauté onion and garlic in margarine and ground beef and combine with bread mixture.

Fill zucchini shells with mixture and top with extra cheese. Bake in greased baking pan in 350° oven for 35 to 45 minutes, until brown. Serves 8 Can be served for dinner with broiled tomatoes or green salad.

Zucchini Bread

This is my own recipe with sour cream for extra special taste and texture. It freezes well — if you have any left over to freeze! Some people might want to add a cup of raisins, but my family likes it without.

2	eggs, beaten lightly
1/4	cup sour cream
1 1/4	cups sugar
1	cup oil (vegetable)
2	cups zucchini, grated
2 1/2	tsp vanilla
2 1/4	cups flour
1	tsp baking powder
1	tsp baking soda
1	tsp salt
3	tsp cinnamon
1	cup walnuts or pecans (chopped)

Mix first six ingredients together. Sift dry ingredients together in another bowl. Combine with zucchini mixture and mix well. Add nuts. Mix. Pour into two greased loaf pans. Bake at 350° for one hour. Turn out onto wire racks to cool. Makes 2 loaves.

Summer Squash Medley

This is best made with garden-fresh vegetables, but in the winter you can use stored vegetables. Or make big batches when these vegetables are abundant and freeze for later use. I like to add cooked green beans to the vegetables, too. These ingredients are approximate.

1/4	cup onion, chopped
1/4	cup green pepper, chopped
2	Tb margarine
2	cups eggplant, peeled (cut in 1-inch cubes)
2	small (4-6 inch) squashes, cut in 1-inch cubes
2	cups tomatoes, cut up
1/4	cup Bell's stuffing mix or herbed bread crumbs
1/2	cup grated cheddar cheese

Sauté onion and green pepper in margarine in heavy skillet. Add vegetables, simmer until tender. Add stuffing mix or bread crumbs and mix well. Sprinkle grated cheese on top, cover and heat until cheese melts. Or slide dish under broiler until cheese melts and bubbles. Serves 6 to 8.

Squash and Apple Casserole

This is one of my favorite ways to serve winter squash. It goes well with any meat dish, and can double as dessert!

1	medium winter squash (Butternut or Acorn is best; the flesh stays firm)
3	cups sliced apples, (peel if desired)
1/2	cup maple syrup or packed brown sugar
1/4	cup margarine, melted
1	Tb flour
1/2	tsp salt
1/2	tsp nutmeg
1/4	cup chopped nuts

Wash squash, cut in half lengthwise, take out seeds, peel and cut in small chunks. Stir sugar or syrup, margarine, flour, salt and nutmeg together.

Arrange squash in an ungreased rectangular baking dish. Place apple slices on top. Sprinkle sugar mixture and nuts over apples. Cover with foil. Bake in 350° oven for 50 minutes or until squash is tender. Serves 4.

Variation: Bake acorn squash halves at 350° for 35 minutes. Fill centers with apples, top with sugar mixture and nuts. Cover with foil and bake about 25 minutes more until squash is tender. Sprinkle with cinnamon, if desired.

Green Mountain Cucumbers

Here's a new way to serve cucumbers. Even heated, they stay crisp and delicious. Serve with fish or a cold meat platter.

4	medium cucumbers
4	Tb butter or margarine
1	clove garlic, crushed
1	cup sour cream
1/2	tsp salt
1/4	tsp pepper
1	Tb fresh dill weed, chopped
1	Tb fresh chives, chopped
	Parsley sprigs

Peel cucumbers, cut in half lengthwise, scoop out seeds, and cut in 1/2 inch slices.

Heat margarine in large skillet. Add garlic and cucumbers. Sauté, stirring often, five minutes.

Add sour cream, salt and pepper. Cook and stir over medium heat five minutes. Stir in dill and chives. Heat one minute. Garnish with sprigs of parsley. Serves six.

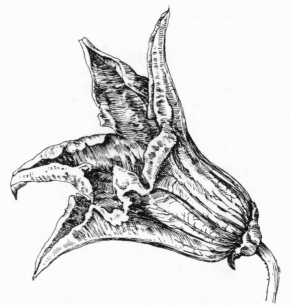

Please, DO Eat the Blossoms

Squash blossoms are a real taste adventure, either fried (in the batter above or your favorite frying batter) or sautéed. Pick a dozen or so blossoms when they're in full bloom, leaving enough male flowers on the vine for pollination. Wash blossoms and remove stems.

To sauté, melt butter or margarine in a heavy skillet and sauté blossoms until heated through.

This used to be an Italian specialty, but more and more gardeners (including us) are discovering how tasty the blossoms can be.

Pumpkin Face Cookies

These are the best Halloween treats I've ever made! The recipe looks more complicated than it really is.

Pumpkin Filling
1/2 cup cooked, mashed pumpkin
1/2 cup sugar
1/2 tsp cinnamon
1/2 tsp nutmeg
1/2 tsp ginger

Cook and stir all ingredients until bubbly; cool.

Cookie dough
3/4 cup shortening
1/2 cup brown sugar, packed
1 egg
1/4 cup light molasses
1 cup quick-cooking rolled oats
2 cups all-purpose flour
1/2 tsp baking soda
1 tsp salt

Cream shortening and sugar; beat in egg and molasses. Place oats in blender or food processor; cover; blend until finely chopped. Mix oats, flour, soda and salt. Stir into creamed mixture. Cover. Chill.

On floured surface, roll dough 1/8-inch thick. Cut into 36 3-inch circles. Place a teaspoon of Pumpkin Filling on only 18 circles. Cut faces in remaining circles. Place on top of filling. Seal edges. Press on stems cut from scraps of dough. Bake on greased cookie sheets in 375° oven 12 minutes. Makes 18 cookies.

Roasted Pumpkin Seeds

Save the seeds from pumpkin carving at Halloween, wash them well to remove the "goop," and soak seeds in salted water overnight (2 tsp salt to each cup water). Drain and pat dry.

Spread seeds on a cookie sheet and bake in 300° oven for 25 minutes or until golden. Crack and remove shells before eating. Shelled seeds may be sprinkled with salt or garlic salt.

If you grow a variety of pumpkin that has shell-less seeds (Lady Godiva, for example), there's no need to soak them before roasting. Try sautéing these seeds in olive oil or sprinkling with garlic salt before roasting.

After roasting, cool seeds and pack in airtight jar for storing.

Pumpkin (or Squash) Pie

1 8 or 9-inch pastry shell
2 cups cooked pumpkin (or Hubbard squash)
2 eggs, beaten
1 3/4 cups milk
1/2 tsp salt
3/4 cup brown sugar
1/2 tsp ginger
1 tsp cinnamon
1/4 tsp nutmeg
2 Tb flour

Preheat oven to 425°. Combine all ingredients in large bowl and pour in unbaked pastry shell. Bake for 15 minutes and turn oven down to 350° for 30 minutes or until set. Pie may be served warm or cold with whipped cream topping. This tastes just as delicious if made with cooked winter squash.

Pumpkin Ice Cream Pie

The "Crust"
1 1/2 pts vanilla ice cream

Put 9-inch pie pan in freezer when you remove the ice cream. Allow ice cream to stand at room temperature until slightly softened. Then spread ice cream evenly over bottom and sides of pan. Keep in freezer while you prepare the filling.

The Filling
1 cup pumpkin purée
3/4 cup brown sugar, firmly packed
1/2 tsp *each* ground ginger and cinnamon
3 Tb dark rum *or*
1/4 cup orange juice
3/4 cup whipping cream

Combine first three ingredients in saucepan and cook over low heat to just below simmering point. Remove from heat, add rum *or* juice and chill thoroughly. Whip cream and fold into pumpkin mixture. Pour into ice cream–lined pan and freeze. Remove from freezer a few minutes before serving time. May garnish with pecan halves and more whipped cream.

CHAPTER 5

Beans

If you've ever walked by containers of bulk seed in a garden store, you may have been surprised by all the many different colors, sizes and shapes of the beans — even by the variety of designs on the seed coats and their descriptive names: Soldier Bean, Wren's Egg Bean, Yellow Eye, Black Eye, etc.

Maybe you were impressed, too, with how big some of these seeds are. Underneath the large, hard seedcoat is an embryo, a tiny plant ready to spring to life. When you plant a bean seed, the right amount of water, oxygen and a warm temperature (65° to 75° F) will help it break through its seedcoat and push its way up through the soil.

Most of the energy the young plant needs is stored within the seed. In fact, there's enough food to nourish bean plants until the first true leaves appear without using any fertilizer at all.

As the tender, young beans come up, they must push pairs of folded seed leaves through the soil and spread them above the ground. Beans also quickly send down "tap" roots, the first of a network of roots that will anchor the plants as they grow. Most of the roots are in the top eight inches of soil, and many are quite close to the surface.

Beans need plenty of sunlight to develop properly. If the plants are shaded for an extended part of the day, they'll be tall and weak. They will be forced to stretch upward for more light, and they won't have the energy to produce as many beans.

The bean plant produces nice, showy flowers,

and within each one is everything that's necessary for pollination, fertilization — and beans. Pollination of bean flowers doesn't require much outside assistance — a bit of wind, or occasionally a honeybee or bumblebee visit, and the job is done. After fertilization occurs, the slender bean pods will emerge and quickly expand. The harvest won't be far off.

Although beans love sun, too much heat reduces production. Bean plants, like all other vegetables, have a temperature range that suits them best — they prefer 70° to 80° F after germinating. When the daytime temperature is constantly over 85° F, most beans tend to lose their blossoms. That's why many types of beans don't thrive in the South or Southwest in the middle of the summer — it's simply too hot.

Beans don't take to cold weather very well, either. Only the Broad bean or Fava can take any frost at all. The rest must be planted when the danger of frost has passed and when the soil has warmed up.

Snap Beans

Snap beans are by far the most popular home-grown beans. They are easy to plant, grow well even in poor soil and furnish a tasty harvest in only seven or eight weeks. They used to be called "string" beans because of the fibrous string that ran the length of the pods.

Most of the varieties now grown in home gardens are stringless. They are called "snap" beans because when they're fresh, they snap in pieces easily. Snap beans are also often referred to as "bush" beans because many snap bean plants are bushy. Other snap bean varieties are called "pole" beans because they grow up poles.

Snap beans are very productive. In my experience you may expect about 15 pounds of bush beans from a narrow, single row 30 feet long or 40 to 50 pounds from a rake-width row that's 30 feet long. (For more about wide-row growing, see page 121.)

There are two basic types of snap beans: green-podded and yellow-podded or wax beans, and they come in different shapes: long, short, flat, round, broad. There are more green bean varieties than yellow ones, and for green snap beans, I have three favorites: **Bountiful**, **Tendercrop** and **Tendergreen Improved**.

In my garden I am an experimenter, and I don't know how many bean varieties I've planted over the years. But Bountiful is still an old favorite with me because it produces early, and as long as I keep harvesting, I'll get more beans. They're particularly good, too, for freezing and canning. Tendergreen is resistant to some major diseases (see page 126 for diseases), and Tendercrop is a heavy yielder for me.

There are some purple-podded snap beans, too. One good one is **Royal Burgundy**. The pods are flavorful, and as the name says, they're purple. (They turn green when they're cooked.)

Southern gardeners sometimes grow a different type of bush snap bean, called "half-runners." One reliable variety is the **White Half Runner** that matures in about 60 days.

Pole Beans: Skyscrapers of the Garden

Pole bean vines twirl around all kinds of supports: strings, poles, fences, and they'll climb as high as 10 to 15 feet if you let them.

Community gardeners and other people with smaller plots love pole beans because they can have a long harvest of beans using very little space. A lot of pole bean fans also grow them because they think they taste "beanier."

Southern gardeners prize them because with their long season they can have a really long harvest from just one planting. In the North, I expect a harvest about two or three weeks long from my pole beans.

Pole beans dry off fast after a rain or sprinkling because they grow straight up where the air can dry them. Therefore, bean diseases, which thrive in humid conditions and spread easily when leaves are wet, are kept at bay.

I prefer growing bush beans to pole beans. Although they take up more space, they require less work planting, staking, weeding and watering. But pole beans are beautiful and bountiful, especially if you don't like bending over to reap your harvest.

Although they mature later than bush beans, most of the pole bean varieties are really prolific. As long as you keep them harvested, they will keep bearing.

Pole snap beans have a more distinct and nuttier taste than bush varieties, and **Kentucky Wonder** and **Romano** are probably the two most popular varieties.

Shell Beans

Shell beans are becoming increasingly popular with home gardeners, but because of the many varieties, uses and harvesting stages, they may seem confusing at first. It's really quite simple, though, to get them straight.

There are three harvesting stages for most shell beans:

1. You can eat many shell beans young — pods and all — just like snap beans.

2. You can let them grow, so the beans inside mature, and shell them green when the beans are tender. You just eat the green beans and not the pods. Lima beans are the most popular example of green shell beans.

3. You can let the shell bean plants mature fully until the end of the season. The pods and plants dry up, and the beans become hard. After soaking, these shell beans are used in such dishes as chili and baked beans.

Though there are some climbing varieties, most shell beans grow short, bushy plants.

My favorite shell beans are fresh, home-grown **lima beans**, or **butter beans** as they're known in the South. Once you eat some, you'll know what makes them so popular with home gardeners. Harvested at peak freshness, their taste is much livelier than the processed limas you find in the store. Jan and I really like them as succotash with corn, butter and milk, and I even enjoy them fresh out of the pod, right from the garden.

One of the nicest things about growing and freezing your own limas is that they lose very little flavor. A dish of our own limas in January almost makes me feel like it's summertime again.

There are large-seeded limas and small-seeded variety or "**baby**" **lima beans**. If the conditions are right, large-seeded ones give you more beans, and they're easier to shell.

The baby limas grow short, bushy plants and produce smaller beans, but they are very productive for the small space they take up, especially if you plant them in a wide row as I do.

Next to limas, my favorite shell beans are the **French Horticultural**, the **Red Kidney** and the **Vermont Cranberry**. These can be harvested all three ways. I generally harvest them, though, when they are fully mature and store the beans dry. They're fine as baked beans, and in chowders

and chilis. But they're also wonderful harvested in the "green shell" stage and served as succotash.

Although I'm not a nutrition expert, I understand that dried beans are a very good source of protein. Proteins are comprised of 22 amino acids, eight of which are essential for us because our bodies cannot produce them. Beans contain only some of the essential eight. And, from what I've gathered, it's an all-or-nothing situation with protein; it's really important to eat all the essential amino acids at one sitting to derive their full benefit. However, if you supplement beans in the same meal with the right amount of grains, seeds or nuts, which contain complementary vegetable proteins, or with animal proteins found in milk, eggs, cheese, meat or fish, it's easy to do.

Soybeans

Soybeans are regarded as "the meat of the fields" in China. They contain about three times more protein than any other member of the legume family (beans, peas, etc.), only a small amount of sugar and no starch. To top it off, they also contain calcium and B vitamins. What more can one ask of a bean?

In the Orient soybeans have been used for centuries in all different forms. The form we know best, of course, is soy sauce. In this country commerical food processors discovered soybeans after World War II, and they've been using them ever since in all sorts of ways.

The drawbacks to soybeans are that they are almost tasteless, and they can take a long time to prepare. But their versatility outweighs these drawbacks. They can be served as sprouts, dried, whole or ground and served as substitutes for milk, meat, bread or nuts. They can be added to other foods, chopped, baked, fried and steamed. And when they are seasoned and flavored, they can be very tasty.

However, soybeans are low in one of the essential amino acids — methionine. This is not a problem if soybeans are served with a small amount of animal protein, such as a glass of milk. And, of course, soybeans are not a complete food. It's always important to have a varied diet.

For the home gardener **Fiskeby V** and **Kanrich** are two dependable varieties to try. Fiskeby V will mature in northern areas of the U.S., and Kanrich is a standard, garden variety in central and southern states. It needs a long season to mature.

Southern Peas

It may seem odd to be talking about peas in a bean book, but the Southern pea varieties, such as blackeye peas, are not peas at all. They're beans. Still, no one ever calls them beans, but I sure can't tell you why.

And just because they're called Southern doesn't mean they can't be grown successfully up North, either. They just need warm soil to germinate. So, if you can grow lima beans, which need warm soil, you can grow all sorts of Southern peas.

I grow Southern peas in wide rows. The plants grow lush and thick and produce about 1½ pounds of peas per foot of wide row. (See wide-row planting, page 121.)

The peas are picked green when the pods are filled out but before the hulls are dry. If you want to store the peas dry, just leave them on the vine until the plants are thoroughly mature and dry.

Blackeye peas, crowder peas and **cream peas** are the best known kinds of Southern peas. Gardening friends of mine in Georgia often grow wide rows of blackeye peas as a soil improvement crop, but before they till the plants into the soil, they

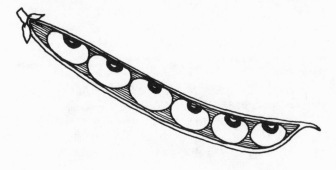

Seeds, Seeds, Seeds

Days to Harvest

Variety	First Harvest	Dry	Comments
BUSH SNAP			
Bountiful	47		One of the earliest beans. Resistant to rust and mildew.
Tendercrop	54		Suited to many climates. Good for freezing.
Blue Lake	55		Big yields. Meaty pods; great for canning.
Kentucky Wonder	65		Prolific bearer of long pods.
Golden Wax	50		Broad, flat, golden yellow pods.
Royalty Burgundy	55		Flavorful new variety of purple-podded snap beans that turn green when cooked.
White Half-Runner	60		Pods are shorter than snap beans; good beany flavor.
Broad bean or Fava bean	85		Plants take some cool soil and frosty weather. Beans cook like limas.
POLE SNAP			
Kentucky Wonder	64		Sometimes called Old Homestead. Probably the all-around, national climbing favorite. Long pods that stay tender.
Kentucky Wonder Yellow Wax	65		Hailed as best pole wax bean. Produces long, deep yellow pods.
Romano Italian	70		Pods wider than most pole beans. Very good for freezing and canning.
BUSH LIMA			
Fordhook No. 242	75		Produces many short, fat pods with 3 to 4 beans in each. Good yield and does well in hot weather.
Henderson Bush Lima	75		Very popular "baby" lima. Keep harvested, and it will really produce.
Jackson Wonder	66		Withstands very hot temperatures, so a favorite in all parts of the South.

Variety	First Harvest	Dry	Comments
POLE LIMA			
King of the Garden	88		The standard for many years. Long pods that contain up to 6 beans.
Christmas Pole Lima	80		Big seeds and pods.
Florida Butter Pole Lima	85		Known in the South as "large, speckled bean."
DRY SHELL			
Dwarf Horticultural	65		Good northern bean.
French Horticultural	64	90	Easy to shell fresh and very tasty.
Red Kidney		100	Excellent in baked bean and soup dishes.
Great Northern White		85	Excellent baking bean.
Pink	60	85	Good for chilis.
Soldier		85	New England favorite.
Navy Bean or Navy Pea Bean		90	White, medium-sized beans. Excellent baker.
Yellow Eye		85	Another good baking bean.
Pinto		90	Sends out vines and can climb poles.
Vermont Cranberry	60	90	Easy to shell. Cook the same way as limas. Also good dry.
SOYBEAN			
Fiskeby V	70		Will mature in northern U.S. or Canada. Medium size seed.
Kanrich	103		The standard in central and southern U.S. Needs long season to mature.
SOUTHERN PEA			
Pink Eye Purple Hull Cowpea		85	Bush type. Freezes very well.
Mississippi Silver		64	Easy to harvest and shell.
California No. 5 Black Eye		60	Can be harvested as a snap bean or shell.

harvest the peas. They've mixed up a dish of these peas with corn, peppers and onions for me, and they are very tasty as well as nutritious.

The name "crowder" is tagged to all kinds of Southern peas, but I've heard it's supposed to refer to the varieties with the peas really jammed together in the pod. The name "cream" can cover a lot of varieties, too, but the cream peas I know have a smooth pod and small white peas.

BEFORE YOU PLANT

Soil Preparation

Most of the work of growing a good crop of beans (and all other vegetables, too) comes before you put the seeds in the ground. Simply, get your soil in the best possible shape and prepare a smooth seedbed, and you'll have the fewest problems.

Tips on Buying Seeds

Be sure to buy bean seeds from a reputable seed source. *Just about all commercial bean seeds sold in garden centers and available through seed catalogues are grown in the West, where the climate is quite dry — an excellent condition for growing healthy seed. Beans are much more susceptible to disease in the wet conditions we often have in the East, and bean diseases are carried from one season to the next in the seed. Many Eastern gardeners save some of their home-grown bean seeds for the following year, but they sometimes have disease problems.*

Select resistant varieties if you have a recurring disease problem. *For example,* **Tendercrop, Topcrop, Contender,** *and* **Kentucky Wonder** *and* **Blue Lake** *pole beans have some resistance to common bean mosaic. Some seed packets and catalogues may also list resistance qualities of varieties. You can learn more about your area's best bean varieties from your local Cooperative Extension Service.*

Buy "treated" seed, or you can "treat" it yourself. *Some seed companies pre-treat their bean seeds with a fungicide, which protects the seeds from organisms in the soil that cause seed rot and "damping off." Damping off can prevent newly germinated seeds from coming up, and if they do come up, they may just keel over and die. Rotting is most common during cool, moist weather. If you buy untreated seed (most seeds in packets are not treated), I recommend treating the seeds yourself. The fungicide is sometimes called "seed protectant," and it usually comes in small packets, available in most garden stores. It's easy to use; just follow the instructions on the packet carefully.*

Those people who avoid using chemicals in gardening usually avoid treating their seed with protectant.

Inoculating seeds. *Right before planting, many gardeners "inoculate" their bean seeds. Inoculating is simply coating the seeds with a small amount of a special powdery bacteria that enables the plants to draw nitrogen from the air and deposit in their roots.*

This ability to draw nitrogen from the air and store it in nodules on the roots of the plant (or "fix" it in gardeners' terminology) is unique to beans and other plants in the legume family, such as alfalfa and clover. Some soils contain the bacteria in sufficient amounts for fixing, but by treating the seed, you are assured you have the right amount.

Inoculating seed is especially important to commercial growers, because they are restoring a substantial amount of nitrogen to the soil. This is essential because nitrogen is one of the three major nutrients for good plant growth.

Inoculant comes in small packages, and it's usually available where you buy your seeds. A little goes a long way. Put the bean seeds in a pan, add a little water to moisten them. Add a small amount of inoculant, and stir the beans with a stick until most of them have a little powder on their seedcoats. After they have been inoculated, plant them right away.

To improve your soil, it's most important for you to chop, spade or till your bean plants into the soil immediately after the last harvest. You will be adding valuable organic matter to the soil and releasing the nitrogen from the roots, also.

To get beans off to a good start, till or spade a sunny section of your garden to a depth of 6 or 8 inches, making sure the soil is as free as possible of clumps of earth or sod. A seedbed of deep, loose soil allows bean roots to stretch rapidly and to take in water, food and oxygen easily.

To get a jump on the weeds, I like to work the soil two or three times over a period of several days or so before planting (the more, the better). Each time I do this, I kill a lot of weeds that have just begun to germinate, and I always till one last time just before planting. Working the soil this way takes care of half my weeding chores before I even plant!

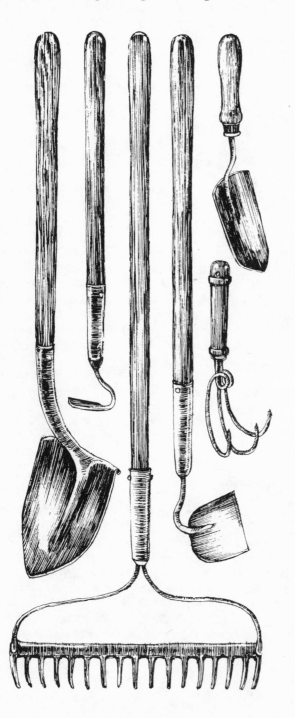

Most beans are not too choosy about where they'll sink their roots. They'll give you a good crop in soil that's loamy, sandy, rocky, rich or poor and even in clay. But you should avoid planting beans in the shade or in soil that stays wet and doesn't drain well. Bean diseases thrive in wet conditions, and the roots may not get enough oxygen with water and mud clogging their air channels.

Beans like soil that is slightly acid with the best pH range for them around 6.0 to 6.5 — pH is just an acid-to-alkaline scale. They will grow outside that range, but they make best use of the nutrients and fertilizers in the soil when the pH is 6.0 to 6.5. If you are unsure about your garden soil's pH, you can purchase an inexpensive, easy-to-use pH test kit. Or contact your local County Extension Agent, who can advise you about soil-testing. The test will tell you how much lime or sulfur to add to bring your soil into the proper growing range. If you have to add lime or sulfur, it should be mixed into the top 6 to 8 inches of soil. Although you can add it anytime, the fall is the best time because it takes time for the lime or sulfur to work.

Fertilizer

As mentioned earlier, beans are "light feeders." They don't require much fertilizer. It's easy to give them just about all the nutrients they'll need by mixing a light dose of fertilizer into the top 2 or 3 inches of soil on planting day or the day before. About 3 or 4 pounds of commercial fertilizer, such as 5-10-10, per 100 square feet is sufficient for most garden soils.

The numbers on the fertilizer bags indicate by weight what percentages of each of the three most important nutrients — nitrogen (N), phosphorus (P), and potassium (K) — are present in the mixture. Although the percentages may vary, the order is always the same: N, P, and K.

For instance, 5-10-10, which is good for beans, indicates the fertilizer contains 5 percent nitrogen, 10 percent phosphorus and 10 percent potassium. Nitrogen promotes healthy green leaves and stems, and you don't need much of it for beans. If you have too much, the plant will spend more time making leaves and less time making beans, which isn't what you want. Phosphorus promotes strong roots, and potassium conditions the whole plant, helping it bear fruit and resist disease.

Non-chemical fertilizers are well-rotted manure, compost, bone meal and cotton seed meal. Dehydrated manures are also available.

PLANTING

Wide Rows: More Beans, Less Work

For years, gardeners have planted their bush bean seeds in single-file, straight-line rows with lots of room between the rows, and most still do. I've always considered this method a waste of valuable growing space and, frankly, not a very productive way to grow beans.

Over the years I've worked on a method to double and sometimes even triple my bean crops. It's called "wide-row growing," and you simply spread seeds over a wide seedbed, instead of putting one seed behind another in a row. The wide area contains many more plants than a single row of the same length, so I harvest much more from the same area.

I've found that a row about 16 or 18 inches across — about a rake's width — is very easy to plant, care for and harvest. With a little wide row experience, you may want to try even wider rows.

The advantages to wide-row growing I have found are:

You can grow 2 to 4 times as many beans in the same amount of space. It really helps people grow as much food as possible on the land they have, which is what home gardening is all about.

Weeding is reduced to a minimum. Because the beans grow quickly, their leaves group together and form a "living mulch." This mulch blocks the sun, so weeds don't grow.

Many gardeners spread mulch — organic matter such as hay, pine needles or leaves — around all their plants in the garden to fight weeds and retain moisture in the soil. Since the wide row mulches itself, you only need to use small amounts of mulch to keep weeds down in the walkways and to help retain moisture. You'll also have fewer walkways using wide rows, so you really can save a lot of time, effort and mulch.

Moisture is conserved by the shade because the sun can't scorch the soil and dry it out as much. Moist soil stays cooler, so beans in very hot climates don't wither as much or stop producing as quickly.

The plants in the middle of the rows are protected from the full effects of hot, drying winds. They don't dry out rapidly like those in a single row. This can be especially important in water-short areas of the country.

Harvesting is easier with wide rows. You can pick much more without having to continually get up and move down the row. It's pleasant to take a stool into the garden, sit down and enjoy picking beans by the bushel.

Don't waste your gardening space on walkways. Concentrate your gardening in wide rows.

For twice the yield in half the gardening space, wide rows is the way to go.

How to Plant Wide-Row Bush Beans

Prepare the soil, and using a steel garden rake, smooth out the seedbed. Be careful not to pack the seedbed down by stepping on it. Do all your work from the walkway beside the row.

Stake out a row about 15 or 18 inches wide (or wider if you like) to whatever length you want. Drop the seeds 3 or 4 inches apart from each other in all directions in the row. It takes about a 2-ounce package of snap beans to cover about 10 feet of rake-width row. Firm the seeds into the soil with the back of a hoe, and cover the seeds with about 1 inch of soil. Just pull the soil with a rake from the side of the row and smooth it evenly over the seeds. Firm the soil again with the back of a hoe.

If the soil is dry, water after planting — not before. If you water before, you pack the soil down, which you don't want to do.

Leave a path or walkway wide enough to walk when the plants grow and spread out. I recommend at least 16 inches — and more, of course, if your cultivator or tiller is wider.

Wide-row planting — stake out the length of the row, and rake the tilled seedbed smooth. For beans the seedbed can be rake-width or wider.

Firm the bean seeds into the soil, and cover them with about 1 inch of earth. Firm soil again.

Remember, wide rows work well with bush snap beans, southern peas, lima beans, horticultural beans and other winter storage beans. In fact they're great for all beans except the pole varieties.

Other Planting Methods

Single row. The best way to plant a single row is to make a shallow furrow with a hoe, and every 3 or 4 inches drop in a bean seed, cover the furrow with 1 inch of soil and then firm it. A 2-ounce packet of bush snap bean seeds will sow a single row 30 to 40 feet long.

Double row. Make 2 shallow furrows about 4 or 5 inches apart, and plant in the same manner as for a single row. This double-row arrangement is especially handy if you need to irrigate regular-

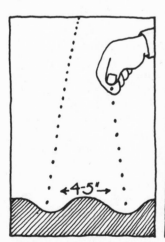

Double-row planting — make 2 shallow furrows about 4 or 5 inches apart, and plant the same as for single row.

Soaker hoses work well in double rows for irrigating. Place the hose between the two rows for efficient watering.

ly. You can put a soaker hose — a kind of garden hose with little holes in it — between the two rows and water the plants quite efficiently.

Another easy irrigating system with the double row is to dig an additional shallow furrow in between the two seed rows. You make this channel when you are planting the beans. To water the beans, you simply run water down the channel between the two rows of plants.

Raised beds. If you garden where it's very rainy, where the soil stays damp or you have clay soil, planting in raised beds is a good idea because the soil drains better. Good drainage helps to prevent diseases and to warm the soil more quickly early in the season.

I try to build up the seedbeds about 4 to 6 inches above the walkway. To get the most for your extra effort, plant a wide row or at least a double row to guarantee a plentiful harvest.

Mid-channel furrows can aid in watering double rows.

Raised beds are a good idea if your soil has poor drainage. Simply pull the soil from the walkway with a hoe onto the seedbed, and plant as usual.

Continuous Planting for Bountiful Harvests

Since you can start harvesting snap beans in just about 50 days, they're a great crop to plant several times over the season for a continuous supply of fresh, tender pods. In many parts of the country you can plant about every two weeks until about 8 or 10 weeks before the average first fall frost date, or you can use beans as a succession crop. For example, when my spinach starts to go to seed or 'bolt' in early summer, I till it under and immediately plant a wide row of beans. Beans can follow beans, too, of course, if you've got a long season. After your last harvest, simply spade or till the plants under, thoroughly chopping and mixing them into the soil, and plant again right away.

Where it gets too hot in the summer for good snap bean production, you can often sow two crops in the spring and one or two more in late summer. Gardeners I know in Georgia plant at short intervals from February to April and then again in late August and September and have bountiful harvests.

However, if you like to plant your entire garden on one warm, spring weekend, plant both bush and pole snap bean varieties. Because pole beans bear a little later and longer than bush types, the harvest won't all happen at once. You will be able to enjoy fresh beans longer, and you won't have to worry about preserving a lot of beans at one time.

Planting Pole Beans

Pole beans like to send their vines up poles, strings or wire, but they don't like chicken wire or fences with a lot of horizontal wires or small mesh. Horizontal wires cause the vines just to wind around each other and choke.

A pole diameter of about 1 or 2 inches is good, and poles with rough surfaces are better than smooth ones.

A good height for a pole is about 6 or 7 feet. A variety like Blue Lake can easily grow to 13 feet if you let it, but who wants to harvest from a step ladder? Not me. By using just 7-foot poles, the vines will head back down, and all the harvest will be within easy reach.

Short poles are okay, too. A friend of mine in California plants long rows of pole beans using stakes just 4 feet high. He plants Kentucky Wonder beans, and they grow quickly to the top of the stakes and then fall back down. The ease of planting and care outweighs the occasional nuisance of harvesting in dense foliage.

Sometimes when I grow pole beans I use tepees. I hitch the tops of three 9-foot wooden poles together, spread the bottoms out 3 or 4 feet from each other and shove each pole in the ground 4 or 5 inches deep for support. It's a pretty sturdy arrangement.

I plant 5 or 6 seeds around each pole about 6 or 8 inches away from it. I firm them into the soil, cover them with 1 inch of soil, and firm them again. If it's dry, I make sure the soil stays moist until they are up. Later, I thin, leaving only the healthiest 3 or 4 plants per pole. With this system, 1 ounce of seed is sufficient for 4 or 5 tepees.

At different times, I have put up these tepees right in the garden and also on the lawn,

have more foliage and tend to dry out quicker. A good time for sidedressing them with extra fertilizer is after the first pods develop. Use about a tablespoonful of 5-10-10 fertilizer around each support, sprinkled about 3 or 4 inches away from the plant stems and covered with soil. (You don't need to sidedress if planting next to corn or sunflowers.) Be careful not to get any fertilizer on the plants or it will burn them. Compost or well-rotted manure is okay for sidedressing, too. It won't burn, so you can put it near the plants.

Planting Dry Shell Beans

When I'm planting shell beans for winter storage, I plant them in a very special place — I put them between the rows of my winter squash.

I plant my winter squash when the soil is really warm in rows about 10 to 12 feet apart, because their vines crawl all over the place. I plant the squash seed in rows, not hills. When the squash plants are just coming up, I have lots of room between the rows. I plant the bean seeds there, in rows about 2 feet wide or more. The beans grow quickly and shade the ground, helping to keep the weeds down. Because I prepare the soil well at the beginning of the season, these two crops pretty much take care of themselves until harvest time. Of course, if it gets very dry, I'll water, but there's very little weeding or cultivating to do.

The squash vines sneak through and around the beans, but neither crop seems to mind the congestion a bit. I harvest both crops at the same time — right around the time of the first fall frost.

Planting Lima Beans

Lima beans, like all beans, need warm soil temperature to germinate and full sun for best growth.

If you garden in a short-season climate, you may have to gamble a little and plant your lima beans early. If it works, you're ahead of the game.

To get a jump on a short season, some people advise starting lima beans indoors in pots or flats to transplant later. I don't advise it because bean roots are extremely sensitive and easily injured when transplanting.

Instead, to speed up germination, try soaking lima bean seeds for an hour in clean, 70°F water before planting. The water temperature is important. If a lima bean seed absorbs cold water as it starts to germinate, it suffers permanent injury. The chances of injuring lima bean seeds when you plant them in cool soil are greatly reduced if you soak the beans in warm water first.

clearing an area for the seeds and poles. Kids love to play in them, but they're also a good, shady place for a cool weather crop, such as lettuce.

I've also planted pole beans "Indian style." They planted corn and beans together using the corn stalks as poles. If you want to try this, plant the beans on the sunny, southern side of the corn-field on the outer rows. Plant one bean at every third stalk or so when the corn is about 10 or 12 inches high. The beans don't get as much sunlight when grown this way, but they'll still produce. If you're growing sunflowers, they make good bean poles, too.

In the beginning you may have to aim the tendrils of the vines toward the poles, strings or corn stalks. Once the vines get hooked, though, they'll do the rest of the climbing themselves.

Pole beans usually need a little extra fertilizer during the season. Their water needs are greater than bush beans, too, because they are bigger,

Soak them only if you live in the North where you really need the jump on the season. You shouldn't soak any other bean seeds before planting because they may crack, and germination will be poor.

CARING FOR BEANS: A SNAP

Once you've planted beans, you can relax because growing them is easy. They grow very well all by themselves, and I think that's one of the prime reasons they are so popular with home gardeners. To have a satisfactory bean harvest the two most important things are: stay out of the garden when it's wet to avoid spreading diseases, and keep picking snap beans when they are young for a continual harvest.

Weed-Beating Beans

Beans grow quickly and shade out weeds, particularly if they are grown in wide rows. If you've prepared the soil well, your weed worries will be few. The only time to be concerned is when beans are very young, before they have developed their leafy shade.

If you are working around young bean plants with a hoe or other weeding tool, or if you are cultivating between rows, remember to stay near the surface. Weed seeds are tiny and must be very close to the surface to germinate — not like beans which are planted at least one inch deep. A gentle stirring of the top ¼-inch of soil every 4 or 5 days pulls the germinating weeds out of the soil

and exposes their roots to the sun which kills them.

Deep cultivation is bad for two reasons: It injures the roots of the beans, and it brings more weeds up near the surface of the soil where they'll germinate.

A good time to cultivate is after a rain but when the plants are completely dry and the soil has dried out a little. This is when many weeds start to germinate.

Once the bean leaves grow enough to shade the ground, there shouldn't be any weed problem within the row, and a good heavy mulch or regular cultivation in the pathways should take care of weeds there.

Watering

Beans need about one inch of water a week for good growth. So if the garden doesn't get sufficient rain, you must water.

Watering the garden is probably the most critical summer gardening chore for many people, but it's the job most often done wrong.

Let me briefly go over some of the watering fundamentals:

Avoid frequent, light waterings. That's the biggest mistake people make. They think splashing a little water on the beans will make them happy, just as a wake-up splash refreshes us. The reverse is true for plants. Water them deeply but gently to a depth of 4 to 6 inches. Thorough soaking encourages the roots to seek water deep in the soil. With a deep root system, the plants can survive hot, dry weather a lot better.

Don't water by the calendar, but rather when the plants need it. Check the appearance of the plants, the condition of the soil on the surface and the condition 4 or 5 inches down. Plants will often look wilted on a hot afternoon — that's okay; they will probably perk up overnight. If the plants look wilted in the morning, they need watering.

A good mulch will save water, protect the soil from the sun's scorching heat, keep the root area of the plants cooler and reduce evaporation.

Water early in the day if you sprinkle or hose from above. Then there's plenty of time for the leaves to dry. If the leaves are wet overnight, diseases can quickly invade the plants.

With furrow irrigation, drip irrigation or soaker hoses, which all deliver water at the soil surface and not on the leaves, you can water in the late afternoon, evening or even at night.

Try to avoid watering during the middle of the day because evaporation losses are usually highest then.

Don't overwater. The soil, while anchoring the plant, also acts like a sponge. It can only hold so much water. Learn the water holding capacity of your soil, so you don't waste precious water or smother the roots of your plants.

Disease Prevention

Anthracnose, bacterial blights, common bean mosaic and rust are the most common bean diseases.

Anthracnose is caused by a fungus which is carried in seeds and lives in the soil on remains of diseased plants. Rotating the crop is important for control. You can recognize the disease by brown, sunken spots that develop on the pods.

Bacterial blights cause large, brown spots on the leaves and water-soaked spots on the pods. Disease spreads quickly on wet foliage.

Common Bean Mosiac is caused by a virus carried in seed and spread by aphids. Leaves become mottled and then curl. Some bean varieties are resistant to this disease.

Rust shows as red or black blisters on the leaves, which turn yellow and drop. The problem is caused by a fungus that lives through the winter on remains of diseased plants.

When anthracnose, blights or other bean diseases hit, there is not too much a home gardener can do except to pull up and destroy seriously affected plants, so they don't spread the disease to others nearby. There are some sprays that are recommended to fight diseases, but you should contact your Extension Service for more information before using them. The Extension Agents are usually aware of which diseases have developed in an area and what the best controls are.

Here is a quick review of the basic steps to preventing disease problems in your garden:

Stay out of the garden when plants are wet, because water is often the carrier of diseases.

Rotate the bean crop each year to avoid soil-borne diseases.

Select disease-resistant seed varieties, and buy seed from a reputable company. You can use seed protectant on beans, too.

Well-drained soil is important for growing beans.

If soil stays wet, raised beds are your best bet for beans. With raised beds the soil will be warmer at planting time, and the seedbed will drain better. Raised beds are also good for heavy soil, because it won't pack down as much.

Use mulch in the walkways and wide-row growing to prevent raindrops from spashing soil and disease spores up onto the plants.

Pests

The Mexican bean beetle is the worst bean pest. The beetles usually first appear before the beans blossom. They feed for a week and lay yellowish-orange egg masses on the undersides of the leaves. The average female lays more than 400 eggs. If you see any, pick them off and destroy the egg clusters right away. Beetles in advanced stages of growth can be controlled with applications of malathion, Sevin or rotenone. Also spade or till the plants into the ground as soon as the harvest is over. It will improve the soil, and the beetles won't have anything to eat, so they'll leave.

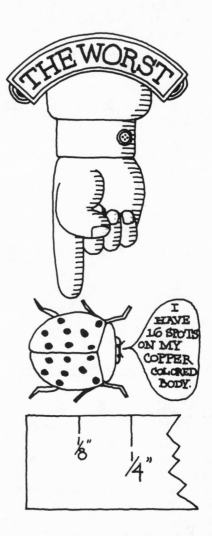

If you do not like using chemicals on your plants and still want to deter pests, some people say they have had some success planting marigolds, onions or garlic near their bean plants to keep the bugs away. Others use rotenone, which is an organic pesticide. And others buy

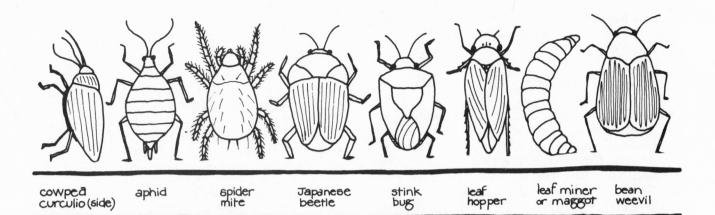

cowpea   aphid   spider   Japanese   stink   leaf   leaf miner   bean
curculio (side)   mite   beetle   bug   hopper   or maggot   weevil

praying mantises and put them in their garden, hoping the mantises don't find the pests at their neighbor's tastier.

Another pest is the **bean leaf beetle**, which will eat large holes in leaves, feeding from the underside. Rotenone or Sevin is effective against them.

A very destructive pest in the South is the **cowpea curculio,** which eats holes in pods, beans and Southern peas. Regular application of Sevin helps keep them in check.

Root-knot nematodes may also be a problem, particularly in the South and West. These very small, eel-like creatures live on the roots and damage many crops. If you have a bad infestation of nematodes, your plants will be quite stunted. You should contact your Extension Agent for advice.

Other insects such as aphids, spider mites, Japanese beetles, stink bugs, leaf hoppers, lima bean pod borers and leaf miners may be problems for some gardeners in different parts of the country. Most of these can be controlled by spraying them with malathion or Sevin. For the most effective time to spray, check with your County Extension Agent.

The steps for crop protection are the same with all these pests: early detection, correct identification of the pest and carefully following recommended procedures for control.

The best source for help and advice is the nearest Cooperative Extension Service office or county agent. Many offices publish local guides which help you identify the various pests in your region and what controls are possible. Remember to follow all directions carefully if you use sprays or dusts in your garden.

Bean weevils may also attack dry beans in storage. You can avoid the problem by heating the beans (130-140°F) or chilling them (35-40°F) for half an hour and storing them in tightly covered containers.

HARVESTING

Pick, Pick, Pick

It's best to harvest snap beans when they are just about the diameter of a pencil or even a bit smaller. Simply snap them off — but take care because any hard jerking or tearing of the vines will cut down on later harvests.

You'll have the best flavor and nutritional value if the snap beans are picked young and tender. So don't wait — when there's something to eat, start harvesting.

You really can't over-harvest snap beans. When you pick the pods, you encourage more blossoms and more pods. That's because the plant is trying to produce large, mature seed to complete its life cycle. When it produces seed, the plant will stop blossoming and producing pods, so keep picking.

After your first picking, you can probably pick again in 3 to 5 days. Just pick, pick, pick, and don't let any seeds develop inside in order to keep the harvest going as long as possible.

Green Shell Beans

When shell beans are young, they are greenish. When they are ready for picking at the green shell stage, the beans start turning color. Horticultural beans turn a strawberry roan color, kidney beans turn red. When you pick them, pick only the pods without damaging the plants.

Dried Shell Beans

It's easy to get nice, dry, mature shell beans for winter storage. In warm parts of the country, the beans and pods will mature and dry very well right in the garden. In Vermont, it is cool and sometimes wet in the fall, so they often require additional drying. I pull the plants up and pile them up around a fence post, roots to the post, like spokes in a wheel, to dry them some more. So if you're having a wet fall, get the bean plants out of the ground and put them somewhere that's airy and relatively dry. Hang the plants from rafters in your garage, carport or in your attic if you're lucky enough to still have one. You can hang them plain or put them in burlap or mesh bags.

It's easy to tell when the beans are dry. They're so hard, biting into one won't even make a dent.

It was important to hold onto the long handle and use the shorter one to flail. The short stick couldn't whirl back and rap our knuckles. After flailing a while, we used a hay fork to lift and shake the plants, and then we tossed the plants aside for the compost heap. This left us with just a pile of beans and chaff.

Threshing

Threshing by hand is an old-fashioned chore, but it's simply removing the beans from the pods once the beans are dry. To thresh I just take some of the plants by the roots — pods, beans and all — and whack them back and forth inside a clean trash can. The dry pods shatter, and the beans drop into the can. I toss those plants aside and start on the next bunch.

There are other ways to thresh beans, too. A fun way is to put the plants, again pods and all, in a big burlap or cloth bag. Then get a bunch of kids to walk and jump on the bag for a few minutes. Roll the bag over, and let them jump some more. Because the beans are dry and hard, the kids won't hurt them a bit. You can also let them have a good time hitting the bag with a baseball bat.

Then open the bag, vigorously shake the plants to make sure all the beans are out of the pods, and remove the plants. You'll just have beans and small bits of debris, or chaff, in the bag. You can also just cut a corner on the bag and let the beans drop out, leaving the plants in.

When I was a kid, we threshed beans with a homemade bean flail. The flail was made of two wooden sticks — one short, one long — hitched together at one end by a leather strap. We gripped the long stick and whirled the short one against a pile of dried bean plants laid out on a canvas on the floor of the barn. When we really got flailing, we appreciated the design of the flail.

Winnowing

Once you've removed the beans from the pods by any of these threshing methods, you need to separate the chaff from the beans, and that's called winnowing.

On a windy day, take a basket of beans — chaff and all — and holding it up high, pour the beans slowly into an empty basket on the ground. Repeat this a few times. The wind will blow all the

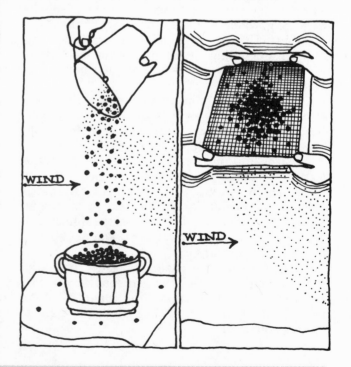

chaff away as the beans fall. (It's a good idea to put a sheet or canvas under the basket on the ground to catch the beans that miss or bounce out.)

If you have a friend to help you winnow, spread the beans and chaff on a spare window screen outside on a windy day. When the two of you lightly jiggle and shake the frame, the chaff will blow away, leaving only the beans.

Sorting

The final step before storing shell beans is sorting. It's important to remove the discolored, immature and misshapen beans from the good ones, because the bad ones could affect the taste.

When I was growing up, we sat around the kitchen table and sorted the beans on a white sheet. The sheet made it easy to roll the beans and check them carefully, and stop them from rolling off the table. If we were doing white beans, it was especially easy to spot bad ones. Sorting was a chore, but it was also time for a chat.

Dry beans will keep well in tightly capped, air-tight containers, stored in a cool, dry, dark spot.

Jan and I work in the garden together, and we both know about growing. What happens in the kitchen is more her specialty, though. So, now that I've shared what I know about growing and harvesting, she can tell you how she preserves and prepares beans.

Garden to Kitchen

Fresh beans taste wonderful! I have yet to meet anyone who doesn't like them. We eat a lot fresh — served hot, cold, all different ways — but we put up a lot, too.

The best days for harvesting beans — sunny, dry and hot — are also the best days for summer fun. I've figured out a way to be able to go on picnics, swim with our grandsons in the pond or just "go fishin'" and still be able to put up plenty of beans: work nights!

After a beautiful summer day, the whole family — Dick and I, the girls and their husbands, even two of our grandsons (the baby is still too little) — will pick beans in the late afternoon or early evening before the dew forms. We can, pickle and freeze the beans in the evening when it's cooler to work but while the beans' flavor is still at its best.

Come winter when we eat and share our homegrown vegetables that we've stored, we don't even remember that we were tired a few mornings during the summer.

On the following pages are some of my thoughts about the best ways to preserve beans and also some of our favorite recipes. I hope you'll try them and enjoy them as much as we do.

FREEZING IS FAST

Snap Beans

Sure, fresh beans taste best. But at the height of the season, you can expect that your garden will produce more than you and your family want to eat fresh.

For the best-tasting frozen beans — even months after they're harvested — I pick the beans young and freeze them as soon as possible after I've picked them. In any one day, prepare about 2 to 3 pounds of beans per cubic foot of available freezer space. By not trying to freeze more than the freezer can handle efficiently, the beans freeze hard quickly, which is very important for the best flavor.

To prepare a batch of snap beans for freezing, thoroughly wash about one pound at a time in cool water. Don't let them soak because they may get soggy. String them if necessary. (Yes, some varieties still have strings. To string them, hold the bean in one hand, stem end up. Grasp the

NO STRINGS ATTACHED!

stem in the other hand and pull down. It's easy to see that the bean has sort of a seam on one side, and that's where the string is. So, holding onto the stem, zip it down that side, and the bean is strung.)

After trimming off just the stem end, you may leave the beans whole, cut them or snap them into 1 or 2-inch bits or slice them diagonally or lengthwise. Lengthwise slicing is known as the French-cut. (Why it's called French-cut I don't know. The French like to use very young beans, which they don't slice at all.) Prepare each batch in only one way, so they'll cook uniformly.

Beans must be blanched prior to freezing. Blanching or scalding stops the plant enzymes from working, which stops the ripening process.

To blanch, put the cleaned, trimmed beans in a wire basket and plunge the basket for 2 to 4 minutes into a large kettle filled with vigorously boiling water. (Purple-podded beans have a built-in thermostat indicating when they have had sufficient blanching — they automatically turn

green after a couple of minutes.) If you live above 5,000 feet, add one minute to the scalding time.

After blanching, remove the basket of beans and quickly plunge it into ice water. The beans stop cooking, remain firm and retain their color. The cooling takes as long as the blanching.

Drain the beans well and pack them in freezer containers. Do not add salt or other seasonings. Pack them firmly but not tightly, leaving little room for air. Air causes freezer burn (dehydration), which reduces flavor, so leave only about 1/2-inch headspace.

There are quite a few different kinds of freezer containers. Plastic bags and paper or plastic boxes are the most popular for beans. If you use paper boxes, plastic bags are used as liners. The boxes act as molds, shaping the plastic bags and contents for convenient stacking. When the vegetables are frozen, the outer boxes can be removed and re-used. With plastic boxes, which I prefer, it's one step: pack them and put them in the freezer. Plastic boxes are more expensive, but they can be re-used many times.

Seal the packages and label them with contents and date. To freeze quickly, place the containers separately in a single layer an inch apart in the coldest part of the freezer. After 24 hours, they will be completely frozen and may be stacked together.

Keep an up-to-date inventory of what you have in your freezer and plan to use the beans within one year. The flavor isn't as good after that, and by that time, fresh beans will be in season again, anyway!

Lima Beans

Harvest the limas when they are green and plump with beans. Wash in cold water, shell them and sort them according to size. To shell a lima bean, hold the pod in both hands, placing your thumbs on the outer seam. Simultaneously, squeeze and twist the pod, pushing down on the seam, and the pod will pop open. Rinse the beans and blanch them: small beans, 1 minute; medium, 2 minutes; large, 3 minutes. Then follow the process outlined for freezing snap beans.

Soybeans

For freezing, soybeans are harvested when they are young and green. After washing, trim off the blossom ends. Soybeans should be blanched for 5 minutes while still in their shells. After they are quickly cooled in ice water, it's easy to squeeze the beans out of the pods. Rinse again, drain, package and freeze.

Baked Beans

Fully cooked baked beans can be frozen very successfully. You can cook a double portion of beans and freeze half for use later. This saves time and energy.

Bean Soup

All bean soups (see recipes, page 138) can be frozen and reheated beautifully. In the old days, they never served soup the day it was made. As a matter of fact, in winter it was often kept frozen in a large vat in the snow, and the amount needed was cut out and heated. Now we just put it in the freezer in well-labeled containers and heat the amount we need.

CANNING IN 10 EASY STEPS

A curious thing happens to me almost every time I open a jar of our own homegrown, home canned vegetables. At the same moment, I feel a sense of accomplishment, recall a pleasant instance from the past summer, and I look forward to the next one. It's just a fleeting emotion, but it's really a nice bonus. Reward enough really would be just the fine taste, beautiful color and excellent texture of the vegetables we put up ourselves.

If you've never canned before, I urge you to give it a try. Here are the ten easy steps I follow to can beans:

1. For safety and health, it is important to be careful canning, and the first requirement is to use a pressure canner with an accurate gauge for canning all vegetables.

For complete instructions and precautions for pressure canning, please carefully read and follow the instruction booklets that accompany your canner and your jars. There are also several books available that deal at greater length with pressure canning. One that's clear, complete and concise is *Keeping the Harvest* by Nancy Thurber and Gretchen Mead, and another 'bible' is the *Ball Blue Book,* which always has the most current U.S. Department of Agriculture information in its frequent updates.

2. Assemble all utensils: Pressure canner, Mason jars, lids, bands, tongs or jar lifter, timer, cooling racks, wide-mouth funnel, slotted spoon, wooden or plastic spatula or "bubbler," colander.

Use only Mason jars for home canning. These self-sealing, air-tight jars are safe for canning because the glass is heat-tempered, which is especially important for pressure canning. If you have saved other jars, such as mayonnaise jars, do not use them for canning vegetables; use them only for putting up jellies or jams with safe paraffin seals.

Do not re-use dome lids. The rubber compound loses its ability to seal perfectly after one use. Screw bands and jars may be re-used, but replace screw bands when they rust.

3. Examine and clean all equipment. Check all bands for rust, dents or nicks and jars for chips and cracks. Recycle them or use them elsewhere (your workshop, for instance) if they are not perfect.

Wash all equipment in hot, soapy water, but do not immerse top of pressure canner in water — just wipe it with a clean, damp cloth.

Keep clean jars and screw tops hot. Keep dome lids in hot water until ready to use.

4. Prepare freshest, cleanest produce possible. One bushel of fresh beans will result in 15 to 20 quarts of canned beans!

Prepare beans in the same manner as for freezing, but do not blanch.

5. Cold Pack or Hot Pack: Vegetables may be canned either cold pack (using raw vegetables) or hot pack (some degree of pre-cooking). Cold pack is less work, and better for delicate vegetables such as tomatoes. Hot pack is better for beans, because more beans fit into each jar. No matter which method you choose, the flavor is the same.

Cold Pack

Snap Beans: Put raw, prepared beans into hot jar, packing firmly. They will shrink during processing. Leave 1-inch headspace. (Correct headspace allows for proper venting and sealing of the jars.) Add boiling water to jar, making sure the liquid covers the food, retaining the 1-inch headspace. Salt, 1/2 tsp per pint, is optional. It is important to eliminate air bubbles from jar by running spatula or bubbler around inside of jar. Wipe jar top and threads clean with damp cloth. Put lid, rubber side down, on jar and screw band on firmly.

Green shell beans: Put raw, shelled beans in hot jar, without packing. They will expand during processing. Leave 1-inch headspace. Continue packing procedure as detailed in snap beans.

Green soybeans: Prepare the same as other shell beans.

Hot Pack

Snap beans: Put clean, trimmed beans in pot, covering them with boiling water. Boil 5 minutes. Pack hot beans in hot jars, and cover with cooking liquid, leaving 1-inch headspace. They will not shrink during processing. Continue procedure as detailed in cold pack snap beans.

Green shell beans: Wash and shell beans. Put shelled beans in pot with boiling water to cover. Boil 3 minutes. Put hot beans in hot jars, and cover with cooking liquid and continue packing procedure as detailed in cold pack snap beans.

Green soybeans: Prepare the same way as other green shell beans.

Dried shell beans: It's not too common to home can dried shell beans. But if you want some presoaked beans on hand for a quick chili, perhaps you should try canning some. Any variety of dried beans can be canned. After soaking them (see page 137), boil them for 30 minutes. Pack hot in hot jars, and continue packing procedure as outlined in cold pack snap beans.

6. Process in pressure canner. Pack only the number of jars your pressure canner can accommodate at one time. Put the canner on the burner, and put the jars on the rack in the canner. Add 2 inches of water to the canner, boiling for hot-packed jars, just hot for cold-packed jars. Allow enough space between the jars and the sides of the pot, so that steam can flow freely. Clamp the lid securely.

Leaving the valve or petcock open, set the canner over high heat until steam has escaped for 10 minutes. Now close the petcock or put on the weighted gauge, and let the pressure rise to 10 pounds. Start timing and keep adjusting the heat, so the pressure remains constant. If the pressure drops below 10 pounds, the processing time must be started again.

You may want to familiarize yourself with the canner by staging a dress rehearsal. Put a quart of water in the canner, and bring it up to 10 pounds of pressure. Notice how much heat is required to maintain constant pressure and how long — just with hot water — it takes to return to zero pressure. Let the canner cool naturally. Do not run it under cold water as you may with ordinary pressure cookers.

Processing time

Vegetable	Pint	Quart
Snap beans	20 minutes	25 minutes
Lima beans	40 minutes	50 minutes
Soybeans	55 minutes	65 minutes
Dried shell beans	75 minutes	90 minutes

If beans are large, process 10 minutes longer.

Your canner instructions may differ with the times given above. If so, follow your canner instructions.

Altitude affects pressure canners. You need to use more pressure and longer cooking time the higher you go.

Feet above sea level	Increase pressure	Increase cooking
1,000		2 minutes
2,000	to 11 pounds	4 minutes
3,000		6 minutes
4,000	to 12 pounds	8 minutes
5,000		10 minutes

If using a weight control canner, increase pressure to 15 pounds at elevations higher than 2,000 feet, and do not cold pack beans for pressure processing at altitudes above 6,000 feet.

Do not skimp on processing time. This is very important to ensure that all bacteria are killed. After the processing is complete, remove the canner from the heat and let it slowly return to zero pressure. Be patient! When the pressure has returned to zero, open the petcock or slowly remove the weight gauge, then remove the top, opening it so that it faces away from you.

7. Complete the processing. Using tongs or jar lifter, remove the jars and place them upright on a rack or thick towel in a draft-free area, allowing enough room between jars, so that air may circulate freely. Do not tighten the rims on the dome lids; you may break the seals.

8. After twelve hours of cooling, test the seals. There are three tests for checking the seal on a dome lid:

1. As the vacuum forms, the lid pulls down into the jar and makes a kerplunking sound.

2. The lid will be dished in the middle and should stay that way as long as the vacuum is present; you can feel it.

3. Push the center of the lid down with your thumb. If you get a clicking sound, the seal is not complete.

If you find some jars with incomplete seals, put the jars in the refrigerator, and use the food soon. The food is perfectly good to eat; it just won't last in storage.

9. Wipe the jars with a clean, damp cloth, label and store. You may remove the screw bands for re-use. Label the produce clearly, including the date. Store the vegetables in a cool, dark, dry area. It is important that the area be dry because moisture may affect the lids and seals on the jars. If your cellar is damp, keep the jars well off the floor. Or store them in an unused closet. (That's something hard to find these days!)

10. Before serving, reheat all canned beans by boiling them in an open kettle for 15 minutes — without tasting — to make sure any bacteria are killed. If the beans smell "off" or if the color or appearance doesn't look right, don't taste them. If in doubt, throw them out — carefully and without tasting.

Sprouting Beans

All bean seeds can be sprouted. In winter and early spring, when you are about to go batty from a lack of fresh, new greens, try sprouting some. They taste great in salads and sandwiches and are good in soups, too.

Sprouting is easy. All you need to start is 2 wide-mouth quart jars, 2 pieces of plastic or nylon screening, and screw bands, rubber bands or string to hold the screening in place over the mouths of the jars plus a few teaspoons of beans. I recommend starting out with mung beans. They're easy and tasty. And after that, try any beans you like.

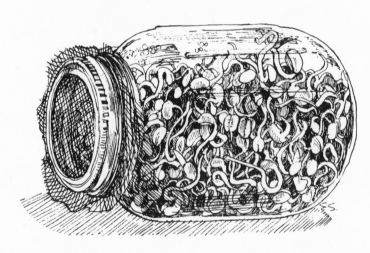

Wash beans in a colander and pick out any dirt, stones or broken seeds. Put the beans in one jar and add 2 cups of water. After an overnight soaking, the beans will have doubled in bulk. Secure the screening over the jar, and drain the water from the beans. Divide the beans between the two jars, and put screening over both jars. Rinse the beans in cool water and drain well. The beans should be just damp. As the beans do not need light to germinate, put the jars on their sides in the dark or away from direct light. Rinse with cool water 2 or 3 times a day, making sure you drain them well. On the second day the sprouts will start to appear, and you can start to eat them on the third or fourth day. If you do not use them all by the fourth day, refrigerate them in a closed container.

FAVORITE RECIPES

I enjoy cooking beans, and I know there are lots of wonderful ways to eat them. Three cookbooks I use as sources of ideas are *The Bean Book* by Crescent Dragonwagon, published by Workman Publishing, *The Complete Bean Cookbook* by Victor Bennett, Prentice Hall and a recent addition is *The Soybean Book* by Phyllis Hobson, Garden Way Publishing.

The recipes here are favorites of our family along with some ideas you may want to try. I am assuming you know cooking basics, but if I am wrong, I suggest referring to more complete cookbooks, too.

Boiled Snap Bean Accompaniments

In varying amounts and in various combinations, everything listed here goes very well with cooked snap beans. I've found it's fun experimenting with the amounts — I start out using a little bit and gradually become more adventurous.

Butter	Oregano	Minced green onions
Tarragon	Cream	Marjoram
Mint	Honey	Crisp bacon bits
Parsley	Chives	Sweet basil
Chervil	Dill	Slivered almonds
Sauteed shallots	Stuffing mix	Buttered bread crumbs
Croutons	Water chestnuts	Sauteed mushrooms
Sour cream	Cream sauce	Chicken stock
Savory	Cheese sauce	Lemon juice

Naturally Tender Beans

When you're cooking beans, you're cooking protein, so treat them tenderly. Avoid cooking in hard water or over too high heat.

And it's best not to add salt, fat or molasses to shell beans during the first half-hour of cooking. Why? Well, fat coats the outside of beans, preventing moisture from penetrating, and it's the water that makes them tender. Salt draws water out of the beans, rather than putting it in, and this lengthens the cooking time, toughening the beans. I'm not sure why you should hold back on the molasses until later in the cooking process, but my beans are tender, so it works.

Don't add baking soda to fresh or dried beans to make them tender. Baking soda just destroys many of the B vitamins that beans contain.

Green Bean Salad

4   cups cooked green beans (or combination
of green and wax)
1   medium onion, chopped
3   slices fried bacon, crumbled
3/4   cup Italian salad dressing

Combine first two ingredients. Pour salad dressing over them and chill well. Serve on bed of lettuce and sprinkle with bacon just before serving. Serves 6 to 8. For extra color garnish with 2 Tb of chopped pimiento.

Tuna & Green Bean Salad

2   cups fresh green beans, cut and cooked
6 1/2   oz can tuna, drained
1/3   cup celery, thinly sliced
3   Tb salad oil
2   tsp lemon juice
1   small onion, minced
      salt and pepper to taste
      lettuce leaves

Drain beans, mix with tuna and celery. Add remaining ingredients. Toss lightly. Chill 1 hour and mix again before serving on bed of lettuce. Serves 4.

Other additions to this salad: 3 or 4 quartered tomatoes, potato salad using oil and vinegar dressing, 1/2 cup pitted black olives, 2 or 3 hard-boiled eggs, 6 to 12 anchovy fillets and 2 to 3 tablespoonfuls of mixed green herbs. If all of these are used, it's a Salade Nicoise.

Vermont Three Bean Salad

A quick salad that I like to make a day ahead.

2   cups green beans, cooked and drained
2   cups wax beans, cooked and drained
2   cups Kidney beans, cooked and drained
1/2   cup green onions, chopped
1/4   cup chopped parsley
1   cup Italian salad dressing
1   Tb sugar
2   garlic cloves, crushed
      crisp lettuce

Combine beans, onions and parsley in large bowl. In a small bowl mix dressing, sugar and garlic together and pour over the beans. Combine well. Cover and refrigerate for at least 3 hours, so flavors can blend, stirring occasionally. Drain and serve on bed of lettuce. Serves 6 to 8.

Snap Bean and Salt Pork Supper

This is a surprisingly good and inexpensive main dish.

1/2   lb salt pork (or picnic ham, but we like salt
pork best)
4   cups snap beans
12   small, new potatoes (1 1/2″ diameter), unpeeled
3-4   cups milk
2   Tb butter
      salt and pepper to taste

Cook salt pork in boiling water, covered, for 1 1/2 hours. Add cut up snap beans, either yellow or green, and the new potatoes and cook until tender, approximately 1/2 hour. Drain and add butter and milk to cover. Season to taste and reheat.

Savory Beans, Squash and Tomatoes

A favorite family dish and a great filler for buffets.

2   Tb oil
1   large onion, sliced
1   garlic clove, minced
1/4 tsp each pepper, thyme, sage
1/4 cup chopped parsley
     salt to taste
2   cups green or yellow snap beans
2   cups zucchini or summer squash, diced
3   large tomatoes, chopped

In a skillet brown onion, garlic, parsley and seasonings in oil for about 3 minutes over moderate heat. Add beans and squash and simmer covered for about 20 minutes. Add tomatoes and heat through. Serve hot or cold; 4 to 6 servings.

Harvard Beans

2   cups yellow or green snap beans
1   cup water
3   Tb sugar
4   pimiento strips
3   tsp cornstarch
3   Tb vinegar

Cook beans in boiling water until tender and reserve liquid. Mix sugar and cornstarch and 3/4 cup of cooled cooking water together and stirring occasionally, heat until cornstarch becomes clear. Add vinegar. Combine beans and sauce. Keep warm for 20 minutes until flavors blend. Add a few strips of pimiento for color. Serve hot or cold. Serves 4.

Accompaniments for Fresh Lima Beans and Broad Beans

These are all good on their own with beans, and some are good in combination. Some work well cold; others are best hot. If you use cream and lemon juice together, they'll curdle.

Heavy cream	Cheese sauce	White wine & sliced onions
Sour cream	Tomatoes	Chilled in French dressing
Lemon juice	Sausage	Sauteed mushrooms
Chives	Ham chunks	Crisp bacon bits
Parsley	Garlic	Cinnamon
Dill	Mint	Hot pepper sauce

Dried Bean Equivalencies

White	1 lb	2 cups uncooked = 6	cups cooked
Kidney	1 lb	2 2/3 cups uncooked = 6 1/4	cups cooked
Lima	1 lb	3 cups uncooked = 7	cups cooked

The Little Known Bean Water Controversy

There is disagreement about whether or not you should use the water in which you soak dried beans. Some say there is a lot of valuable protein in the water and that it's important to use. Others say the bean gases are released into the water and you just end up eating the bean gases, so obviously, don't save the water. Until I became aware of this controversy, I usually threw out the water, but now I may use half of it, which I think is a reasonable compromise. I also hear that you should pour bean cooking water over plants and flowers in the garden rather than down the drain. Of course, make sure it's cooled.

Your own home-grown, dried beans need to be soaked before cooking. But not all store-bought beans need soaking; to find out which do, read the directions on the package.

There are quite a few methods to soak dried beans. I either just wash them and soak them overnight in 3 to 4 times as much water. Or using the same amount of water — but boiling hot — I just drop the beans in it. I don't leave the beans on the heat, but let the water cool off. This method reduces the soaking time to just 2 hours.

Boston Brown Bread

The best accompaniment to good baked beans.

1	cup rye flour
1	cup cornmeal
1	cup graham flour
1 1/2	tsp baking soda
1	tsp salt
3/4	cup molasses
2	cups buttermilk
1	cup chopped raisins
1	cup chopped nuts

Sift all dry ingredients together. Mix in molasses, buttermilk, raisins and nuts, but don't beat. Divide batter and place in 3 buttered 1-pound coffee cans, filling them about 3/4 full. Molds must be tightly covered, with buttered foil lids, tied and taped, so the bread won't force the cover off on rising. Place molds in pan filled with enough boiling water to reach half-way up the mold and steam for 3 hours, keeping water at the half-way mark.

Cold Baked Bean Sandwich

This is a French Canadian specialty, and a lot of Vermonters really love it. It tastes great if you're hungry from chopping wood or working outside on cold winter days.

Spread really cold baked beans on bread — if it's brown bread, so much the better. Some people like to add a little parsley or chopped celery and catsup or mustard. Others think a thick slice of onion is mandatory. The important thing is to have cold beans, so they don't ooze out the sides.

Best Bean Soups

Bean soups are inexpensive, filling, nutritious and taste good. They take time to cook, but the amount of time actually spent preparing them is minimal. Some bean soups, such as Lima Bean Chowder or Minestrone, can be meals in themselves. Protein can be added by grating cheese on top or serving an egg custard for dessert.

Bean soups can also be filling and delectable starters. Black bean soup with sherry and a slice of lemon floating on top looks good and tastes better.

Bean soups should not be hurried by using a pressure cooker. Because the beans expand so much in cooking, they may plug the pressure escape valve, and that could be very dangerous.

Vermont Baked Beans

Baked beans were a traditional Saturday night supper both at Dick's house and at mine when we were growing up, and they're still a favorite at our house.

2	cups or 1 lb dried beans (yellow eye, Navy, Great Northern, kidney)
1	medium onion, chopped
1/2-1	cup maple syrup or 3/4 cup brown sugar with 2 Tb dark molasses
2	Tb catsup (optional)
2	tsp dry mustard
1/2	tsp salt
1/2	lb salt pork, cubed
3-4	cups apple cider or water (only 1 cup liquid if using crock pot)

Soak beans if necessary. Then boil the beans for 20 minutes. Mix drained beans and all other ingredients together, except for the liquid, and put in bean pot. Add cider or water to just cover beans. Cover pot and bake at 350° for 7 to 8 hours. If beans look dry, stir them and add cider or water if necessary. Remove cover for last hour of baking.

If using crock pot, use only 1 cup of cider or water and cook on low for 10 to 12 hours or on high for 4 to 6 hours. Stir occasionally.

Black Bean Soup

2 cups dried black beans
1 qt water
  ham bone with meat, ham hock or smoked
  pork bones
2 medium onions, chopped
2 carrots, chopped
3 celery stalks, chopped
4-5 parsley sprigs, chopped
3 whole cloves
1/8 tsp allspice or mace
1/8 tsp thyme
2 bay leaves
1 tsp dry mustard
1 tsp Worcestershire sauce

To bind:

1 Tb butter
1 Tb flour
  small amount of cold water, stock or milk

Garnish to finish:

1/2 cup sherry
2 hard-cooked eggs or
1 lemon slice per bowl or
1 dollop of sour cream per bowl

Wash and soak beans. In large, heavy soup kettle combine all ingredients except binder and garnish. Bring to a boil and reduce heat, simmering gently for 2 to 3 hours until beans are tender. Remove ham and bone, cutting any meat into small pieces. Work soup through sieve or in electric blender or food processor. Blend butter and flour and small amount of liquid. Blend with 3 cups of smooth soup. Return all to pot and simmer for at least 5 minutes. Add diced ham and sherry and season to taste. If soup is too thick (it should look like heavy cream), stir in a little water. Serve with sliced, hard-cooked eggs or lemon slices or dollops of sour cream floating on top of each serving. Serves 6.

Senate Navy Bean Soup

This soup is on the menu of the U.S. Senate every day of the year because a senator on a hot summer's day in 1904 arrived in the dining room to find no bean soup on the menu. "From now on, hot or cold, rain, snow or shine, I want bean soup on the menu," he declared. He also had a resolution passed in committee to that effect, so now it's the law of the land!

2 lbs Michigan Navy beans
1 1/2 lbs smoked ham hocks
4 qts hot water
1 onion, chopped

Wash and soak beans. Boil beans slowly in water for approximately 3 hours, adding the ham hocks after the first half hour. Saute chopped onion in butter and when light brown, add to soup. Season with salt and pepper and serve.

A lot of things can be added to this basic soup to make it more interesting: chopped celery, 2 cloves garlic, 1/2 tsp marjoram, 1 cup tomato sauce, 1 cup minced parsley, 1 cup minced carrots, 2 large potatoes, 1 chopped turnip, 1 beet, 1 cup cream. These can be added, but remember, then it won't be authentic Senate Navy Bean Soup.

Minestrone

1/2 cup dried green beans
1/4 cup chick peas
1/2 cup brown lentils
1/2 lb pork rind
1 ham bone with meat
1/4 cup olive oil
1/4 cup finely chopped salt pork
1 clove garlic, chopped finely
3 sprigs parsley, chopped finely
2 carrots, diced
4 large, ripe tomatoes
1 bulb fennel, finely chopped (optional)
1 cup fresh lima beans
2 cups shelled green peas
4-5 fresh mint leaves
  pepper
1/2 lb fresh spinach, cut in ribbons
1/2 lb short, thick noodles (optional)
  grated Parmesan cheese

Wash and soak the dried beans and partially cook them. In another pan cook pork rind and ham bone in salt water until meat is tender. Drain the meat and cut into small pieces.

Heat the oil and fat salt pork in the pan in which the soup is to be made, and saute the garlic, parsley and carrots until the garlic is golden but not brown and the carrots have softened. Add the tomatoes, drained beans and remaining fresh vegetables, except for the spinach. Season and add 12 cups of water. Bring to a boil and simmer gently for about 1 hour. Add the spinach and the meat and cook until the spinach is just tender. Noodles may be added for a thicker soup, but do not overcook them. Serve hot or cold, sprinkled generously with grated Parmesan cheese.

Chili con Carne

Peter Halpin, the chef at Painter's Tavern in Vergennes, Vermont, a town 5 miles south from where we live, has a wonderful recipe for chili con carne. The vegetables in the chili retain their crispness. This makes it more interesting to eat than most chilis, which have rather predictable texture.

5	cloves garlic, finely chopped
1 1/4	lbs ground beef
1	green pepper, cubed
1	large Spanish onion, sliced
2	stalks celery, sliced
1	qt tomatoes, crushed with their juice
2	cups water
1	Tb thyme
2	Tbs oregano
2	Tbs basil
3	Tbs chili powder
2	Tbs cumin
3-4	drops Tabasco
3-4	drops Worcestershire sauce
	salt and pepper to taste
1	qt red kidney beans

Sauté garlic and add ground beef to brown. Add green pepper, onion and celery and saute until onion is translucent. Add remaining ingredients and simmer until vegetables are cooked, approximately one hour. May be cooked longer, but the texture changes, of course.

Hopping John

In the South, Hopping John is a traditional dish on New Year's Day. Without it, they say a year of bad luck follows.

1/2	lb slab bacon in one piece
2	cup blackeye peas
1	tsp salt
1	cup long grain or brown rice
1	onion, chopped
	hot pepper sauce to taste

Wash and soak blackeye peas. Cook bacon in 2 quarts of water for 1 hour. Add beans and continue cooking until beans are almost tender. Add rice and onion and boil, covered, over low heat 15 to 18 minutes, until rice is cooked. If you use brown rice, cook for 45 to 50 minutes. To serve, remove bacon and slice it. Serve with rice and beans. Hot pepper sauce is a good accompaniment. Serves 8.

Kidney Bean Relish

From the Waybury Inn in East Middlebury, Vermont, which is a lovely family-style restaurant not too far from home.

1	small onion
1-2	hard-boiled eggs
2	cups cooked kidney beans
1/4	tsp white pepper
3	stalks celery, chopped
1	Tb mayonnaise
2	tsp relish
1	tsp curry powder
1/2	tsp salt

Chop onion, celery and eggs together. Add beans and mix with mayonnaise, relish and other seasonings. Chill. Serve on crackers or in celery sticks.

Dilled Green Beans

This is an especially good pickled bean recipe because they really stay crisp. Makes about 8 pints.

4	lbs green beans
	mustard seed
	dill seed or 8 heads of dill
	garlic cloves, halved
	crushed red hot pepper
5	cups distilled vinegar
5	cups water
1/2	cup salt
	Mason jars and tops

Wash beans well and trim off ends. Cut beans to fit lengthwise into pint or half-pint Mason jars. Rinse jars in hot water and stack beans snugly in hot jars.

For each pint, add 1 tsp whole mustard seed, 1/2 tsp dill seed (or 1 head of dill), 1/2 clove of garlic, 1/4 tsp crushed red pepper. Halve the amount per jar if half-pints are used.

Combine vinegar, water and salt in saucepan and heat to boiling. Pour boiling solution over beans, filling to within 1/2 inch of top of jar. Adjust lids and place jars on rack in large kettle filled with boiling water, 1 or 2 inches above jar tops. Cover. When water returns to rolling boil, boil 10 minutes.

Remove jars from kettle. Set jars upright on rack away from draft to cool.

Store in cool place for 2 weeks to develop full flavor.

CHAPTER 6

Peas and Peanuts

Northerners and Southerners have different ideas about the meaning of the word "pea." To Southerners, peas are black-eyeds, crowders and creams; to Northerners, these same varieties are known as beans. The northern version of the "pea" is called the English pea, the green garden pea, or just plain peas, and if you ask home gardeners to name their favorite vegetable, a large percentage will tell you the English garden pea.

As far as I can discover, the garden pea originated in Western Asia and Eastern Europe. We know they existed as far back as the Stone Age because dried pea seeds were discovered among relics in lake villages of Switzerland. Apparently 1,000 years ago the pea, which was small and dark colored, was grown only for its dry seeds. At the turn of the millennium, people started eating them fresh, too.

The popularity of peas increased during the 18th century. The Anglo-Saxon word for peas was "pise," later to be called "pease," but nobody knew whether that was one pea or a whole lot. So, the word "peas" was coined. Because our green garden peas were derived from varieties that thrived in England, they are called "English peas."

When and Where to Plant Peas

While the snow is still falling in Vermont and the temperature is hovering below freezing, Jan and I spread out the seed catalogs and start planning our garden on paper.

By planning early, we can start planting as soon as the ground is ready to be worked.

When you're deciding where to plant which vegetable, there are a couple of reasons why it's a good idea to locate your peas in a section that receives full sun:

1. Sunny spots will be the first places to thaw in the spring, and you want to get your peas into the ground as early as possible.

2. If peas are planted in the shade, they'll grow. However, the sugar content will be low, and they'll taste like peas that have been sitting around the store for a few weeks.

Even though peas need full sun, be careful not to plant the tall varieties where they'll shade other plants.

No matter what size your garden, you'll have the best results if you plant peas in wide rows — at least 16 inches wide — with walkways at least the same width (see page 147). Not only will you harvest more, but it will take you less time and less work. There is no need, generally, to have trellises or fences for support if you plant in wide rows because the vines will support each other. Also, wide-row vines form a living mulch canopy which helps to eliminate weeds. Wide rows also keep the soil cool and moist.

Peas are a cool weather crop that can withstand frost. I usually plant my first crop around the end of March, as soon as the garden has thawed and the soil can be worked. There are some varieties that are happier being planted when it's warmer and harvested during midsummer. Seed catalogs and individual seed

English Peas

No matter where you live, English peas should be planted as soon as the garden can be worked. In the North that means early spring because they can survive late frosts.

The two basic types of English peas are dwarf, which grow to a height of about 16 inches, and telephone or tall varieties, which will grow to more than three feet. While both dwarf and telephone peas can be grown without a trellis if you plant in wide rows, the taller varieties need a fence or some type of support if grown in single or double rows.

If you are wondering how much to buy when selecting varieties, it helps to know that one-quarter pound of seed will usually produce enough peas for one person to eat fresh. Multiply this figure by the number of people eating, and you'll know about how much to plant. If you plan to preserve some for winter use, double the amount.

Edible-Podded Peas

Snow or sugar peas are usually harvested when they are young and crisp before their pods have filled out. These peas are eaten pods and all. However, if the pods develop too fast, the peas can be shelled, cooked and eaten as English peas. Most varieties will begin producing 63 to 72 days from planting. Their need for support depends on whether or not they're grown in wide rows and how tall they grow.

Sugar Snap peas are sweet-flavored, edible-podded peas which are delicious raw or cooked. They have the tenderness and fleshy pod qualities of young beans with the flavor of peas. The wilt-resistant vines, which grow to a height of at least four to six feet, need some type of support. The delicious, medium-green pods grow to a length of two and one-half to three inches.

Seeds should be planted early and may be sown again for a fall crop.

packets will often indicate the preferred time for planting different varieties.

In the far north, garden peas can be harvested almost all summer if you use a little ingenuity. Plant peas every three to four weeks for a continual summer harvest. Once you've harvested your first crop of peas, pull out and compost the vines or till them in and replant a second crop of peas in the same space. Or you can plant another short-season vegetable.

In the west, peas can be harvested year-round, and in the south they are best if grown in the fall, winter and very early spring before the weather gets too hot. However, using the wide-row method, I have grown English peas successfully in Florida *almost* in midsummer.

Choosing Varieties

Peas are fun and easy to raise because they take very little work and they mature rapidly. It's possible to grow them in any part of the country, even though English and edible-podded peas prefer cool, moist weather.

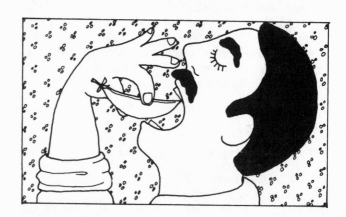

Varieties

ENGLISH PEAS

Variety	Days to Harvest	Comments
Alaska	52–55	Earliest of all. Hardy, smooth seeded. Low sugar content. May be used as dried split peas. 2½-inch pods. 30 to 36 inches tall.
Alderman	70–74	High quality. Very productive. 4½ to 5 inch pods. 54 inches to 72 inches tall.
Burpee's Blue Bantam	64	Heavy yield. Medium early. Long bearing season. 4-inch pods. 15 inches to 18 inches tall.
Burpeeana Early	63	Heavy yield. Early. 3-inch pods. 18 inches to 24 inches tall.
Early Frosty	64	Wilt resistant vines. 3 to 3½-inch pods. 24 to 28 inches tall.
Fordhook Wonder	79	Late season. 5 to 5½-inch pods. 28 inches tall.
Freezonian	63	Exceptionally fine quality. 3½-inch pods. 30 inches tall.
Frost Bite	62	Frost and wilt resistant. 26 to 30 inches tall.
Green Arrow	68–70	Disease resistant. High yield. 4 to 4½-inch pods. 24 to 28 inches tall.
Lincoln	67	Extra sweet. 3-inch pods. 30 inches tall.
Little Marvel	63	Early. Heavy yield of high quality. 3-inch pods. 18 to 20 inches tall.
Maestro	61	Nearly immune to powdery mildew. Disease resistant. Healthy and prolific. 4½-inch pods. 24 to 26 inches tall.
Midseason Freezer	63	Recommended for freezing.
Mighty Midget	60	Early type. Requires little space. 3½-inch pods. 6 inches tall.
Perfection	65	Heat and drought resistant. 4½-inch pods. 24 inches tall.
Progress #9	60–65	Early. Resistant to Fusarium wilt. 4½-inch pods. 20 inches tall.
Thomas Laxton	60–65	Early. Heavy cropper. 3½-inch pods. 30 to 36 inches tall.
Victory Freezer	65	Wilt resistant. High yield. 3½-inch pods.
Wando	66–68	Warm weather variety. Very productive. Tolerant to heat and cold. 3-inch pods. 28 to 30 inches tall.

EDIBLE PODDED PEAS

Variety	Days to Harvest	Comments
Dwarf Gray Sugar	57–65	Prolific. Later variety than Dwarf White. 2½ to 3-inch pods. Two to two and one-half feet tall.
Dwarf White Sugar	50–65	Wilt resistant. Very early. 3-inch pods.
Mammoth Melting Sugar	68–75	Wilt resistant. 4-inch pods. Four to five-foot vines.
Oregon Sugar	58–68	Prolific. Hardy. 5-inch pods. One and one-half to two and one-half feet tall.
Snowbird	58	Very early. Ideal for short season or limited space. 3-inch pods. 16 to 18 inches tall.
Sugar Snap	70–100	Frost and heat tolerant. Wilt resistant. High yield. 2½-inch pods. Four to six-foot tall vines.

SOUTHERN PEAS

Variety	Days to Harvest	Comments
Big Boy	75	Excellent flavor. Heavy yielding.
Brown Crowder	60–80	Brown seeded, all-purpose. 7 to 8-inch pods. Mild flavored. 14-inch pods.
Calico Crowder	65	Mild flavored. 14-inch pods.
California Blackeye	75	Disease resistant. Heavy yielding. 7 to 8-inch pod.
California No. 5 Blackeye	60–75	Disease resistant. Abundant crop. Resistant to wilt, nematodes and other diseases.
Colossus Crowder	58	Extra large peas. 7 to 9-inch pods.
Dixielee	60	Yields two crops per season. 8-inch pods are light yellow with brown peas.
Lady	70	Prolific. Small and tender.
Magnolia Blackeye	65	Small sized. Good for canning and freezing.
Mississippi Silver (cowpea)	64–80	High yield. Easy to harvest. All purpose.
Pink Eye Purple Hull	50–85	Excellent for freezing. Pods are deep purple with creamy white seeds and pink eyes.
Texas Cream 40	75	Cross between extra early and mid-season. Long, cream-colored pods.
Queen Anne	68	Early variety. 7 to 8-inch pods.
White Acre	65	Prolific. Large plants.
White Purple Hull Crowder	60–85	High yielding. Disease resistant.

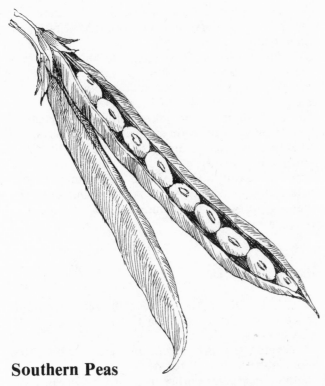

Southern Peas

Confusing as it may sound, Southern peas are not really peas but beans, and I can't tell you why they're called peas.

Black-eyeds, crowders and creams are the best known types of Southern peas, which are also known as shell beans to Northerners. They can be grown successfully in the North as well as in the South. Unlike green peas, Southern peas need warm soil to germinate. The cool, damp weather that English peas love is exactly what Southern peas don't like. Because they are drought resistant, excess moisture may cause a reduced yield. I plant and grow Southern peas in wide rows the same way I do English peas.

Soil

If this is your first gardening venture, you may be curious about what kind of soil you have in your garden: sand, clay, loam or combination of these soils.

Your local Cooperative Extension Service Agent will be able to tell you where to send a soil sample for various tests, including type of soil and its organic content. The service will also provide you with suggestions for improving your soil.

If your soil is less than perfect — and most are — you'll want to start building it up. The healthier the soil, the healthier your vegetables.

The best method for improving any type of garden soil is to incorporate organic matter into it: old leaves, hay, grass clippings, compost, organic kitchen garbage or even harvested pea and peanut vines. You'll find that organic matter will serve like a glue, holding particles together, when added to sandy soils. On the other hand, it will wedge in between particles, loosening or lightening clay soil, allowing water and air to reach plant roots. There is no special season for working organic matter into your garden; do it anytime except when crops are growing.

Green Manures

You may have heard gardeners discussing "green manures." They're talking about certain crops that are grown and plowed or spaded back into the soil to increase the organic content and improve the texture of the soil.

Peas, peanuts and other legumes are especially beneficial when used as green manures. After you've harvested your pea and peanut crops, till the plants back into the soil. Not only do the vines of these delicious legumes add organic matter to your soil, but symbiotic bacteria living on the roots have the ability to capture large amounts of nitrogen from the soil air and fix it into the root nodules. This nitrogen goes back into the soil when the green manure is tilled in, making it available for future crops.

One way to start a soil improvement program, is to plant an early variety of English peas (**Alaska, Laxton, Little Marvel**) as soon as the ground can be worked in the spring. Once the peas have been harvested, turn the vines into the soil. A few days later, plant another vegetable crop. Because it will still be early in the season you will be able to expect a full crop if you plant a summer crop, such as tomatoes, peppers, or corn, in the same place.

GETTING STARTED

Soil preparation is one of the most important steps in growing a good crop of peas or peanuts (or any vegetable for that matter). The reason it is so important is your vegetables will be only as good as the earth in which they're grown.

As soon as the ground can be worked in the spring, till or spade your garden (with a shovel, heavy spading fork or rotary tiller) to a depth of eight to ten inches. If the soil is soggy from melting snow or spring rains, wait until it's dry enough to work. To test it, step on the soil, and if your foot print is *not* shiny, the earth is dry enough to work. If it is shiny, wait a few more days. When you've thoroughly worked the soil, it should be loose, friable and free of clumps.

If you're breaking lawn or areas that have been

in sod, make sure that the clumps of grass are turned over so that the grass is facing down into the garden soil. This will help prevent the unwanted grass from making a reappearance in the garden.

Seeds need oxygen and loose soil to germinate properly, so I work my garden soil at least two or three times before planting. I've always found that the looser the soil, the easier it is for plant roots to stretch out to take in the necessary food, water and oxygen.

In addition to creating a well-prepared seedbed, the more you work the soil, the less weeding you'll have to do later on. Each time you cultivate, tiny weed seeds are brought to the surface where they die. Others are buried too deeply to germinate. Either way it's less weeding later on.

Once your seeds are planted there is little you can do about improving the soil's texture and organic content, so it is essential that you spend time before sowing seeds.

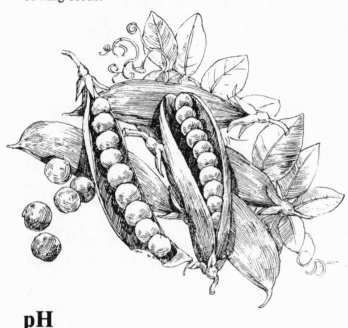

pH

To test your garden's pH, which is simply the degree of acidity or alkalinity of your soil, buy a test kit at a local garden store or contact your local County Extension Service. The test will indicate the present pH and give recommendations for the addition of lime or sulfur to bring the soil into proper growing range. Lime sweetens the soil, and sulfur makes it more acid.

Peas prefer a soil that has pH range of about 5.8 to 7.0. On a pH scale of 0 to 14, 7.0 is neutral, with 5.8 tending to the acid side.

It's a good idea to have your soil tested every few years to make sure that the pH level remains balanced. This ensures that fertilizers will be more efficient and symbiotic nitrogen-fixing bacteria will be able to thrive.

When growing peas, pay particular attention to your soil's pH. Very acid soils will inhibit nitrogen-fixing bacteria on pea roots.

The easiest way to sweeten the soil is to spread one 12-quart bucket of lime over every 1,000 square feet of garden space (four to five pounds per 100 square feet). Lime should be applied to soil about once every three or four years if it needs sweetening.

If you've been searching for a place to use wood ashes accumulated from your stove or fireplace, here's your answer. Wood ashes may be substituted for lime and can be worked into the top three to four inches of soil to sweeten it. Apply about the same quantity (forty to fifty pounds per 1,000 square feet) as you would lime.

Raised Beds

"Raised bed" is simply a term used when soil is raised so that the seedbed is higher than the soil in the adjacent walkways.

There are many reasons why growing on raised beds can be beneficial for peas:

You can plant earlier in the spring because the soil on a raised bed warms up and dries out faster than it does in the rest of the garden.

You'll have better drainage because rain water runs off into the walkways, eliminating the problem of water standing too close to the plants' roots. The better garden drainage, the fewer diseases plants will have.

You can irrigate more easily. Simply run water from a hose between the beds and allow the water to seep into the root zone. Raised beds are an especially good idea if you live in a dry area or if you have a dry spell.

You'll find that preparing raised beds will be well worth the extra time and effort. Here's all you have to do.

1. Decide on the width and length of your raised beds as well as the space in between. This will depend on whether you're planting single rows or wide rows.

2. Spade or till your soil to a depth of six to eight inches.

3. Measure your rows and walkways. Stake out the dimensions of your raised beds with sticks and strings. One to two feet wide is fine, and the length can be as long as you want. Allow at least 18 inches between the edge of one raised bed and the edge of the next. I like rake-width raised beds myself. Therefore, the center of one raised bed is almost three feet from the next if I have an 18-inch walkway.

4. Use a hoe to pull the loosely tilled soil from the walkways up onto the bed until it's four to eight inches higher than the walkway. By drawing only two inches of soil from the walk, you will have a four-inch raised bed.

5. Rake the top of the bed smooth, leveling the surface as you go. Now you're ready to plant.

Fertilize, plant and harvest the same on raised beds as you do on level ground. However, as long as you are going to make raised beds, it only makes sense to make the best of the space. For my money that means growing in wide rows — or double rows at the very least! Otherwise, you waste too much valuable growing space. So plan to make your raised beds rake width for wide-row planting.

Fertilizer

Because peas are good foragers, they don't need much fertilizer — especially nitrogen. A day or two before planting, I broadcast three to four pounds of 5-10-10 commercial fertilizer over each 100 square feet of garden space. Then I work it into the top two to three inches of soil.

You may prefer to use organic fertilizers, such as well-rotted manure, bone meal or dehydrated manures. If you use manure, be sure it is very well aged or dehydrated. Animals' digestive tracts do not destroy weed seeds, and if you put fresh manure on your garden, most likely you'll also be planting weed seeds.

The primary ingredients of synthetic fertilizer are three nutrients that are vital to all plants: nitrogen (N), phosphorus (P), and potassium (K). If you have a 100-pound bag of 5-10-10 fertilizer, it contains 5 percent nitrogen, 10 percent phosphorus and 10 percent potassium. (The order is constant.) The remaining 75 pounds is sand or other filler plus some trace minerals.

Each of the three major nutrients contained in fertilizer has a unique job to accomplish while your plants are growing.

Nitrogen helps plants have healthy green, lush foliage. However, too much nitrogen can "burn" seeds or plants if it comes in direct contact with them, and it can also generate too much vine growth rather than pods with peas inside.

Phosphorus is necessary for the development of strong, healthy roots.

Potassium, or potash, helps the plant to grow, bear fruit and resist diseases.

It is important to mix chemical fertilizers thoroughly into the soil before you start planting.

Inoculating Seeds

Nitrogen is one of the three most important nutrients in plant growth, and it is necessary to get as much of it into the soil as possible. One way to do this is to grow peas, peanuts and other legumes because of the unique ability of the symbiotic bacteria that live in the nodules of these plants' roots. They can draw elemental nitrogen from soil air and "fix" it into usable form.

To make sure your plants "fix" the most nitrogen possible, inoculate the seeds with a nitrogen-fixing bacteria just before you plant. Inoculating seeds has proven to increase the number of nitrogen nodules and has a positive effect on yield as well. Inoculant, usually in the form of a wettable powder, comes in small packages and can be purchased in seed stores and through seed catalogs.

It's easy to inoculate seeds. Simply place the seeds in a pan, add enough water to moisten them, and add a small amount of inoculant to the water. Stir the seeds with a stick until they have a little powder on their seedcoats and then plant them immediately.

PLANTING

Wide Rows — A Winner

Although peas can be grown successfully in single rows, years of gardening have taught me that I'll have a more abundant harvest with much less work if I grow peas in wide rows. With wide-row growing, less time is spent weeding, watering and harvesting, and more time is spent shelling, because the harvest is larger.

It's easiest to make your wide rows the same width as your rake, which is normally 14 to 16 inches. To mark off a wide row, put a stake at both ends of the row. Stretch a string close to the ground between the two stakes. Hold one edge of an iron rake next to the string, and drag the rake down the length of the row. This will level and smooth the seedbed at the same time it marks off the width of the row.

Remove large stones and any debris from the seedbed and really smooth the soil before you plant. Once you've smoothed the seedbed, don't walk on it because you'll only pack it down. You want the soil loose for your seeds.

Broadcast pea seeds over the entire raked area about one and one-half to two inches apart.

Using the back of a hoe, gently tamp down the seeds, so that they are pressed into the soil.

Pull enough soil from outside the row with a rake to cover the seeds. The amount of soil covering each seed should equal four times the diameter of the seed or about to one and one-half inches for peas. Gently level off the row.

Finally, the soil should be firmed down again, so that there is good contact with the seeds.

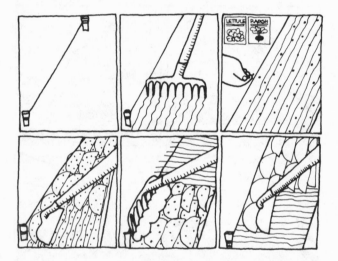

It's a good idea to gently water the rows *after* planting, especially if the soil is dry. If you water before planting, you'll pack down the soil, which you don't want to do.

I always leave at least 16-inch walkways between rows. This allows enough room for the plants to spread out, and it is also wide enough to walk through, to cultivate and harvest easily.

Single Rows

The simplest way to make a single row is to put a stake in the ground at each end of the row and stretch a string tightly between them. Draw a shallow furrow with a hoe beside the string in the well-spaded seedbed.

Plant seeds one to two inches apart in rows at least 16 inches apart. After planting the row, cover the seeds with soil using a hoe so that the seeds are planted one to one and one-half inches deep. Then

gently firm the soil with the back of the hoe and water well.

Double Rows

Although they're similar to single rows, double rows use the space more productively. Make two shallow furrows four to five inches apart. Drop the seeds into the furrows, one to two inches apart and one and one-half inches deep. Continue planting as you would for single rows.

The double-row method is especially helpful for trellising tall pea varieties. Simply place the vine supports between the double rows.

If you have irrigation problems, place a soaker hose (a garden hose made of porous material that allows the water to seep out slowly) between the two rows for efficient watering.

Another way to irrigate double rows is to dig a shallow furrow between the two seed rows. To water the peas, simply run water down the middle furrow.

CARE FOR PEAS

Support for Climbers

Alderman and *Sugar Snap* peas are two examples of climbing pea varieties. Because both of these varieties grow about six feet tall, they usually need some type of support, like a fence, trellis or brush.

In single rows, the support should be placed about three inches behind the row. For double rows, the support should be placed in between, so that the peas can grow up either side of the support. Or to maximize space, you can plant a double row on each side of the trellis.

Supports are not difficult to make. A simple one uses four to five-foot stakes placed five feet apart down the row. Three wires are run horizontally between the stakes, one foot apart. If you prefer,

chicken wire with a two-inch mesh can be used instead of the separate wires.

Unlike other climbing vegetables, peas naturally grasp the support with their tendrils, and they do it without any help from the gardener.

Watering

Because watering is so important, the following fundamentals should be helpful in producing a more abundant pea crop.

Water after planting your seeds, if the soil is dry. If you water before planting, the soil will pack down too much.

An inch of water a week is the rule to ensure good growth, no matter whether vegetables are grown in single rows or wide rows. The amount of rain that falls during the week affects how much you should water your garden.

To determine how much time it will take to water a certain section of your garden with a sprinkler, use a rain gauge or put a straight-sided can in the garden near a plant. Turn on the sprinkler and check the time. When an inch of water has fallen into the can, check the time again. Now you know how long it takes to supply one inch of water to your garden.

To determine the amount of rainfall, place a can or rain gauge in your garden and check it after every rain. Add up the amount to see if it totals an inch each week. If not, you will need to water.

Water early in the day. This gives the plants plenty of time to dry before night falls and discourages the spread of disease organisms.

Avoid frequent, light waterings. When you water, soak the soil to a depth of three to six inches. By watering deeply, your plants will survive hot, dry weather, How do you know how deeply the water has gone? Dig down and feel.

Soil type affects the amount of water needed for good growth. Sandy soils, in general, drain much faster than heavy, clay soils.

Don't water for the sake of watering. Just because your plants look wilted on a hot afternoon, doesn't mean they need watering; they'll probably perk up overnight. You may find the top of the soil is bone dry but moist as you dig deeper. However, if plants look wilted in the early morning, they probably do need to be watered. The best way to check your soil's moisture is by digging down into the soil three to four inches. If the soil feels dry at that depth, water.

Don't overwater. The soil can hold only so much water, so don't waste precious water and smother the plants' roots. However, if you've been without rain for a while, it's a good idea to water.

Watering wide rows. When many of our neighbors complain about watering every day during dry spells, my wide rows are usually doing very well without watering. I've discovered that because wide rows form a mulch canopy, the moisture is held in the

ground. However, I still check to make sure the soil has enough moisture, especially during hot spells.

Weeding

Once your seedlings start to emerge, weeds will also begin to appear. Weeding is the scourge of gardening to most people, but it doesn't have to be. Honestly! If you stay ahead of it, which is easy with wide rows, you won't have to think of bribing the neighborhood kids to do it for you.

With wide-row growing, you usually drag an iron rake across the row as soon as the seedlings emerge in order to thin the row and get rid of early-germinating weeds. *Do not do this with peas or beans.* The plants are tender, and they may break. The plants will grow quickly and form a canopy, soon shading weed seedlings from the sun, which will inhibit their growth.

Mulch

When your single and double row plants are a few inches tall, one way to put an end to weeding is by putting mulch in the walkways. A three to six-inch layer of mulch completely shades the ground, preventing weed growth.

Mulch also conserves moisture and helps to keep the ground at a constant cool temperature. Mulch is almost a necessity if your soil is sandy, warm and too dry.

I prefer organic mulches such as bark, hay, lawn clippings, leaves, pine needles and straw. Although black plastic is effective, I don't use it, mainly

because it's hard to lay and can't be turned back into the soil.

To keep moisture in the soil and weeds out, mulch should be applied soon after you cultivate following a soaking rain. Be sure not to add trouble where there wasn't any before. Use only mulch that is free of weed seeds. This sounds obvious, but I know a few gardeners who are still fighting weeds they got from mulch that had weed seeds in it.

Tackling Trouble

The best way to deal with problems is to avoid them in the first place. Here are my suggestions about how to prevent disease and insect problems in your garden before they even begin.

Select disease-resistant seed varieties.

Well-drained soil is important in eliminating diseases. If soil tends to be wet, raised beds are the best idea.

Plant in wide rows and use mulch in walkways to prevent raindrops from splashing soil-borne disease spores up onto the plants.

Stay out of the garden when plants are wet. The less plants are disturbed when they're wet, the better. It's too easy to spread water-borne bacteria and fungi if you're in the garden shortly after a rainfall or shortly after you've watered.

Keep the garden area weeded and clean of debris.

Rotate your pea crop each year to avoid soil-borne diseases. A good rule of thumb is to avoid planting legume crops in the same area three years in a row.

Pull out and burn disease-ridden plants.

Pesky Pea Problems

If you practice good garden hygiene, you won't have to worry about insects or diseases harming your pea crop. But if something does crop up, it's important to know what you're dealing with. Northerners will find that aphids and pea weevils are the most prevalent insects, while Southerners most often have to contend with the cowpea curculio. Blight, fusarium wilt, mosaic and root rot are the most common diseases of peas.

My best advice is to keep a careful watch over your garden, and if problems arise, contact your Cooperative Extension Service. They can advise you about how to deal with specific garden problems that you may have.

Here is a guide to the most common pea crop pests and diseases. This is not to say that these insects and diseases will all suddenly appear in your garden. It is simply to help you decide what could be bothering your crop.

Pea Aphids are pear-shaped, long-legged, soft,

green insects only one-sixteenth to one-eighth inch long. By sucking juices from the leaves and stems, they may cause the withering of plants and stunting of crops thus reducing yields.

Control aphids by gently rubbing them off leaves or spray with a mild solution of soapy water. Ladybugs and aphid lions, which may be in your garden, are natural enemies of aphids. Pea aphids can also be controlled with the commercially available spray malathion.

Cowpea Curculio, a very destructive pest found in the South, eats holes in peas and pods. To control, spray or dust with carbaryl (Sevin) or rotenone regularly.

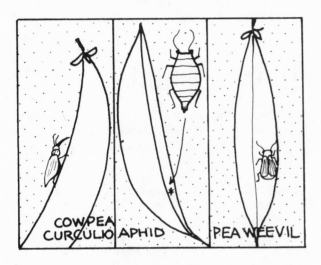

COWPEA CURCULIO | APHID | PEA WEEVIL

Bacterial Blight, a bacterial disease carried on infected seeds. Large, water-soaked spots appear on pea pods, irregular dark spots appear on leaves, and cream-colored, shining ooze will show up in the center of these spots. To avoid blight, plant certified disease-free seed on well-drained soil. Make sure that old pea vines are removed and rotate crops.

Fusarium Wilt can be a deadly disease for peas. The leaves turn yellow, and the plant is stunted and it eventually wilts. Fusarium wilt symptoms are similar to root rot. The main difference: the base of the stem of the plant affected with wilt is not withered and the inside of the stem shows discoloration. This fungus lives in the soil and enters the plant through the roots. Check seed catalog or seed packet to see if the seeds are resistant to the disease. If seeds are resistant, the seed packet should be marked with an "F." For other control measures see root rot.

Mosaic is a virus disease spread by aphids and carried within infected seeds. The plants usually become stunted, leaves turn light colored and mottled, and pods are few and poor in quality. To reduce infection, remove pea plants that show leaf mottle and control aphids.

Powdery Mildew is a fungus disease that is most troublesome in warm weather. A white or grayish powdery mold apears on the pods, leaves and stems. To combat this problem, turn under or compost the pea vines as soon as the harvest is over.

Root Rot is caused by fungi that live in the soil, and they often kill plants at flowering time. Plants turn pale yellow, and they may also be stunted. The stems wither near the ground, and the plants often die back or collapse. To avoid root rot, plant peas in well-drained soil. Remove and destroy affected plants. Rotate crops.

Damping-Off Fungi, which cause seed decay are prevalent during cool, moist weather. To avoid this problem, plant only after the soil is dry enough to work easily.

Precautionary Note

If you feel you must use commercially available sprays or dusts, *always* purchase the least toxic preparation that will do the job effectively. Use them only according to directions.

When using a commercial spray or powder, make certain to *read the instructions three times: before buying* to make sure you are buying the right substance; *before using* to make sure you are using it correctly; and again *before storing* to make sure you are putting it away properly.

It is often best to contact your local County Extension Service for advice when a problem arises. Not only can they help you to identify the unwanted pests in your garden, but they will suggest the best remedy.

HARVESTING PEAS

One of the marvelous things about growing your own vegetables is that *you* decide when it's time to harvest. You can pick your vegetables just before preparing them, knowing that you have the freshest in town. Better still, you can have the youngest vegetables. Most commercial gardeners don't pick the youngest vegetables because they know if they wait a few days they can get more money because the crops weigh more. But, generally, the younger the harvest, the more tender and flavorful it is.

English Peas

There's nothing more delicious than the first tender peas, picked right off the vine, shelled and eaten raw. Not only are they sweet and tasty, but they also contain an abundance of vitamins A, B and C.

English peas are very sweet because of their high

sugar content. However, a few hours after picking, the sugar starts turning to starch. That's why it's important to rush the peas into the kitchen right after picking, so you can shell and cook them immediately.

In general, you can begin harvesting English peas between 55 and 80 days after planting depending on the variety. When ready to harvest, the pea pods will be nearly round in shape and the peas will taste sweet. You should have several pickings over a period of seven to ten days.

Always use two hands to pick peas, so that you won't damage the brittle vines or uproot the plants. Hold onto the pea vine with one hand, and pick off the pods with the other. When harvesting, I take a short stool into the garden, relax, and fill several large baskets.

Make certain to pick any pods that are overly mature. If allowed to remain on the vines, your total yield will be decreased.

Once the peas have been harvested, till or spade the whole plant back into the ground. By doing this, the nitrogen in the root nodules will be contributed to the earth. Or pull out the plants and put them in your compost pile.

If your peas were planted early in the spring, you will have time to plant another vegetable in that same location. Broccoli, cabbage, cauliflower, lettuce, root crops and spinach do well in soil where nitrogen-fixing legumes have grown.

Edible-Podded Peas

Snow peas are harvested in the same manner as English peas, only you pick them *before* the peas have filled out in the pods. These pods will be bright green, tender and flat. Sugar Snap peas, on the other hand, should fill out completely, so they're nice and plump. Then remove their strings and blossom ends, and they're ready to steam, boil, stir fry or freeze.

Southern Peas

Southern peas may be harvested at three different stages. They may be picked when the pods are still green, and the peas can be shelled, boiled and served in the same manner as English peas. However, they will not have the sugar content of English peas; rather, they'll have a high level of starch.

They may also be harvested and used in the same way when the peas have matured and the pods have changed color. By this stage, the peas will have started to dry, and their starch content will be even higher.

In either of these two early stages, the harvested and shelled peas may be frozen or canned using the same method as for English peas.

Southern peas may also be left on the vine to ful-

ly mature and dry. If your growing season ends before the peas are thoroughly dry, either pull the vines and hang them to dry in a well-ventilated area, or shell the peas and dry them in the sun or in a dehydrator.

Dried Split Peas

A variety of English peas known as *Alaska* can be grown and dried to produce split peas. This variety has a low sugar content, and it is hardy with a smooth seed.

Although most of these are dried commercially, they can be dried by the home gardener, using the methods explained on page 158. This is the variety of pea that is used for split pea soup.

About Peanuts

It may come as a surprise to some of you, but the peanut is a *vegetable* and not a nut. It doesn't grow on trees. It is not even harvested above the gound. Instead, the peanut pegs (where the nuts form on the peanut plant) bury themselves into the ground and are harvested by digging up the plant. A member of the legume family, gardeners reap this energy-packed vegetable as far north as Ontario, Canada.

Because peanut-shaped pottery jars were uncovered in the Inca tombs of Peru, it is believed that peanuts originated in Brazil or Peru as early as 950 B.C. Similar artifacts found in Bolivia and Argentina indicate that peanuts were treasured there also.

When the Spanish Conquistadors traveled to South America in search of gold, they returned to their native land bearing peanuts as their prize, which became one of Spain's prime crops.

The Spaniards traded peanuts to Africans for elephant tusks and spices. The Africans called this strange looking food "goobers" and believed that the peanut plant possessed a soul.

Peanuts, also known as earth nuts, earth almonds, ground nuts, pendars, monkey nuts or manilla nuts, first came to North America during the 18th century. Slave traders bought them from Africans as the cheapest, easiest, on-board food for slaves.

Until the late 1800's, peanuts were grown in this country principally for fattening farm animals. Since that time, the peanut has grown both in popularity and profitability. Through extensive research, Dr. George Washington Carver found peanuts to be an abundant source of fats, proteins and other nutrients. His pioneering creativity led to the development of over 300 uses for the peanut. These include axle grease, linoleum, wood stains, shaving cream, paper, ink, adhesives, plastics, fertilizer and wallboard. All

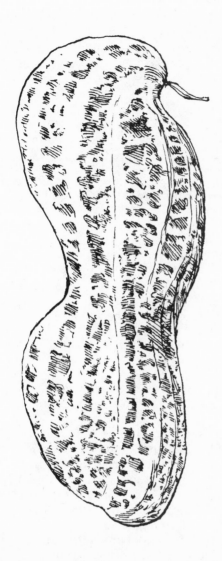

tion in the United States is concentrated in Texas, Oklahoma, Virginia, North Carolina, Georgia, Alabama and Florida. However, this does not mean that peanuts cannot be grown successfully in your home garden, no matter where you live.

How Peanuts Grow

No other vegetable grows like a peanut grows.

The peanut seed germinates about two days after planting, when the soil temperature is between 65 and 75 degrees. A few days later, roots begin to appear and approximately eight days after planting, you'll see shoots appearing on the soil's surface.

Within 14 days of planting, small leaves unfold with each leaf consisting of a slender stem and four leaflets. From these four leaflets new shoots begin to emerge.

The lateral branches that begin developing are the origin of the flowering branches. Extreme care must be taken not to injure or bury these branches when cultivating

Attractive yellow flowers appear approximately six weeks after planting, and the peanut plant starts to resemble a yellow-flowering, sweet pea bush. As each small flower withers, stalk-like structures called "pegs" develop on the base of the flowers. These pegs, pulled by gravity, curve downward and penetrate the soil to a depth of one to three inches. As the pods begin to form, they shift to a horizontal position. The pods grow and form the tan fruit that we know as unshelled peanuts.

The plants signal that the pods are maturing by starting to turn yellow. The color change is due to the food supply being consumed by the peanut kernels instead of by the plant. The plants continue to grow and flower for several weeks until they reach about one to one and one-half feet tall, and each produces

parts of the peanut — the shell, nutmeat and plant — have diversified uses, and they may each be incorporated in a variety of food products including chile sauce, cheese, mayonnaise, milk and candy.

One product that most of us keep on hand is peanut butter. Peanut butter was created in the late 1800's by a St. Louis physician, who had been searching for a nutritious, easy-to-digest food for elderly patients.

Around 1900 housewives found a new gadget on the market — a money saving device that they could use in their own kitchens. It was a small hand device used to make peanut butter. A few years later, owners of small country stores were making their own peanut butter with the same gadget that housewives had been using, and selling peanut butter from large, wooden tubs.

Today, with its high energy content, at least 200,000 tons of peanut butter are consumed yearly in the United States. One pound of peanuts provides the approximate energy value of one pound of beef, one and one-half pounds of Cheddar cheese, nine pints of milk or three dozen medium eggs.

For the most part, commercial peanut produc-

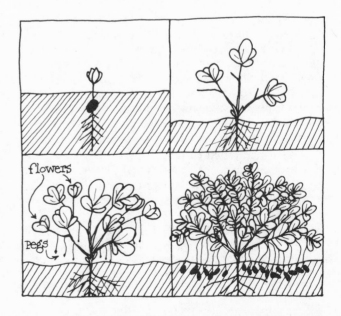

Variety	Days to Maturity	Comments
Early Bunch Virginia	120	Vigorous producer. One or two large kernels per pod.
Early Spanish	100	Excellent for northern climates. Small nut with good flavor.
Jumbo Virginia	120	Productive. Vines spread three and one-half feet across. One or two large kernels per pod.
Spanish	110	Quick grower. Dwarf plants. Two or three small kernels per pod.
Valencia Tennessee Red	120	Large, sweet kernels. Two to five kernels in a pod.

at least 40 mature pods. Once the plants turn almost completely yellow, it's harvest time. Don't wait long to harvest because the pods are apt to break off and become lost in the ground.

Peanuts fall into four basic types: **Virginia, Runner, Spanish** and **Valencia.**

The low-growing Virginia and Runner plants, which contain two seeds per pod, tend to spread and produce larger nuts than the Spanish type.

Spanish and Valencia, both bunching plants, are small-seeded with the Spanish having two to three seeds per pod and the Valencia having three to six seeds per pod.

Because our summers are short in Vermont and peanuts cannot tolerate frosty nights, I plant the fastest growing variety, **Early Spanish,** to make sure that the peanuts can be harvested before there's any sign of frost.

PLANTING PREP

Soil Type

Peanuts prefer a well-drained soil with a sandy or sandy-clay subsoil. The nut-forming pegs will penetrate a sandy soil easily, but they will have trouble penetrating a clay soil. During the harvest, sandy soils won't cling to the nuts nor will pods be lost because the soil becomes hard.

It is possible to grow peanuts in any type of soil *if* you make certain that the seedbed has been well worked to the point that it is loose and friable.

As I mentioned earlier, to determine the type of soil in your garden as well as the pH level and the needed nutrients, it's best to test your soil. For information about testing, contact your local Cooperative Extension Service.

Peanuts are no different from any other vegetable. Their seedbed must be prepared well (see p. 145) for a prolific harvest.

Inoculating Peanuts

As with all legumes, your peanut yield will often be increased if you inoculate the seeds at planting time with a nitrogen-fixing bacteria (see p. 147).

pH

For best results when growing peanuts, your soil should be slightly acid with a pH of 5.9 to 6.3. If the pH is below 5.9, broadcast limestone over the row and work it into the top three to four inches of soil where the peanut pods will develop. Although limestone can be applied during the spring, it's more effective if you apply it in the fall, because it takes a while for the lime to work. To raise the pH level one full point, I use about five pounds of ground limestone per 100 square feet.

Gypsum, which contains a lot of calcium, is often used on peanut plants especially in the West where the soil tends to be more alkaline. When the plants start to bloom, the rows should be sprinkled with gypsum, about six pounds per 100 square feet, which will help to satisfy their need for calcium. If the pegs don't receive enough calcium, you may be left with unfilled pods and no peanuts.

Fertilizer

In addition to supplying the soil with organic matter, I broadcast three to four pounds of 5-10-10 fertilizer over each 100 square feet and work it into the top two to three inches of soil just before planting time. Because peanut seeds and young plants are sensitive to fertilizer burn, don't apply fertilizer directly to the rows where you'll be planting peanuts.

A member of the legume family, peanuts have their own supply of nitrogen. For this reason, I use 5-10-10 fertilizer because it contains less nitrogen than some other commercial fertilizers. If the peanut seeds have been inoculated with a nitrogen-fixing bacteria, they'll be able to draw elemental nitrogen from the soil air, change it into usable form and store it in the nodules of the plant roots.

PLANTING

I'm very careful not to plant peanut seeds until frost dangers have passed — at least two weeks after the last spring frost.

Because of their heat-loving nature, peanuts need all the sun and warmth they can get while they're growing. Plant peanut seeds in a spot where they'll receive as much sun as possible.

Single Rows

Shelled peanut seeds (with their little jackets still on) should be planted about one and one-half to two and one-half inches deep (shallowest in clay soils). Again, the general rule of planting the seed to a depth four times the diameter of the seed applies. Drop the seeds into well-worked single rows (see p. 148), two or three seeds to a foot. Cover the seeds with soil and pack it down firmly with a hoe. I like to leave about 36 inches between the rows because the plants spread, and become attractive bushes.

Raised Beds

Because peanuts thrive in warm soil and their pegs must have loose soil to enter the ground, raised beds are best for this legume. (See page 146 for information on how to raise beds.)

PEANUT CARE

Hilling

It's a good idea to "hill" peanut plants when they've reached about two-thirds their full height, which is one and one-half feet. Hilling makes it easier for the peanut pegs to bury their tips into the ground.

To hill, use a hoe to pull up loose soil around the stems of the peanut plants.

However, once you've hilled your plants, don't disturb them with any tools, including a hoe. If they need weeding, do so by hand, allowing the roots and pegs to remain undisturbed.

Hilling peanut plants buries and kills weeds around the plants as well as taking care of most walkway weeds. It also creates a natural irrigation ditch by pulling soil from between the rows up around the plants and helps heavy soils to shed water. Hilling keeps the soil better drained and more productive because the earth is not packed around the plants. The biggest advantage is that it allows the pegs to penetrate the loose soil easily.

Mulch

Mulching peanut plants can be a little tricky. Because the peanut pegs penetrate the soil, they'll first have to penetrate the mulch. Therefore, if you decide to mulch, make sure that you put down a very thin layer of the material. Also make certain that you use a type of mulch that the pegs can easily go through.

Mulches that are best for nuts include grass clippings and straw. Don't use fresh grass clippings; let them dry for a day or so by spreading in the sun. Grass clippings help condition the soil by adding nutrients.

Watering

Although peanuts are relatively tolerant of dry soils, it's a good idea to check the amount of moisture in the soil before planting. Dig and if the soil feels moist one foot down, you probably won't have to worry about watering until after your plants start to bloom.

Even though the plants don't need a regular supply of water, the critical times for moisture are when the plants bloom and when the pegs enter the soil. A shortage of water at these times will reduce your total peanut yield.

Be careful not to water the plants when harvest time draws near. Nuts may not mature if it's too wet, or mature nuts may sprout.

Weeding

With young peanut seedlings, it's better to weed by hand than to use a weeding tool. The seedlings could be injured or killed if you're not very careful.

Continue to control weeds and loosen the soil as the plants grow, so that pegs can penetrate the surface easily. When you're weeding, be extremely careful not to cover branches and leaves with soil; this could kill the plants' leaves and interfere with flowering.

Once the pegs thrust themselves into the soil, the weeds should be pulled by hand to eliminate damaging the near-surface pods.

Remember that the best time to get rid of the weeds is after a rain once the plants have dried off.

Peanut Problems

Home gardeners don't have to worry much about diseases and pests infesting their peanut crops. The most common disease is leaf spot. Insects that cause the most trouble are aphids. See page 150 for ways of preventing problems in your garden.

Insects and diseases that may appear on your peanut plant include:

Leaf spot, a fungus, which is especially prevalent in areas where the weather is warm and moist. Small spots with light centers start appearing on plant leaves, and eventually, the leaves may turn yellow and drop off. To check leaf spot, contact your Cooperative Extension Service.

Nematodes can be a serious problem for Southern gardeners. There are several species of nematodes, microscopic eel-like creatures, that can stunt plant growth, kill root systems and cut down yield. In addition to feeding on the roots, they may also carry and spread disease. Above ground symptoms of nematode damage to plants are stunting,

yellowing and wilting. Preventive measures include adding loads of organic matter to your garden in advance of planting and thoroughly tilling it into the soil. Rotating crops also helps. For further information, contact your Cooperative Extension Service.

Potato leaf hoppers suck on the underside of leaves, spread diseases and cause peanut leaves to turn yellow, especially at the tips. These tiny, green, hopping insects are sometimes referred to as "sharp shooters" because of their wedge-like shape. To prevent leaf hopper damage, keep weeds down around garden and cover plants with cheesecloth. If they do infest your plants, spray with pyrethrum, carbaryl or malathion.

Aphids can cause peanut growers some concern. These tiny bugs, about one-sixteenth inch long, are light green. Not only do they multiply rapidly, but they do a lot of damage in a short time by sucking sap from plants. They weaken the plant as well as spread disease. In general, you should check plants every so often for the appearance of aphids. Home remedies include spraying the plant with soap and water mix. Carbaryl (sold as Sevin) or malathion may also be used.

Southern corn rootworms bore into young plants and feed on peanut pegs and pods in soil. These insects can slow healthy growth or even kill entire peanut plants. They're about one-half inch long, slender and yellowish-white with a brown head. Southern corn rootworm is the larval stage of the spotted cucumber beetle. Soil can be treated with an insecticide such as diazinon.

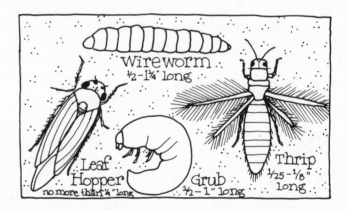

White grubs are smooth, grayish-white with hard brown heads. Mature grubs have curved bodies about one-half inch to one-inch long with six prominent legs. Grubs live in the soil and feed on the underground parts of the peanut plants. Home remedies include growing green manure crops (see page 145) and not planting peanuts where grass recently grew. The soil may be treated with diazinon or milky spore powder.

Wireworms vary in color from dark brown to yellowish and reach one-half to one and one-quarter inches long when fully grown. Their bodies are segmented, hard and shiny, and they feed on roots. Damage is the same as that for white grubs, and the wireworms can be treated with diazinon.

HARVESTING

When it's time to start harvesting peanuts, our children, grandchildren and neighborhood children gather. There's nothing more wonderful than to watch children's faces as peanuts are pulled out of the ground. Most of them think that peanuts come either in cellophane bags or that they grow on trees. When they watch them pulled out of the ground, their expressions are beyond description.

Peanut plants should be inspected every couple of days as harvest time approaches. Check plants in different parts of the row to determine if the pods directly under the main part of the plant are ready to harvest.

Prior to harvesting, the plants start to lose their green color and the leaves turn yellow. This happens because the kernels need the plant's food supply for their own growth. Inspect a few pods. The veins inside the mature pods should be a dark color, and the peanut skins will be papery thin and light pink. When the majority of plants are mature, start digging.

If you harvest peanuts before they have ripened, the pods will contain shriveled kernels. If they're harvested too late, many pods will break off in the soil and never be found.

Keep in mind when harvesting peanuts that the soil should be neither too wet nor too dry. In either extreme you might lose some of the nuts.

I've found that the best way to harvest peanuts is by slowly prying up the whole plant with a pitchfork

or shovel. Once the plant is out of the ground, gently shake off the loose soil. Using other methods, it's very easy for pods to break off and get lost in the ground. Place the plant in a shaded, warm and airy spot with the peanuts facing upward.

If weather conditions permit, it's best to leave the harvested plants exposed for two to three weeks, allowing the moisture content of the peanuts to drop.

Within a couple of weeks, when the plant leaves become dry and crumbly, pull the nuts off the plants and they are ready for storage.

Garden to Kitchen

Although you can't beat the taste of peas fresh from the garden, I think those preserved at home come close, especially in the middle of the winter when a foot of snow is on the ground. Here are methods I use for freezing and canning the peas we grow.

Canning: Hot Pack — Harvest tender peas and shell while fresh. Wash, drain and blanch peas in boiling water for three minutes. Drain peas, reserving the liquid. Fill hot, sterilized jars with peas. Add a half teaspoon salt to each pint or one teaspoon to each quart, then add the retained liquid, leaving one inch head space. Adjust lids. Process pints and quarts 40 minutes at ten pounds pressure (240° F). If your peas are extra large process ten minutes longer.

Canning: Cold Pack — Harvest tender peas and shell while fresh. Wash peas and pack loosely into hot, sterilized jars, leaving one inch head space. Don't press the peas down. Add a half teaspoon salt to each pint or one teaspoon to each quart. Cover peas with boiling water, leaving one inch head space, and adjust lids. Process pints and quarts 40 minutes at ten pounds pressure (240° F).

Freezing: Harvest, shell and wash tender peas while fresh. Blanch in boiling water for two minutes. (Three minutes for those in edible pods.) Cool quickly in ice water and drain. Package peas in containers and seal. Date and label the containers, and place them in a single layer in freezer for a quick freeze. They may be stacked the next day.

Drying peas: It isn't difficult to dry Southern and English peas — even if you live in areas with short growing season.

Allow Southern peas to ripen completely and dry as much as possible on the vine. Then either pull the vines and hang them in a well-ventilated area to allow the peas to dry, or harvest and shell the peas.

Spread these shelled, partially dried peas in a thin layer on cookie sheets and place them in an area that receives full sunlight and is well ventilated. The best drying days are those with low humidity and few clouds — it will take about three of these to dry the peas. Stir the peas occasionally while they are drying, and rotate the trays. It is best to bring the trays inside at night.

The peas are dry and ready to store if they split when tapped with a hammer, or if they are hard, wrinkled and white.

These peas may also be dried in a dehydrator. Spread them in single layers in the trays. Dry at 120° F for about 10 to 12 hours, depending upon dryness when harvested.

English peas can be dried in the same manner; but they should be harvested when young, and they need to be blanched after shelling for two to three minutes. The drying process will take longer for green peas, yet when the peas are dry they will split in the same manner when hit with a hammer. Store in airtight container when dry.

Shelling peas: After the peas are harvested, we relax on the porch or in the shade and shell pods. I still haven't found a quick and easy way to shell peas, but inviting family — grandchildren and all — and friends over to help makes an enjoyable afternoon, and the job goes quickly.

Pick and shell the peas just before you are ready to use them because sugar within the peas turns to starch quickly, and then peas lose their flavor and quality. If it's inconvenient to use English peas right after they're harvested, I simply place them in the refrigerator or in a cool place. Cool temperatures slow the sugar to starch conversion process.

It is just as important to use edible-podded pea varieties right after harvest, because they also have a high sugar content.

English peas, here are some vegetables and herbs that combine beautifully with peas. Use them to create some new dishes of your own.

asparagus	fennel	pimiento
allspice	garlic	potatoes
almonds	green tops	rice
bacon	ham	rosemary
basil	honey	saffron
bayleaf	leeks	savory
butter	lettuce	shallots
buttermilk sauce	maple syrup	sorrel leaves
carrots	mint	sugar
celery	mint jelly	sweet majoram
chervil	mushrooms	tarragon
chives	nutmeg	thyme
coriander seed	onions	turmeric
cream	parsley	turnip
curry	pepper	water chestnuts

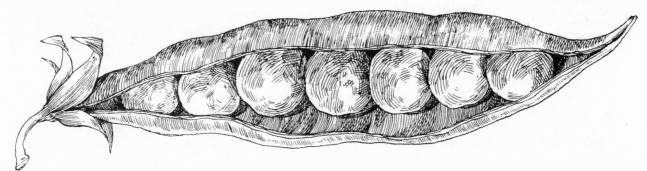

FAVORITE RECIPES

To Cook Peas Fresh

Heat salted water until boiling (one-half teaspoon salt to one cup water), add peas and boil about eight to ten minutes. If the peas are slightly overmature, a teaspoon of sugar may enhance their flavor. I usually allow one-half cup of shelled peas, or one-half pound unshelled for each person.

Snow peas are cooked for less time. They may be boiled in salted water for about two minutes and served with melted butter, or steamed with a little butter for five minutes. They are also delicious stir-fried for five minutes with other vegetables and cooked rice or packaged stir-fry rice.

To cook Sugar Snap peas simply blanch them briefly until they are cooked through or steam them for seven minutes. They are also wonderful stir fried.

Fresh English peas are delicious when they are boiled or steamed until they are just tender and then served hot with melted butter. But they are also a versatile vegetable, and I like to be creative with them. In addition to a few of my favorite recipes for cooking

Green Peas with Lettuce and Cream

The combination of peas and lettuce originated in France. Cooked with seasonings, they make a nice fresh, spring side-dish, which goes particularly well with baked ham and new potatoes.

3	Tb margarine or butter
1/4	cup water
2	cups peas
2	Tb chopped onion
1	tsp chopped parsley
2	Tb chopped celery
1/4	tsp ground nutmeg
2	cups shredded lettuce
	salt and pepper to taste
1/2	cup light cream

In a medium saucepan heat margarine, water and peas. Add onion, parsley, celery and nutmeg. Cover and simmer for six minutes or until peas are almost tender.

Mix in lettuce, salt and pepper. Cook five minutes more. Stir in cream and heat through. Serves 6.

Variation: Substitute one-quarter cup of chicken broth for water and eliminate cream. Add a sprig of fresh thyme and serve garnished with parsley.

Sauces for Peas

Buttermilk Sauce

2 Tb butter
2 Tb flour
3/4 cup buttermilk
1/4 cup mayonnaise
salt and pepper to taste

Melt butter in top of double boiler. Blend in flour, salt and pepper. Add buttermilk and cook until mixture is smooth and thickened. Blend in mayonnaise and cook until very hot. Serve immediately over hot, cooked vegetables. Serves 4.

Sour Cream Sauce

2 Tb margarine
2 Tb flour
1 cup milk
1 cup sour cream
1 small onion, minced
1/2 tsp sugar
1 Tb lemon juice

In saucepan, sauté onion in margarine. Add flour and mix well. Gradually add milk, stirring constantly over low heat until mixture thickens. Add sour cream and blend. Remove from heat and add sugar and lemon juice and stir. Pour over hot, cooked vegetables and serve.

Pot Luck Peas and Potatoes

For a church supper or even if unexpected company drops by, this dish is tasty and surprisingly quick and easy. We like it with meat loaf.

1/3 cup margarine
1/3 cup flour
1/2 tsp salt or to taste
1/2 tsp seasoned salt (optional)
1/4 tsp pepper
2 1/2 cups milk
2 cups shelled, raw peas
2 1/2 cups small, raw white onions, peeled
2 cups peeled, sliced potatoes
1 cup shredded Swiss cheese

Melt margarine in saucepan over low heat. Stir in flour, salts and pepper. Add milk gradually, stirring constantly, and cook until sauce is smooth and thickened.

In a buttered, two-quart casserole, combine half the peas, onions and potatoes. Pour half the sauce over the vegetables and sprinkle half the cheese on top. Repeat with remaining vegetables, sauce and cheese. Bake in 375° oven for about one hour or until vegetables are tender. Serves 6 to 8.

Peas and New Potatoes

One of the reasons we look forward to spring is fresh-from-our-garden peas and potatoes. Both Dick and I as children had them served this way, and it's still a favorite one-dish supper at our home.

1/2 lb lean salt pork, sliced to the rind or diced
12 tiny new potatoes, in their jackets
2 cups shelled peas
2 cups milk (or 1 cup milk, 1 cup light cream)
2 Tb butter
pepper to taste

Simmer salt pork, covered with water, 1 1/2 to 2 hours.

Wash potatoes, but do not peel them. Add potatoes and peas to salt pork and water. Cook about 10 to 15 minutes, or until vegetables are tender. Drain.

Add milk (or cream), butter and pepper. Be sure to taste before adding any salt. The salt pork imparts a salty flavor. Heat but do not boil and serve immediately. Serves 6 to 8.

Shrimp Pea Salad

On New Year's Day, Dick and I have had a party every year for over 25 years. Every year we have served this salad, which our friends and family have come to expect. I use our home-frozen peas. They're bright green, tender and sweet. Of course, in the summer we enjoy it with peas fresh from the garden.

2 cups cooked green peas, cooled
2 cups cooked elbow macaroni, cooled
2 7-ounce cans tiny shrimp
1/4 cup chopped onion
1/4 cup chopped celery
1/2 cup chopped dill pickle
1/2 cup mayonnaise
1/4 cup sour cream
2 Tb catsup
salt and pepper to taste
1/4 cup sliced ripe olives (optional)
lettuce leaves

Combine all ingredients. Chill and serve on a platter of lettuce leaves. Serves six to eight. Sprinkle paprika on top or add 1/4 tsp to other ingredients.

Peas in Pattypan Squash Cups

This not only tastes delicious, it's an attractive and unusual vegetable dish to serve guests. I like to make it as soon as this variety of summer squash is ready for harvest.

4 to 6 small pattypan squash, whole
2 cups peas, cooked
2 Tb margarine
2 Tb chopped onion
2 Tb chopped red or green pepper
1 tsp sugar
1 tsp lemon juice
1/2 cup sour cream
   salt and pepper to taste

Wash squash. Cook whole in a little boiling salted water for 15 minutes or until just tender. Drain.

Sauté onions and pepper in margarine. Add peas, sugar, lemon juice, sour cream, salt and pepper.

Scoop out seeds of squash to form cups. Butter inside and fill with pea mixture. Serves 4 to 6.

Variation: Cook a large pattypan squash in boiling salted water until tender. Drain and scoop out seeds from center. Fill with buttered peas and carrots.

Creamed Peas on Toast

Creamed peas are delicious prepared in a variety of ways. Dick loves them for breakfast, but they're also good for lunch.

2 Tb margarine or butter
2 Tb flour
2 cups milk
2 cups peas, cooked
   salt and pepper to taste
4 slices toast

In a medium-sized saucepan, melt margarine or butter over low heat. Blend in flour, salt and pepper. Cook, stirring the mixture until it is smooth and bubbly. Remove from heat. Gradually add milk, stirring constantly until it is well blended. Replace on heat and stir until boiling. Stir constantly and boil for one minute. Add peas and serve on hot, buttered toast. Serves 4.

Variation: Add a seven-ounce can of tuna-fish and one-quarter cup of shredded cheese when adding the peas. Our grandchildren like this for lunch when they visit.

Green Peas and Tomatoes

3 slices bacon, chopped
1/2 chopped green pepper
1/2 cup chopped onion
1 cup bread cubes or 1 slice bread cut in cubes
   salt to taste
1 tsp sugar (optional)
1/8 tsp paprika
2 cups chopped tomatoes, fresh or canned
2 cups green peas, partially cooked

Sauté green pepper and onions with bacon. Add bread, sugar, salt and paprika. Add tomatoes, juice and all, and simmer for about 15 minutes over low heat. Stir in peas, heat throughly and serve as a side dish. Serves 6 to 8.

Creamed Curried Peas

Curry powder is a blend of several ground spices, which adds an exotic flavor to dishes. I like to serve curried peas with roasted chicken and baked potatoes.

2 cups cooked green peas
3 Tb onion, chopped
2 Tb margarine
2 Tb flour
1/2 tsp curry powder
   salt and pepper to taste
1 1/2 cups milk

In a saucepan, cook onion in margarine until tender. Remove from heat. Stir in flour, curry powder, salt and pepper. Cook over low heat, stirring until it bubbles. Remove from heat, and stir in milk. Heat to boiling, stirring constantly. Boil and stir for one minute. Add peas, stir and heat thoroughly. Serves 4.

Variations: Add mushrooms, tiny onions or carrots; add one-quarter tsp minced garlic.

Peas and Mushroom Casserole

2 cups fresh, raw peas
1/2 lb fresh mushrooms, sliced (2 cups)
1/4 cup chopped onion
2 Tb margarine or butter
2 Tb flour
2 cups milk
   salt and pepper to taste
1/4 cup shredded Cheddar cheese

In a two-quart casserole, layer half the peas, mushrooms and onions. Dot with half the margarine and sprinkle with half the flour, salt and pepper. Repeat with remaining vegetables, margarine, flour, salt and pepper. Add milk and sprinkle top with cheese. Bake in 350° oven for one hour or until vegetables are tender. Serves 4 to 6.

Traditionally, dried peas are soaked overnight before cooking. They are just washed, put in three to four times as much water, and then drained the following day.

Another method reduces soaking time to just two hours. Drop peas into the same amount of water as you have peas. Make sure the water is boiling hot. Let the peas stand in the water as it cools for two hours.

Split Pea Soup

To take the chill off a cold winter night when I was a child, my mother would make hot split pea soup and serve it with warm johnny cake — that's cornbread to some. She still makes it, so do I, and so do my daughters.

1	lb dried split peas
2	quarts water
1	ham bone (or 3 ham hocks or 1 cup ham pieces)
1	cup chopped celery
1/2	cup chopped onion
1	bay leaf
1/4	tsp pepper

Presoak peas if they need it. Combine peas, ham, celery, onion, bay leaf, pepper and water in large pan. Bring to boil, reduce heat and simmer 2 1/2 to 3 hours, or until peas are soft. Stir occasionally. Remove bay leaf and ham bone. Trim meat from bone, cut into chunks, and add to soup. Serves six.

Variation: Add one cup sliced carrots to other ingredients, and substitute four whole peppercorns and four whole allspice for pepper. Tie spices in a small piece of cheesecloth before adding to soup, and remove cloth when removing ham bone.

Fresh English Pea Soup

Here's a quick soup in which you can use fresh or frozen peas. It's delicious piping hot or cold, garnished with a sprinkling of chopped parsley chives.

2	cups green peas
1	bay leaf
1/4	tsp thyme
1	scallion chopped (optional)
1	cup boiling water
1	cup milk or cream
	salt and pepper to taste
	butter

Cook peas, bay leaf, thyme and optional scallion in water for five minutes. Remove bay leaf. Pour peas and liquid into a blender. Blend until smooth. Add milk, salt, pepper and reheat. Dot with butter. Serves 4 to 6.

Variations: Substitute one tablespoon chopped fresh mint for bay leaf and thyme. Garnish with croutons.

Substitute chicken broth for water, and a half-teaspoon paprika, a quarter-teaspoon nutmeg, and an eighth-teaspoon curry powder instead of bay leaf and thyme.

To Soak or Not to Soak

Not all dried peas need soaking. If you're using your own home-grown dried peas, they do need to be soaked. Some store-bought peas do not need soaking, so before proceeding read the directions on the package.

Cardamom Rice with Split Peas

1	Tb margarine
1	medium onion, chopped
2 1/2	cups beef or chicken broth
1/4	cup green or yellow split peas
2 or 3	whole cardamoms
2 or 3	whole cloves
1	tsp parsley
	dash paprika
	pinch turmeric
1	cup long grain or brown rice
	soy sauce

Sauté onion in oil. Add broth and bring to boil. Add peas slowly, simmer covered 15 minutes. Open cardamom pods and add cardamom seeds, cloves, parsley, paprika and turmeric. Bring to boil and add rice slowly. Cook covered about 40 minutes. Serve with soy sauce. Serves 6 to 8.

Indian Split Pea Soup

1	cup split green peas, soaked one hour
	oil
1	large onion, chopped
	marrow bone optional
2	cloves garlic, crushed
1	2-inch cinnamon stick
2	cloves
2	whole cardamoms, bruised
5	cups water
1/4	tsp peppercorns
1/2	tsp minced ginger
1	tsp turmeric
1	tsp cumin
1/2	tsp crushed red pepper (optional)
2	tsp salt
2	medium tomatoes, chopped

Heat oil and brown onion. Add and fry five minutes everything but peas, tomato and water. Add tomatoes and cook five minutes. Add drained peas and stir several minutes. Cover with boiling water. Simmer 2 to 3 hours. Adjust spices to taste. Garnish with chopped green onion and fresh coriander leaves or parsley.

Hoppin' John

Hoppin' John, a traditional New Year's Day dish in the South, is supposed to bring good luck to those who eat it. Our friend Caroline Riggins from Atlanta, Georgia, tells us that many folks have it with pork chops, sweet potatoes, turnip greens and cornbread. Traditionally, Hoppin' John is made with field peas, but in many parts of the South, black-eyed peas are used, too.

1	cup dried peas, washed and sorted
1/4	lb lean slab bacon, cut in cubes
2 1/2	cups water
2	Tb minced onion
	salt and pepper to taste
3	cups hot, cooked rice

Place dried peas, bacon and water in a medium-sized pan and bring to boil over moderate heat. Reduce heat so that the liquid simmers. Cover and simmer until peas are firm but tender. Field peas need about 20 minutes and black-eyed peas take about 45 minutes. Drain liquid from mixture. Add remaining ingredients, simmer to blend flavors and serve hot. Serves 6.

Peas Porridge

When I was a little girl, I often heard the rhyme:
"Peas porridge hot,
Peas porridge cold,
Peas porridge in the pot,
Nine days old."

Only recently did I find the apparent origin of that rhyme. In the 1800's, porridge was a staple for lumbermen in the northern woods of New England. It was cooked over the wood stove in a big pot, and then poured into small bowls. A length of string was laid in it with a loop dangling over the edge, and then the pot was put out where the porridge would freeze. Later, when the dish was held in hot water, the porridge could be slipped out and hung by its string in the freezing cold pantry. It was considered best "when nine days old," and then the woodsmen would wrap it in a towel and hang it on their sled to take into the woods for lunch. At noon they would heat the porridge in a kettle over the fire and eat it with brown bread kept unfrozen in their pockets.

4	lbs beef
1	lb salt pork
2	cups dried peas
4	Tb flour or cornmeal
2	cups corn (canned or frozen)
	salt and pepper to taste

Heat peas and meat in boiling water and simmer until both are tender. Skim fat off pot, and remove bones from meat. Cut meat into small pieces. Wet flour with water until it is a paste, and then add it to meat and peas to thicken porridge. Add corn and seasonings. When meat and peas fall apart, cool and freeze — for nine days. (Or less, if you like.) Serve piping hot. This is good to take camping in the winter or for long cross-country ski trips or ice skating.

Fried Black-Eyed Peas

Gather and shell tender peas, and boil them until they are tender. Heat margarine or vegetable oil in skillet. Mash drained peas and form into patties and fry until light brown. Garnish cake with bits of bacon. Peas can be fried whole, but they must be boiled less and fried with great care. Peas can also be boiled until tender and served.

Cornfield or Black-Eyed Peas

I love to read cook books, and occasionally I come across a recipe that makes me chuckle. This old recipe from "Housekeeping in Old Virginia" published in the late 1800's did just that.

"Gather your peas about sundown. The following day, about eleven o'clock gorge out your peas with your thumbnail. . . . Rinse your peas, parboil them, and fry them with several slices of streaked middling (bacon), encouraging the gravy to seep out and inter-marry with your peas. When moderately brown, but not scorched, empty into a dish. Mash them gently with a spoon, mix with raw tomatoes sprinkled with a little brown sugar and the immortal dish is quite ready. Eat a heap. Eat more and more. It's good for your general health of mind and body. It fattens you up, makes you sassy, goes through and through your very soul. . . ."

Black-Eyed Pea and Ham Salad

A wonderful salad to serve a crowd or take to a pot luck picnic. I also like to serve it at home with rolls, sliced tomatoes, cucumbers and pickles.

4	cups cooked and drained black-eyed peas
2	cups diced cooked ham
1	cup celery, chopped
1/2	cup chopped green pepper
1/2	cup onion, chopped
2	cups shredded lettuce
1	cup salad dressing or mayonnaise
	salt and pepper to taste

Combine all ingredients, chill and serve. Ten large servings.

Peas and Peanut Salad

The combination of ingredients in this recipe sounds funny, but it really is tasty. I dare you to give it a try! We like it for lunch on hot days as a change from cole slaw.

2	cups cooked peas
1/2	cup unsalted peanuts
1/2	cup sweet pickle
1	Tb prepared mustard
2	tsp sugar
1/4	cup sour cream

Place peas in a bowl. Grind peanuts and pickles together. Add to peas and mix. Make a salad dressing by mixing the mustard, sugar and sour cream together. Stir into the pea mixture. Chill. Serve on a lettuce leaf or in a tomato cup. Serves four.

COOKING WITH PEANUTS

It isn't the nutritional value of peanuts alone that keeps them around my kitchen. They have a wide variety of uses, they're tasty, and they're fun!

The following includes some methods, tips, and recipes which I use for peanuts. I hope you'll enjoy them.

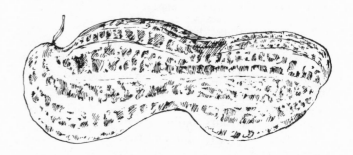

Roasted: You can store peanuts up to two months after harvesting before roasting. Roasting crisps the nuts and brings out their flavor.

To roast peanuts unshelled, spread them on a baking sheet or in a wire basket, and bake them in a 300° F oven for 20 to 25 minutes, stirring occasionally. Remove a few skins to test for brownness.

To roast shelled peanuts, spread them on a baking sheet and bake at 300°F oven for 20 to 25 minutes, stirring occasionally. Coat with melted margarine and salt to taste.

Boiled: Although roasted peanuts are more common, I have eaten boiled peanuts while traveling in the South, and they are a delicacy.

Green, freshly picked unshelled peanuts may be covered with salted water and boiled for about two hours, or until tender. For serving, more salt may be added if desired.

Toasted: Toasting is another way to prepare peanuts before serving them as a snack. Spread raw, shelled peanuts in a shallow pan, and heat over low heat 10 to 15 minutes, stirring frequently. The nuts continue to brown slightly after removing, so avoid overbrowning. Remove skins. Sprinkle hot nuts with salt and cool on absorbent paper.

Peanut Butter

For smooth, creamy peanut butter, process roasted, shelled peanuts in blender until desired consistency is obtained. For a smoother consistency, add one to three tablespoons of vegetable oil for each cup of peanuts used. If unsalted nuts are used, add about one-half teaspoon of salt per cup of peanut butter to reach desired taste. For crunchy peanut butter, put roasted, shelled peanuts through a fine meat grinder or food processor instead of a blender and continue as with smooth peanut butter.

Peanut butter may be canned for storage. Pack the peanut butter into hot, sterilized jars, leaving one inch of head space. Adjust lids. Process half-pints in boiling water bath for one hour.

Peanut Storage

Because peanuts have a high content of fat, they become rancid quickly if not stored properly. Keep these nuts (raw or roasted) in a refrigerator or freezer in a moisture-proof container.

Peanuts in the shell keep approximately nine months when refrigerated. If they are frozen at zero degrees or lower in air-tight containers, they'll keep indefinitely.

Although shelled peanuts may be stored approximately three months if refrigerated, they will also keep indefinitely if they are frozen in tightly closed containers. For best results, do *not* salt the shelled peanuts.

You should blanch raw, shelled peanuts before freezing. Place them in boiling water for three minutes; cool in ice water three minutes, drain, package and label.

Skinning Peanuts

If you prefer the flavor of skinless peanuts, you can remove the skins easily after either blanching, roasting or toasting the nuts. Simply slide the skins off with your fingers.

Sparks and Garnish

Peanuts and peanut butter can add an unexpected flavor to food. Sprinkle one-quarter cup chopped peanuts on top of squash or sweet potato casseroles before baking, or perk up cole slaw with chopped nuts. Use your imagination and add them to casserole and dessert dishes.

On a rainy day, get out the peanut butter. Put it on crackers, bananas and celery. And a p.b. and jelly sandwich is fun, tasty and nutritious.

FAVORITE RECIPES

Chicken Malay

5	lbs chicken breasts and legs
3	cloves garlic, crushed
4	Tb paprika
1	Tb salt
1	tsp pepper
1/2	tsp poultry seasoning
1/2	cup flour
1/4	cup butter or margarine
1/4	cup salad oil or peanut oil
1	cup chopped onion
1	Tb flour
1	10-ounce can condensed chicken broth
1	cup dry white wine or dry vermouth
2	packages cut green beans
1	cup salted roasted peanuts.

Rinse chicken in cold water. Drain, pat dry and cut in serving-sized pieces. Rub pieces with crushed garlic. Combine paprika, salt, pepper and poultry seasoning and roll chicken in mixture. Roll chicken in flour. Brown the chicken pieces in butter and oil over medium-high heat in a heavy skillet. When all are browned, remove chicken and drain off fat.

Return 2 Tb of fat to skillet. Reduce heat to medium. Stir in onions and sauté until golden. Stir in 1 Tb flour and cook for one minute. Slowly stir in chicken broth and wine or vermouth. Cook, stirring constantly, loosening brown bits from pan until mixture thickens and comes to a boil. Cook two to three minutes. Pour half of sauce into a second skillet and divide chicken into the two skillets. Let the chicken cook slowly over low heat for 20 minutes or until tender. Add beans and cook 10 minutes longer. Add the peanuts just before serving. Serves 6 to 8.

Peanut Tuna Casserole

1/2	cup chopped salted peanuts
1/2	lb cooked macaroni
2	7 oz. cans tunafish
1/2	cup shredded sharp cheese
1	can cream of mushroom soup
2	Tb chopped onion
2	Tb chopped celery
	pepper to taste
1/2	cup milk

Combine all ingredients in two-quart casserole and mix well. Bake in 350° oven for 30 minutes or until well heated. Serves 6.

Peanut Butter Spread

This blend may sound doubtful but give it a try. It's tasty served on crackers or in celery sticks.

2 Tb margarine or butter
1/2 cup chopped mushrooms
3 slices bacon
8 ounces cream cheese, softened
1-2 tsp horseradish
2 Tb smooth peanut butter

Sauté mushrooms in margarine for five minutes. Fry bacon until crisp and drain. Beat cream cheese, horseradish and peanut butter until fluffy. Add crumbled bacon, and mushrooms. Chill.

Variation: Form into a ball, and roll in one-half cup finely chopped peanuts.

Squash Peanut Pie

This recipe of mine first appeared in the "Gardens For All News," but I think it's worth sharing again. It's easier than it looks and really delicious.

1/4 cup margarine
1 1/4 cups light brown sugar, packed
1 1/2 tsp pumpkin pie spice
2 eggs, beaten slightly
1/4 cup sour cream
2 cups cooked, mashed winter squash (butternut or Hubbard are best)
1 3/4 cups milk
1/4 tsp salt
1 1/2 tsp vanilla
2 Tb margarine
2 Tb brown sugar
1 cup unsalted peanuts, chopped
1 pint whipped cream
  nutmeg

Preheat oven to 400°F. Prick bottom and sides of pie crust, bake 10 minutes and cool. In medium saucepan, cream 1/4 cup margarine with 1 1/4 cups brown sugar and the pumpkin pie spice. Add eggs and mix well. Gradually blend in sour cream, squash, milk, salt and vanilla. Pour into pie crust. Bake 15 minutes and remove from oven. Lower oven temperature to 325°F.

In small saucepan mix 2 Tb margarine and 2 Tb brown sugar. Cook and stir over low heat until sugar is dissolved. Remove from heat. Add peanuts to the butter and sugar and stir until well coated. Top pie with mixture. Return pie to oven and continue baking about 40 minutes or until knife comes out clean when inserted. Cool completely. Garnish each serving with a spoonful of whipped cream and a dash of nutmeg. Serves 6.

Peanut Butter Milkshake

2 Tb peanut butter (smooth style)
1 cup cold milk
2 Tb honey
4 ice cubes

Mix all ingredients together in blender at high speed until ice cubes have disappeared.

G.O.R.P.

Good Old Raisins and Peanuts is a tasty, nutritious snack for any cross-country skier, hiker or hunter. It's a great source of energy, and easy to carry. Any of the following are great to combine into a creative mixture, which can then be packaged into baggies.

Peanuts	Roasted pumpkin seeds
Raisins	Sunflower seeds
Sliced Almonds	Sesame seeds
Cashews	Walnut halves
Chopped dates	Grated coconut
Dried fruit	M&M's

Peanutty Coffee Cake

A quick and tasty coffee cake, which is nice for breakfast or to bring out for guests along with coffee. It's also delicious topped with vanilla ice cream for a special dessert.

```
3/4  cup brown sugar, packed
1/2  cup flaked coconut
  1  cup flour
  1  tsp baking powder
1/2  tsp baking soda
1/2  cup chunky peanut butter
  2  Tb salad oil
1/2  cup milk
  1  egg
```

In a large bowl combine sugar, coconut, flour, baking powder and baking soda. Mix. Stir in peanut butter and oil. Beat until crumbly. Save 1/2 cup of mixture for top of cake. Add milk and egg to remaining mixture, beating at medium speed for three minutes. Pour into a 9-inch, greased baking pan. Sprinkle mixture over top. Bake in oven at 350° for about 30 to 35 minutes. Serve warm or cold.

Peanut Cookies

Delicious, chewy cookies. Perfect to make for lunches and snacks.

```
  1  lb salted peanuts
  3  eggs, well beaten
  1  cup light brown sugar, firmly packed
  3  Tb flour
1/4  tsp baking powder
  1  tsp vanilla
```

Grind or coarsely chop peanuts. Beat eggs and sugar together. Sift flour and baking powder together and add to egg mixture. Blend in vanilla. Add peanuts, mixing well. Drop by teaspoonfuls onto greased cookie sheet and bake in 400°F oven for about 10 min. Makes about 4 dozen.

Chinese Peanuts

An excellent and unusual snack.

```
1/2  Tb peanut oil
1/2  Tb sesame oil
  2  cups raw peanuts
  1  tsp soy sauce
  1  chili pepper, minced
     salt to taste
```

Heat oils in skillet and stir fry peanuts at medium heat for 5 to 10 minutes. When peanuts are golden, remove from heat. Mix remaining ingredients together and sprinkle over peanuts. Mix well and serve hot.

Peanut Brittle

Delightful plain, crushed and sprinkled over vanilla ice cream. It is a great gift.

```
  2  cups sugar
  1  cup light corn syrup
1/2  cup water
  2  cups peanuts, preferably raw
  1  Tb margarine or butter
  1  tsp soda
1/2  tsp salt
  1  tsp vinegar
```

In a three-quart pan, heat sugar, syrup and water to boiling. Cook over medium heat until mixture reaches soft ball stage (236°F). Add peanuts. Cook slowly, stirring constantly, until mixture reaches 300° on candy thermometer, or when it spins a thread when dropped in cold water. Remove from heat, and add butter, soda, salt and vinegar. Pour onto buttered baking sheet. Cool. Break into pieces and store in air-tight container. Makes about two pounds.

Variation: After candy is poured onto baking sheet, lift candy around edges with spatula. While candy is still warm, but firm, turn it over and stretch the brittle until it is thin.

Nutty Banana Bread

This bread is wonderful served warm for breakfast, and it is also good served with soup or salad for lunch. Children double their pleasure by spreading the bread with peanut butter for a snack.

```
  3/4  cup peanut butter
  1/3  cup shortening or margarine
  2/3  cup sugar
    2  eggs
       grated rind of one orange
1 3/4  cups sifted flour
    2  tsp baking powder
  1/2  tsp salt
  1/8  tsp baking soda
    1  cup mashed banana, very ripe
  1/3  cup chopped peanuts
```

Cream shortening with peanut butter. Then blend in sugar, eggs and orange rind. Beat thoroughly. Sift flour with baking powder, salt and baking soda, and add to the first mixture alternately with banana. Mix in peanuts. Turn into greased, standard-sized bread pan, and bake at 350°F for one hour. Cool on wire rack.

CHAPTER 7

Onions

There are more than 300 widely scattered species of onions in the world, and the bulb onion we grow is just one of them. The onion is a biennial plant, which means that it grows one year and produces its seeds the second (but they're ready for eating even the first year). Onions have a dormant phase between these two seasons — and this ability to stop growing only to grow again later really helps us as gardeners.

The first year the onion plant begins its growth by putting out its green top leaves in cool weather. It stores a lot of energy in those leaves. When the weather gets warmer and the days get longer, the plant stops putting out new top leaves. Instead, the plant takes the energy from the leaves and stores it in the expanding bottom bulb. The leaves fall over and shrivel up and the plant appears dormant. But inside the bulb the plant is storing the energy to put out a flowering seed stalk when it starts growing again. That's the goal of any plant — to produce the seed to keep its species going.

However, the onion bulb is best for eating, cooking and storing *before* it has started to put its energy into making seed. That's why gardeners harvest it after just one season and try to pick off the seed pods as soon as they appear.

Because there is such a wide variety of onions, it is helpful to know what characteristics to consider in selecting them for your garden.

Grouping onions according to **taste** is one way to select them. There are basically the strong-flavored onions and the milder (and usually bigger) kinds. The mild varieties are sometimes called "European" onions. These include the kinds we slice for hamburgers and onion rings, like Sweet Spanish, Bermuda and the big red onions.

Onions vary in **keeping qualities,** too. For an onion that you can keep long after the growing season, the strong-flavored, yellow ones are your best bet. They are the most widely grown in this country and keep extremely well. The commercial growers really like them because they store onions for long periods of time and ship them long distances. The Stuttgarter and Yellow Globe onions we bag and hang in our root cellar each September will last through the winter and following spring. A recent yellow variety for home gardeners, "Spartan Sleeper," can keep 18 months or longer under good storage conditions.

The milder Bermuda, Portugal and Spanish onions won't keep that long. They don't develop the really firm outer skin needed for long storage. In fact, some Bermuda white onions will keep for just a few weeks. They're definitely worth growing, though, for their sweet, mild taste. And they're essential at our house for a good hamburger.

It may also help to sort out varieties by **how much daylight** they need to make a bulb. If an onion is called "short-day" variety in the seed catalog description, it will bulb when it gets about 12 hours of light per day. A "long-day" variety will bulb only when it receives about 15 or 16 hours of daylight. There are long summer days in the North, and the short-day varieties are generally intended for use in the South.

Here's a good rule of thumb: the stronger the skin and flavor of the onion, the longer it keeps. Jan and I use our white onions first for pickling and boiling, then the red ones are ready to slice for salads and hamburgers. We save the yellow ones, generally for cooking throughout the year.

The following onion varieties are by no means the only ones you have to choose from. It may take you a few seasons to find varieties that are the best for your garden soil and climate. That's why it's important for you to talk with experienced local gardeners or to get in touch with your local County Cooperative Extension Agent for more information on which kinds of onions grow best in your area. Across the country, the Extension Agents recommend over 50 different onion varieties to home gardeners, so do contact them.

Of course, your own garden is your "laboratory." Don't be afraid to experiment and have fun with different varieties. Planting any onion variety will at least give you something tasty to eat.

Popular in the South

Granex This is one of the deep South's most popular varieties. The shape of the large, yellow bulbs may be thick-flat or almost globed. It's an early onion, and it keeps well if cured and stored properly.

Red Bermuda A good table onion that has a growing season of 95 days. It has crisp bulbs with mild flavor.

Texas Early Grano 502 Another popular variety in the South; it has some resistance to thrips that can pester crops, and can produce some very large onions.

Excel Mild-tasting, early onion. It's a yellow Bermuda-type and popular.

Crystal Wax Steady performer over the years in southern states. Mild flavor, short storage.

Popular in the North

Southport Yellow Globe Very popular bulb in the North. Medium-size bulbs with good taste.

Elite Will produce a tall globe-shaped bulb. Stores quite well.

Autumn Spice A good one for northern states. Flesh is hard with strong flavor. Stores well.

Early Yellow Globe This medium-size onion is grown a lot in the Northeast. 100 days to maturity usually. Keeps well.

White Portugal You can plant seeds directly in garden for green tops and pickling-size bulbs in many parts of the country. White bulbs won't keep too long.

Ebenezer Mostly available in sets. Plant the sets to get big bulbs. Pretty strong flavor. Stores well. White and yellow varieties available.

Yellow Sweet Spanish and other Spanish types They need long growing season, but they produce large, globe-shaped, mild-flavored bulbs. Many gardeners buy transplants grown in South and shipped North for spring planting. 120 to 130 days to mature.

Scallions

Most any onions sown can be scallions (also called bunching onions, green onions, spring onions or green tails). Plant them thickly, pick them young, and you've got scallions.

To have scallions in the summer, plant seeds of an onion variety such as Beltsville Bunching or Evergreen Bunching as early in the spring as you can. Pull them up when the stalks are about 8 inches tall, and the small bulbs will be tender and tasty. (Some varieties, such as Long White Bunching, don't ever form bulbs. So, even if you let them grow taller, you won't have scallions with oversized bulbs.) White Portugal, a bulbing onion, is a variety that's grown all over the country as scallions when harvested young.

You'll sometimes see bunching onion transplants for sale. Although they are ready to eat a little sooner, I don't think they're worth buying. Bunching onions planted from seed will be at the eating stage in just a matter of weeks, so why pay the extra cash?

A few years ago I planted bunching onions in a 2-foot by 6-foot section of the garden, and they're still producing. I've never replanted them. (They're very hardy and survive winter temperatures as low as -30°F.) They go to seed each season, so the crop comes back year after year. All I do is keep the weeds out. If you want to keep a perennial bed going, plant a hardy variety, like Evergreen White Bunching.

Early Scallions

Here's how to be the first in your neighborhood to have scallions in the spring. Three to four months before frost in the fall, plant a variety such as Stuttgarter in a foot-wide row, scattering the seeds onto smooth soil and raking them in lightly. If it's dry, soak the area before planting, and keep the soil moist until the seedlings are up.

Don't thin them at all! Around the first of November, bend the tops over and mulch them with 3 to 4 inches of hay or leaves. In the spring take the mulch off early, and your spring onions are 4 weeks ahead of your neighbors'! You can start harvesting as soon as there's something big enough to eat.

Varieties

White Lisbon Regular A hardy, mild-flavored onion. For a long time it was the most popular bunching onion among American gardeners.

Evergreen White Bunching ("He-shi-Ko") This onion won't form a bulb. It continues to grow and form new shoots throughout the growing season. Will winter over well in the North. Good flavor.

Long White Globe Bunching Won't form bulb. Produces clusters of stalks, and winters over to produce early scallions.

Long White Tokyo This variety can take some hot weather well. Single stalk will form.

Beltsville Bunching Withstands hot, dry weather better than any other green onion variety. Crisp, very mild and excellent eating quality.

Chives

Chives are a great windowsill crop. But you can also plant them in a permanent location in an herb garden or as a border for a flower garden. They are just about disease-free and need very little attention once you get them producing.

You can start your chive bed from seed in a window box or flower pot or by using some plants from a neighbor. Six or eight plants are plenty — and since they are perennials, you'll get plenty of chives each year. When you set out plants, put them 8 to 10 inches apart, and they will expand to fill the area.

Chives like rich, well-worked soil and fertilizer. Rake some compost or manure into the soil before planting. Trim off the tops of the transplants, leaving an inch or two, and put the plant in at the same depth. Do this early in the spring.

Clip off the tops whenever you need them. The plant will produce more.

Keep the chives producing through the winter by digging up part of a cluster of plants and potting it inside. It won't hurt the next year's crop.

Garlic

You can buy garlic bulbs or sets from garden stores or the local grocer. Elephant garlic is the variety to look for at the garden store as it produces large, mild-flavored clusters. They peel easily, too.

Plant the little, individual cloves that break off from the bulb. The outer cloves of each garlic will produce the largest bulbs. Don't break them up until you plant them, though.

Like onions, garlic is great for wide-row growing. Plant them the full depth of the bulb — about 3 or 4 inches apart, and firm the soil. Try a row 10 to 12 inches wide.

To grow big garlic bulbs, plant the cloves in the late fall. They'll mature the next summer. Northern gardeners can mulch garlic over the winter, but next season they have to watch out for seed stalks and pick them off right away. They can also plant the cloves in the spring as soon as the ground can be worked.

If you live in the South or Southwest, plant the cloves anytime from the fall through early spring.

Plant early, because garlic isn't fond of hot weather. They don't like competition from weeds, either.

Harvest them when the green tops turn brown and die down. It should take 90 to 100 days for spring-planted garlic. Pull them up and let them dry for a few days, and then cure them in an airy place, like onions (see page 183). They'll keep for quite a while at 40° to 60°F. Braiding is a very good way to cure and store them.

I sometimes like to leave garlic bulbs in the ground over the winter. The next season I let these bulbs go to seed. At the top of the seed stalk you can get 10 to 15 tiny bulbs which you can plant — it's fun.

Shallots

Shallots have a unique flavor — sort of halfway between garlic and onion, but better. We like them pickled or fresh with scrambled eggs, and they are fine used in cooking. They are very expensive to buy, which has always struck me as strange, because they are so easy to grow. It's one crop that's always a success.

You need shallot "sets" to get started. They are usually available from a good seed supplier or garden store. Plant them very early in the spring — freezing weather doesn't hurt them. Fall planting is best where summer gets very hot.

If you have difficulty finding shallot sets, try the grocery store. Small packages of shallots are often available. Each single set will form a cluster of shallots, so they're worth buying even though they're expensive.

Plant the sets about 4 to 6 inches apart in a row 10 to 12 inches wide. Push them into the soil the full depth of the bulb. Shallots like lots of fertilizer.

You'll get a big clump of shallots for each set you plant. You can harvest bulbs for use fresh or pickling anytime or at the end of the season for storage. When the tops die down — that's the sign to pull them up and dry them, just as you would onions (see page 183). They store really well.

Remember to keep some to plant as sets the next season.

Leeks

A lot of people enjoy vichyssoise, which is just cold leek and potato soup, but they may not have tried leeks other ways. They think leeks are strange and hard-to-grow vegetables. They're not.

You can start them easily indoors, like onions, and set them out as transplants, or you can sow the seeds right in the garden in a wide row. Leeks like lots of fertilizer. Seeds start slowly, so don't let any weeds overwhelm them.

In the South, sow seeds or set out transplants in the fall. Northern gardeners should get underway in the spring. Remember to keep the young plants watered well. If you don't use a wide row, you can plant the young transplants in the bottom of a shallow furrow. After the plants have grown some, gradually fill the furrow back up with soil. This is one way to get nice, white stems of about 4 to 6 inches. This stem-whitening or blanching method is also used with some other vegetables such as celery and asparagus.

To blanch leeks in a wide row, you can put on several inches of compost, leaves or dirt on the row. This mulch is hilled up a few inches around each stem. It may sound like some work, but it's worth it.

If you plant early in the spring you should get some nice leeks a few weeks before the first fall frost. A lot of gardeners leave their leeks in the ground over the winter under a layer of mulch. (Pull the mulch back a bit when the end-of-

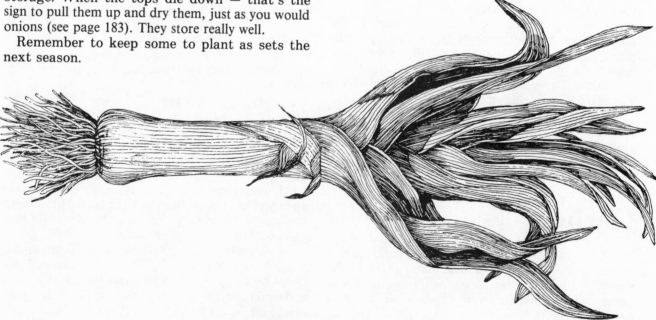

winter temperature gets into the 20's.) Of course, go out and harvest them anytime.

GETTING STARTED

As with most vegetables, you can start onions from seed in the garden. But many onions have relatively long growing seasons and onion seeds don't germinate quickly, so it's often better to start the crop another way. You can set out transplants, or you can plant 'sets,' which are simply half-grown onions.

Buying Sets

In Vermont we see our first onion sets at the garden stores when there's still snow on the ground. The welcome sight and smell of a basket of sets reminds us that planting time isn't far away.

Using sets is probably the most popular, convenient and dependable way to get onions started. They're very easy to plant, and you can harvest your first eating onions sooner than if you started from seeds.

Usually stores sell only a few varieties of sets, such as good-keeping white and yellow varieties and a red type. You can also grow sets yourself during one season for use the next year.

Sets are sold by the pound or by the scoop, and each set is one onion. When you buy onion sets, watch the size. Sets that are smaller than ½ inch in diameter take longer to grow, but they'll still produce. Sets larger than ¾ inch in diameter are very apt to 'bolt' or grow seed pods in a hurry after you plant them. If you let them grow seed pods (a pod looks like a miniature version of the domes on the towers of the Kremlin in Moscow), the plants put energy into the seeds and not into the bulb. The bulbs will be small, tough and won't keep, so pick the pods or seed stalks off as soon as you see them.

The most dependable sets are around ½ to ¾ inch in diameter — the size of marbles — and are quite firm.

Where Sets Come From

Most sets are grown from seed on big farms near Chicago. The onion seeds are planted very thickly. Super-crowding of the plants makes the competition for water and fertilizer fairly stiff, so the plants never get very big. The resulting bulbs are quite small.

The small onions are harvested in the late

Onion sets larger than ¾ inch in diameter may quickly grow seed pods. Pinch off these pods, so the plant's energy goes into the bulbs and not the seeds.

summer or fall and dried for a month or more to rid them of moisture which could cause rot. Then the sets are stored until gardeners need them the following spring.

I've heard that Chicago got its name from onions. Indians, who once lived nearby, called the place "Shikako" which means "Skunk Place" after the strong smell of wild garlic, onions and leeks that once flourished there.

Growing Your Own Sets

To save some money and have a little onion fun, you may want to grow your own sets. Here's how I do it: sometime in July in a small section of my garden I plant a good keeping onion, such as Yellow Globe. (Further south, in the middle states, you can plant in August.) I sow the seeds about ¼ inch apart in foot-wide rows. I give the plants some fertilizer and just let them grow without thinning them at all.

About frost time I bend the tops over. (In a big garden I've even mowed the tops down with a rotary mower.) I wait a week or so and then dig the small bulbs out of the ground. After curing them for a few weeks, (more about curing, see page 183), I store them in mesh bags in a very cool, dry, dark place. The following spring — plenty of sets on hand. I may buy extra sets to back up my supply.

Most Southern gardeners don't bother with growing sets because they have a pretty long season and don't always need the head start that sets give.

But if you're an experimenter, here's one method that works pretty well in the South: Select an onion seed variety that's a good keeper, and in early March sow it thickly in a wide row. Just let them grow. As they are very crowded, the bulbs won't get oversized. Harvest the bulbs when the tops wither from the hot summer sun. Dry them in the sun for a day or so and store them in mesh bags in a very cool, dry place. In the fall you can set them out in the garden again. They'll put on a little root growth before it gets cold, and when the weather warms up in the spring, they'll pop back to life, giving you very early onions. Of course, in the deep South, where the winters are quite often mild, you can plant sets in the fall and harvest onions throughout the winter.

Buying Transplants

The best way to start big bulb, European-type onions is from transplants. They are thin, young onion seedlings, and the best planting size is when they are just the size of a pencil. You can send away to seed or plant companies for bunches of transplants, or you can often buy them at your local nursery. To get mail-order transplants, you order the kind you want sometime during the winter from companies in southern states, and they ship them to you in the spring. You have to order by the bunch (75 to 100 plants in each bunch). As with many other things, if you order a lot, it'll be cheaper, so getting together with friends on a big order can save you a little money.

Mail-Order

The first thing to do when the plants arrive is to unwrap them. The onion plants develop a lot of heat when banded together, and heat encourages rot in onions. Then put ½ inch of water in a shallow pan, such as a baking pan, and stick the roots in the water. Just get their "toes" wet. They'll revive quickly. And plant them as soon as you can.

If you can't plant them within a few days, forget the bath. Put the unwrapped plants in plastic bags and store them in a cool, dry place until you can plant. The refrigerator is a good spot!

You can also "heel in" your transplants until you have time to plant them where they belong in the garden. Just dig a shallow trench out in the garden (or use some kind of container if you want), put the plants in the soil a couple of inches deep and firm the soil tightly around them. Soil in the spring is usually wet enough to keep the roots from drying out.

If some plants have a bad odor or they are slimy or slick, they are probably rotting. Separate them from the others right away. They won't make it in the garden.

Growing Your Own Transplants

There is a tremendous satisfaction in growing your own plants indoors for transplanting. For one thing you have the benefit of choosing from more varieties.

Buy your seeds early enough to start your plants anywhere from 8 to 16 weeks before the last hard frost in your area. I start mine in a flat that is 4 or 5 inches deep, filled with very rich, sterile, loose soil. Sterile soil is free of weed seeds and harmful disease organisms, so the onion seeds have a better chance at the start. The various potting soil and starter mixes on the market are good, but mixing in extra fertilizer before you plant is a must. I find that 1 or 2 tablespoons of 5-10-10 fertilizer added to every gallon of potting soil works fine for onions and other vegetables.

Sprinkle the seeds into the soil and gently press them into it. I try to space my seeds about ¼ inch apart, but I don't fuss about it. It's impossible to get them spaced exactly right, and you can always thin them if they get too close. After sowing, I just barely cover the seed with a little more soil or sand and tamp it down.

Then I moisten the soil and wrap the flat with a sheet of plastic and then some newspaper. The plastic creates a greenhouse effect retaining the moisture, and the newspaper keeps the temperature even. (Onion seeds do not need light to germinate.) You won't need to water again until you take off the newspaper or plastic.

Put the flats in a nice, warm spot around 65° or 70° if possible. (Don't worry too much about the temperature being exactly right. Onion seeds *will* germinate anywhere from 40° to 80°. They prefer a steady 65° to 70°, that's all.)

Don't put the flats on a windowsill before the seedlings come up. The temperature there fluctuates too much. On a sunny day it will get up to 90° or more, and then at night it's the coldest place in the house. That's not good for germination. What onions want is an *even temperature*.

When the seedlings sprout, remove the plastic and newspaper and put the flats by a window or under lights. They won't need too much attention. Just make sure they get enough water, and you should add a little fertilizer from time to time — about a teaspoon in water every two weeks is good. Pour it around the edges so that it runs and covers the whole area.

In a few weeks, you'll notice the tiny plants getting tall and spindly. That can be a problem, unless you turn it into a plus. It's very important that your onion seedlings not fall over and get too skinny to transplant, so when they are 3 inches tall, cut them back to 1 inch. Your first harvest! The trimmings are delicious in dips, salads, sandwiches or as a garnish.

After you cut them, the plants will naturally produce more tops. When the tops reach 3 inches again, mow them back to 1 inch. As long as the plants are indoors, cut them back whenever they grow to 3 inches. With short tops the plants can put more energy into developing healthy roots, and that will help them get a good start when you put them in the ground. When it gets close to planting time, don't trim them anymore. Top growth will be important outside.

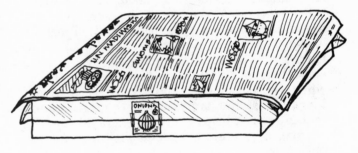

BEFORE YOU PLANT

Soil Preparation

Onions will grow in practically any kind of soil, but a soil that is very rich in decayed organic matter and humus and having good drainage is best. A heavy soil that sticks together after a rain will bake hard when the sun comes out. That makes it difficult for the bulbs to expand.

Another problem with very heavy soils is that water stays on the surface in puddles. That can drown plants! I know some gardeners in Georgia who overcame this problem by making raised planting beds — about 4 or 6 inches high. When it comes time to plant onion sets in Jan-

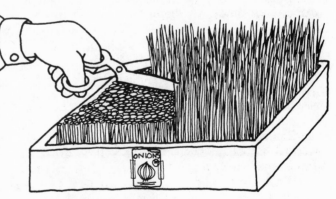

Give seedlings sunshine as soon as they poke through the soil, and trim them back to 1 inch to encourage root growth and to prevent spindly plants.

uary, their seedbeds aren't too wet to plant. The planting beds, which are about 10 inches wide, drain well and leave the soil moist but not packed, soggy or impossible to work.

Adding plenty of organic matter to heavy soil will help to loosen it up and improve drainage. With light, sandy soil, the organic matter will help hold the water after rain or irrigation. If your soil has plenty of organic matter — like decayed leaves or compost — worked into it, I'm sure it will stay moist after a rain or irrigation. Organic matter acts like a sponge, holding moisture near the surface. That's good for onions. Their roots are shallow, and they can't tap water or nutrients deep in the soil.

If you're wondering about soil acidity or alkalinity (pH), onions do best if the soil pH is between 5.5 and 6.5, a little on the acid side. They'll grow outside this range, but perhaps not as well. You can easily test your own garden's pH by using a soil-testing kit, available at gardening stores. Soil testing is also done by County Cooperative Extension Agents.

Fertilizer

I've never known onions to refuse some fertilizer — they like a lot of it. In my experience they can take twice as much fertilizer as most other vegetables. Your onions won't mind it a bit if you add plenty of well-rotted or dried manure, compost or commercial fertilizer to the soil before planting. A neighbor of mine always includes some bonemeal, which is high in phosphorus, when he prepares his soil for planting. Phosphorus stimulates early bulb formation and root growth. It helps give onions a rapid start. By the size of his crop, I think his little handful goes quite a way.

To determine how much fertilizer you should mix in your onion row before planting, this chart may help.

Onion Row	5-10-10	Fertilizer 8-16-16	10-10-10
10 ft. long, 15″ wide	2¾ cups	1 cup	½ cup
25 ft. long, 15″ wide	6¼ cups	2 cups	1¼ cups
50 ft. long, 15″ wide	12½ cups	4 cups	2¼ cups
100 ft. long, 15″ wide	25 cups	8⅓ cups	5 cups

Consider this a minimum requirement. Some extra compost or dried manure will be great for the onions, too!

While my onions are growing I like to 'sidedress' them. A sidedressing is simply an extra ration of nutrients; it can be more compost, dried manure or commercial fertilizer. Onions like a steady supply of nutrients all season long, but they need a little more fertilizer once the bulbs

start forming than they do at the beginning. That's because they use a lot of energy making bulbs.

One of the best times to apply sidedressing is when the bulbs *begin* to swell. That's when they can really use a boost. A pound and a half of 5-10-10 fertilizer will nourish a 15-inch wide-row about 20 feet long, and if your onions are in a narrow, straight-line row, this amount will be good for a row 100 feet long.

There are a couple of easy ways to apply sidedressing. If you plant a single row, you can make a *shallow* furrow down both sides of the row, about 2 or 3 inches from the plants and sprinkle the fertilizer in the furrow as you go down the row. Then cover it with soil.

Or, in wide rows you can sprinkle fertilizer a few inches from the bulbs. I'm careful *not* to get any on the onion top leaves where it might 'burn' them. There's no danger of burning if I sprinkle good compost around the bulbs. In either case, the next rain or watering will start carrying the fertilizer or compost toward the roots of the onions.

If you have a very sandy, porous soil, your fertilizer will tend to leach straight down instead of spreading out to all the roots. Really sandy soils don't hold water and nutrients very well — they drain away too fast. You may have to side-

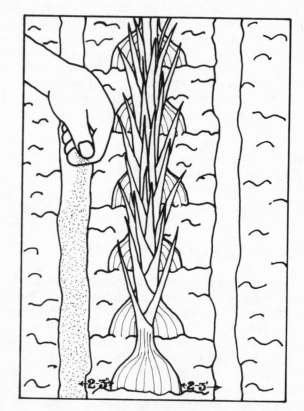

Onions need extra energy during the growing season. To side-dress single-row onions, apply fertilizer band 2 to 3 inches away from bulbs and cover with soil.

With wide rows, simply sprinkle fertilizer around bulbs, being careful not to get any on plant leaves.

dress more often in sandy soil than you would with a clay or loam soil.

If you plant your onions in soil that has plenty of compost or rotted or dried manure worked into it and feed them as they grow, I can almost guarantee they won't have any diet problems.

Here are the signs that indicate onions need more nutrients:

* *Pale yellow or greenish-yellow leaves. Onions could lack nitrogen. (Leaves can yellow after long, wet periods of weather because a lot of rain washes nitrogen from the soil.)*
* *Plants grow slowly and there are many thick-neck bulbs. (Thick-neck bulbs will not keep as well.) Phosphorus may be lacking.*
* *Onions have thick necks; bulbs are soft with thin skins and tips of leaves turn brown. Onions may lack potassium.*

Important: It's difficult to overfertilize onions. As I said, they use quite a lot of nutrients.

Caution: *Don't give onions fertilizer when the tops are starting to fall over.* It's just not needed that late in the season. The extra boost of energy could cause them to sprout new leaves at harvest time. New growth at the neck of an onion will keep it from completely drying out, and it may rot in storage.

PLANTING

I always put my sets in the ground *early* in the spring. Onions do best if the temperature is cool when they start to grow and warm as they mature. Our Vermont springs are certainly cool — and often frosty! But I have a saying, "You can't kill an onion — even with a hammer!"

Frost just won't harm sets. As soon as the ground can be worked in the spring, put them in. In Vermont that's usually in late March and early April. Gardeners in the mild winter areas of the deep South can plant their sets in the fall and get a plentiful supply of fresh onions throughout the winter months. Most other southern gardeners can get under way early. Why, I know gardeners in Atlanta, Georgia who plant their sets on New Year's Day!

Onion sets you plant in early spring will put on a lot of green top growth before they make bulbs. You may ask, "Why don't the bulbs start forming right away?"

Before the plants can make bulbs, they first have to store energy in the top green leaves. Then they have to wait for Nature's signal to put this energy into bulb making.

The plants usually get the message when the day length and the temperature are right. The onions don't care how old they are or when they were put in the ground; when conditions are right, they simply stop making new leaves and start using the energy they've stored to make bulbs.

So, the size of the onion bulb is determined by how much energy there is in the top green leaves. The more green growth, the more energy there is, and the bigger the bulb will be.

Early planting is important because it gives your plants plenty of time to grow tops and to store a lot of energy for the bulbs. If you put your sets in late, they won't have the time for a lot of top growth. As a result, there won't be much

You can't kill an onion — even with a hammer! So plant sets even if it's frosty

energy available when Nature whispers to the onion plant, "Make a bulb."

The Wide-Row Method

You should plant sets about 3 to 4 inches away from each other in wide rows (or a little closer if you plan to harvest them when they are small). I like wide rows for onions and many other vegetables because I can grow much more using less space. That's especially important if you only have a small plot. Here's what I mean:

If I plant 100 onion sets 3 inches apart in a single row, my row will be 25 feet long. If I allow a few inches, say 3, on each side of the set, the row will be 6 inches wide. That's a total of 12½ square feet of garden space for 100 sets. But with a wide row 15 inches across, putting the 100 sets 3 inches apart in all directions, my row will be just 5 feet long and 6¼ square feet. The garden space I use for 100 sets is half the space of a single row! A wide-row is easier to water, weed, fertilize and harvest, too.

I received a letter from a home gardener in Wyoming who tried growing onions in a wide row on a big scale. He wrote, "Whew! I may have overdone it, but a 150-foot by 4-foot wide row of onion sets (1 bushel of sets) will surely supply a small village."

Plant sets to the full depth of the bulb.

In the Ground

There's no need to make trenches or special holes for the sets. Just grasp them at the top (the pointed end) with the root end down and push them into well-prepared soil the full depth of the bulb. The soil should just barely cover the top of the onion sets. If you have some tiny sets, plant them at least an inch in the ground, so they get good contact with the soil. The sets will get a better start. After you've got your sets in the ground, firm the soil around them with a hoe.

Remember, if a set is planted too shallow, it takes a long time to get started. It's important to push the bulb all the way into the soil. It gets the onion off to a good start to produce a lot of top growth. If the onion sets are a little too deep, it won't hurt. Later, when the bulbs are expanding, pull some of the dirt away from the sides to give the bulbs room to expand.

A Florida gardener recently told me he likes to plant his sets deeper than usual to get better scallions (see page 170). He said, "Plant them extra deep, and you'll have a lot more white stem to eat."

I don't plant all my sets at once. I keep a few handfuls in the refrigerator. When we start harvesting some small onions to eat raw or use in salads and other dishes, I replace them with sets from the icebox. It's one of the many ways we keep the harvest going.

Planting Transplants

Hardening Off

Hardening off transplants is simply getting them used to being outdoors instead of in a warm house. Plants are like people — they can get sunburned, windburned or chilled, too. To harden off your seedlings, take your flats outside around the time of the average last frost in your area. Set them in partial shade, protected from wind, for a couple of hours the first day. Increase their time outside by an hour or so a day the first week.

Then place the flats in full sun for most of the day, and if there's no danger of frost, leave them out overnight. If you suspect a freeze, bring them in or protect them well outside.

After about a week or 10 days of gradual exposure to the outdoors, your plants will be tough enough to take the shock of transplanting.

Remember: Plants are more tender than sets, so transplant after the danger of hard freezes in your area has passed. Light frosts won't hurt them, though.

Transplanting

When you plant your seedlings, make sure the seedbed is smooth and the soil has compost or fertilizer worked into it. Putting the transplants in is easy: Lay the plant on your index finger, and push your finger with the onion on it into the soil about 2 inches. Lift up just a bit (this gets the roots headed in the right direction) and firm the soil around the plant. (You can also use a pencil to make the holes for the plants.)

Don't be afraid to transplant small seedlings — even those as small as toothpicks. I put some tiny ones in each year, and they make it.

Starting Seeds Outdoors

Half your weed problems can be eliminated if you prepare your soil properly before you plant. First your soil should be finely tilled and as free of clods and chunks of earth as possible. Like many other vegetables, onions get under way better in rich, smooth soil.

Combine the onion seed with some radish seed (about 5 per cent radish seed) and sprinkle or "broadcast" this mixture in a wide row about 15 inches across. I let the seed fall where it may, because I know that by harvesting the fast-growing radishes (they will also serve as row markers) and many young onions early for eating or pickling, there will be enough space between the remaining onions for them to grow to full size.

To make sure the seed has good contact with the earth, I spread a light layer of soil on top of the seed and firm it into the soil by tamping it down with a hoe or rake.

When the plants are up and going — about ¼ inch high — I thin some of them out with a steel garden rake. You may feel cruel doing this the first time, but do it. The end results will be worth it. I just drag the rake lightly through my onion wide row. The teeth thin out some of the plants, and they also cultivate within the row uprooting many little weeds as well.

When the bulbs start reaching ½ to ¾ inch in diameter (about the size of a marble or English walnut), I start pulling some of them to use right away for pickling or boiling.

Whenever enough bulbs reach the size I want, I harvest them. This way we have a continuous supply, and we don't have to do all the pickling and canning at the same time.

The small white onions are best for canning, pickling and boiling, and the varieties I prefer are Silver Queen, White Portugal or Eclipse. In April or May, I sow them close together after preparing the soil as I would to grow big onions.

For storage onions, I sow Early Yellow Globe onions because they are a convenient, all-around cooking size. I plant them fairly thickly and really give them a good thinning by dragging a rake through the row after they're first up. When the onions get good top growth, I pull some up and we eat them as scallions. After all our scallion-eating, the plants will stand 3 or 4 inches apart.

GROWING
Weeding

Onions hate weeds! Onions are slow-growing and have shallow roots, and weeds are just the opposite. Onions are thin plants, while weeds often have thick foliage that blocks out the sun onions need. All in all, onions can't give the weeds much competition. I've heard some gardeners come out of the onion patch moaning, "The weeds have won!"

It doesn't have to be that way.

Give your onions a head start in their battle with weeds by planting them in a spot where the weeds were previously kept down. For example, put them where a wide-row of some shade crop, such as bush beans or peas, kept weeds out the previous season. There won't be as many weeds to sprout in that area, and the onions will have a better chance.

Important: Just before you plant onions, till or cultivate the seed bed to destroy any weeds sprouting near the surface. At least those few weeds won't get a head start on your onions.

Don't wait until you can see the weeds! Weed seeds are very tiny, and they usually germinate about ¼ inch from the surface. An easy, shallow cultivation can kill weeds that are starting to germinate right under the surface.

The best time to cultivate is a few hours after a rain or watering. Since disease can spread very fast when the garden is wet, don't work around the plants until the leaves are dry. Also, wait until the top of the soil has dried out somewhat. If the sun is shining — all the better. When you stir the tiny weed seedlings out of the ground, the sunlight will dry up and kill their roots.

While you're keeping a watch on weeds, don't

forget to look for seed pods on your onions. Pinch them off as soon as you spot them. I can't emphasize this enough.

For most of my weeding I use an In-Row Weeder, a tool I invented that lets me cultivate very close to the plants and pass safely over and around them. It works extremely well with onions. It stirs up only the top quarter-inch of soil, so there's no cutting the roots. (A big broad hoe is more likely to damage the shallow onion roots near the surface, and that keeps the plants from taking up essential moisture.) As in any good cultivation, this tool also aerates the soil and keeps it from forming a crust. I use it all through the season with onions to get rid of young weeds and to keep the soil in good condition.

If you miss a few chances to cultivate, some weeds will grow past the point where a shallow cultivation can uproot them. That's when I use a hoe with a very slim blade and curved neck. I can stay on my feet to pull weeds away from the onions. It's easy to use very close to the plants; it's not cumbersome like a broad hoe. I can work

Quicker Sprouting

You can gain a week or more on the onion season by soaking the seeds in lukewarm water for a few hours before planting them.

Another way to sprout the seeds is to spread them on a wet paper towel and roll up the towel. Then put it on a wet terrycloth towel and roll that up. Put the towels in a plastic bag and seal it. Check it after 4 or 5 days. When the sprouts are tiny, plant them just as you would onion seeds.

quickly without any fear of cutting the roots or bulbs.

To help onion bulbs when they're swelling, you should loosen or pull away some of the soil around them. I like to leave just the bottom third of the bulb in the ground. In very hot, sunny parts of the country, you may want to throw some mulch over the exposed bulbs to keep them from getting sunburned. (Sunburn produces green spots and strong taste.)

Weeds aren't much of a problem in my garden as long as I plant in the right spot, cultivate as soon as I can and regularly keep after the weeds — about once a week. I rarely have much hand-weeding to do.

Here's my weeding strategy in a nutshell:
* *choose relatively weed-free spots for onions*
* *till or rake the soil right before planting*
* *cultivate gently when seedlings appear or after transplants or sets take hold*
* *do the job regularly — don't wait to see weeds*
* *get busy when the sun shines after a rain (be sure foliage is dry and soil is drying out)*
* *use good, lightweight weeding tools*
* *remember, shallow cultivation is best*

Mulch

Mulch is a covering of leaves, grass clippings, peat moss, etc. spread on the ground around plants to keep the soil moist, the weeds under control and to act as insulation for the plants. Mulching around the bulbs just as they're getting big is a good way to keep them supplied with vital moisture. It helps keep the soil soft for good bulb expansion, too.

If your garden is in an area that's very hot at harvest time, you can throw a thin layer of mulch or soil over the bulbs to protect them from sunburn.

Onions that you want to winter over in the garden don't require a lot of mulch. I use just a couple of inches. This insulates the top of the soil and keeps it at an even temperature. Without mulch, onions could freeze, then thaw. If that happens several times, it will cause them to rot. It's okay if they freeze once and then gradually thaw out with the soil in the spring.

If you have planted onions in a wide row and don't like weeding much, when the soil is nice and warm and the green tops are up a few inches, you can put on a layer of mulch around the onions. By blocking the weeds from the sun, they never have a chance, and the onions thrive.

Watering

It's especially important for onions to get water just after planting. A well-hardened transplant can survive almost two weeks in dry soil. But, in the long run, early dryness will hurt the crop. The bulbs just won't measure up at the end of the season.

If soil is allowed to dry out during bulb formation, the onion may split and form two bulbs. It helps to apply mulch (see page 181) when the tops get 10 to 12 inches tall, because mulch helps retain moisture.

Because their roots are so shallow, onions dry out faster than many other crops during a drought. When that happens, the onions often mature early, and that doesn't help the size of the bulbs. *Watchword: don't let onions dry out.*

Many people in the West and Southwest must irrigate their home gardens all season long, while gardeners in other parts of the country may face a dry spell of several weeks during the season. Where water is in good supply, people turn to sprinklers and furrow irrigation to keep gardens supplied with water. In areas where water is not plentiful, moisture-saving drip or trickle irrigation is now important.

If you use a hose or sprinkler to water your garden, remember it's best to water early in the morning rather than during the heat of the day. Too much water is lost to evaporation if you water when the sun is high.

Watering onions and other plants from above in the evening can leave plants with wet foliage overnight. Often that can be an invitation to trouble because with moisture remaining on leaves, disease can spread rapidly.

Onions do need a lot of water, but the soil shouldn't be soggy all the time. "Just enough" water is better than "too much." A thorough soaking to a depth of 6 inches once a week is what onions require rather than just a light sprinkling each day.

Here are some guidelines for watering:
* *if the soil is dry, water immediately after planting or transplanting*
* *keep the soil moist until seedlings come up or until plants and sets take hold*
* *in well-drained soil, onions need a thorough soaking of 1 inch of rain or water per week to grow best*
* *watering when onions are bulbing can keep some soils from hardening around the bulbs allowing for bulb expansion*

Pests

I've yet to get a call from a Vermont neighbor saying, "Insects are getting my onions!" Onions in the North aren't usually bothered by insects like onion thrips or onion maggots, but I've heard from many gardeners in the South who have to deal with them.

Thrips are very tiny insects that feed on the leaves of the onion plant. The plants weaken, and the yield of the crop can be reduced quite a bit. A spray or dust with rotenone or malathion is usually all it takes to control thrips. Follow spray directions on all sprays carefully when you use them.

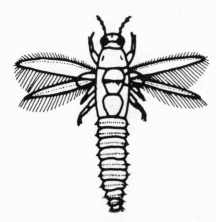

The **onion maggot** is the offspring of a small fly that lays its eggs near the base of the plant, or late in the season right on the bulb itself. The small maggots kill the plant by burrowing into the stem and the bulb. Pull up and destroy any plants with maggots before the maggots mature into flies.

There are some insecticides that can handle a bad case of onion maggots, but please check with your local Extension Service Agent and read directions carefully before using these insecticides in your garden.

Diseases

Neck rot is probably the most common onion disease. It often hits just after the harvest or while the bulbs are in storage. All onion varieties can develop neck rot, but the mild-flavored, Bermuda-type onions are especially susceptible. Drying the onions at warm temperatures with good ventilation can help prevent this disease.

There are some fungus diseases such as **pink root, mildew** and **bottom rot** that are carried in the soil itself, but rotating the onion plot is just about all a home gardener has to do to avoid these.

It's a good idea to spread your onions out, planting them in several sections of the garden. You not only reduce the chance of onion disease, but, because onions repel many insects, you create a kind of defense network that protects your other vegetables.

Harvesting

There's never a time when onions aren't ready for harvesting. They can be picked and eaten at any stage.

But no matter how many onions we use during the season, it's nice to have a crop of big onions mature at the end of the summer to store for the fall and winter months.

You can always tell when onions have stopped growing. The leaves will lose their color, weaken at the top of the bulb and flop over. Each year a few new gardeners watch the leaves die and ask me, "What's wrong?" There's nothing wrong; it's Nature's plan. The leaves' job is done — they've put the last of their energy into the bulbs.

We like to let most of our onion tops fall over by themselves — maybe 80 or 90 percent of them. We bend over the rest of them. Once the tops are down, we leave the bulbs in the ground to mature fully — maybe 10 days to 2 weeks. It's not good to leave the onions in the ground for longer than two weeks after the tops die because they become very open to organisms which can cause rot in storage, or they might even start growing again.

We pull our onions up on a sunny day if we can, and let them sit in the sun for a day or so to dry. In hot climates this usually takes just a few hours. This drying kills the little root system at

the bottom of each bulb. The roots will be like little brittle wires when they're dry.

We have a friend in Alabama who says that picking the right day to pull the onions can determine how well the onions will keep. He keeps an eye on the weather and, if possible, harvests the onions after 3 or 4 sunny days. "If you harvest them after some rainy weather," he says, "they have a heck of a lot of moisture in them. They don't dry out as well."

Curing

Now after drying the onions in the open for a day or so, it's time to bring them under cover for a second, longer drying or 'curing' process.

Some people cut the tops off the onions before curing, but we don't think it's necessary. But *if you trim the top leaves, don't cut them any closer than 1 inch from the bulb.* Otherwise the neck won't dry out, and the onion could rot in storage.

To cure them, spread your onions out in any warm, airy place out of the sun, such as a porch. We have quite a lot of onions each fall and not enough porch, so we spread them out near the edge of our gravel driveway and cover them with a light cotton sheet (not plastic!) to provide shade.

The sheet, held in place by stones along the edge, keeps the sun from burning the bulbs but still allows a lot of air circulation. We turn the bulbs a couple of times to promote even drying.

Heavy coverings like canvas or plastic trap moisture inside, so the onions will never get really dry. With our sheet system we don't worry about a few scattered rains. The sheets and the onions dry out rapidly after a shower.

We don't want any wet spots on the onions when we put them in storage, so we give them a darned good curing, maybe two or three weeks. Then we hang them in mesh bags in our carport and dry them some more before putting them in our root cellar. It doesn't take that long in the South, but we find the more people cure the onions, the better they keep.

Here are the basics of curing:
* *sun dry for just a short time*
* *cure just the onions you'll store; separate the soft, young and thick-necked bulbs and use them first*
* *cure in warm, well-ventilated area away from direct sun*
* *don't crowd onions during curing; give them room to breathe*
* *onions are ready to store when the skins rattle and the roots are dry and wiry*
* *cure thoroughly for best storage*

One more thing about growing and harvesting: The gardener and the cook have to work together pretty closely, we've found. It doesn't do you a bit of good to grow something, harvest it, and then find out your partner had something else planned either for the crop or the day it comes in!

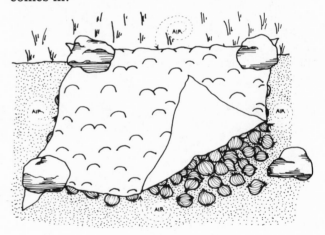

Garden
to
Kitchen

PRESERVING ONIONS

The onion is such a versatile vegetable, one that we use in so many different ways, that we spend time through the summer pickling some of the white ones, freezing or drying some of the larger ones that don't store well in the root cellar, and then storing most of the yellow ones we grow. Because we like them, we eat a great many onions. We figure we use about 10 pounds of onions per family member during the year.

I hope some tips or ideas here will encourage you to try some new ways with onions, as well as with other members of this tasty family.

Storing

Storage is the great thing about onions — there aren't many vegetables that keep as well and taste as fresh as onions do after storage.

Let me give you a few pointers:

Don't wash your onions before storing them.

You probably can't store all your onions. Use up the immature, soft and big-necked ones, and store just the mature and thoroughly cured bulbs. Hanging them in mesh bags (sorted by size) is a good way to store them in a root cellar.

Onions will keep best at temperatures between 32° and 40°F, and the closer to 32° the better. The temperature in a root cellar is usually a little higher. That's okay — root cellar temperature is a compromise anyway. (You can't please all the vegetables.)

The humidity should be low, too, to slow down root development and the spread of rot organisms. Good ventilation is important also.

A 96-year-old gardener recently wrote us about his curing and storing system. He drops a dried onion in a nylon stocking, then ties a knot in the stocking above it, adds another onion, ties another knot, etc. Then he hangs the stocking in a warm, dry, shady place to cure. When the curing is done, he just transfers the stocking to his root cellar. With this system, the onions never touch each other, so they can't pass on rot organisms easily. During the winter our friend takes a pair of scissors to the root cellar and just snips off the onions he needs for a meal.

It's not necessary to have a root cellar to store onions. If you follow the basics of onion storage, you'll have satisfactory results.

The storage basics are:
* *store only mature, well-cured onions*
* *keep onions in a cool, dry, dark spot*
* *allow for good ventilation*
* *check occasionally for soft spots, sprouting, etc.*

Pickling

Pickling is our favorite way to preserve a lot of the small, white onions we grow. We like to eat pickled onions, and so do our neighbors. The onions don't mature all at the same time, so we don't have to rush and do all the pickling at once, which makes it easier.

Our older daughters, Barb and Brenda, like to come over at pickling time with their onions and other vegetables. We mess up only one kitchen, talk, have lots of fun experimenting with different recipes and just enjoy being together. We work on an assembly-line basis; it's easier because we can move along more quickly. Everything is out and easily available before we begin. We are fairly strict about this because when we're pickling, canning or freezing, we can get in an awful mess with blanching pans, cooling-off pans and containers all over the place.

Braiding

If you want to braid onions together — an old, effective and attractive way to store onions — do it soon after the harvest while the tops are still flexible. You may use some twine to reinforce the tops, and be sure to hang the braids in a well-ventilated, warm, shady spot to cure. After they are cured, store them in a cool, dark place, and bring out one braid at a time to use. The braids are pretty to look at, and they are a handy way to keep onions. (Garlic can be braided, too.)

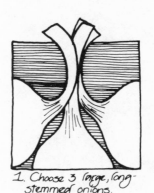

1. Choose 3 large, long-stemmed onions.

2. Wrap the 3 onions with another onion top or with natural twine

3. Begin to braid the onion tops as you would braid hair.

4. Work in another onion every inch or so to continue the length of braid.

5. After the last onion has been added, braid to the end of the tops.

6. Loop the braided end around & secure with twine.

Drying

This is one method of preservation with which we have been experimenting. It seems to work pretty well. I peel and slice the onions in rings about 1/8 inch thick and put them in an electric dryer at about 140°F until they're nearly dry. To keep the pieces from browning, I usually bring the temperature down to 130° for the last hour or so and just keep testing for dryness.

When I'm satisfied the onions are dry, I take them out of the dehydrator, cool them and store them in sealed containers in a cool, dry place. Because the onions are light and reconstitute easily, they're handy.

We keep a jar or two of them at our camp in the mountains. They're not affected by the severe changes in temperature that occur in the unheated cabin. It's great for when we go to camp; we can get a fire going in the woodstove and make a pot of soup or stew quickly. We don't have to go to the bother of slicing, dicing and peeling the onions — they're all ready to use.

If you like snack foods, onion rings which have been French-fried and then dried in a dehydrator are a delicious party treat. They do not store well unless vacuum sealed, but they're so good that they won't stay around long enough to need storage!

Freezing

Honestly, I don't freeze onions much. I find they're one vegetable that's easy to have fresh all year long. One thing I have tried, though, and find quite handy if some of my onions aren't keeping or are starting to sprout is to peel some and mince them in my blender. I quick-freeze them in my refrigerator freezer, covering the trays with plastic so the odor doesn't affect other foods. After they're frozen, I put the onion cubes in a plastic bag in my food freezer. They're good for gravies and taking the 'canned' taste away from canned soup.

But, if you want to freeze onions, here's how: To freeze whole onions, peel and wash them and blanch them in scalding water until the centers are heated (3 minutes for small onions to 7 minutes for medium to large ones). Cool, drain and put them on cookie sheets, and place the sheets in the freezer. After they are frozen, put them in a plastic bag for convenient storage. Freezing them in this two-step way makes them easier to use; they stay separate, so it's easy to take out only the amount you need.

To keep large, European onions that don't store well, wash, chop and freeze them without blanching. Pack them in small containers, leaving ½-inch headroom.

No matter how I freeze onions, I find they have better taste if I use them within a month or two.

Canning

Onions can be canned in a pressure canner, but I don't recommend it. The onions discolor and lose their shape. It's easier and more satisfactory to pickle them, freeze them or just store them. Even the 'canned' onions you find in the store aren't plain — they're usually pickled with a brine and spices.

Scallions

Scallions or green tops are one of the first vegetables we can harvest each spring. It's a real pleasure to go in the garden and pull them. Good scallions are young, green and tender and usually have several inches of white skin above the roots. They are either grown from a variety of bulbless onion or they are green tops — thinnings from the entire onion family: garlic, shallots, leeks, as well as onions.

Scallions keep a few days if wrapped in plastic and kept in the refrigerator, but they're best if picked the day you use them. To prepare scallions, wash them and cut off the roots. Peel off the outside layer of skin and cut off the top green tail, leaving about 4 to 6 inch scallions. (The green tails are good as garnish. Excellent with sliced tomatoes, on baby boiled potatoes and fish.)

Preserving Scallions

To dry scallions, cut them crosswise, tops and all, into 1/8 to 1/4-inch bits. Put the chopped scallions into a cheesecloth bag and blanch them in boiling water for 30 seconds. Plunge the bag in cold water, then take it outside and shake it to dry. Put the scallions in a single layer on the dryer screens, and when thoroughly dry, seal them tightly in containers. When using dried

scallions in dips or spreads, let them stand in the mixture for 2 hours before serving.

To freeze them, simply chop them up and put them in small, plastic containers and put them in the freezer. Use them within a month or so for their best flavor.

Chives

Chives are chopped finely and used as garnish and in spreads, dips and eggs. Their flavor gets stronger the longer they are mixed with cottage cheese or cream cheese, so only combine them at serving time.

To cut chives use scissors and trim a few of the stalks to a height of 1 inch rather than cutting the tips of the whole plant. When they grow back to 6 or 7 inches, they may be trimmed again.

Shallots

The queen of the sauce onions, the shallot, imparts a delicate flavor to sauces somewhere between garlic and onion. Shallots should not be browned as they turn bitter, and 3 to 4 shallots are the equivalent of 1 medium-sized onion and are rarely eaten alone, but are used in cooking. However, pickled shallots are special (see page 191). Shallots are cured, dried and stored in the same way as onions.

Leeks

Leeks are the king of soup onions and are regarded in France as the asparagus of the poor.

The patron saint of Wales, Saint David, exhorted his countrymen who were faithful to King Cadwaldr to distinguish themselves from their Saxon foes by wearing a leek in their caps. Even now on Saint David's Day, March 1, Welshmen sport leeks, the emblem of Wales, on their lapels.

To prepare leeks for cooking, they must be washed very carefully, flushing water down into the white part to remove the dirt that has accumulated from the blanching process during growing (see p. 172). Trim off roots, remove any bruised or dried leaves; cut off tops leaving only the white stem and tender part of the green leaves. The leeks will be about 7 inches long. Flush out sand from the leaves by washing thoroughly under cold water.

FAVORITE RECIPES

Cheese and Onion Pie

The wife of the retired minister next door, Mrs. Waldo, gave me this recipe. Her family likes it, and so does mine. This pie is similar to quiche.

1¼ c coarse cracker crumbs
½ tsp curry powder
6 Tb margarine, melted
1¼ c sliced onions
¼ tsp paprika
1¼ c milk + 1 Tb cold milk
1½ c grated cheese, Parmesan
2 beaten eggs
1 tsp salt
2 Tb margarine

Preheat oven to 325°. Mix cracker crumbs, curry powder, salt and 6 Tb margarine together. Line 9-inch pie plate with this mixture, keeping ¼ cup for topping. Saute onions in 2 Tb margarine in saucepan over medium heat. After onions are transparent, put them in pie crust. Heat 1¼ cups of milk in top of double boiler. Blend paprika and 1 Tb cold milk and add with the cheese to the hot milk. Stir until cheese melts. Slowly stir in the beaten eggs. Pour over onions. Sprinkle remaining cracker crumb mix on top. Bake at 325° for 40 minutes.

Leeks may be substituted for the onions in this recipe. Swiss or Gruyere cheese is good to use with leeks.

Glazed Onions and Carrots

2 c cooked tiny onions
2 c cooked, sliced carrots
½ c maple syrup
1 c apple juice or cider

Combine syrup and juice or cider in heavy saucepan. Cook over low heat until the mixture thickens. Then add the drained, cooked vegetables and simmer over low heat 30 minutes. Stir the vegetables frequently to glaze them evenly. Keep them hot until served.

Creamed Onions

1½ lbs small, white onions
1½ c shredded carrots (optional, but a must at our house)
  For the sauce:
2 Tb butter or margarine
2 Tb flour
½ tsp salt
1/8 tsp black or white pepper
1½ c light cream or milk
½ c shredded cheese (optional)

Peel the onions and cook them gently in boiling water until tender, approximately 15 minutes. Drain and keep warm.

Melt the butter in a heavy saucepan over low heat. Blend in flour and seasonings. Cook over low heat, stirring until the mixture is smooth and bubbly. Take the saucepan off the heat and cool. Then gradually stir in the milk or cream. Heat the sauce just to boiling, stirring constantly. Simmer and keep stirring for one minute or until sauce thickens. If you're using carrots, stir them in and cook 5 minutes longer over moderate heat, stirring often. You may also add ½ cup shredded cheese if you want — it's good.

Pour the hot sauce over the hot onions. Mixing them together while hot will prevent curdling. Serves 4 to 6.

Firehouse Onions

Our son-in-law, Noel, told me about this one. It's his favorite way to have onions. His family invented the recipe, and I guess that's why it got the name — his dad is a retired fireman.

5 lg onions, sliced
1 c catsup

Saute the onions in the catsup in a heavy skillet over low heat until the onions are tender. Serve as a relish, side dish or vegetable. They're good — maybe even better — the next day, cold or hot.

Baked Onions and Apples

When Dick is curing our storage onions in the early fall, it's time for this harvest specialty.

1 lb onions
1 lb tart apples
3 Tb flour
1 Tb brown or white sugar, honey or maple syrup
½ tsp salt
2 Tb butter

Peel the onions. Wash and core the apples. Slice both the onions and apples thinly. Don't pare the apples unless the skins are tough. Dredge the apples in the flour mixed with sugar and salt. If maple syrup or honey is used instead of sugar, make sure it is mixed well with the onions. In a greased baking dish, alternately layer the onions and apples. Dot the top with butter, cover the dish and bake at 350° for about 30 minutes. To brown the top, remove the cover during the last few minutes of baking. Serves four to five. Good accompaniment to meat loaf and baked potatoes, which can be baked at the same temperature and thereby save energy.

Baked Stuffed Onions

4 lg Spanish onions
1 c chopped onions
1 c whole kernel corn
bread crumbs
½ lb pork sausage
1 Tb chopped parsley
2 Tb melted margarine
½ tsp paprika

Peel the onions and cut about ½-inch slice from tops. Blanch until just tender. Cool and remove centers, forming ¾-inch shells. Chop the onion centers and tops, cook with pork sausage in a heavy skillet until browned, stirring to break the sausage into small bits. To the sausage and onions add the bread crumbs, parsley and corn. Fill onion shells with this mixture and place in greased baking pan.

Mix margarine and paprika. Brush mixture on onion skins with pastry brush. Cover with tin-foil and bake for 15 minutes at 400°. To brown, take cover off and bake another 5 minutes.

Good served with broccoli or green beans and fruit salad. Other fillings: rice and cheese; mushrooms, onions, cream cheese and parsley; chicken livers; rice and onions — something nice you can do for leftovers!

French-Fried Onion Rings

1 lg Spanish or Bermuda onion
½ + ⅔ c milk
½ c water
½ c flour
¾ tsp baking powder
¼ tsp salt
vegetable oil or fat for deep frying

Peel the onions, and cut them into ½-inch slices. Separate them into rings and soak them for ½ hour in mixture of ½ cup of milk and ½ cup water. Heat the oil (1 inch deep) to 375° in a deep pan or fryer. Mix smooth batter of ⅔ cup milk, flour, baking powder and salt. Dip each ring in the batter, and fry a few rings at a time until golden brown, turning once. Drain the rings on absorbent paper and serve immediately. One big onion makes 3 or 4 servings.

Braised Leeks

12 washed leeks, about 1½ inches in diameter
3 to 4 c water or chicken stock or broth
6 Tb butter
½ Tb salt
2 to 3 Tb chopped parsley

Use heavy, fireproof baking dish or casserole long enough to hold leeks. Make 2 or 3 layers of leeks and pour in enough water or stock to cover ⅔ of the leeks. Add butter, salt and parsley.

On top of stove, partially cover casserole and set over fairly high heat. Boil 30 to 40 minutes, until tender when pierced with a knife. Most of the liquid should have evaporated or been absorbed.

Place casserole in 325° oven, covered loosely with aluminum foil and bake for 20 to 30 minutes until leeks are pale gold.

Excellent with roast lamb or beef. Good served with cheese melted on top, too.

Leeks are wonderful served cold with french dressing if butter is omitted during braising.

Real French Onion Soup

(12 servings)

For the stock:

1 c butter or margarine
3 lbs yellow onions
2 cloves garlic
8 c beef consomme or stock
½ tsp black pepper
salt to taste

Melt the butter or margarine in a large, heavy pot. Add thinly sliced onions and garlic and cook over very low heat 20 minutes until the rings are pale gold but not brown. Add consomme or stock and bring to a boil. Add pepper and salt; simmer gently for 30 minutes.

You can freeze part or all of the stock at this point to serve later. To save on containers when freezing stock, I put two plastic bags, one inside the other, in a half-gallon milk carton, pour in the cooled stock, use "twist-em" ties to close, and place it in the freezer. When the stock is frozen, I tear off the carton, label the bags using freezer tape and just store the plastic bags. These square bags stack well in the freezer and use up less space than round, plastic freezer containers.

To finish six servings:

½ c red wine, port or whatever wine you like to use in cooking
6 slices of toasted, buttered French bread
¾ c grated Swiss cheese

Heat the soup and stir in the wine. Divide the soup into six small individual casserole dishes. Top each with a slice of toasted, buttered, French bread and sprinkle each slice with about 2 tablespoons of grated cheese.

Bake in preheated oven (375°) for ten minutes or until cheese melts and becomes crusty. Excellent with a fresh, green salad for lunch.

Easy Vichyssoise

3 medium-sized, washed leeks
1 medium-sized onion
2 Tb butter
4 medium-sized potatoes
1 to 2 c cream
¼ tsp mace (optional)
salt & white pepper
chopped watercress or chives
4 c chicken stock or broth

Mince white and tender green part of leeks and onions and sauté them in butter in large, heavy saucepan until just transparent. Peel potatoes and slice very finely. Add potatoes and chicken stock to leeks and simmer, covered, until tender, about 15 minutes. Puree mixture in blender or food processor. Add cream, salt and pepper and serve hot or cold. (Cold it's vichyssoise, hot it's leek and potato soup.) Garnish with watercress or chives.

This also makes an excellent soup base before adding the cream. Different vegetables may be incorporated, such as carrots, string beans, watercress, asparagus or turnip.

Sautéed Scallions

7 to 12 scallions per serving, peeled
1 Tb butter or margarine per serving

In a skillet melt butter or margarine and add scallions. Stirring frequently to prevent burning, sauté them over medium heat until they are tender and golden. Excellent accompaniment for meat, especially hamburgers.

Scallion-Sour Cream Dip

2 Tb minced scallions
2 c sour cream
½ tsp lemon juice
dash of pepper

Mix all ingredients together. Chill well. Serve with fresh, raw vegetables such as pieces of cauliflower and broccoli, carrots, cucumbers, eggplant strips and green pepper slices. Makes 2 cups.

Green Onion Top Cheese Spread

1 lb softened cream cheese
¼ c milk
¾ c minced green onion tops

Mix ingredients together until the mixture is light and fluffy. Serve on crackers.

Pickled Onions or Shallots

This is the recipe I use most often for pickled onions. Dick took a few jars to deer camp this year and only came home with the jars. (Oh, yes, and a 6-point buck!)

4 qts tiny, peeled onions or shallots
1 c salt
2 c sugar
¼ c mustard seed
2½ Tb prepared horseradish
2 qts white vinegar
7 bay leaves
7 small, red, hot peppers
7 pint jars and lids

Sprinkle the onions with salt. Cover with water. Let stand 12 to 18 hours in a cool place. Drain, rinse and drain again. Mix together sugar, mustard seed, horseradish and vinegar. Heat, simmer for 15 minutes. Pack onions in hot, clean jars leaving ¼-inch headspace. Add 1 pepper and 1 bay leaf to each jar. Heat pickling mixture to boiling. Pour over onions, retaining ¼-inch headspace. Remove air bubbles with spatula. Adjust lids. Process pints 10 minutes in boiling water bath.

(If you have never canned, you may want to read more before starting. There are several really good canning/preserving books available; one is "Keeping the Harvest" by Nancy Thurber and Gretchen Mead, Garden Way Publishing. Or consult your County Cooperative Extension Service.)

Pickled Onions and Cucumbers

8 medium, unpeeled cucumbers, cut in 1-inch chunks
¾ lb small, peeled white onions or 2¼ c onion slices
2 c water
5 tsp salt
4 c white vinegar
2 c sugar
5 ½-pint jars and lids

Cover the onions and cucumbers with 2 cups vinegar and water; bring to a boil. Remove the vegetables immediately from the vinegar and water mixture. Throw away the liquid.

Fill hot, clean jars with the cucumbers and onions. Add 1 tsp salt to each ½-pint jar. Combine 2 cups sugar and remaining 2 cups vinegar; boil 2 minutes. Pour over onions and cucumbers leaving ½-inch headspace. Remove air bubbles from jars with spatula. Adjust lids. Process in boiling water bath for 5 minutes. Makes 5 half-pints.

Dill Onions (Quick Method)

30 to 40 small, peeled onions
1 qt white vinegar
1 qt water
¾ c sugar
½ c salt
3 tsp mixed pickling spices
2 heads fresh dill or 1 Tb dill seed per jar
3-4 pint jars and lids

Combine vinegar, water, sugar and salt. Tie spices in a cheesecloth bag and add to the vinegar mixture. Simmer 15 minutes. Pack onions in hot, clean jars, leaving ½-inch headspace. Put a head or two of dill in each jar. Cover onions with boiling vinegar mixture retaining ½-inch headspace. Remove air bubbles with spatula. Adjust lids. Process in boiling water bath for 5 minutes.

ET CETERA

Aroma

People seem to make a big deal about onions on your breath, but I don't let it bother me. If it does, I brush my teeth or have a mint. Some other tips I've heard are eating parsley, celery leaves or a slice of bread.

After working with onions, I end up with the smell on my hands. Unless I'm going to sew or something, I don't worry about it. But you can rub them with a few drops of lemon juice, vinegar or a little salt to remove the odor.

And I think the smell of onions cooking is good! But if you don't like it, light wooden matches. The sulfur from the matches will take the odor away. So will lighting a tablespoonful of coffee (or at today's prices — ground chicory root!) in an old pan or ashtray.

Peeling Onions

No recipe I know calls for unpeeled onions, and peeling onions is one chore many people don't like because it makes them cry.

There are a few tricks that have helped me that I'm happy to pass on. I find I can cut down the irritation if I breathe through my mouth as I

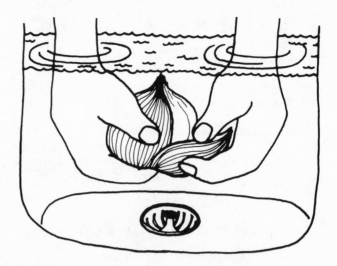

peel and slice onions. Also, I often peel them in cold water, which prevents the onion chemical from becoming airborne.

Another trick, especially handy when peeling a whole lot of small onions, is to soak them for a few seconds in boiling water and then in cold water. The skins will then slip off more easily.

And last pickling season my daughters and I used a new, hand-powered spinning peeler. It also doubles as a lettuce dryer because of an inner basket, and it works great for peeling quantities of onions, potatoes and carrots. We just cut both ends off the onions, put enough water in the peeler to touch the bottom of the onions, put on the cover, take a few turns of the crank — peeled onions!

CHAPTER 8

Cole Crops

Gardeners often group broccoli, Brussels sprouts, cabbage, cauliflower and kohlrabi together as "cole crops." Cole is the German word for cabbage, hence the term "cole slaw." Cole crops are hardy and grow best in cool weather, and an easy way to remember is to think how much "cole" sounds like "cold" or "cool."

Cole crop seed is slightly more tender than the mature plant. In order to sprout, it must be planted in rich, moist soil with the air temperature about 60°F.

Once the seed sprouts, it sends down the start of its taproot while the stem and first leaves develop. These first leaves are called seed leaves.

The true leaves appear next and the plant is on its way toward fulfilling its natural goal: to produce flower buds that will eventually open and give way to a seed stalk.

Cabbage and Brussels sprouts actually surround a seed case with their tightly folded leaves, forming a head. Broccoli and cauliflower heads, or "curds," are tight bunches of the buds themselves.

Once the heads have formed, they gradually loosen (unless you pick them, of course) to make room for the seed stalk to develop. This loosening action is triggered under certain temperature, daylight and growing conditions, causing the plant to bolt, or go to seed.

Broccoli — Sprouts with Clout!

When broccoli first came to this country from Italy, it was considered exotic. Now, it's as much a part of our garden and kitchen as peas or carrots.

The bluish-green mature heads of broccoli can be harvested from early summer to late fall, depending on your climate and growing conditions. Once the first large head is harvested, most broccoli varieties produce smaller side, or lateral, shoots that extend the harvest for weeks.

I always plant broccoli in the early spring and again in midsummer for a fall harvest. The only time the plants don't produce heads is during the hottest weeks of the summer, but at that time there are plenty of other fresh vegetables to keep us well-fed.

We love broccoli because our fall crop keeps bearing shoots after the rest of the garden is spent. The green leaves and stems are a welcome sight in the chilly September and October days. We've even harvested them for our Thanksgiving dinner here in Vermont.

There are quite a few dependable early varieties of broccoli, along with purple-headed and late season types. I stick with these four good-growing producers: **DeCicco** takes 60 days to the first harvest of large, tight, dark green budded center heads, followed by weeks of many side shoots. **Green Comet Hybrid** is extra-early, maturing in only 40 days. Its disease and heat resistant qualities make up for the fact that it only produces a single, large head with few, if any, side shoots. **Italian Green Sprouting** broccoli is widely available and good for both spring and fall crops. The head reaches 5 or 6 inch harvestable size in about 70 days from transplanting and produces many light green tender side shoots. **Spartan Early** is another favorite that develops tightly packed, medium heads on short stems about 55 days from transplanting.

Cabbage — King of the Garden

I've heard more stories about cabbages than just about any other vegetable. Giant cabbages, cracked cabbages, headless cabbages and bolting cabbages. They really are a snap to grow, and they are one of the few salad vegetables you can have available from your garden well into winter. Raw cabbage is said to possess great healing power, and at one time it was prized by the Egyptians.

Cabbages can be either early, for spring planting; midseason, for planting anytime; or late, for a fall crop. One thing to remember is that the late varieties need a longer growing season than the others, so you may end up planting your fall harvest earlier than a midseason variety. Check the seed packet for the days to maturity. Count back from the time you'd like to begin harvesting, and you'll have a handy planting and harvesting timetable.

Because cabbages are biennial plants, you don't have to worry about them going to seed in the garden. The main problem that gardeners have with cabbages is splitting heads, or no heads at all; I'll show you how to avoid these troubles.

Following is a list of cabbage varieties, including red cabbage and Savoy cabbage, that should do well in most gardens.

Stonehead — 65 to 70 days to maturity — Extremely solid heads; 6 inches in diameter; yellows resistant; early variety; short core.

Early Round Dutch — 71 days — Heads are round and firm; slow to split or bolt; mature at different intervals for extended harvest; grow to average weight of 4½ to 5 lbs.

Early Flat Dutch — 85 days — Large, flat heads; good winter keepers; average weight 10 to 12 lbs.

Penn State Ballhead — 90 to 110 days — Extremely hard, nearly round heads; can be harvested young (about 4 lbs.) or when mature (7 to 9 lbs.); good for krauting or winter storage.

Ruby Ball — 68 days — Extra early, firm, round, dark-red heads; small-cored; resists splitting; delicious raw or steamed.

Savoy King — 80 to 90 days — Crinkly-leaved, dark green, semi-flat heads; heat resistant for summer growth; average weight 4 to 5 lbs.

Brussels Sprouts

Even though Brussels sprouts have been a mealtime tradition for hundreds of years, I must admit I used to avoid eating them, until we grew our own. The difference between those frozen in the supermarket and your own, fresh from the garden, is unbelievable. Now we really look forward to the fall harvest of "mini-cabbages."

Growing Brussels sprouts is almost as much fun as eating them. They start out looking just like cabbage or broccoli, but as they grow, the stem becomes tall and thick and sprouts pop out above each large leaf along the main stem. They look like miniature palm trees — at least that's what my grandsons call them. You add to this look by breaking off the lower leaves once the harvest begins. The stems can end up 2 to 3 feet high, loaded with sprouts.

This vegetable originated in Brussels, Belgium and is still extremely popular in Europe. As more Americans try them, Brussels sprouts are becoming better known and enjoyed in this country, too.

Long Island Improved is the most popular variety of Brussels sprouts, and **Jade Cross** is desirable

because it is disease-resistant. Both mature in 80 to 90 days after transplanting, and they grow best as a fall and early winter crop. The sprouts not only withstand frosts, their flavor improves after a freeze.

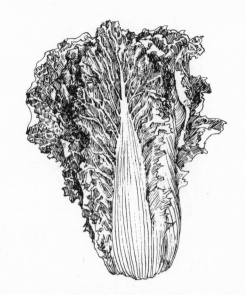

Cauliflower — "Cabbage with a College Education"

I have talked with many gardeners in different parts of the country and their feelings about growing cauliflower sometimes shocks me. I hear things like, "Cauliflower's only for city folks." "I can't be bothered with blanching." "We're afraid to try cauliflower; we've just started gardening." Nonsense! Cauliflower grows exactly like cabbage, and to make the heads white or blanch them, you simply cover the heads with their own leaves for 4 or 5 days.

Cauliflower can be used in any recipe that calls for broccoli, but we actually prefer to serve it raw as cauliflowerettes with dips or in salads. Kids will often eat vegetables raw that they refuse to eat cooked. They're better for them, and easier for you, too. Try them on raw cauliflower.

Unlike broccoli, cauliflower produces only one head per plant. The head is called the "curd," and your only concern is to keep light away from it as soon as it's about 3 to 4 inches across. After that, it's just harvest and enjoy. Since it freezes so well, be sure to plant enough.

Snow King and **Early Snowball** are both popular strains of early cauliflower, reaching maturity in 50 to 60 days. The first is heat tolerant, so it will do well in the South.

Purple Head is an unusual cauliflower variety that doesn't need blanching. The head matures in 80 to 85 days, and it really is purple. It turns green when you cook it and is an interesting variety for freezing or pickling.

Chinese Cabbage

Oriental vegetables seem to be showing up in gardens all over America, and as an amateur wok chef, I'm delighted to try them all. I've had the best results growing Chinese cabbage, a close cousin to the rest of the cabbage family.

The leaves of this vegetable form a loose, oblong head that grows 18 to 20 inches tall. It's sometimes called "celery cabbage" since it also resembles the tall, ribbed stalks of celery.

The flavor of Chinese cabbage is much sweeter than standard cabbage, with a nice nut-like aftertaste. The leaves are crisp and tender and can be used in any combination salad or stir-fry dish.

Michihili — 72 days — Most common variety. Grows well in partial shade and will take a few autumn cold snaps. Can be harvested until November here in Vermont, so in many parts of the country, Chinese cabbage can easily become a fall, spring and even a winter delicacy.

Kohlrabi

This strange-looking vegetable is sometimes called a "stem turnip" since the stem just above the ground forms a fattened bulb that tastes like a sweetened turnip. The name is derived from the German words **kohl** (cabbage) and **rabe** (turnip).

Kohlrabi is started from seed right in the garden. The plants are very durable, and will thrive in just about any kind of soil in any temperature. Kohlrabi is the one garden vegetable that seems to be insect and disease free. We've grown it for years, and have never had a single problem. Naturally, it's bound to be a popular plant!

We always plant lots of kohlrabi in the early spring, and we include raw slices in all our summer

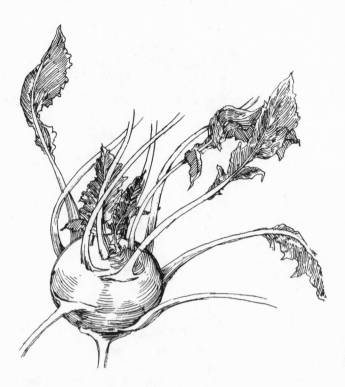

pH

Like most garden vegetables, cole crops grow best in soil that is slightly acid with a pH of 6.0 to 6.8. You should have your soil's pH tested every couple of years to determine its acidity or alkalinity, either by your County Cooperative Extension Service or with a home soil-testing kit available at most garden centers.

If the test indicates that your pH is too high or too low, or that your soil is deficient in certain vital nutrients, you can remedy the situation by adding the prescribed corrective substances. This might be lime, sulfur or other minerals.

The fall is the best time for soil testing and for taking necessary corrective measures. There's plenty of time for the additions to work their magic on the soil. Of course, you can test and add lime in the spring. However, because lime takes a few months to work down into the soil, it is best added in the fall. The new seasons' crops will be that much better if you take care of the pH four to five months ahead of planting time.

Site Selection

Cole crops can be planted just about anywhere in the garden. As long as they get 6 to 8 hours of sun each day, they don't mind a little shade from neighboring rows. Your only considerations will be crop rotation and how long the crop will occupy the spot you give them. For instance, Brussels sprouts take the entire growing season, yet some varieties of broccoli will be finished in as little as 30 days from transplant time.

Crop Rotation — A MUST!

One final word before you plant your cole crops. Be sure you don't plant any member of the cabbage family in the same place in successive years. Also, rotate if you plant more than one crop the same season. The insects and diseases that bother cole crops remain in the soil, and your crops will be spared considerable damage if you plant them where beans, peas, tomatoes or other vegetables grew previously.

If you garden in a community plot, it can be worth your while to find out what crops were in that plot during the previous year, and rotate your cole crops.

Earlybird Spring Gardening

Plan to start your first crop of cole family plants indoors and transplant the seedlings early, waiting only until the ground is dry enough to work and you're not expecting another hard freeze. Allow

party dips. Our guests sometimes have to guess what they're tasting, but they always enjoy the flavor. Kohlrabi is excellent in stir-fry dishes, too.

The two most common kohlrabi varieties are the **Early White Vienna** (it's really pale green in color) and **Early Purple Vienna** whose skin is bright purple and looks jazzy in the garden. Both plants mature in 50 to 60 days, but we prefer the flavor of the white kohlrabi.

GETTING STARTED

Soil Savvy

Cole crops will produce well in nearly any type of soil, as long as you take the time to till or spade the planting spot thoroughly two or three times before planting. These vegetables grow best in loose soil that is rich in organic matter. So while you're preparing the soil, mix in plenty of old leaves, manure, compost, straw or kitchen garbage to enrich the topsoil.

Spring cole crops thrive in sandy soils that drain well. Spring showers can sometimes waterlog roots in heavy soil. If you have mostly clay soil, don't fret; work in some organic matter to loosen up the clay particles. Fall cole crops, on the other hand, actually prefer a heavier soil because it retains moisture better. Rainfall at the end of the growing season can sometimes be scarce.

Even if you've turned over your soil with a spade or tiller, always work your planting area one more time on planting day. This adds fresh air to the seedbed and loosens the soil there.

about four to six weeks from planting the seeds indoors to transplanting. For example, here in Vermont I plant the seeds indoors around the end of March and transplant them in early May.

Since certain varieties are designed as early-maturing and others as late-maturing, you can extend the harvest by planting more than one variety. In general, the early varieties are meant for the spring planting, but you can mix and match with very few, if any, problems.

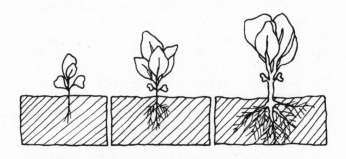

Starting Seeds Indoors

The only time you need to start cole crops indoors is in the spring, since you want to be sure your plants can mature before hot weather hits. If you're planning a fall garden, or if you live in an area where the summers don't get very hot, you can start cole crops from seed right in the garden.

You can buy transplants in garden stores or farmers' markets. However, by growing your own, you save money, you can grow varieties you choose, and you have the added satisfaction of doing it yourself.

Here's what you need:

— Sterile, fertilized potting soil or seed starter mix.
— Flats or individual pots.
— Seeds. Choose varieties that are right for your climate and soil conditions. Check with your Extension Agent and local gardeners for advice.
— Water.
— Small, flat board or shingle.
— Newspaper and plastic covering.
— Light — sun or artificial.

Here's what you do:

1. Fill the flats with sterile soil or soil mix to about 1 to 1 1/2 inches from the top.
2. Smooth the soil with a board or shingle.
3. Sprinkle the seeds fairly closely, about 1/2 inch apart.
4. Firm the seeds into the soil.
5. Cover the seeds with 1/4 to 1/2 inch of soil.
6. Level and firm the top layer of soil.
7. Carefully moisten the soil thoroughly until the soil is damp but not muddy.

8. Cover the flats with a layer of plastic, then a few sheets of newspaper. The newspaper insulates the flat, ensuring a more even temperature. Most vegetable seeds do not need light to germinate.
9. Place the flats in a warm spot with an even temperature. Don't place them on a windowsill; the temperature there fluctuates too much. The top of a refrigerator works fine for me.
10. When the seedlings first show, remove the plastic and newspaper cover and place them in a sunny window or under lights.
11. Keep the soil moist, not soaked, by watering once (maybe twice) a week. Check for dryness by pressing your finger into the soil; if it feels dry, water.
12. Once the seedlings are up, give them a small dose of balanced fertilizer or plant food, dissolved in water, about once a week.
13. When the seedlings grow at least two true leaves, transplant them into another container, leaving about 2 inches between each plant. Give the seedlings water when needed and a steady supply of light.
14. Ten days before you want to plant the seedlings outside start preparing them for the transplant shock by hardening them off.

Shock-Proofing

If your seedlings are to live through the shock of being transplanted outdoors, you need to gradually expose them to the sun, wind and spring temperatures. Just like people, plants can become sunburned, windburned or chilled if they aren't toughened before they're exposed. This process is called "hardening off."

Cole crops are hardier than many of the vegetables that you transplant in the garden, but their yield will be much better if you give them time to harden completely.

Here's how to harden off:

1. Withhold water for a few days before moving the plants outdoors.
2. Move the plants outdoors for a few hours, placing them in a sheltered spot protected from wind and direct sun.
3. Gradually increase the length of time outdoors and amount of exposure until the plants are outdoors 8 to 12 hours at a time.
4. After 5 or 6 days of daytime hardening, leave the plants out overnight for 2 or 3 days. Bring them indoors if there's a danger of frost.
5. After a week to 10 days of hardening off, your seedlings should be strong and ready for transplanting.

Fall Garden Bonus

Fall cole crops taste better than spring crops, I think. Cole crops seem to do best if they are planted in warm weather and mature when the nights are cool and the days are crisp and sunny.

A fall cole crop garden is a bonus because it gives you fresh vegetables long after most of your crops have been harvested. Plant your cole crops (plus onions, greens, and root crops) twice: once in the spring and again in late summer for a full harvest. In the fall, the ground may be cold and brown and covered with leaves, but you can still be cutting fresh broccoli and cabbage. You can expect Brussels sprouts into January, since they withstand hard frosts and a fair amount of snow.

A major benefit of a fall cole crop garden is the lack of diseases and insects. Pests hit hardest in the spring and summer, and many harmful insects and bacteria are killed by the first cold snap.

You also don't have to bother with flats or peat pots indoors for your late crops; you can start the seeds right in the garden toward the end of summer.

For storage purposes, the fall garden has still another selling point. Late cabbage varieties are bet-ter keepers, so use the fall growing season to make the most of your garden space.

Food to Grow On

Luckily, cole crops don't have special fertilizer needs; a moderate dose of a fertilizer is fine. Work it into the transplant hole for seedlings or for seeds the top 3 to 4 inches of soil on planting day.

Chemical fertilizers supply the three elements that are vital to plant growth. These are nitrogen, phosphorus and potassium. Their presence in a bag of commercial fertilizer is indicated as a percentage of the total (for instance, 10-10-10 or 5-10-10). The elements are always listed in the same order: nitrogen (N), phosphorus (P) and potassium (K).

Organic fertilizers, such as dehydrated animal manures, are also excellent sources of plant nutrients. They should be mixed into the soil at the same time and at the same rate as chemical fertilizers, about 5 to 6 pounds per 100 square feet. Organic fertilizers also condition the soil while providing nutrients to the plants.

No matter what type of fertilizer you use, if you know your soil is already very rich in organic matter such as leaves or compost, you can add a little less fertilizer. I use a combination of organic and commercial fertilizer in my garden. The organic material conditions the soil, and the plants get their fair share of nitrogen (which aids in leaf and stem growth), phosphorus (for strong roots) and potassium (for the overall health of the plant).

Since you will be planting seedlings, take special care not to overfertilize. Even after hardening, transplants are tender, and if they grow too fast when you first set them out, they may be weak in the long run. It's better to go easy on the fertilizer when they are transplanted and sidedress later in the growing season. I use only a small handful of fertilizer for each plant at transplant time.

Make the Most of Space

After trying many different cole crop planting arrangements and judging the pros and cons of each, I now have favorite ways of spacing the plants and laying out the rows. Of course, my suggestions aren't hard and fast planting rules; plant according to your own instincts and needs once you understand the options.

There is a simple formula for spacing cabbage: the closer you plant them, the smaller the heads. Commercial growers have started planting these vegetables closer, since most shoppers prefer a 3 or 4-pound head to a larger one. I plant cabbage closer than most seed packets instruct, and I save space by

staggering the plants in 10- to 20-inch wide rows. At our house, we make much better use of 20 smallish heads than we do 10 giant cabbages, and we think smaller heads taste better.

Start by planting the first two cabbages on each side of the row, 10 to 12 inches apart. Then measure down 10 inches and place the third cabbage in the center of the row. Continue alternating two plants, then one plant, until the row is complete. The row ends up looking a domino design of cabbage plants. You can also plant wider rows with a 3-2-3 arrangement.

There are other advantages with this method than just saving space. The plants in staggered wide rows mature at different speeds, so the harvest is stretched over a number of weeks. You'll also notice that the leaves of closely planted cabbages shade the ground keeping it cool, moist and weed-free. This saves some gardening headaches like weeding, mulching and frequent watering.

Cauliflower takes up about the same amount of space as cabbage, and can be spaced the same in staggered wide rows.

Broccoli and Brussels sprouts need a fair amount of room, since their broad leaves extend a foot or more. I plant them in single rows, one behind the other, 15 to 18 inches apart. I leave 2 feet between each row.

Kohlrabi and Chinese cabbage are exceptions in the cole crop family, since you plant them right from seed in the garden. Plant kohlrabi like root crops: sprinkle the seeds in 15-inch wide bands with 3 to 4 inches between seeds. Here again, you can grow lots of food in just a small amount of space, and the shaded ground helps the plants to grow trouble-free. It's almost a matter of just waiting until they're ready to harvest.

Chinese cabbage can be planted the same way. The seeds should be spaced 4 to 5 inches apart in the wide row.

It's perfectly all right to plant all the cole crops in conventional single rows. Just leave the same amount of space between each plant as suggested here for staggered or wide-row spacing.

Cole Crop Spacing

	Transplants inches apart	Seeds in Rows inches apart
Broccoli	15 to 18	4 to 8
Brussels Sprouts	18 to 24	4 to 8
Cabbage	10 to 12	4 to 8
Cauliflower	10 to 12	4 to 8
Chinese Cabbage	—	4 to 5
Kohlrabi	—	3 to 4

No matter which spacing method you choose, allow 16 to 24 inches between the rows, depending on the vegetable and your method of cultivation. You need more room if you use cultivating equipment than if you rely on hand-cultivating.

In the Ground

At last! You're ready to transplant your broccoli, cauliflower and cabbage seedlings. If you have a choice, pick a day that's overcast and moderately cool. Too much hot sunshine or cold wind will be hard on the plants. Planting late in the afternoon also helps protect them.

Have everything ready before you lift a single transplant: well-worked soil; your rows marked off; water; fertilizer; 2-inch wide newspaper strips to use as collars for cutworm protection; trowel or spade for making holes; seedlings.

Water the seedlings thoroughly while they're still in the tub, pots or flats. This causes the soil around their roots to adhere to the roots, protecting them from exposure to air and light.

I like to prepare each row step-by-step, rather than starting and finishing one transplant at a time.

The plants get uniform amounts of fertilizer, even spacing and water, and the rows are generally neater.

First, I make all the holes for the seedlings. Cole crop roots need large enough planting holes and loosened soil around them to take hold quickly. Use a trowel to dig 4 to 8-inch holes — deep enough to plant the seedlings slightly deeper than they were in the pots or flats. Space the holes 10 to 18 inches apart, depending on the crop.

Next, drop a small handful of compost or fertilizer in each hole and cover it with 1 to 2 inches of soil. This soil covering is crucial because the nitrogen in the fertilizer will burn any roots that touch it, meaning trouble for the plant.

Douse the hole with water. By making it muddy and soupy, you create a complete moisture seal around the roots that helps each plant take hold.

Carefully lift a seedling from the flat and cup the roots in your hand to protect them. The ideal transplant has more roots than leaves, and you can create this situation by removing some of the leaves. I pinch off the big outer leaves on each transplant, making certain to leave the center "mouse ear" leaves.

Place a cutworm collar around the stem of each seedling so that it extends 1 to 2 inches below the soil surface and sticks up 1 to 2 inches above the soil surface.

Quickly place the seedling in the planting hole. Remember to put it slightly deeper than it was in its original container. Scoop soil back in the hole to fill it back to level ground. Firm the soil around the plant; then water the plant well before moving on to the next.

You can't overwater these vegetables at transplant time. Most gardeners make the mistake of underwatering instead.

Transplant Insurance — Cutworm Collars

Unless you protect your seedlings, cutworms can wipe out whole rows of newly planted transplants overnight. These smooth, black or grayish two-inch worms chew through tender, young stems at ground level.

Luckily, it's easy to prevent cutworm damage when you're setting out your plants. The simplest way is to wrap the seedling stem with a 2 to 3-inch strip of newspaper. You can also make a collar from a paper cup with the bottom cut out, a strip of cardboard or a tuna can with both ends removed.

Cutworms chew stems either right at ground level, just above or just below. In order to make your collar an effective barrier, place it so it extends 1 to 2 inches below and 1 to 2 inches above the soil surface. A strip of newspaper will last long enough to keep the damaging cutworms away from your younger plants without interfering with their growth. Paper cups, cardboard or tin can collars can be left around the plants all season.

Fast Fall Gardening

You can plant an entire fall feast of cole crops in about 15 minutes. In most parts of the country, wait until midsummer, pick a garden spot that's produced an early crop such as peas, carrots or onions, and prepare it for replanting.

Work the top 3 or 4 inches of soil and add 3 to 4 pounds of fertilizer to each 100 square feet of growing space. If you know your soil is very rich, add less fertilizer. Some fertilizer from the previous crop is bound to be left in the soil. Work the fertilizer into the top few inches of soil.

Rake out a 15-inch wide band for your row and sprinkle the seeds evenly down the row 4 to 8 inches apart. Don't worry about planting too thickly. You'll be taking some plants from the row in just a few weeks.

Firm the seeds into the soil with the back of a hoe. This contact with the soil ensures good germination.

Cover the seeds with 1/2 to 3/4 inch of soil and firm again.

Since you start these plants for the fall garden during hot weather, you have to prevent the seeds and seedbed from drying out. Keep the seedbed moist by sprinkling it every few days or by putting down a light layer of grass clippings or straw to serve as a mulch. This is one of the major keys to a successful garden.

When the plants come up and are about an inch tall, thin them by removing enough seedlings so they stand 10 to 18 inches apart, depending on the variety. Or you can wait another week or so and transplant all the seedlings to another garden spot. I often compromise by thinning the row carefully and transplanting only the thinned seedlings.

After that, just keep the rows weed-free and watered, and you can look forward to a harvest that will last weeks after the first frost.

GROWING

Away with Weeds!

Weeds don't have to be much of a problem with cole crops you transplant, especially if you plant in wide rows. Once the plants take hold and develop broad leaves, they shade the soil under the plants. Weeds — like all plants — can't grow without adequate light.

Watch out for weeds in your rows of outdoor-started seeds for fall, however. The first few weeks your plants are growing is when weeds can damage the crop.

By working the soil and raking it four or five times before planting, I prevent quite a few weeds. Stirring the top few inches of soil exposes or buries weed seeds that would otherwise sprout.

Once you've planted some cole crop seeds, you can continue this invisible weed-killing method by using a rake or weeding tool to scratch the top 1/4 inch of soil. Be careful, however, not to stir up the seeds you're trying to grow.

When the seedlings are well established, you can cultivate the soil near them as well as the walkways between to keep out weeds. Use a hoe or other weeding tool to disturb the top 1/2 inch of soil every 4 or 5 days. Cultivating also aerates the soil, permitting air to get down to the roots of the plants.

Don't ever use a hoe right under the shallow-rooted cole crops. No matter how shallow you cultivate or how careful you are, you're bound to injure some roots. It's safer to pull weeds there by hand.

Mulch

Mulch is a protective layer of material such as straw, hay, leaves or grass clippings. Placing 4 to 8 inches of mulch around your garden vegetables prevents weeds, keeps the soil cool and helps retain moisture in the ground around your plants. Mulch is practically a must in the South.

Cole crops don't need to be mulched when the weather and soil are cool. But you can use mulch to provide the cool, moist growing conditions they need if it's hot.

Since Brussels sprouts have to be in the garden for a number of months before they mature, it's likely they'll be subjected to some hot, sunny days. Mulching them will help them endure the heat with fewer problems.

One of the benefits of mulch is that it cuts down on weeds by shutting out light to the ground it covers. If you really hate to weed, you can mulch the walkways between your garden rows as well as the vegetables themselves. Try to use a mulching material that contains few, if any, weed seeds, so you aren't planting more weeds than you prevent. Also, rodents and insects are sometimes attracted to the organic environment of mulch, so think twice about mulch if these pests are already a problem.

Black plastic is another type of mulch, but it is used mostly to warm up the soil for heat-loving plants, such as melons and tomatoes. Don't use it on cole crops.

Sidedressing

Some plants need extra nutrients during their growing period. They either use the initial fertilizer completely or they take such a long time to reach maturity that the fertilizer has been washed away. Giving plants a second dose of nutrients is known as sidedressing.

Usually, I sidedress broccoli, Brussels sprouts and cabbage. The best time is just before they start to head. They'll use this boost to produce a second crop once you've harvested the first. Since Brussels sprouts are in the ground a long time and the foliage is quite dense, they really respond to a second dose of fertilizer just before they start budding.

To sidedress simply draw a circle in the soil around the base of the plant, about 4 inches from the stem. Sprinkle a handful of 5-10-10 or dehydrated manure in the ring and cover it with an inch of soil.

Don't let the fertilizer touch the plant because the tender foliage can be burned by the nitrogen in the mixture. Burning is avoided by placing the plant food a few inches away from the base of the plant. You also ensure that the nutrients will seep gradually into the soil, reaching the roots a little at a time rather than all at once.

If there's no rain soon after sidedressing, water around the base of the plant to send the nutrients to the roots.

Water

Your cole crops will be fine as long as they stay moist as seedlings and receive a steady supply of water from the time they're up. They need about one inch of water per week.

If you have a rainy spring or fall, you won't have to worry about watering. Unfortunately, every gardening season seems to be drier at times than we'd like, so most of us have to supplement nature's watering occasionally.

Don't water out of sheer habit. If you have clay soil that retains moisture or if it rains hard every week or so, you may not have to water much. But, if you have light, sandy, quick-draining soil, you may have to water more often.

The easiest way to monitor rainfall is with a rain gauge. You can also check the soil for dryness by digging down a few inches. If you find dry soil below 3 or 4 inches, water!

Water the garden thoroughly to a depth of 5 or 6 inches to encourage deeper root growth and to spread nutrients throughout the soil.

Evaluate your own garden and use every drop of water wisely; your plants will be healthier for it.

Trouble-Free Gardening

Sometimes weather conditions cause cole crops to fail to produce quality heads. If seedlings suffer from stress in their first month or so of growth (temperatures below 55°, lack of nutrients or water), they may form small heads or no heads at all. This is especially true with cauliflower. Even though you can't alter the weather, raising your own seedlings and staggering your plantings can give you a hedge against these problems.

Many problems can be avoided simply by timely harvesting.

Cabbage — The most common cabbage problem seems to be cracking or splitting heads. This is usually caused by too much fertilizer or water that makes the new inner leaves of the heads grow faster than the older outside leaves.

To avoid cracking, don't overfertilize cabbages, and try to maintain an even moisture supply. If a head should start to split, you can stop it by "shutting off the faucet." That means simply grasp the head and rotate it about one half turn. This root prunes the

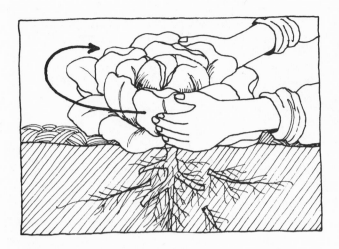

soon as the tight buds start to loosen. A head that is past its best harvest time is "ricey;" the buds separate and become somewhat granular. There are self-blanching cauliflower varieties that also work well.

Brussels Sprouts — You can affect the growth of the Brussels sprout plants two ways: by pruning the leaves along the stem and by pinching off the growing tip, called the terminal bud, on top.

I have the best results by snapping off all the leaves on the bottom six inches of stalk. I do this when the plant is well established and the buds have just started to develop. The leaves break most easily in the morning when they're crisp from the dew. This encourges more leaves to form higher up on the stalk and makes the plant grow taller. The sprouts are formed just above each leaf, so more leaves mean more sprouts.

plant, cutting some roots so the head draws less food and water. Then the outer leaves have a chance to catch up with the inner leaves, and the cracking ceases to be a problem. However, if it keeps splitting, just give the plant another half turn.

Sometimes a head that is overmature will crack, so try to harvest cabbages while they're still in their prime, firm and smallish.

Cauliflower — Most gardeners run into needless trouble with cauliflower when it's time to blanch the heads. The reason you blanch cauliflower when it's growing is to make the head nice and white. It sounds like it might be hard to do, but all you need to do is cover the young head before the sunlight hits it.

As soon as the head is 3 or 4 inches across, shield it from light by loosely tying or pinning the large outer leaves over the cauliflower head. I make it even simpler by bending the leaves over on all sides of the head and tucking them under it on the opposite side. Light stays out, but air circulation seems better than securing the leaves at the top.

Check the heads daily after blanching, and start harvesting as soon as the first head is snowy white. You may have to harvest one or two heads a day because cauliflower loses its fine texture and taste as

Pinching the growing tip directs the plant's energy into making more leaves, less stalk and earlier, larger sprouts. It also causes the sprouts to mature at about the same time, which is more helpful to commercial growers than to home gardeners. I generally leave the terminal bud alone, but if you want to remove it, wait until sprouts have formed on about 10 or 12 inches of the stem.

Although it's not necessary to prune or pinch back the top of Brussels sprouts, breaking off the leaves does make harvesting easier. You can begin harvesting when the first sprouts are marble-sized.

Broccoli, Chinese cabbage and kohlrabi don't need any special attention other than protecting them from diseases and insects that often bother the cabbage family.

DISEASES AND INSECT PESTS

Disease Basics

Some gardeners complain that their cole crops are constantly hit by diseases. Although occasionally there's nothing you can do, understanding how diseases strike can help you get on the road to healthier crops.

An agricultural professor once told me, "The number and complexity of diseases possible in the garden might seem overwhelming, but remember this: **three things are necessary for a disease problem — a susceptible plant, a disease organism, and the right weather and environmental conditions.**"

This simple reminder applies to all vegetables, and it also helps to explain why cabbage family diseases can be light one year and troublesome the next. **If one of the three requirements is missing, you can't have a problem. It's as easy as that.**

Unfortunately, there are usually plenty of disease agents in the garden and a number of susceptible plants. So the weather is often the key factor in determining whether a plant will remain healthy or contract a disease.

It's especially important to be on guard during extended wet weather, because most diseases flourish in cool, wet periods. Stunted plants, blotchy or spotted leaves, drooping foliage or changes in color . . . these and other signs indicate plants may be diseased.

Common Cabbage Family Diseases

Yellows — Lifeless, yellowish-green color appears in plant 2 to 4 weeks after transplanting. Caused by a fungus that lives in the soil indefinitely. Especially troublesome in wet areas during hot weather. Use resistant varieties (indicated on the seed packet by the initials "YR"), plant on raised beds if drainage is a problem and rotate crop every year.

Blackleg — Caused by a fungus, this disease infects young plants, causing them to wilt because it rots away the stem. As the disease progresses, dark sunken areas develop on the stem. Disease spreads in humid, rainy weather. Crop rotation and good garden sanitation are the best prevention.

Root Knot — Primarily a Southern disease caused by nematodes. Knots form on smaller roots and nearer the tips than clubroot. Although crop rotation can help somewhat, the only sure treatment is to fumigate the soil before planting. Check with Extension Agent for fumigating recommendations if root knot is persistent.

The U.S. Department of Agriculture publishes a complete disease identification guide available to the home gardener (Bulletin #380, available from the U.S. Government Printing Office, Washington, D.C. 20009).

Some diseases, including several bacteria and fungus-caused wilts, cannot really be checked once they appear. Other diseases may be slowed by applying a fine sulfur dust or other organic fungicide to the plants. The best way to avoid diseases in the cabbage family, and in all your vegetables, is to stop trouble before it hits.

Black Rot — A bacteria that can invade plants at any stage, blackening veins and affecting head formation. In severe cases, no head will form, or the existing head will rot. Rotate crops and remove plant debris.

Clubroot — Swelling of roots caused by a slime mold introduced through the roots. Lives in soil once mold is present. Crop rotation is best remedy and prevention. Disease doesn't thrive in alkaline soil, so adding lime to acid soils may help.

Crop rotation is probably the most important precaution a home gardener can take. Many disease organisms, such as those that cause yellows and clubroot, can live in the soil for several seasons. Depending on your garden size and its exposure to the sun, you might be able to solve a persistent problem with a three-year rotation plan. Don't plant any cole crop in the same garden area for three seasons.

Keeping Bugs Out

Insects seem to plague members of the spring-planted cabbage family more than some other vegetables. This isn't because bugs would rather chew on

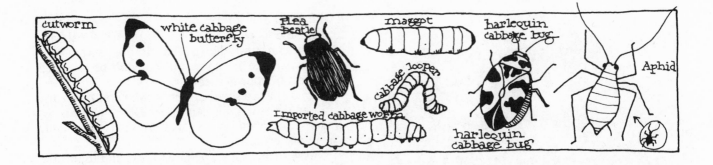

broccoli than beans. It's partly because many insect populations emerge — hungry — early in the season. Often, your cole crops are the only food in sight. Also, the distinctive odor of cabbage family vegetables may make them especially easy prey for insects.

One way to cut down on insect problems is to depend largely on the fall garden for your supply of cole crops. Insect populations are generally past their peak by the end of the summer, and increasingly cool temperatures discourage those that remain. You can also encourage insect-eating birds such as martins by providing a bird house in the garden.

Learn to recognize harmful insects (listed below), and make daily visits to your garden to pick off or destroy any unwanted pests before they ruin large amounts of your crops.

Cabbage Aphid — Small, sap-sucking insects that are often found on undersides of leaves. May introduce fungus, bacterial and virus diseases. Leaves of infected plants will crinkle and growth will be stunted. Remove and destroy parts of leaves where colonies occur. Spray with malathion.

Cabbage Maggot — Small, whitish larvae of a black fly. Bores into stems and roots, causing plants to wilt and die. Cover transplants with cheesecloth or nylon netting tent to prevent flies from laying eggs in surrounding soil. To remedy very bad infestations of maggots treat soil, before planting, with Diazinon.

Cabbage Looper — Pale green worm that crawls in distinctive looping or "measuring" movement. Feeds on undersides of leaves; breeds two or more generations each season. Pick off or spray with Dipel, rotenone, malathion, or methoxyclor.

White Cabbage Butterfly — Harmless in itself, but lays eggs on the underside of foliage to produce populations of destructive imported cabbage worm (see below). Keep butterfly from depositing eggs in garden by covering plants with protective netting.

Imported Cabbage Worm — Larvae of white cabbage butterfly. Green, with light and dark stripes, about 1 1/2 inches long. Eats very large holes in leaves; bores into cabbage heads. Handpick worms (locate from brown-black droppings on lower leaves). Some people have luck sprinkling worms with small amounts of salt, wood ashes or flour. Spray with Dipel, rotenone, malathion or methoxychlor.

Cutworm — Fat larvae of dull-colored, medium-sized moths. Can feed underground, on the surface, or above ground, but does most damage by chewing through young plant stems at ground level. Use cutworm collars at transplant time; cutworm baits later in the season.

Harlequin Bug — Barrel-shaped eggs emerge as black, shield-shaped adults with bright red markings. Nymphs may kill young plants by sucking out sap. Handpick bugs and destroy egg masses regularly.

Flea Beetle — Black, brown or striped jumping beetles, about 1/16 inch long. Attacks young plants by chewing leaves so they look as though they've been shot full of holes. Spray with malathion.

Note: One easily practiced preventive measure against many of the insects attacking cole crops is sanitation. Be sure to till in or cull and destroy plants that have been bothered by imported cabbage worm, cabbage looper or harlequin bugs. To survive, these pests must winter-over on some plant part, such as leaf or stem. Depriving them of a home during the cold months will reduce their numbers in your garden the following season.

A Note on Dipel

Bacillus thuringiensis (B.T.), the biological insecticide sold as Dipel or Thuricide, is extremely effective against worms and caterpillars. It has the added advantage of being harmless to all other forms of life, including humans.

Dipel works because it contains a bacterium that only infects moth larvae — cabbage worms, cabbage loopers, cutworms, even large tomato hornworms that strike just when your tomatoes are prime for picking. Don't worry about Dipel and our gardening friends, earthworms. They are not moth larvae, so they cannot be affected.

Because of the tremendous success I've had using Dipel on my cole crops during the past few years, I recommend it without hesitation. You generally mix

it with water and spray it on your crops. The best time to use Dipel is when you first see the white cabbage butterflies around the garden. If you spray your plants every 7 to 10 days, you shouldn't be bothered by worms in your garden.

If you have a small garden, or you don't own any spray equipment, you can apply Dipel with an ordinary houseplant mister. Just rinse it thoroughly when you're finished.

As with any spray, be sure to read and follow the directions that accompany Dipel, practice the other preventive measures outlined elsewhere in this book and enjoy a fine harvest!

To Spray or Not to Spray . . .

Be sure to consider the alternatives to spraying before deciding on chemical control. Perhaps you can harvest the crop early, or wait for helpful garden predators to restore the balance of power in your garden, or try natural insecticides or home sprays.

Look carefully at the damage to your crops and be sure it is being caused by an insect. Try to observe the pest in action if you can. This way you'll be sure the damage is insect-caused, and you'll have an easier time correctly identifying the pest.

Ask yourself if the damage is serious enough to warrant spraying for control. Insect activity is normal for any garden, and good gardeners often simply plant a little extra of every crop, realizing that he or she will share some of the harvest with various insects that live in or visit the garden.

If you opt for a spray or dust remedy to an insect or disease problem, keep these watchwords in mind for best results:

Once you select a spray to use, read and follow all directions on the label carefully. Pay special attention to waiting times between spraying and harvesting. The "days to harvest" information may change your pest control strategy. Some insect sprays are long-lasting, so be careful about using them on crops *near* those you want to harvest soon. Keep a logbook on all your pest control activities.

Your spray equipment should always be in good working condition. With some chemicals, it's safer to spray only at certain hours of the day. Sevin, for example, should be used very early in the morning or late in the evening because it is toxic to bees. (Bees do not work early and late in the day.) Dusts are more effective when applied early in the day when the dew is still on the plants.

Chemical control for diseases is usually recommended on a season-long basis. Sulfur, or fungicides such as captan and maneb, are often contained in the multi-ingredient, all-purpose tomato and potato sprays. These are used every 7 or 10 days through the season, usually starting within a week or two of planting and not just when disease is evident. As with other substances, fungicides must be handled and applied carefully.

Pesticides, used only when necessary and with caution, common sense and consideration for environment, can be an asset in growing a productive food garden.

If the insect situation warrants chemical control, choose the weakest chemical remedy to control the insect. Your local Extension Agent can provide you with regional guides to insect identification and recommended substances for control of most pests.

All pesticides and fungicides are reviewed regularly by the Environmental Protection Agency. For the latest information about products on the market, contact your Extension Service.

HARVESTING

You can enjoy a rich harvest of cabbage, broccoli, cauliflower and Brussels sprouts — if you use your head at harvest time.

Broccoli is like a trick candle you can't blow out. Once you pick the first head, the plant responds by producing more side shoots for you to eat. The first head is prime for cutting when its buds are packed close together without any sign of blossoming. Cut it off then, even if the head is smaller than you'd like. If you wait until the small yellow flower blossoms appear, the plant won't produce more heads; it has already gone to seed (bolted). If you spot any yellow blossoms, cut the broccoli. You may stop the bolting process in time, and side shoots may form.

Leave 2 to 3 inches of stem on the plant; the second, lateral heads will branch out from there. Harvest these smaller spears on a daily basis, breaking or cutting them off the plant with a few inches of stem in-

cluded. Most of the broccoli stem is tender enough to eat, although the tenderest part is at the top, nearest the newest growth. Again, if you harvest before it blossoms, you should be able to keep the plant producing for weeks!

Brussels sprouts are no problem to harvest, although you might run out of energy trying to keep up with the load of sprouts on each plant! Starting when they're marble-sized, pick off sprouts from the bottom up as you want to eat them. Also pick off any loose or soft buds, even if you aren't going to eat them, so the plant will keep producing new sprouts.

I've harvested Brussels sprouts here in Vermont in December and even January, brushing aside snow to reach the plant. In more temperate climates, these extra-hardy plants will produce throughout the winter months.

Cabbage is kind of a challenge for me at midsummer harvest time because I can coax each plant into producing two, three or up to six heads for a fall harvest. You can, too. To do it, you must harvest the first spring-planted cabbage when the heads are fairly small, about softball size. These small heads make terrific coleslaw for two. Leave 4 or 5 lower leaves on the plant, and from each leaf or two another small head may appear.

Of course, you can settle for just one cabbage from each plant. You have no choice in the fall, since your second crop of cabbage only has time to make single heads. Harvest the largest heads in the row; the larger and firmer they are, the better they'll keep.

Cauliflower heads are ready to harvest as soon as they are blanched pure white and have grown to be 6 to 12 inches across. Each plant produces only one head, so make the most of your growing efforts and keep harvesting any heads that are ready. Simply cut off the head, leaving about 3 inches of stem to keep the florets intact.

Chinese cabbage is best harvested fully grown, although the leaves are edible right from the start. When the loose heads are 12 to 15 inches tall, cut them off at the base with a sharp knife. Harvest the largest heads first to make room for the rest to develop. You will provide a continual harvest this way.

Kohlrabi should be pulled when it's 2 to 3 inches across. Don't let it grow any bigger or the bulb will become tough, bitter and woody tasting. Since it grows so well, you shouldn't have any problem raising enough to satisfy everyone's appetite.

STORAGE

Although all of the cole crops are easy to freeze, cabbages will also keep in a root cellar or other winter storage.

Under the Spreading Broccoli Leaves

Just because a garden row is occupied, don't think you've used up all its growing potential. By planting a few cool-loving seedlings under and around established cole crops, you can get a jump on your fall gardening. You also save space by planting more than one vegetable in a row, and the new plants benefit from the shade of the older plants. This can be a real help in the heat of midsummer. It's not a good idea to rely on this method for your main crop, but it can give you quite a harvest bonus.

When your broccoli plants are up and growing in midsummer, try planting loosehead lettuce seedlings in the partial shade of their broad leaves. Prepare a planting hole four to five inches from the base of each broccoli plant and set in a seedling. If you fertilized or sidedressed the broccoli, the new lettuce seedling will probably have enough food for growing. If not, you can sidedress it after it's established.

The broccoli shade will protect the seedlings from the hot sun. When your broccoli plants have finished bearing, just pull them out; the lettuce will continue growing. You can also try this multiple planting method around Brussels sprouts, but you may have to experiment to see if any extra fertilizer is needed.

You might try planting a few quick-maturing seeds such as radishes, lettuce or cress in the soil around mature plants. Just plant, weed and water as usual, thinning if the plants appear crowded. After that, enjoy the extra harvest.

There's another way to maximize your garden space. Whenever you harvest a cabbage or cauliflower, pull the whole plant from the row. In the gap that's left, plant a new seedling. Depending on your climate and the length of your growing season, you can replace these early-season vegetables with lettuce, kale, tomatoes, peppers or even flowers. The tender seedlings will be partially shaded by the foliage of the remaining cabbage or cauliflower plants, and you won't have to look at empty spaces in your garden.

Cabbage heads will keep well if you harvest them properly and store them correctly. Plant a hardy, late-season variety. Harvest only fully mature cabbages, and handle these very carefully to prevent bruising.

Don't wash the heads or trim off any outer leaves; these will help protect the heads.

Cabbages can be somewhat tricky to store for extended periods. They need cool, moist and dark surroundings with an even temperature. My root cellar is a near-perfect location, and to help preservation, I wrap each head in several thicknesses of newspaper. Check your stored cabbages often, since even slight rot can send out a three-alarm smell.

If you don't have a root cellar, you can make cabbage storage mounds outdoors with very little effort. Dig out a deep hole, and line the bottom with a heavy layer of straw for insulation. Place the heads upside-down in the hole, cover them with more thick straw, shovel 4 to 5 inches of soil around the straw and leave an opening on top. Cover the opening with a board. Whenever you need a cabbage, dig down into the straw pit and repack the straw around the remaining vegetables when you're finished.

One very easy way to keep lots of cabbage is by krauting, and Jan will tell you her secret of 3-week sauerkraut later on. She also gives you her tips for freezing and pickling the other cole crops, along with her selection of our favorite recipes.

Garden to Kitchen

In the Raw

As long as you have the luxury of fresh-picked broccoli, kohlrabi, cauliflower or cabbage, do yourself a favor. Serve these vegetables raw. It takes less time, preserves more of their nutritive value, and provides crunchy, good-tasting, colorful summer fare. I use uncooked cole crops in salads and slaws, with dips, or lightly marinated and chilled.

Hint: To make sure there are no bugs from the garden in your cole dishes always soak Brussels sprouts, cauliflower and broccoli in cold salted water (1/2 cup salt to 1 gallon water) for half an hour before serving or cooking. This soaking brings out any tiny insects that might possibly be hiding in the buds and leaves. Drain and rinse vegetables before using.

Kohlrabi is one vegetable we eat raw more often than cooked. This odd looking plant becomes a crisp, handy, low-calorie treat once you trim away the antenna-like leaves, then peel and slice the bulbs. I serve kohlrabi slices with other summer vegetables as dippers for hors d'oeuvres. Carrots, radishes, celery and green pepper slices all complement their mild, turnip-like taste. Or toss kohlrabi pieces in any summer salad for extra tang and texture.

Use broccoli and cauliflower florets with a dip, or try them in a refreshing marinated salad.

Simple Salad

This is practically guaranteed to convert reluctant cauliflower or broccoli eaters. It's great for a mid-summer party.

1   head broccoli
1   head cauliflower
1   pint cherry tomatoes, halved
1   cup vinaigrette dressing

Soak and wash broccoli and cauliflower heads. Cut into bite-sized florets. Toss florets with tomatoes and dressing in a large bowl. Chill at least 3 hours. Serves 8 to 10.

Colorful Cole Slaw

4 cups shredded red and green cabbage
1/2 cup chopped green pepper
1/2 cup celery
3/4 cup sour cream
1 Tb vinegar
1/2 tsp dill weed
1/2 tsp salt
1/8 tsp pepper

In a large bowl, toss cabbage, green pepper and celery. Cover and chill.

In a small bowl or blender, mix sour cream, vinegar and spices. Cover and chill for at least 1/2 hour.

At serving time, toss cabbage mixture with dressing lightly until evenly coated. Serves 4 to 6.

Variations — Add other grated vegetables to slaw: carrots, onion, Chinese cabbage, kohlrabi. Add other flavorings to sour cream dressing: grated horseradish, dry mustard, celery seed or a pinch of sugar.

Sauerkraut

Sauerkraut is a fine way to store cabbage. In addition to having a crisp, tart texture that spices up meals, sauerkraut is good for you, too. Some say it helps curb "charley horses."

Making kraut involves the same general principle as pickling. Cabbage becomes tart and mildly fermented because of a reaction between the salt and the bacteria released from the cut shreds. As with all home food preservation techniques, if you've never made sauerkraut before, start with small batches. Once you're comfortable with the steps and satisfied with the results, you can increase the quantity.

You really don't need any special equipment to make kraut, but you do need a spot to leave the crock or large jar for 2 to 4 weeks until the sauerkraut is ready.

Have all utensils and equipment clean and assembled before you begin:

- Large, firm heads of cabbage
- Pickling salt
- Clean stone or enamel crocks, large jars or paraffin-lined barrels
- Kitchen scales
- Large, sharp knife or kraut cutting board
- Thin white cloth or plastic cover
- Tight-fitting cover with weighted lid (A plastic bag or glass jar filled with water topping a large heavy plate works fine.)

Steps for Krauting

1. Let the cabbage heads sit at room temperature for a day to wilt. This makes the leaves less brittle, so they won't break or bruise during cutting and packing.

2. To prepare the cabbage, trim the outer leaves and wash the heads. Cut into halves or quarters.

Discard the core or chop it finely. Chop the cabbage with a sharp knife or use a kraut cutting board to make shreds, about as thin as a dime.

3. Weigh the cabbage and thoroughly mix in the correct amount of salt: 1 1/2 teaspoons salt per pound of cabbage. Let the mixture sit for 3 to 5 minutes to soften the cabbage a bit. This makes packing easier.

4. Pack the cabbage in large crock or other container, pressing each layer down gently to release the natural brine. Continue filling to within 3 inches of the top.

5. To keep the cabbage immersed in the brine and to shut out all air which can spoil sauerkraut, place a piece of plastic or a clean, white muslin cloth on top and tuck it in around the sides. Then place a tight-fitting, weighted top inside the crock or jar, right on top of the covered cabbage.

6. Let cabbage cure in the crock at 68° to 72° F for about two weeks. Remove surface scum every few days, and check to make sure cabbage stays immersed in brine, adding more weight to the lid if necessary. If brine bubbles over the top of the container, use less weight on the lid.

7. When the bubbling has stopped, the kraut is finished. If it isn't tangy enough for you, leave it for a few more days, since the fermentation will continue. When the flavor is to your liking, remove it from the crock; it's ready to serve. For long-term storage, it's best to can sauerkraut in a boiling-water bath.

8. Boiling-water bath canning: heat kraut to simmering and pack in hot, clean jars, leaving 1/2 inch headspace, including liquid. If cabbage liquid doesn't cover the kraut completely, mix 1 1/2 tablespoons salt in 1 quart hot water and pour into jars to fill them within 1/2 inch of the top. Seal jars and process in boiling water bath: pints, 15 minutes; quarts; 20 minutes.

Serving: Serve sauerkraut cold as a relish, a sandwich topper or a different summer salad, or heat kraut 10 minutes and serve as a vegetable side-dish. For added flavor, stir in 1/2 tsp caraway seed, 1/2 cup minced onion, 1/2 tsp celery seed, 1/4 cup bacon bits, 1 grated apple or 1/2 cup shredded, cooked potato. Heat thoroughly.

In case your sauerkraut becomes too tart, or you're serving guests with sensitive stomachs, it's handy to know that the longer you heat sauerkraut, the milder it becomes.

Freezing

I have found that freezing cole crops preserves their color, flavor and texture better than any other storage method. Except for making a supply of cauliflower pickles and sauerkraut, most of our cole crops end up "on ice."

Broccoli — Use only tender, firm heads and don't use any that have started to blossom. Wash broccoli and remove leaves and woody stem parts. Cut through stalks lengthwise to make individual spears.

Soak heads in salt water (1/2 cup salt to 1 gallon water) 1/2 hour to remove insects. Rinse in cold water and drain.

Scald medium-sized stalks (about 1 inch thick) 3 minutes, slightly more or less depending on varying size. To complete the blanching process, cool broccoli immediately by plunging into ice water for 3 minutes, or the same time you allowed for scalding.

Drain and pack in freezer containers leaving no headroom. Label, date and freeze.

Brussels sprouts — Select firm, dark green heads. Remove tough outer leaves, wash heads and soak in salt water for 1/2 hour. Sort according to size and freeze according to the directions for broccoli.

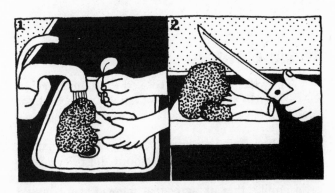

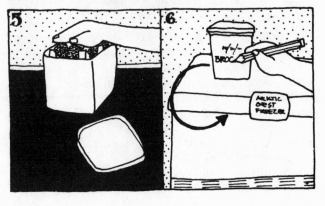

Cauliflower — Pick well-formed, compact white heads. Soak for 1/2 hour in salted water. Trim off leaves and stems, wash heads and drain. Break into florets, about 1 inch across. Scald and freeze as for broccoli.

Cabbage — Pick fresh, solid heads with crisp leaves. Discard the tough outer leaves, wash heads and cut into wedges or shred coarsely. Don't freeze the core; use it in soups for added flavor.

Scald wedges 3 minutes; scald shredded cabbage 1 1/2 minutes. Cool, drain and pack into containers. Label, date and freeze. Frozen cabbage is fine in any recipes that call for cooked cabbage, but it can't be substituted for fresh in salads or slaws.

Kohlrabi — Use tender, fully grown bulbs. Trim off leaves and side shoots, peel and wash. Leave small bulbs whole; cut larger kohlrabi into thin slices. Scald whole bulbs 3 minutes; slices 1 to 2 minutes. Cool, drain and pack into containers. Label, date and freeze.

Basic Cooking

The watchword for all cooked vegetables is *crispness*. There's nothing worse than limp broccoli or soggy cabbage; this is the fastest way to turn people off!

Although there are conflicting theories among cooks and home economists about the best way to prepare the "strong-flavored" members of the cole crop family, they all agree that the end result should be served heated through, tender but still crisp.

Here are the different methods, from which you can choose, unless you already have a preferred way.

Steaming — I find that steaming vegetables over boiling water in a heat-proof, perforated steamer (blancher or colander works fine) cooks them evenly without overdoing it. Trim away coarse outer leaves, soak heads in salt water, rinse, cut into serving-size pieces or leave whole, and place in steamer. Set steamer over 1 to 2 inches of rapidly boiling water in a large pot. Cover tightly and steam 6 to 10 minutes, depending on the size of the pieces. Steaming is especially good for Chinese cabbage.

Boiling — Trim, soak and rinse vegetables as for steaming. There are two ways to boil, so try both and take your pick. I boil all vegetables in very little water, about an inch, covered, until tender. Allow 5 to 7 minutes for cut-up pieces of cauliflower, broccoli or shredded cabbage. Larger pieces or cabbage quarters may take 12 to 18 minutes. You may have to allow a little longer for large, mature cabbages and the Savoy varieties.

Cauliflower and cabbage tend to discolor during cooking. You can avoid this by adding 1/2 Tb vinegar

or lemon juice to the cooking water. Or before cooking, rinse in 1 cup water mixed with 1 Tb vinegar.

Some experts advise cooking all members of the cole crop family in enough water to cover them completely, and boiling them in an uncovered pot. This is supposed to eliminate the harsh flavor that can make these vegetables hard to digest, but I've found that this sometimes causes overcooking, which I think tastes worse. If you choose this cooking method, boil only until vegetables are tender. Again, prevent discoloration with a little vinegar or lemon juice.

If you intend to use precooked vegetables in another recipe that will require more cooking, cut steaming or boiling time by 2 to 3 minutes to ensure crispness.

After boiling or steaming, drain vegetables immediately and serve. Or proceed with another recipe.

Vegetable Sauces

Use your imagination when it comes to cooking vegetables. Broccoli, cauliflower, kohlrabi, cabbage and Brussels sprouts can all be enhanced with sauces.

I used to avoid making sauces because I thought they would be too tricky or too time-consuming. How wrong I was! Starting with a few basic recipes, I soon became an expert "saucière." You can, too.

Here are some secrets for foolproof sauces. Use a wire whisk or wooden spoon for stirring to give your sauce smooth, uniform texture. Use a heavy saucepan that distributes heat evenly and prevents scorching. And never use high heat for bringing sauce to a boil; heat it gradually over medium to low heat.

Finally, when the directions say "stir constantly," don't be lazy. Be patient. You'll be rewarded with a rich, delicate, velvety-smooth result.

You can add spices or seasonings to any basic sauce recipe to give it your own special touch. Some flavorings I use are celery seed, nutmeg, lemon juice, Worcestershire sauce, onion juice, parsley, chives and curry powder. Start out with no more than 1/4 teaspoon or pinch of anything you add, adding more according to your taste.

Spoon sauces over tender-crisp, hot vegetables and serve immediately.

Short-Cut Sauce

1 cup cream of celery soup
2 Tb butter or margarine
2-4 Tb chicken stock
1 Tb chopped chives, dill or parsley
Salt and pepper to taste

Heat all ingredients over medium heat 5 minutes. Makes 1 1/4 cups sauce.

Basic White Sauce

2 Tb butter or margarine
2 Tb flour
1 cup milk
   Salt and pepper to taste

Melt butter over low heat. Stir in flour and continue stirring over low heat until smooth, 3 to 5 minutes. Gradually add milk. Stir constantly until sauce is smooth, thickened and hot. Simmer one minute. It is important to cook the sauce long enough to make sure the flour is cooked. Otherwise it may have a pasty flavor. Add seasonings if desired. Makes 1 cup sauce.

Cheese Sauce: When sauce is thickened, stir in 1/2 cup grated Swiss or Cheddar cheese. Heat and stir until cheese melts.

FAVORITE RECIPES

Tangy Kohlrabi

5   medium kohlrabi, peeled
2   Tb margarine
2   Tb honey
1   Tb prepared mustard (I use the hot stuff!)
1/2 tsp salt

Cut kohlrabi in cubes or 1/4 inch slices. Cook in boiling, salted water for 20 minutes, or until tender. Drain.
Melt margarine in a frying pan. Stir in mustard, honey and salt. Add kohlrabi and stir until well-coated with mixture. Cook over medium heat, turning until nice and brown. Serves 6.

Indian Apples and Cabbage

1   large head cabbage, cut in wedges
1   cup chopped apples
1/2 tsp curry powder
2   Tb margarine or butter
1/2 cup sour cream
1   cup White Sauce with Swiss cheese (see pg. 213)

Cook cabbage wedges in boiling water until tender-crisp, about 10 minutes. Sauté apples with curry powder in margarine or butter for 3 minutes. Add sour cream to cheese sauce. Combine cheese sauce, apple/curry mixture and cabbage. Bake at 475° for 10 minutes. Serves 6.

Polynesian Red Cabbage

Delicious and different vegetable and fruit combination that will add color to meals.

5   cups shredded red cabbage
1   Tb lemon juice
1/2 cup boiling water
1   Tb margarine
2   Tb brown sugar
1   Tb cornstarch
1/2 tsp salt
1   cup or can pineapple tidbits
2   Tb vinegar

In skillet, cook cabbage and lemon juice in boiling water. Cover, cook until cabbage is tender, 10 to 12 minutes. Add margarine.
While cabbage is cooking, mix together brown sugar, cornstarch and salt. Drain juice from pineapple, and combine it with vinegar. Combine cornstarch mixture with juice and vinegar and mix until no lumps remain. Add cornstarch/juice mixture to cabbage and blend. Complete by adding pineapple tidbits to cabbage. Cook over medium heat, stirring until sauce thickens and bubbles. Serve hot. 6 servings.

Spiced Pickled Cabbage

Serve this cold as a sweet-sour relish or heated as a side dish.

4   quarts shredded red or green cabbage
1/2   cup pickling salt
1   quart vinegar
1 1/2 cups sugar
1   Tb mustard seed
4   tsp horseradish, grated
1   tsp whole cloves
4   cinnamon sticks

Layer cabbage and salt in a large kettle or crock. Let stand overnight. The next day, drain cabbage, pressing out all the juice. Rinse thoroughly and drain again.
In a saucepan, combine vinegar, sugar, mustard seed and horseradish. Bring to a boil. Tie the cloves and cinnamon in a cheesecloth spice bag and add to saucepan. Simmer 15 minutes.
Pack cabbage into hot, clean, pint Mason jars and fill with vinegar mixture, leaving 1/4 inch headspace. Remove air bubbles by running non-metallic spatula down sides of jar. Seal and process in boiling water bath 20 minutes. Makes 4 pints.

Stuffed Cabbage Roll-Ups

10	large cabbage leaves
1	egg, beaten
1/4	cup milk
1/3	cup onion, minced
1/2	tsp salt
1/4	tsp pepper
3	Tb celery, finely chopped
1	lb ground beef
1	cup cooked rice
1	cup tomato sauce
1	Tb brown sugar
1	Tb lemon juice
1	tsp Worcestershire sauce

Cook cabbage leaves in large pot of boiling water for about 3 minutes, so they fold easily without breaking. Drain. To make filling, mix together egg, milk, onion, salt, pepper, celery, beef and rice. Spoon about 1/4 cup filling onto each cabbage leaf. Fold up sides and roll over meat. Place in heavy skillet, seam side down.

Combine tomato sauce with sugar, lemon juice and Worcestershire sauce. Pour over cabbage rolls. Cover and cook at 350° 45 minutes. Serves 5. (This dish can also be cooked in a slow-cook crock pot on low for 6 to 8 hours, great for the cook who works.)

Easy Chicken Divan

1 1/2	lb. fresh broccoli, cooked until just barely tender
3	cups cooked chicken or turkey (white meat is best)
2	cans condensed cream of chicken or cream of mushroom soup (10 1/2 oz. each)
3/4	cup mayonnaise
1	tsp lemon juice
1/2	cup American cheese, shredded
1	cup soft bread crumbs
1	tsp margarine, melted

Arrange broccoli stalks in greased 13 × 9 baking pan. Layer skinned, sliced chicken or turkey on top. Combine soup, mayonnaise and lemon juice and mix until well-blended. Pour over chicken. Sprinkle shredded cheese over sauce. Combine crumbs and margarine; sprinkle over all.

Bake at 350° about 35 minutes until heated through and golden brown on top. Serves 6 to 8.

Broccoli-Potato Soup

This recipe was invented by a friend of ours who lives in Georgia, Caroline Riggins.

2	cups chopped raw broccoli
1	small onion, chopped
1	Tb margarine or butter
1	cup water
2	chicken bouillon cubes
2	cups potatoes peeled and diced
1	cup milk
	salt and pepper to taste

Sauté onion in margarine until transparent. Add water, bouillon cubes and potatoes. Cook until almost tender, about 20 minutes. Add broccoli and cook 5 minutes, until barely tender. Let cool slightly. Purée cooled mixture in blender with 1 cup milk. Reheat gently. Do not boil. Season to taste and serve immediately. Serves 4.

Broccoli Bouquet

This simple and elegant one-dish meal was served at a special luncheon. It was delightful and delicious.

1	large head broccoli
1	large lemon
3	medium tomatoes
	lettuce leaves to cover platter
	salad filling of your choice (recipes follow)

Break broccoli into individual stalks and steam until just crunchy-tender. Do not overcook. Chill. Prepare salad filling and chill.

Cover large (about 14 inch diameter) round platter with lettuce leaves. Arrange chilled broccoli spears in spoke fashion with florets around edge of platter.

Slice tomatoes and place them in an overlapping circle over the broccoli, about midway between the center and the platter edge. Slice lemon wedges and arrange them near the outer edge, placing them individually among the broccoli spears.

Push the salad filling down into a bowl with a broad spoon to "mold" it into a round shape. Turn bowl over center of broccoli spears and place rounded salad filling gently on the broccoli. Garnish with a small broccoli floret or sprig of parsley.

Salad Fillings

Egg Salad: Combine 6 hard-cooked eggs, 1/4 cup sliced, stuffed olives, 2 Tb chopped onion, 1/3 cup salad dressing or mayonnaise, salt and pepper to taste.

Tuna Salad: Combine 1/2 cup chopped dill pickle, 1/2 cup salad dressing or mayonnaise, 1/4 tsp salt, 1 large can drained tuna.

Salmon Salad: Combine 1/2 cup thinly sliced celery, 1/4 cup salad dressing, mayonnaise or sour cream, 1 large can salmon, drained and with skin and bones removed.

Cauliflower Dill Pickles

4   pounds cauliflower, broken into small pieces
3/4   cup pickling salt dissolved in 4 quarts cool water
5   cups vinegar (4% to 6% acid strength)
5   cups water
3   Tb salt
2   Tb mixed pickling spices
2   cloves garlic
1   head dill or 1 1/2 tsp dill seed, per jar
1   tsp mustard seed, per jar
1   small hot pepper, per jar

Wash, rinse and drain cauliflower pieces. Make brine of 3/4 cup pickling salt and 4 quarts cool water. Cover cauliflower with brine and let stand 3 to 4 hours. Rinse, drain and taste. If overly salty, rinse and drain again.

In saucepan, mix vinegar, 5 cups water and 3 Tb salt. Crush garlic and tie in a cheesecloth bag with pickling spices. Add to vinegar mixture and bring to a boil. Keep hot.

Pack cauliflower in jars with dill, mustard seed and hot pepper. Fill to within 1/2 inch of top. Reheat pickling liquid to boiling and pour over cauliflower to cover. Remove air bubbles with plastic spatula inserted down sides of jar. Leave 1/4 inch headspace. Seal and process jars 10 minutes in a boiling water bath. Makes about 6 pints.

Cauliflower Casserole

1   medium head cauliflower
1/2   lb sliced mushrooms
1/4   cup diced green pepper
1   small jar pimientos (or 1/4 cup diced red pepper)
1   cup milk
1/3   cup margarine or butter
1/4   cup flour
1   tsp salt
6   slices American cheese
    paprika

Separate cauliflower into bite-size pieces. Boil or steam until barely tender; set aside. In skillet, brown mushrooms lightly in margarine; add green pepper and cook until tender. Blend in flour, then gradually stir in milk. Cook and stir over medium heat until thickened. Stir in salt and pimientos.

Place half of the cauliflower in greased casserole, cover with half the cheese and half the sauce. Repeat. Sprinkle with paprika. Bake in 350° oven 20-25 minutes or until top is browned. Serves 4 to 6.

Sweet and Sour Brussels Sprouts

4   cups fresh Brussels sprouts
10   slices bacon
2 1/2   Tb vinegar
3   tsp sugar
1/2   tsp salt
1/4   tsp garlic powder
1/8   tsp pepper

Wash Brussels sprouts and remove any dried or wilted leaves. Cut crosses in bottoms to cook more evenly. Cook in 1 cup boiling, salted water, covered, for 10 to 15 minutes and drain. At the same time cook bacon until crisp. Drain and save 1/4 cup of the drippings. Crumble bacon and set aside.

In frying pan, combine bacon drippings, vinegar, sugar, salt, garlic powder and pepper. Stir in Brussels sprouts until heated and well-coated. Sprinkle with crumbled bacon. Serves 6 to 8.

Variation: Sprinkle 1/4 cup grated Parmesan cheese on top along with the bacon. Cover and bake in 350° oven for 15 minutes.

Brussels Sprouts and Tomato Bake

This dish is as colorful as it is tasty.

1 1/2   cups cooked Brussels sprouts
1/4   cup cracker crumbs (herbed or seasoned crackers add flavor)
1 1/4   Tb melted butter or margarine
2   tsp cornstarch
1/2   tsp salt
1/8   tsp black pepper
1   cup stewed tomatoes
1/2   cup grated Cheddar cheese

Place Brussels sprouts in a greased casserole dish.

Drain liquid from stewed tomatoes and stir cornstarch into it until smooth.

Combine cracker crumbs and butter. Toss lightly to coat crumbs and set aside.

In saucepan combine tomatoes, cornstarch liquid, salt and pepper. Cook over medium heat, stirring constantly until thickened. Spoon over Brussels sprouts. Sprinkle crumb mixture and cheese on top. Bake at 350° for 30 minutes. Serves 4.

Brussels Sprouts and Carrots

- 1/2 cup onion, chopped
- 2 Tb melted margarine
- 2 cups sliced carrots
- 1/4 tsp salt
- 1/4 tsp Tabasco sauce
- 1 cup chicken broth
- 1/4 tsp marjoram
- 2 cups Brussels sprouts

Sauté onions in margarine until tender. Add carrots, salt, Tabasco sauce and chicken broth. Cover and simmer over low heat 10 minutes.

Add marjoram and sprouts. Cover and simmer 15 minutes more. Serves 4.

Chinese Cabbage

The crisp, succulent lettuce-like heads of this cabbage are available in our garden well into the frosty days of late fall. Like lettuce, you can't store Chinese cabbage for any length of time, but it will stay fresh for quite a few days in the refrigerator.

Generally, I use the leaves of Chinese cabbage in salads and the tender midribs in stir-fry dishes. They're also tasty steamed and served with butter and salt. Here's still another serving idea.

Chinese Custard

This is an unusual, protein-packed dish that needs only a loaf of crusty bread and perhaps a green salad to turn it into a complete lunch or light supper.

- 4 cups Chinese cabbage, cut in small pieces
  paprika
- 2 eggs, beaten
- 2 cups milk
- 1/4 tsp salt
- 1/8 tsp pepper
- 1/4 cup grated cheese

Boil cabbage 5 to 7 minutes in salted water just to cover. Drain and place cabbage on the bottom of a greased baking dish. Sprinkle with paprika.

Mix eggs, milk, salt and pepper together until well-blended. Pour over cabbage and place baking dish in a pan of hot water.

Bake at 350° for 45 minutes, or until custard is firm. Remove from oven and sprinkle grated cheese over the top. Place dish under broiler for 1 minute, until cheese melts and browns. Serves 6 to 8.

Dick's Garden Stir Fry

This brightly-colored dish is designed for wok cooking, but you can also cook it in a large, heavy skillet. Use whatever vegetables you have on hand. The Chinese cabbage adds bright green color just before serving.

- 1 lb venison steak, sliced in 1/4" strips (or use strips of beef or chicken)
- 4 Tb vegetable oil
- 2 cups diagonally sliced celery
- 2 cups fresh mushrooms, sliced in "T" shapes
- 1 cup fresh snow pea pods, whole
- 6 scallions, cut in 1/2 inch lengths
- 1 cup broccoli, chopped
- 1 kohlrabi, peeled and sliced thin
- 1 cup cauliflower, cut in small florets
- 1/2 cup onion, diced
- 1 green pepper, diced
- 1 6-ounce can bamboo shoots, drained
- 1 6-ounce can water chestnuts, drained
- 1/2 cup Chinese cabbage leaves, cut in 1-inch pieces
- 1 1/2 cups cooked rice (We use a long grain/wild rice combination.)

Pour 1 Tb oil into wok and heat to 350° or hot enough for frying. Stir-fry meat strips for 2 minutes. Push up the side of the pan.

Add another Tb oil and stir-fry celery for 1 to 1 1/2 minutes. Push to the side, add 1 Tb oil and stir-fry all remaining vegetables except the last three. Add remaining oil and stir-fry bamboo shoots and water chestnuts. Top with Chinese cabbage leaves.

Toss all foods together in wok and reduce heat to keep dish warm for serving. Serve with hot rice and soy sauce. Serves 6 to 8.

Variation: Add one drained can of tiny shrimp to rice. In a heavy skillet, stir-fry shrimp and rice in 1 to 2 Tb hot oil 2 to 3 minutes before serving.

Lettuce and Greens

The green gardening season at our place starts as soon as the sun and rising temperatures start to warm up the top few inches of soil in early spring. We don't delay our first garden chores — we've planted early crops of lettuce, spinach and chard in April with snow still covering the ground in the shady woods near the garden.

You see, most green crops thrive in cool spring and fall temperatures (50-60°F). Just compare the crisp, flavorful lettuce leaves harvested in spring with the often flaggy, bitter leaves of a summer cutting and you'll agree. A few greens can handle summer heat, but most of them prefer the spring and fall climate.

A steady flow of moisture and nutrients is important for good greens growth. And for some greens, these supplies have to be near the surface. The roots of lettuce, for example, are rather limited — they're close to the surface. They don't grow deep in the soil to search out food and water. If you've gardened in dry times, you know lettuce is not too drought-resistant. Big-leaved plants give off a lot of moisture. When it's dry, they get very thirsty!

Leafy crops need plenty of nitrogen, too. That's the key element in the good growth of leaves and it influences the crispness and quality of leafy crops, too.

A lot of heat is what most greens don't need. Spinach, for example, will quickly develop a seedstalk and start to stretch upward when it gets too warm. This is known as going to seed or "bolting."

When it happens, spinach leaves start to lose some of their flavor. A long hot spell can spoil heads of iceberg-type lettuce, too. The heat loosens the leaves of the head, and they get soft and sometimes bitter. If you can shade some of these crops as hot weather approaches, you can often keep the harvest going pretty well.

But, basically, greens are straightforward to grow — so, let's get started!

Lettuce

"Lettuce" is synonymous with "salad" for people all over the world. It's by far the world's most popular salad plant and has been cultivated for more than 2,000 years. Ancient records note that lettuce was served at the royal table of Persian kings as early as 550 B.C. And today you rarely see a home garden without some kind of lettuce growing in it.

The unitiated may think, "Lettuce is lettuce." Not so! There are wonderful varieties. Each has a distinct flavor, texture and color, so you can have remarkably different salads just by varying the lettuces you use. Here's a rundown of what you can expect in the lettuce department:

With the way **head lettuce** prices have jumped around the last couple of seasons, head lettuce is always in my garden plan. Some people refer to all head lettuce as "crisphead" or "iceberg" lettuce. Crisphead is probably a better catch-all term, since technically iceberg is just one variety of head lettuce. Early each season I put out several dozen young plants that I've started inside. Starting the plants early indoors enables us to get a good harvest of firm, crispy-leaved heads before the summer heat stops production.

Great Lakes, Iceberg and **Ithaca** are head lettuce varieties which have been good in my garden. Gardeners in the South may want to try varieties which do better when the weather gets hot, such as **Premier Great Lakes.**

Butterhead or **'loosehead' lettuce** plants form a head, but the leaves don't wrap themselves tightly together. They're more open and greener. My favorite loosehead variety is **Dark Green Boston.** I devote quite a bit of space to it each year, planting the seeds as early as peas and growing them in wide rows 15 or 16 inches across. You can harvest many tasty heads from a row 6 to 10 feet long.

The taste and crispness of Dark Green Boston is terrific. The leaves are crunchier than leaf lettuce. The outer leaves of the head are dark green, and the inner leaves are lighter-colored, sometimes even whitish.

Buttercrunch and **Bibb** are two other good and popular loosehead varieties. You can harvest some loosehead plants before they form a head to have an early harvest of tasty leaves. A second crop will follow. To harvest, simply take a knife and cut the entire plant off about 1 inch above the ground.

Leaf lettuce doesn't form a head at all — it grows up and out. It's very easy to plant and will grow anywhere, almost anytime. Make regular plantings every few weeks over the entire season, starting as soon as you can work the soil in the spring. That way you always have lettuce that is young and fresh. Never give the crop time to get old, tough and bitter — harvest at the peak of freshness and taste.

The flavor of **Black Seeded Simpson** is probably my favorite. I like **Oak Leaf,** too, because it is ready to eat so quickly. After harvesting Oak Leaf by cutting the plants back to an inch above ground, it'll come right back. Sometimes you can get 3 or 4 good-tasting cuttings from one planting of Oak Leaf or any other kind of leaf lettuce, too.

Make sure to include some **Ruby Leaf** lettuce, too. It adds great color and taste to a salad, and looks beautiful in the garden.

Cos or **Romaine lettuce** always has a spot in the garden. Plant the seeds very early like other varieties, but plant them a little thicker because Romaine lettuce doesn't germinate as well as other kinds of lettuce.

The plants produce a tall head — 10 inches or

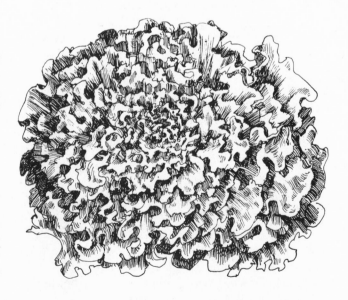

more — of dark green leaves and close up firmly. The tight, inner leaves are especially tasty in tossed salads because they often have a pleasant, mild taste.

Romaine lettuce takes a little while longer to form a full-grown head — about 70 or 80 days. You can harvest them earlier, of course, just like loosehead lettuce. Cut it before it forms a head, and it will come back to give you an additional harvest.

Parris Island Cos is the Romaine variety we grow most often.

Spinach

Spinach is the most versatile green because it fits into almost any part of the menu. But if you want to feature spinach as the main vegetable of a meal, you need to plant a lot to have enough to go around.

The leaves of a robust spinach plant are large, and if you've ever grown spinach, you know it doesn't take many leaves to fill a basket. But, when you cook them, they really wilt, and a lot turns to a little.

To get a lot of spinach from a small space, I plant it in wide rows, perhaps 15 to 20 inches across. Because spinach thrives in cool weather, I plant early in spring and again in late summer for a fall harvest.

I like to see gardeners expand their spinach production because it's one of the most nutritious greens. Raw spinach is very high in vitamin A and tasty in salads. Very little of this important vitamin is lost in canning or freezing, so you can pack a lot of nutrition in your canning jars or freezer cartons. Spinach has a lot of vitamins C and E plus others, too.

We used to think the iron content of spinach was its leading asset. Remember how ''Popeye the Sailor Man'' created instant muscle by downing a serving of spinach? Well, nutritionists have now shown that it is impossible for the body to use all the iron in spinach. The iron is present in a form the body can't assimilate. Sorry about that, Popeye.

Don't be afraid to start your spinach plantings early. Otherwise, early summer heat may send your plants into the seed stage before your harvest — you'll know you waited too late to plant.

There are two varieties that I often plant: **Avon Hybrid,** which has large, somewhat crinkled leaves; and **Bloomsdale Long-Standing,** with very large and crinkled leaves. The big leaves are easiest to cook and freeze. Bloomsdale Long-Standing has a tendency to bolt, though, if not harvested properly.

Another good variety is **Winter Bloomsdale.** It's a nice fall-harvested spinach; and many gardeners, especially those in the South where winters are mild, plant it in the fall to harvest through the cool winter months and early spring.

And then there's **New Zealand Spinach.** I wish this spinach substitute tasted as good as spinach. The first year I grew it I ate some leaves raw: Ugh! Don't use them in a salad. To approach the taste of spinach they must be cooked.

People grow New Zealand Spinach because it produces in hot weather when spinach won't. It's not a true spinach, though. It's a member of a different plant family and native to New Zealand. It hasn't ever gone to seed in my garden, so we use it for spinach-like flavor in cooked dishes when our true spinach has gone by.

I know one man with a small garden, though, who has kicked the regular spinach off his crop list

in favor of the New Zealand type. In his small space, he wants a crop that will give him a season-long harvest.

Some gardeners advise soaking the very hard New Zealand seeds for a day before planting, to help germination. But you can have good stands of this green without soaking; just plant it early in the season when the soil is quite moist.

The plants grow a foot or two high. To harvest, pick off the leaves you need — don't cut the plant back and don't pick off the top.

Chard

As a gardener I like chard because it'll grow in cool *and* warm weather. This ability to grow through the summer sets it apart from most greens, and should put chard at the top of your planting list!

Chard is actually a bottomless beet. It's in the same family as beets, but chard doesn't develop roots like beets. In the large, fleshy stalks and broad, crisp leaves, there are plenty of minerals and vitamins, just like the highly nutritious beet tops.

Plant chard in rows about 15 inches wide, scattering the seeds an inch or so apart. After thinning, the plants will be 4 to 5 inches apart. Harvest the first plants when they are about 6 inches high, and cut the entire plant an inch above the ground. In a short time the chard leaves come on again. Harvest only a few feet of the row at a time, so by the time you cut your way to the taller plants at the end of the row, the plants you harvested first are about ready to

cut back again. This way the wide row of chard will keep producing all the way into fall and early winter.

If you really enjoy chard, make two plantings: one in early spring and another one in mid or late summer. You can plant it in the fall down South.

Chard comes in different colors. **Swiss chard** is green with white stems, and **rhubarb (or ruby) chard** has bright red stems and reddish-green leaves. I prefer ruby chard, partly because I like the color it adds to the greens. Ruby chard also has more of a beety taste to me, and when the stalks get ahead of me and grow large, they are more tender than large Swiss chard stalks.

Those chard stalks, by the way, are a bonus vegetable for the greens grower. You can cut the stalk and thick mid-rib out of the leaves and have two entirely different vegetables from the same plant. Just cook up the leaves using your favorite greens recipes and prepare the stems as you would asparagus or braised celery.

GETTING READY

Planning on paper

When you think about greens to plant — you've got a big group of plants to consider, as well as different varieties of some salad crops. So plan your greens garden on paper when the temperature in the middle of the winter really drops down. It's a nice time to spend an evening or two thumbing through the summery, colorful seed catalogs.

In addition to my 'big three' of spinach, lettuce and chard, I make room for cabbage family greens, and some lesser known greens, such as chicory, corn salad, rocket and escarole. They don't take up much room, and a new green can really spice up a summer salad.

We plan to put our rows of lettuce, spinach, endive and other salad greens close to the kitchen door. Because we have salad so often and like it very fresh, we like to have the greens on the near side of the garden, so it's easy to gather what we need for a salad.

If you're going to plant your lettuce in space-saving wide rows for the first time, you'll have room to try several varieties. Buy an extra seed packet or two of varieties you'd like to try. Planting just 3 to 6-foot rows of 3 or 4 kinds of lettuce will give almost any family more than enough lettuce to eat.

If you live in the South, you may want to design your garden to give lettuce and spinach some

shade, so they'll last a little longer when the warm temperatures come and push these crops toward bolting.

Planning Tips

Plan in advance to use methods of shading cool-weather greens, or try these planting ideas:

Plant lettuce under pole bean teepees to provide some shade. The bean foliage will shade some of the sun and keep the plants and soil cool. Plant the beans early.

Plant some lettuce or spinach between your corn rows, or on the shady side of a row of tomatoes.

Try multi-planting. Plant lettuce, carrots and onions within the same wide row (15 or 16 inches across). Harvest the lettuce when young, leaving expansion room for carrots and onions. You can mix and match with other crops, too, including beets and spinach.

Save a window box for a hot green like curli-cress. Or, plant lettuce in a small section of your flower garden, or use it as a decorative, edible border. The foliage is lovely and contrasts beautifully with flowers.

Rich Soil: Greens Love It!

The healthiest and best-tasting greens are those that grow quickly. The important contributors to rapid growth are a steady moisture supply and a fertile soil, one rich with decomposed organic matter or humus.

Make it a point to regularly work plenty of organic matter into the top 6 to 8 inches of soil. Use leaves, compost, grass clippings, garden residues or easy-to-grow cover crops (buckwheat, cowpeas, annual rye grass).

Organic matter in the soil helps it to act like a sponge, retaining moisture. Without organic matter, the soil may drain too quickly, and shallow-rooted crops, like lettuce, will dry out and stop growing. When growth is interrupted like that, food quality goes way down.

When you spade or till all this organic matter into the soil, you are feeding the teeming soil life — those millions of micro-organisms that break down the organic matter into nutrient-rich humus. Feed them, and they'll feed you in return.

The micro-organisms in the soil and the plants' roots have to breathe, too, and organic matter gives the soil a porous quality so that oxygen can reach the roots.

If you have a heavy soil that doesn't drain well and crusts over after a rain, the particles of organic matter will wedge themselves between the tight, locked soil particles, so that air and water can circulate better.

I plant most of my greens in the spring — but the previous fall I add as much organic matter to my garden soil as possible. In mid-summer when I plant my fall crop of greens, I till in a spent spring crop such as peas or spinach — along with grass clippings or old mulch I have on hand — add some fertilizer and plant!

I'm wary of adding manures to the soil unless they're dehydrated or well-composted. Straight from the barnyard, manures contain many weed seeds that can germinate in your garden. Who needs extra weeds? The heat process of dehydrating or thorough composting kills most of the weed seeds. I know the dehydrated manures (available in 25, 40 or 50-pound bags in garden shops and supermarkets) are just about free of weed seeds.

To make your soil lighter you can also add sawdust to it, but don't overdo it. Mix only a layer of an inch or so into the soil in any one year, and add some nitrogen fertilizer along with it. Sawdust takes a long time to break down. Nitrogen is necessary for the soil organisms to do the job of decomposing, but that nitrogen is also needed by your plants for healthy, green leaves.

About pH

Lettuce, spinach, chard, beet and turnip greens, and most of the other greens, prefer slightly acid soil — soil with a pH of 6.0 to 6.5. pH is the measure of soil acidity or alkalinity. The pH scale of measurement runs from 1 (very acid) to 14 (very alkaline), with 7 as neutral. (In nature you would find the range between 4.0 to 8.3.) If your soil pH is too high or too low, your crops may disappoint you. Spinach, for example, will be stunted and less tender when the soil pH is down below 6.0.

A Scratch in Time Saves

When it's early in the season and nearly time to plant a host of greens, put in a little time with your garden soil to prevent weed problems.

For a week to 10 days before planting time, spade or till the soil every 2 to 3 days. This puts the soil in good tilth — no clods or soil chunks — and kills early-growing weeds. You see, weed seeds are quite small and must be near the surface where there

is moisture and warmth before they can sprout to life.

When they do sprout, you have to look hard to see them. Working the soil — even raking it — will get rid of the tiny weed seedlings before they shoot up.

By periodically going over the soil before planting, you destroy most of the weeds that could be a problem later on. Work the soil one last time just a few minutes before planting. This eliminates most weed seeds that have germinated since your last outing and will give your greens an even chance against the few remaining ones.

Fertilizer

Most gardeners understand that vegetable crops need fertilizer to produce well, but sometimes the questions of what kind, when and how much can cause some confusion.

The nutrients your leafy greens need are available in commercial fertilizers such as 5-10-10 or 10-10-10, and in organic fertilizers like bonemeal, bloodmeal and dehydrated manures. By the way, the numbers 5-10-10 or 10-10-10 refer to the percentages of nitrogen (N), phosphorus (P) and potassium (K) in the bag of fertilizer. They're always listed in that order, too: N-P-K.

Nitrogen is essential to all growing vegetation for healthy, dark green leaves. Phosphorus helps plants grow strong roots and potassium or potash conditions the whole plant, helping it to bear fruit and resist disease. A balanced diet is important for plants, but remember that we're really looking for quick, steady leaf growth. Nitrogen is the key here. It gives our salad crops their dark green color and encourages stems and leaves to grow.

Of course, plants need more than just the three

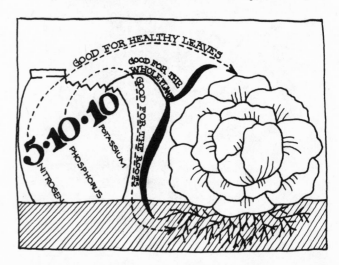

major plant nutrients to grow normally. There are secondary plant nutrients, such as magnesium, and some minor elements such as zinc and iron — all important, but usually plants need only small quantities. Most soils have most of these elements, but mixing good compost or a lot of organic matter like leaves or mulch into the soil insures the presence of these minor elements.

The best time to apply fertilizer is on the day you plant, because you want greens to grow fast.

To apply fertilizer, use this standard recommended amount: a 10 to 12-quart pail of balanced fertilizer, such as 5-10-10, for each 1,000 square feet. For smaller plots, that comes to a couple of quarts for each 100 square feet. Simply toss it over an area as evenly as possible. You don't want to get a lot of the commercial fertilizer or dried manure in one place. Always mix the fertilizer into the top 2 to 3 inches of soil before planting. Seeds are sensitive and can get burned by any fertilizer that touches them, so spreading it evenly and mixing it into the soil prevents any trouble.

PLANTING

Wide Rows — Greener Garden

I've told you I plant my big three in rows 12 to 15 inches wide. Here's why:

Years ago, I planted my seeds like everybody else, in single rows — one seed behind another in a straight line. But after the plants were up, I got discouraged looking at the number of walkways in the garden and all the rich soil that would produce nothing but footprints.

So I started to experiment with wide-row growing. Briefly, it involves broadcasting seeds in a wide band, thus creating thicker rows with fewer paths in between.

Not all vegetables, of course, are meant for wide rows. Squashes, tomatoes, cucumbers and melons are examples of crops that need room to run.

But for greens — including head lettuce, collards and kale — wide rows offer many advantages. Most importantly, we harvest over half again as much from wide rows as from single rows using the same space. With wide rows, it is finally possible to grow lots of spinach in a little space — plenty to eat fresh, plus enough to put by.

Many seasons of wide row growing and experimenting have shown more benefits than simply greater yields:

Wide rows mean less weeding because after the closely-planted greens grow up to shade the ground, they create a "living mulch" or ground cover that blocks out light from weeds, thus checking their growth. Some hand weeding is still necessary, but living-mulch wide-rows take care of most weeding.

Living mulch shades the soil, keeping it cool and moist, which is very important for crops like lettuce and spinach that get bitter and bolt when the weather warms up. Wide-row growing extends the harvest into summer because the soil in the row stays cooler. The cooler the soil — the better-flavored crop you'll enjoy.

With summer greens like Swiss chard, the moist soil of a wide row helps maintain continuous growth. There's less drying out of the soil, and consequently, less stop-and-go growth.

Planting is simple. You scatter seed over the wide seedbed with no worry about straight lines or precise spacing. Broadcasting seed is quick. I'm convinced you get a better stand of plants, too.

Wide rows are proven space-savers. You can do away with long single rows of one variety and plant more varieties of your favorite crops. For example, in a 10-foot-long row, 15 inches wide, you can grow 3 or 4 kinds of lettuce.

Harvesting is fast because you can reach so many more plants from one spot without moving. It sure beats the non-stop stooping and straightening it takes to harvest or weed single rows.

The garden looks nice. I couldn't believe the change in appearance of my garden when I started using wide rows. Try some wide rows — and give your garden a clean, lush look that will surprise you and your neighbors.

Time to Plant — Wide Rows

After you've prepared and fertilized your soil on planting day, follow these easy steps to plant your wide rows of greens and salad crops:

Mark the wide row. Stretch a string between two stakes close to the ground for the length of row you want.

Smooth the planting bed. With an iron garden rake, smooth the soil along one side of the string. The rake will mark the width of the row. Don't pack the seedbed down by stepping on it. Always do your work from the side of the row.

Sprinkle the seeds onto the seedbed. Roll seeds off the ends of your fingers with your thumb. Try to scatter them across the seedbed as evenly as

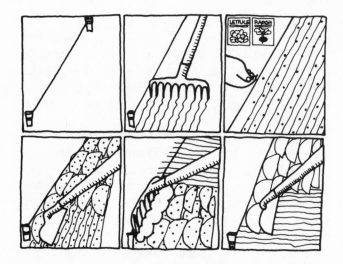

you can. The spacing of crops will vary a bit. Lettuce seeds can be planted much thicker than kale or collard seeds, for example. Don't worry if you plant too thickly, thinning will correct that. To give you an idea of how much seed you need, the average packet of lettuce seed will cover about 3 to 6 feet of a row 15 inches wide.

Sprinkle in a few radish seeds. After you've broadcast the main crop, sprinkle some radish seed down the row. They'll come up quickly and mark the row. I use about 5 percent as much radish seed as the main seed.

I have a hunch that radishes are decoys for some garden insects. Hungry pests seem to zero in on the first crop that appears in a row — radishes — and leave the others alone. After the regular crop is established, you can harvest the radishes.

Firm the seeds into the soil with a hoe, so the seeds make good contact with the earth.

Cover the seeds with soil from the sides of the row, pulling it up with your rake. The rule of thumb for the amount of soil to cover seeds is four times the diameter of the seed. So for most seeds in the green group, that's about 1/4 to 1/2-inch of soil. In midsummer or late-summer plantings, an extra 1/4-inch of soil will help keep the seeds from drying out.

Finally, firm the soil once more with the back of a hoe and water gently if the soil is dry.

Single Row Planting

Use a string to plant a single row, too. Rake the seedbed smooth right over the string and with the handle end of your rake, make a shallow furrow or planting line along the string.

Sprinkle the seeds in the shallow furrow, and walk by a second time and drop radish seeds every 5 or 6 inches. After firming the seeds into the soil,

cover them with 1/4 to 1/2-inch of soil and firm down gently again. Mark the row with the seed packet or a small sign, remove stakes and string and proceed to the next row to be planted.

Double or Triple Rows

The double row planting system is just two single rows separated by 4 to 5 inches. It's a garden space-saver, and it is easier to irrigate, which is very important for gardeners in the West and South.

One irrigation system I've seen is simply placing a soaker hose between the two rows. A soaker hose has many tiny holes in it so water oozes gradually from it, irrigating only the soil around your plants. This is a big water-saving advantage over sprinklers which also water the walkways.

You can even put three or four single rows 4 to 5 inches from each other and move the soaker hose to each aisle to water all the plants. This arrangement has the space-saving characteristics of wide-row growing and lets you water all the plants evenly, too.

To Win — Thin!

To give your greens the best possible chance for success, thin! Whether you plant in wide, single, double or multiple rows, you'll need to thin. Because the seeds of most greens are so tiny, we all inevitably plant a little too thickly. That's not bad, though — it helps guarantee a good stand of plants.

You just have to thin out the crowd, so that the plants will have enough room to grow without too much competition from their neighbors. Thinning also provides good air circulation around plants to keep them from staying wet and becoming diseased.

Now, you can spend hours thinning by hand — or you can spend one minute using an iron rake. I pick the rake every time. To thin a row, simply pull the rake *across* it — with the teeth digging into the soil only about 1/4-inch. The teeth remove just enough seedlings, leaving the remaining ones properly spaced. Perhaps they look a little beat up, but don't panic. The plants will snap back quickly and

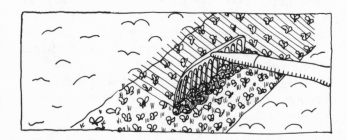

get growing again, better than ever. Rake thinning also gets rid of many small weeds that may have started to germinate, again saving you tedious hand weeding time.

Thinning by hand has always seemed like too much work for me. But if you want the exercise, simply bend over and gently pull up enough plants, so the remaining ones are spaced correctly. For example, in the case of leaf lettuce, the plants should stand 3 to 4 inches apart, butterhead lettuce, 4 to 8 inches (6 to 10 inches if you want a bigger head). You can leave 6 to 10 inches between plants if you're thinning collards, kale or mustard.

THE WORLD OF GREENS

Two for the Price of One

Beets and turnips are special greens because their roots are also edible. Beet greens are most nutritious and taste best when they're harvested young and tender. Fortunately, there's an easy way to have a lot of young greens and still keep plants in the garden for a long time to produce plenty of mature beet roots for later.

The secret is to plant beets in fairly thick wide rows. Beet seeds resemble tiny scraps of cork — they're bigger than most other salad and green crop seeds. They're easy to space correctly — about an inch apart.

Try about a 15-inch wide row if you haven't planted wide-row style before.

Plant early in the season. After the seedlings are up, thin with a rake and then sit back and wait for the green bonanza.

Start gathering your greens when the plants are about 6 inches tall. Pull up the entire plant, and if there's a small beet on the bottom, so much the better. Cook it right along with the greens for added flavor.

Detroit Dark Red and **Lutz** are the two good varieties. These produce excellent greens and good-sized, tasty beets, too.

A dish of turnip greens may sound like dreary eating — but only if you've never tried them. Cooked with salt pork or bacon, and served with butter or vinegar, greens can be a real taste treat — and very nutritious, too. Turnip greens are high in vitamins A and C, iron and calcium and are low in calories.

Turnips are a cool-weather crop, so plant them

early in the spring — as soon as the ground can be worked — and again toward the end of summer for a fall crop. Spring is a great time to concentrate on their greens — you don't have to worry about summer heat spoiling any turnips underground. You simply harvest the plants when the roots are small before hot weather comes.

Fall plantings are popular in the South, too, because in most places you can plant anytime from August to October. The cool fall and mild winter temperatures keep the harvest going for several months. Of course, Southern turnip-lovers plant in the spring, too. In some Southern areas, you can plant every couple of weeks from February to May. With a system like that you'll have nothing but young, tasty greens.

Of course, I use wide rows when I plant turnips, usually about 15 to 16 inches across. In the South, where gardeners have boasted to me they were practically raised on turnip greens, I've seen 10 to 15-foot squares of greens in backyard gardens. Hardly anyone grows them in single rows because you get so few greens that way.

Plant turnips thickly, and once the plants are 4 to 5 inches tall, start thinning them by hand and boil up the tasty greens. You can eat a lot of greens this way and still afford to let some plants put on a good turnip root below ground.

Some people harvest just the big outside leaves from turnips, so the plants can produce more leaves from the center bud. I prefer to pull up the whole plant because the small leaves are the most tender.

You can have greens from any turnip variety, but a couple — **Seven Top** and **Shogoin** — are favorites because of their lush, tender foliage.

There's more information about growing and cooking beets and turnips in the next chapter.

Cabbage Family Greens

Mustard

Mustard — it's not yellow and you don't spread it on the backside of a ham sandwich. Garden mustard is leafy, curly, green and very nutritious. Down South I've seen mustard growing not only in vegetable gardens, but also in flower gardens as border plants.

Mustard planted in late summer for fall harvesting is tops. To me, cold weather and light frosts improve mustard's flavor, just as cold weather does good things for the taste of collards and kale. If you live where the winters are mild, plant mustard in late summer, and you'll harvest greens through the fall and into winter — mustard is quite hardy.

Of course, you can plant mustard early each spring, too. In as little as 30 days or so, you can be harvesting young leaves, or even the entire plant, if you grow mustard in wide rows. **Green Wave** and **Tendergreen** varieties give excellent results. Green Wave is peppery when raw, and Tendergreen has a nice mellow-green flavor when cooked.

Sow mustard seeds in rich, well-worked, fertilized soil. After the seedlings poke through the soil, thin them with a garden rake. After thinning, the plants should be 4 to 6 inches apart in the row. Start harvesting as soon as there is enough for a meal.

Collards — Headless Cabbages

The mild cabbagey taste and long tradition of collard greens at mealtime are really special for Southern gardeners. Collards are well-adapted to the climate in the South — unlike most greens, they'll survive not only the cool spring and fall weather, but also the intense heat of summer.

Some gardeners in the South plant a spring crop, harvesting the lower leaves as they need them early in the season. Then they simply keep the plants growing through the hottest months, and begin harvesting again in the fall. It's much more common, though, to plant collards twice, in early spring and again in late summer.

In the South, collards are so widely grown that garden stores and nurseries provide young collard plants for sale at planting time. Setting out these plants is a convenient and pretty reliable way to have a good harvest before hot weather slows things down.

The 4- to 5-inch seedlings resemble cabbage plants, but they'll never "head up" in the garden like cabbage. Some folks even refer to collards as "headless cabbages."

In the North you have to start collard seeds yourself. Most years I plant seeds directly in the garden for a fall crop, planting in mid or late July. I like the **Vates** variety of collards, but there are probably other good ones, too.

Fall collards profit from the cool nights and light freezes we have. That puts the zing and succulence into the leaves.

If you plant collards in wide rows, thin them, so that the plants will be 8 to 10 inches or so apart.

Like other greens, you can start harvesting collards as soon as some of the leaves make enough for a meal. If you harvest only the bottom leaves of the plant, the center bud (where the action is) will keep putting out branches.

Kale

Kale used to be more popular in our country. Before the days of trucking lettuce thousands of miles to market, local growers provided some of the big Eastern city markets with fall, winter and early spring kale. It helped fill the need for fresh, nutritious greens.

Kale is one of the very best greens if you're shopping for high vitamin and mineral content. It's sometimes called the "Wonder Crop" because its vitamin A and C content is so high. Kale even outranks orange juice in the vitamin C department.

Good taste goes hand in hand with its nutritional excellence. The leaves are tender and sweet-tasting when harvested at the right time, which is after a couple of hard frosts in the fall. The leaves develop a tanginess that is hard to match. Don't stop harvesting if the snows come. The plants stay green and tasty — all you have to do is dig through the snow to get them.

Another peak harvesting period for kale is when the snow melts in the spring and the plants start growing again. The leaves are delicious raw, or you can cook them and use them like spinach.

Kale is not a hard-to-grow or fussy plant. It simply needs well-fertilized, moist soil to get started. But like most cabbage family greens, after it comes up, you have to make sure it has enough moisture and thin the crop.

Kale doesn't like very hot weather — it's strictly a cool-season green. I like to plant the seeds in wide rows in July or August and start harvesting after our first fall frosts. In the South you can plant as late as October and have fresh kale through the mild winter into spring.

A few weeks after planting I thin the plants, so they are 6 to 8 inches apart. Later I can harvest entire plants to put a little more distance between the remaining plants and really give them room to grow.

Don't worry about mulching kale as winter approaches. I've found that while winter weather does kill some of the plants, most survive and put on good growth the following spring. The taste is very good until the plants bolt with warm weather.

Siberian Kale and **Blue Curled Scotch Kale** are the two varieties you'll most likely see in the seed racks. I think the Blue Curled Scotch variety is the better-tasting one.

By the way, the Blue Curled kale makes a nice houseplant in winter. Jan and I dig a couple up each fall, pot them and place them near a south-facing window. The plants lose some color, but the intricate shapes of the curled leaves are quite pleasing.

We also like to plant flowering varieties of kale. Their curly, green and maroon leaves are beautiful at the edge of the garden — and they also can be potted and brought indoors for the winter.

Cabbage Family Pests

Mustard, collards and kale are closely related to the cabbage — and so they suffer from similar pests and diseases.

If you plant any of these greens you'll have to watch for early-season flea beetles, aphids and other insects. Spraying with Sevin or rotenone will control flea beetles — and malathion is recommended for aphids. Be sure to read all directions very carefully before you spray.

The best-known cabbage family pest is probably the cabbage worm — offspring of the white cabbage butterfly. As soon as you see the butterflies making the rounds of your garden, spray every 7 to 10 days with the biological control *bacillus thuringiensis,* available in garden stores as Dipel or Thuricide. It's a bacterium which causes the worms to get sick and die after they ingest it. It does not affect the crop or people who eat it.

To guard against diseases that plague the cabbage family of vegetables, be sure to rotate these crops each year. Do not plant them where any other member of the cabbage family — including cabbage, cauliflower, broccoli — grew the previous year.

Water

You can't beat greens that are crisp and succulent. One of the most important things for highest quality greens is a steady supply of moisture.

Greens thrive in moist, but not wet, soil. They require about an inch of rain or irrigation water per week, and perhaps a little more for summer greens in hot weather.

If the water supply drops, they may be the first crops in the garden to show signs of drought. That's because many of them — especially lettuce — have limited root systems; and because their large green leaves give off quite a lot of moisture. Sometimes on a hot, sunny afternoon many garden plants appear wilted. That's normal — usually they'll recover by next morning. If they don't, it's time to water.

Here are some tips to help you water wisely:

Irrigate early in the day to cut down on evaporation losses and to make your water go further. This also gives the plants plenty of time to dry out during the day. (Wet foliage overnight allows disease organisms to spread rapidly among plants.)

Soak the soil thoroughly enough so that you don't have to come back and water again the following day. Try to moisten the soil to a depth of 5 or 6 inches at least.

If the soil is dry at planting time, water as gently as you can after planting, so you don't wash any seeds out. Be sure to keep the seedbed moist until the plants come up.

Weeds & Cultivation

Weeds are green, too, but we really don't want them growing in among our salad crops. Some weeds are touted as highly nutritious when picked young — such as lamb's quarters and purslane. But I'm not a big fan of eating weeds, so I'll stick to vegetables that taste better, that have a longer harvesting season and that won't interfere with my other crops.

Most of the time weeds don't do us any good. They steal moisture, fertilizer and sunlight. Some of the slower-growing greens can be shaded out of your garden forever by weeds.

There are ways to avoid weed problems in any garden — even if you've suffered from weeding fits in the past:

Try to plant your fine-seeded greens in a section of garden that was relatively weed-free the season before. For example, where your thick, weed-smothering wide-rows of beans grew.

Work the soil with a shovel, rake or tiller every 2 or 3 days for a week or so before planting. This uproots the tiniest weed seedlings and kills them or buries them (which kills them, too).

Always work the soil just before planting. This clears away any newly-germinating weeds and at least puts any remaining weed seeds and your vegetable seeds on even footing.

Make your first thinning timely. When your vegetable seedlings are about 1/4 or 1/2-inch high, drag an iron rake across the row, keeping the teeth 1/4-inch deep. This thins the plants, of course, but it's also your first weeding effort.

Hand weed as often as necessary until the wide-row greens develop enough foliage to shade out further weed growth.

If you set out lettuce, collard or other transplants, work the soil before planting them, and wait a week or so for them to take hold before you cultivate near them.

In the first few weeks after being transplanted, the plants roots are quite close to the surface and gaining root strength by the day. Don't be careless with a hoe and risk slowing them down or killing them. Keep all cultivation very shallow, 1/2 to 1 inch deep at most.

Use a good covering on the soil — a 'mulch' — to stop weeds around head lettuce plants, collards or plants in a single row. The hay, straw or other organic matter will stop most weeds except some stubborn perennials, which will grow through it. Pull those by hand.

Get after weeds when they are small. Don't even wait till they come up out of the ground. After a rain, which will surely cause some weed seeds to germinate, allow the soil to dry slightly and then lightly stir it up with your rake or weeding tool. You kill many weeds before they even appear.

Diseases

I have not had too much of a problem with diseases affecting the greens and salad crops over the years. Occasionally, head lettuce develops a problem, perhaps bottom rot, which can occur during a streak of damp weather. These things happen, but don't be too concerned about them. As a home gardener, you can simply harvest heads no matter what size, cut out any damaged portion, and use them.

Another common ailment of head lettuce is tip-burn, where the ends of many leaves turn brown and die. It's mostly a hot-weather problem, and it's not caused by any pest or fungus in the soil.

Other diseases of head lettuce can be avoided by rotating the crop each year, not over-watering and spacing the plants in the row to ensure they have good ventilation.

Be sure to thin your wide rows of greens properly, so that the plants have enough air circulation to dry off after a rain or watering. If they're too thick, plants may stay wet too long and develop rot. Continual wetness is an invitation to disease.

Beet and chard greens sometimes develop leaf spot trouble. The edges of the greens turn dark brown and spots show up on the leaves, reducing the quality and appearance. However, it's not usually a serious problem. If the problem is bad, simply use a spray or dust containing Maneb, but read the directions carefully.

Also remember to rotate the cabbage family greens (kale, collards and mustard) each season to help avoid disease problems.

If you have any further questions regarding pests and diseases, check with your local County Cooperative Extension Agent. He or she will know about the problems in the area and will be able to suggest remedies.

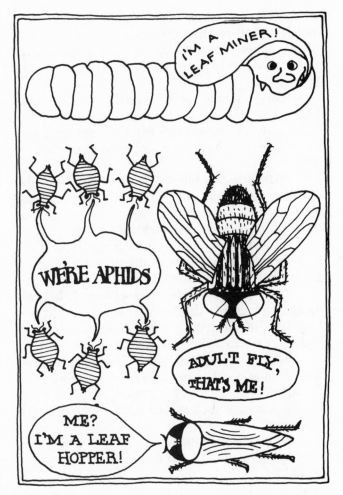

Pests

Aside from the pests of the cabbage family greens, there are few pests that damage greens. Probably the most troublesome in most gardens are the small leaf miners, which feed on spinach, chard, beet and turnip greens. The larvae are 1/8-inch long, yellow and live in the leaves, while the adult fly is tiny, black and yellow. Spraying with malathion can control a bad problem. But at harvest time, just tear out the affected part and eat the rest.

Aphids and leafhoppers can also be a nuisance in some gardens. The six-spotted leafhopper spreads a virus among lettuce plants. They are light greenish-yellow, small but quite active. The United States Department of Agriculture recommends home gardeners spray with Sevin or malathion to control the leafhopper, beginning when the plants are 1/2-inch high and repeating once a week.

Many plants, including spinach and turnip, can be affected by the many kinds of aphids that suck sap from the leaves and spread diseases. Weekly spraying of malathion is recommended to control aphids. If you use malathion, pay attention to the directions carefully, and observe the recommended waiting times before harvesting.

Some of the more pungent greens like chicory, curlicress and celtuce seem to have fewer pest visitors.

Other pests I've noticed on or near my green crops have not really caused me a lot of headaches. Just plant enough of each crop to be able to sacrifice a small portion to insects and diseases.

Curing Lettuce Problems

Let's look at some of the problems you may encounter growing all kinds of lettuce (and some other greens, too.)

"My seeds didn't come up." Don't write to the seed company right away. Most often, poor germination is caused by letting the seedbed dry out. It has to be continuously moist. Drying out occurs more often during hot weather plantings, and not as much with early spring plantings. Sometimes a light mulch of hay or straw to shade the soil after you plant will keep the soil moist until the plants are up. But don't delay in removing the mulch once you see the plants.

Also be sure to cover the seeds correctly — use just 1/4 to 1/2-inch of moist soil. If your soil gets very crusty and hard before the plants are up, gently run a lawn rake over the surface to break up the hard soil.

"My lettuce is bitter." Bitter lettuce is usually old lettuce, and the older it is, the worse it tastes. Harvest lettuce when it is young — as soon as there's something to eat — and harvest often. Don't wait for leaves to get big. Make frequent plantings of different varieties through the summer, so you'll always have tender sweet lettuce coming in.

"My plants go to seed before I harvest much." Seedstalks develop with warm weather and long days. It's the natural urge of a plant, and there's nothing you can do after lettuce bolts.

Bolting won't affect you if you make successive plantings and harvest early. Cut the entire plant off about an inch above the ground. Also, try slow-bolting varieties such as Oak Leaf which can take some heat.

Wide-row planting slows bolting, too, as the close-growing plants keep the soil and roots cool.

Tips for Growing Head Lettuce

A lot of people think crisphead (iceberg-type) lettuce is hard to grow. It's not. Good head lettuce just needs fertile soil, ample sunlight, a good supply of moisture and nutrients — and most importantly, cool weather. The plants like temperatures around 55 or 60°F during the growing season, but sometimes it doesn't always work out that way.

Because head lettuce must grow the most in the spring before it gets hot, plant the seeds indoors in late winter — about 6 to 8 weeks before the average date of the last hard spring frost.

Plant the seeds in shallow seed boxes or 'flats.' Put the tiny seedlings in a sunny spot and keep them watered. About six weeks later, the plants are big enough to set in the garden. But before you do that, harden the plants off to get them ready for outdoor living. Place them in a protected spot outside for a few hours a day, lengthening the time they spend outside until they're out there all day.

Head lettuce can be started in cold frames if you live where the nights don't get too chilly in early spring.

Gardeners in mild winter areas or where the springs are long and cool, you can simply sow head lettuce seeds in the garden and thin the plants to stand 10 to 12 inches apart. In the deeper South, plant seeds out in the garden in the fall, and harvest the heads in late winter and early spring.

Some varieties are noted as "heat resistant" in the seed catalogs. These are worth trying if hot weather comes too quickly in your area.

I can remember years when my head lettuce was doing fine until an extended spring heat wave came along. High temperature over a period of time is nothing but trouble for head lettuce. The heads lose their firmness, the leaves get bitter, and diseases may erupt. So, keep cool — by using mulch, starting seeds indoors and planning a fall head lettuce crop.

Transplanting Head Lettuce

Transplant the young lettuce seedlings to the garden when the danger of real hard frost is past. They'll take a light freeze if they are hardened off properly.

I till the soil on planting day to get rid of any weeds that have germinated and to prepare a good, loose seedbed. I usually make a 20-inch wide row for my head lettuce.

Putting the plants 10 inches apart from each other is the best way to grow them. Some experts recommend 15 or even 18 inches, but I find advantages for closer planting.

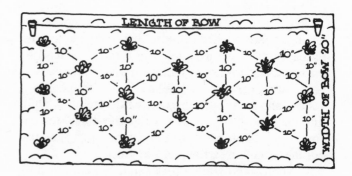

For one thing, you get more heads from a row, and they're better for eating than the larger ones that grow with wider spacing. I start harvesting heads when they're about the size of a softball — a most edible size. There's no waste and no storing.

You also have a continuous harvest if you start when the heads are small. If you wait until the first head you harvest is the size of a basketball, they'll *all* be that big on the same day. Start harvesting early, so that you'll have weeks of prime head lettuce. The quality drops off quickly once they reach maturity.

Another advantage to closer planting comes when the large outside leaves of the plants stretch out toward nearby heads. They form an effective shade cover for the soil. The soil stays cooler and more moist, which is necessary for good production. Weeds are also blocked out.

When setting the plants out, dig all the holes for them at one time, using a 10-inch scrap of wood to measure quickly the distance between holes. Dig each hole 4 to 5 inches deep. In the bottom of each hole put a tablespoon of 5-10-10 fertilizer or a small handful of compost or dried manure, and cover it with 2 to 3 inches of soil.

Water the flats well before transferring the seedlings to the garden. That will help keep soil around the roots and protect them from injury. Before you put them in the ground, strip the outer leaves off the plant. Don't touch the center sprout of the plant, though, because that bud will grow to form the head.

I trim the foliage because some of the roots are killed in transplanting, and the smaller root system can't support all the top growth. The roots, which need time to recover, take hold and start to grow again, and find it easier at first to meet the demands of fewer leaves.

Set the plants in slightly deeper than they were in the flats and give them a gentle watering. Keep them well watered for a few days.

Booster Shot

Head lettuce, like the other kinds of lettuce, has a limited root system and can't go deep in the soil for nutrients. Sometimes an application of extra fertilizer along the way — sidedressing — can help.

Some gardeners like to put down compost after harvesting to help spur new growth. My soil usually has enough nutrients present, so I don't have to do this. But if you have the compost and time to do it —

go ahead. You can sidedress with 10-10-10 or bonemeal, too.

To sum up — good head lettuce needs fertile soil, ample sunlight, a good supply of moisture and nutrients — and most importantly, some cool weather. The plants like temperatures around 55 or 60°F during the growing season, but sometimes it doesn't always work out that way.

Mulching

A thick, organic mulch (straw, leaves, grass clippings, hay, etc.) is almost a must if you're growing head lettuce down South in the spring. It will help retain moisture and keep the soil cool as warm spring weather arrives. It's good in Northern gardens, too, where spring heat or quick-draining soils could hurt the crop.

Cultivation

Cultivation is simply stirring up the soil lightly to kill young weeds and to aerate the soil. Be sure not to till or hoe around your head lettuce plants deeper than 1 inch — their roots are shallow.

Heading into Fall

Not enough people realize it is easy to have nice fall heads of lettuce, too. Gardening in Vermont, I start the seeds in flats in partial shade by the side of the barn. Sometimes I start the seeds directly in the garden toward the end of July.

Most years it requires a watchful eye during the first few weeks of growth to make sure the plants don't get parched and burned by the sun. They must have a good supply of moisture.

If you start seeds indoors, wait until they're 3 to 4 inches high before transplanting them. The best time to put them out is after a few rainy days or during some cool weather.

And Still More Greens

Endive

Endive is a cool-weather green with a distinct, clean, sharp taste. In recent years it has shown up more often in the produce bins of stores but it's still expensive.

Endive doesn't like hot weather too well, but it can take some pretty hard frosts. So it's a good green down South where the winters are mild. Up North we grow it as a spring or fall crop only. I'm usually too busy with other crops in the spring, so I plant endive in late July or so for a fall picking. It's a good green to follow my first crop of snap beans.

Plant the seeds directly in the garden, keeping the soil moist until they come up. Plant them in wide rows and thin later with 6 to 7 inches between plants. You can start endive in flats indoors like head lettuce and transplant them later if you want.

Like other greens, endive tastes best when it grows quickly and steadily. Make sure it gets enough water and fertilizer.

To reduce the bitterness of endive cut off the light to the heads, or "blanch" them, right out in the garden about a week before harvesting them. Gather up the leaves of the plant and tie them together above the head or cut the tops and bottoms out of milk cartons and slip these homemade blanching tubes over the plants.

I like the curly-leaf endive varieties such as **Green Curled.** The green known as 'escarole' is actually a less-curly endive with broader leaves, grown the same way as 'endive.'

Chicory

Chicory grows wild in many parts of the country. It's easy to recognize in fields or along the road when the plants sport many small blue flowers in late summer. But by the time wild chicory flowers, the greens are practically inedible. If you locate the wild plants early in the spring, try harvesting some of the spiny young leaves for salads.

Two different cultivated harvests are possible from a row of chicory: you can pick young leaves early in the season or let the plants grow (but not allowing seedstalk to develop) and harvest the roots after a killing frost in the fall. The roots can be roasted and ground and used as a substitute for coffee — a practice that started 200 years ago in Italy when coffee became a fashionable but expensive drink. Or, the roots can be placed in a cool cellar and the tops "forced" for fresh salad sprouts in winter. The greens in this case are often called **witloof** heads. That's from the Dutch word for "white leaf." In Europe, forcing witloof heads is big business. For an American home gardener, it can be a rewarding winter project.

Chicory should be planted in late spring or

early summer. Sow the seeds in a wide bed, a foot or so across. If you have loose, rich soil somewhere, great! That will encourage the plants to develop large, straight roots. After the plants come up, thin them to 4 or 5 inches apart. You can harvest the greens for salads, or you can let the plants grow if you're interested in the roots.

Winter Chicory or French Endive

Chicory roots can be forced in the fall or in the dead of winter to have nice tight heads of fresh leaves for salads. Forcing simply means encouraging the roots to use their stored energy to send up fresh top growth.

You can do this right out in the garden in early fall if you want. Just cut the top of the plants off about one inch above the crowns, hill 4 to 6 inches of soil over the plants and keep the roots watered.

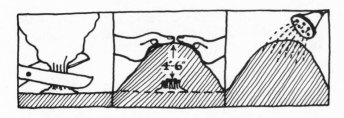

I think it's better to harvest the roots, store them and force them in the cellar in midwinter when a fresh head of chicory is really a delight.

Dig the roots sometime after the first killing frost. Don't brush them or wash them. Just place them in the sun for an hour or so. Then store them in a cool cellar (40°-50°F) in sand, sawdust, peatmoss or in plastic bags.

When winter sets in, take some chicory roots and trim the root ends so they're pretty much the same length — probably around 6 to 8 inches.

Get a box that's twice the height of the roots and half fill it with sawdust, sand, peatmoss or very fine soil. Put the roots in standing upright, close together but not touching each other. The crowns of the roots should just be at the top of the packing material. Water thoroughly and then top off the box with another 6 inches or so of more fine sand, peat or sawdust. Put the box out of the light in a warmer spot (60° is recommended as ideal) and keep the earth moist. Cover the box with plastic or newspaper to keep the moisture in. In 3 or 4 weeks you can harvest the tightly folded leaves that sprout up from the center bud of the crown.

You may have to water again if the lower pack-

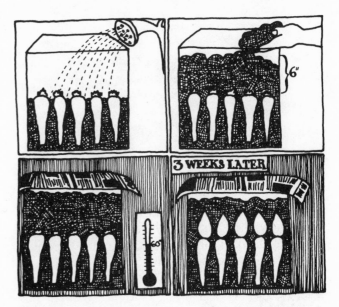

ing material dries out a bit. Make a hole through the top layer to water. You don't want it wet where the leaves are growing.

The heads are usually just an inch or two in diameter and 5 or 6 inches tall. The leaves are yellowish or white because they haven't received any light. Separate the leaves before serving them.

You can start forcing a box of roots every 2 weeks or so to have a supply throughout the cold months.

Dandelion

I've never really met a dandelion I liked. I'm as surprised as most people to see the seeds for sale in garden stores. I've tried eating the young, spiny leaves of dandelions growing wild, but frankly, I've never found them that appetizing. But other people really like them.

Dandelion greens are more popular in Europe, I'm told. It's there that several dandelion varieties were developed to produce larger and curlier leaves. European gardeners make a habit of blanching the plants to reduce bitterness.

If you want to blanch some local dandelions — maybe on your lawn — turn flower pots over them early in the spring, wait a week and then harvest the leaves.

It's just hard for me to think about planting dandelions as they can be hard to root out if they get firmly established in the garden. If you're a determined gardening experimenter and want to grow some, plant the seeds in spring as soon as you can work the soil. Thin them to 3 inches apart and later to about 5 or 6 inches. Keep picking the green leaves

as they reach edible size and as long as you can eat them.

I've heard that you can dig up the dandelion roots — wild or garden varieties — and force them in the cellar like rhubarb or chicory roots, but until I try it, I won't recommend it.

Rocket

Rocket is sometimes called "ruccola" or "rocquette" in seed catalogs. It's one of a number of salad greens I've started to grow in recent years in a special fall section of the garden.

The young leaves are rough and slender, with a taste all their own — hot, with a hint of bean or nut flavor. Chopped into a salad, the leaves can sure keep people guessing about the ingredients.

Celtuce

Celtuce was introduced to U.S. gardeners more than 20 years ago from China, but it didn't meet with much success. I've seen more seed catalogues carrying it now, so perhaps it's getting another try from gardeners.

It was first called "celery lettuce." That's because you can harvest the young leaves of the plants in early spring like leaf lettuce, and then later as the plants get taller, cut the stems, pick off the leaves, peel them and use them like celery, raw or cooked.

Celtuce is a cool-weather plant for the most part. You should plant it as early as you plant let-

tuce, but spaced a little farther apart. Harvest the leaves as they reach eating size.

The late spring warm weather will cause the leaves to become bitter, so let them go. When the plant gets a foot or two high, cut the stalk for the "celery" harvest. Trim the leaves off and be sure to peel the stem before eating raw or cooking.

Upland Cress

I haven't grown upland cress yet, though I have a jar of seeds that a gardening friend saved for me that I'm looking forward to planting. This cress, sometimes called winter cress or spring cress, is a biennial, which means that it will go to seed the second year of its growth.

You plant seeds early in the spring, and soon after start harvesting the young leaves and sprigs. The plants will survive most winters and send up flower stalks early the next season. You can have a spring harvest of some leaves before the seedstalks appear.

The seeds of upland cress must be easy to harvest because my friend sent me a whole handful of them.

Corn Salad

I didn't know very much about this spring and fall green before I planted it. Some U.S. seed companies introduced this European specialty a few years ago and I decided to try it. (It's sometimes called lamb's lettuce, fetticus or maches.)

One of the nice things about corn salad is its hardiness. It's one of the last crops to quit in the fall and early winter. You get plenty of light green leaves for salads. They don't have much taste, so you should mix them with other salad greens.

I sow the seeds fairly thickly toward the end of our hot summer weather. I usually plant a row 10 feet or so long and 15 inches wide, simply by broad-

casting the seed over the seedbed. After thinning, the plants will be a few inches from each other. You can plant it in the spring, too, if you like, but I save it for the fall, since it takes cold weather so well.

Like other greens I like to harvest as soon as there's something to eat — after just 3 to 4 weeks — by cutting the whole plant right above the ground. They are never too tall, but the leaves are fairly wide, so it's easy to fill a salad bowl.

Though our long, wide row probably yields more corn salad than necessary, it's nice to know that we have fresh greens still growing as the early winter snow clouds head our way.

Curlicress or Peppergrass

I like the name curlicress for this zesty, fast-growing green because the plants are low to the ground, frizzy and add a curly look to the salad garden.

It's often advertised as the plant you can start harvesting in 7 to 10 days. I've come pretty close to that in my garden.

Curlicress will grow just about anywhere. Probably the best place for it would be in an indoor flat near the kitchen where you could snip leaves anytime for garnishing salads or sandwiches.

Chew a few leaves before you decide to use a lot of it in any one dish, though. Curlicress has a fiery taste.

Plant it in short, thick rows early in the year and throw more seeds in every couple of weeks. Harvest early because it will produce little flower stalks in a month or so and the quality of the sprigs will go down.

Watercress

Most people think they have to chase around the woods and streams to find watercress. Not so. Though it is more at home in a fast, shallow stream, this snappy, clean-tasting green will grow very well in the garden. You just have to give it a wet spot — preferably some shade, too — to grow in. You'll have to water it often to assure rapid growth.

You can start seeds in small, clay pots set in a pan of water indoors and later transplant them to an outside location when the hard spring frosts are past. Or you can start some plants indoors by sticking some store-bought leafy watercress stems in moist potting soil. Just make sure you keep it well watered.

When the stems start producing new leaves,

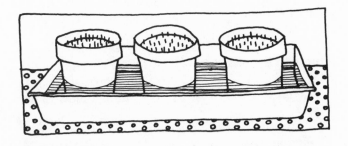

you can transplant them to the garden about 6 to 8 inches apart from each other. In 4 to 5 weeks, you can start harvesting by cutting off the top 3 to 4 inches of the plants.

Giving the plant the moist conditions it needs will be any gardener's main challenge with watercress. Once you find the right spot . . . perhaps next to a small pool, or in a low, wet area of the garden . . . then you can show off your success with this somewhat rare and highly prized green. It really adds flavor to sandwiches, omelettes, fresh-caught trout and jazzes up salads.

Watercress Stream

A friend showed me how to create a false stream on the shady side of the house to grow watercress. Dig a trench (preferably near a downspout or an outside spigot) that will hold a few sections of orangeburg pipe, cut in half lengthwise. (Orangeburg pipe is a man-made fiber pipe — often 6 inches in diameter — used in sewage systems.) You can cut it with a saw. Incidentally, because you're cutting it in half, just buy half the total length you want to end up with.

Butt the sections together and place them in the trench, so the rim of the pipe is at ground level. Just about fill the pipe with small stones or stone chips. Then place narrow, perforated plastic seed flats in

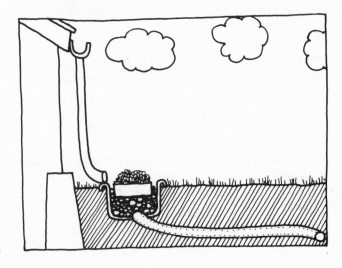

the pipe trench. Fill them with peat moss and soil, and sow your watercress seeds or put in cuttings.

Let the water from a garden hose or the spigot run into the stones in the pipe sections. As long as the stone bed beneath the flats stays wet, your watercress should flourish — from first thaw to last freeze.

If you have a drainage problem where you've built your stream, you can run a "lateral" of perforated soil drain from one of the ends.

Celery

Celery has a reputation for being a fussy, hard-to-grow vegetable. There's a lot of truth to that, but with the right climate and some care, you can grow large, tender celery. A dozen plants will take up just 5 or 6 feet of row, and it's worth trying.

Celery is challenging to grow because it needs a long time to grow — up to 130 to 140 days of mostly cool weather — and it's quite demanding when it comes to water and fertilizer. If your soil stays moist and has plenty of organic matter in it, you're in good shape for growing celery. But shut off the water supply even for a short time, and you're in trouble.

The roots of celery plants are limited — usually stretching just 6 to 8 inches away from the plant and only 2 to 3 inches deep, so the top part of the soil not only has to have enough moisture, it must also contain all the nutrients the plants need.

Celery plants don't like hot weather at all — the crop will thrive only where the winters are mild, or where the summers are relatively cool, or where there's a long, cool growing period in the fall. In Vermont the summers are not blisteringly hot, so we can set out plants in the spring, tend them through the summer and harvest a crop in early fall.

Because celery takes such a long time to grow, it's best to start the seeds in plant boxes or flats indoors to get the jump on the season.

Celery seeds are slow to germinate, so soak them overnight to speed up the process. Plant them indoors around 12 weeks before the last frost.

When the plants are 2 inches high, transplant them to individual peat pots or to another deeper flat with new potting soil. If you use flats, put the plants at least 2 inches apart.

By early May the plants are about 4 to 6 inches high. Harden them off for a week to 10 days to get them used to the spring weather.

Transplant celery a week to two before the average date of the last frost. However, experts say that if the weather turns cold after you set them out

(night temperatures consistently under 55°F) the celery plants may go to seed prematurely. Well, we have our share of cool spells in Vermont, and I can remember only two or three plants going to seed early. Because of the need for a long season, it's worth the gamble to set them out early — they'll take any light frost we have in May.

To transplant celery, first work the soil, mix in the fertilizer (about 1 pound of 5-10-10 per 30 square feet) and dig a straight trench about 4 to 5 inches deep. Plant the celery in the bottom of the trench, spacing the plants 8 to 10 inches apart, and set them half an inch deeper than they were in their pots.

Remove some of the outside leaves from each plant before setting them in. As with head lettuce, this trimming helps the roots recover from the transplant shock and resume normal growth more quickly.

As the plants grow, fill in the trench with sand or soil, mulch or compost. This blanches the lower part of the stalks, and also keeps the roots cool, which celery plants like.

I've also grown celery in 'blocks' instead of furrows. The blocks measured about 3 to 4 feet on each side. It's a real space saver.

Cultivation is important because celery grows slowly and doesn't appreciate any competition from weeds, and remember to keep your weeding shallow, so you don't injure the celery roots.

Sidedressings of 5-10-10 or similar balanced fertilizer in the second and third month of growth will help keep celery growing steadily. Use 1 tablespoon per plant and sprinkle it in a shallow furrow about 3 to 4 inches from the plant and cover it with soil.

Give your plants plenty of water. If celery is short on moisture, or a hot spell hits, the stalks get tough and stringy. They can also develop hollow or pithy stalks in dry spells.

When celery gets big enough to eat, start harvesting the larger, outer stalks as you need them. The center will keep producing stalks. To harvest big plants at the end of the season, simply pull up the whole plant and trim off the roots.

Blanching

Unblanched celery is twice as strong in flavor as the celery you buy in the store. I like celery a little milder in taste, so I take the time to blanch the stalks before harvest — simply keeping the sun from striking the stalks.

Open the tops and bottoms of half-gallon milk cartons and use these 'sleeves' to blanch your celery. Set the cartons over the plants a week, 10 days or even longer before you want to harvest. The color of the stalks will lighten, and their flavor will become milder.

Some people place boards close along each side of the row to blanch celery. Others simply bring soil or mulch up around the plant to block out the sun. If you use soil, wait until the cool weather of early fall arrives and hill up the plants when they are dry and free of disease. This will help prevent rot. There's no need to blanch the top leaves, of course, just the stalks.

Storing

Celery stores really well — you can keep it for many weeks with no trouble. Dig up the plants carefully, disturbing the roots as little as possible. Replant them in boxes of sand in your root cellar or set them close together in a trench in your cold frame where you can keep them from freezing. As long as the roots stay moist and the stalks dry, they'll really keep. Temperatures in the range of 35 to 40°F are best for good storage.

HARVESTING

Harvesting is one of the nicest chores of the gardening season. It's easy to do right:

Start harvesting when there's something to eat. Gardens are for eating, so as soon as your endive, spinach, celery, lettuce or whatever is big enough to toss in a salad — harvest. There will be plenty more to come.

Harvest at peak flavor and freshness. Young greens are the tastiest and most nutritious. Don't wait for prize-winning heads of lettuce — start picking them when they're soft-ball size — still crisp and flavorful.

If you're freezing or canning spinach, chard or beet greens, harvest the choicest leaves and plants and process them right away for the best quality.

Harvest lettuce and other greens close to meal time to retain as much quality and food value as possible.

Try for 2, 3 or even 4 cuttings. Leaf lettuce and chard are the best examples of crops that will "come again" after you harvest. If you cut lettuce and chard an inch above the ground, the plants will send out new, fresh growth in an effort to make seed. This is the way I harvest all lettuce varieties except crisphead. It seems drastic, but it's not.

With Oak Leaf lettuce I sometimes get 4 cuttings in a season. And the produce is much sweeter than what I'd get by just picking off the larger, more mature leaves that can be somewhat tough and bitter.

Incidentally, a long serrated bread knife is the best tool for harvesting wide rows of greens.

Garden to Kitchen

FAVORITE RECIPES

Salads

Good salads are easy to make, and they are wonderful. Unfortunately, bad salads are also easy to make. The two most important rules for excellent salads, I think, are

1) use the freshest, cleanest greens available and

2) use no commercial dressings.

The first rule is challenging for me only in the deep of winter. At that time of year, I am hard-pressed to find nice greens. But many of you don't live as far north, and it's easier for you to have fresh, home-grown greens later in the year.

The second rule isn't challenging at all, because tasty salad dressing is so easy to make. Basic oil and vinegar dressing — vinaigrette — takes me less than two minutes from start to finish. If I want to dress it up a bit, it may take a minute longer. Of course, I can make it more complicated, but it's not necessary. If I really want to save energy, I can make up a whole jar of basic dressing and make additions for each salad right in the bowl — it keeps in the refrigerator for up to a month.

Good quality ingredients are important for the best flavor. Although I have used corn oil and other vegetable oils with success in vinaigrette dressing, I prefer the flavor of olive oil. A mild vinegar — perhaps a wine or herb vinegar — gives just enough tartness without overpowering the flavor of the entire dressing. No matter how much dressing I make, the proportion of oil to vinegar remains the same: 3 to 1.

Greens Preparation

In the summer I like to pick lettuce from the garden just minutes before serving. I wash it well and don't chill it because it's so fresh. Actually, I think that the flavor of lettuce is enhanced if it's close to room temperature rather than icy cold. Others, however, prefer lettuce cold, because it's crisper.

If I need to store lettuce, I wash it first, wrap it in a damp towel and store it in a plastic bag or tightly covered container in the refrigerator.

Washing lettuce is very important, because greens are magnets for dirt. Nothing ruins a salad faster than having grit as the surprise ingredient.

Because oil and water don't mix, lettuce leaves also need to be dried before being mixed with salad dressing. If they are not dry, they won't accept a coating of oil, and the dressing will just end up in the bottom of the bowl.

Wash leafy greens in several changes of water, letting the grit settle to the bottom and lifting out the greens while changing the water. Be careful not to bruise the leaves.

To dry leaf lettuce, wrap the leaves lightly in a clean towel and pat dry. You can also drain them in a colander or swing them in a wire salad basket. Many people also swear by salad spinners for drying and storing lettuce.

To wash head lettuce, core the solid part of the stem and hold the head upside down under running water. Place on a terry towel in the refrigerator and cover with another towel. In a few hours the lettuce will be dry.

Unless you are cutting wedges of tightly-packed head lettuce, such as iceberg, it is suggested that you tear lettuce greens by hand rather than cut them with a knife. I believe there is a difference in flavor, and I like hand-torn lettuce best. I have tried to discover if there were any nutritional reason for recommending tearing, and so far I can't discover any. For many, sufficient reason seems to be — "My mother told me to do it that way." What I recommend is try both and see which you prefer.

Basic Vinaigrette Dressing

3   Tb olive oil
1   Tb vinegar
1/4 tsp dry mustard
     salt and freshly ground pepper

If I make up a jar of dressing, I may add a couple of peeled garlic cloves plus salt, pepper and dry mustard, and that's it until I am ready to make a salad. Dry mustard may not be used by purists, but I find it gives the dressing a little sparkle many people enjoy. (When I first started using dry mustard in dressing, I was a little heavy handed, and everyone could guess my new, secret ingredient — so, go easy!)

I mix the basic dressing in the salad bowl and then decide what seasonings and extras I want to add to complement the meal. It may be fresh herbs — a terrific one is dill, another standby is basil; it may be cheese — almost everyone likes some Roquefort or bleu crumbled in their dressing; perhaps some chopped green pepper or onion. I try to do this as I start preparing the meal, so they have sufficient time to "stew." Then just before bringing the bowl to the table, I'll put the lettuce on top of the dressing and add any garnish I want. Just before serving, the salad gets a good toss, so the greens are evenly and lightly coated with dressing.

One easy way to wreck a salad is to use too much dressing. It can drown the salad and make the lettuce limp and soggy. If you find that there's a lot of dressing in the bowl after the salad is gone, you're probably using too much dressing — hold back a little.

Basic Blender Mayonnaise

Although Vinaigrette dressing is my stand-by, I do use some others. The most basic, of course, is mayonnaise. It's not hard to make because I use a blender. Homemade mayonnaise really does taste quite different and much better than store-bought. As for economy, I think I save about a nickel a gallon, but as I make it in small batches, I probably don't save anything.

```
  1   egg
1/2   tsp dry mustard
1/2   tsp salt
      dash of cayenne pepper
  2   Tb lemon juice
  1   cup salad oil, olive oil or mixture
```

Put egg, mustard, salt and cayenne in blender and blend for 30 seconds at high speed. Add lemon juice and blend for additional 10 seconds. While blending at high speed, very gradually add oil — in droplets, especially at first. Use rubber spatula if necessary to keep ingredients flowing to processing blades.

All of a sudden in the process, the sound will change as the mayonnaise thickens, and then you know it's almost done. Go very gently at this point in adding additional oil. Mayonnaise is an emulsion or suspension of egg in oil, and the oil can only hold so much before the whole thing separates. If it does separate, don't despair. Simply remove the mixture from the blender and start with another egg. After it is beaten thoroughly, gradually add the mixture to it and perhaps just a little more oil until it has reached the right consistency.

For different tastes, add one or a combination of the following to the mayonnaise base:

Almonds, chopped	Dry sherry	Parsley
Anchovies	Egg,	Pickles
Basil	hard-cooked	Pimiento
Catsup	Fennel	Sour cream
Capers	Garlic, minced	Spinach leaves,
Chervil	Green pepper	chopped
Chili powder	Horseradish	Tabasco sauce
Chili sauce	Nasturtium	Tarragon
Chives	leaves	Tomato, chopped
Curry powder	Olives	Watercress
Dandelion greens	Onion, grated	Whipping cream
Dill	Paprika	Yogurt

Honey Dressing

```
1/3   cup honey
  1   cup wine vinegar
  1   clove garlic, finely chopped
  1   cup salad oil
```

Mix or shake all ingredients in a tightly covered jar and chill. Excellent on spinach greens.

Creamy Salad Dressing

```
    1   tsp egg yolk
  1/2   tsp dry mustard
  1/2   tsp minced garlic
        dash of Tabasco sauce
        salt and freshly ground pepper
    1   tsp vinegar
  1/2   cup olive oil (or peanut, vegetable or corn oil)
1 to 2  tsp lemon juice (fresh, preferably)
    1   tsp heavy cream
```

Beat an egg yolk and put one tsp of it in a mixing bowl. Add the mustard, Tabasco sauce, garlic, salt, pepper and vinegar. To blend the ingredients well, beat with a wire whisk. Gradually add the oil, beating vigorously until dressing is thickened and well blended. Add the lemon juice and beat in the heavy cream. Makes about 3/4 cup, sufficient for 10 to 12 cups of salad greens.

Tangy Russian Dressing

```
    2   cups mayonnaise
1 1/2   cups chili sauce
  1/3   cup minced celery
  1/3   cup minced dill pickle
    2   Tb lemon juice
    1   Tb Worcestershire sauce
    1   tsp horseradish sauce
```

Mix all ingredients well and chill. Traditionally served on wedges of head lettuce, especially iceberg. It is also excellent on Swiss cheese and roast beef sandwiches.

Hot Bacon Dressing

```
  1/4   lb bacon
  1/2   cup diced onion
  1/4   cup white vinegar
  1/4   cup red wine vinegar
  1/4   tsp salt
        pinch of pepper
  1/4   tsp sugar
1 1/2   tsp cornstarch
  1/2   cup beef broth
```

Sauté bacon in large pan until crisp. Drain.

Sauté onion in bacon drippings until soft. Stir in vinegars, salt, pepper and sugar.

Blend cornstarch and 2 Tb of beef broth in a small cup. Add remaining broth to pan and stir in corn starch mixture.

Cook over low heat, stirring constantly until thick. Pour over salad greens and toss. Sprinkle with crumbled bacon and serve.

Spinach

Although a lot of people don't agree with me, I love spinach! It's got to be cooked right, though. Overcooked, I think it's mushy, slimy and bitterly metallic. Cooked gently, it has a distinct flavor, which I think is a wonderful accompaniment to fish, eggs, chicken, roasts or as a separate course in quiche or soufflé and raw as a salad. One pound of fresh spinach cooks down to about one cup, and that is almost enough for two people.

Spinach, like other greens, must be washed well. To serve it plain, just leave the water of the last washing on the leaves, and put the spinach in a large enamel, Pyrex or stainless steel pot.

Or use a steamer that has an inner container full of holes that sits over, not in, about 2 inches of boiling water in the outer container. Cover and cook over low to medium heat. In a few minutes, the spinach will be tender, tasty and ready to serve. Some people like to add vinegar. I prefer salt, pepper and butter, and occasionally a sprinkling of nutmeg.

Precooked, chopped spinach is tasty baked in cream sauce, cheese sauce or with grated Swiss cheese and topped with bread crumbs.

Spinach Ring

2 Tb margarine or butter
3 Tb finely chopped onions
2 cans cream of mushroom soup
3 cups cooked spinach or chard, chopped
1/2 cup bread crumbs
 salt and pepper to taste
 nutmeg to taste
2 eggs, separated

Preheat oven to 375°. Sauté onions in margarine or butter until tender. Heat the soup, undiluted, stirring until smooth. Add the onions and margarine, spinach, bread crumbs, salt, pepper and nutmeg.

Beat egg yolks until thick. Stir the egg yolks into spinach mixture, very slowly. Set aside. Beat egg white until stiff but not dry. Fold into spinach mixture and pour into buttered ring mold. Set the mold in a pan of hot water and bake 45 minutes or until set. Unmold and serve hot. Very good with baked or roast chicken. Serves 6.

Lamb and Spinach Stew

2 Tb flour
2 lbs boneless lamb stew meat
2 medium onions, chopped
1 1/2 cups stock or bouillon
1 bay leaf
3 lbs fresh spinach, well-washed and chopped
3 cups diced tomatoes
1 tsp salt
1/2 tsp dried rosemary
1/2 tsp freshly ground black pepper
2 Tb flour
2 Tb butter

Dredge cubed stew meat in flour and brown in Dutch oven. Drain fat, leaving only about 1 Tb. Add onions and cook until they are translucent. Add stock and bay leaf and simmer, covered, until tender, about one hour. Add spinach, tomatoes, salt, rosemary and pepper and cook for about 10 minutes or until spinach is wilted. Blend additional flour with butter and add gradually to stew to thicken. Stir constantly and cook for additional minute. Serve with rice. Serves 6.

Spinach/Noodle Casserole

1 pound noodles
1 1/2 pounds fresh spinach, well washed
1 Tb lemon juice
3 Tb butter
1 Tb finely chopped onion
1 garlic clove, finely minced
3 Tb flour
1 cup light cream or milk
 salt and pepper to taste
 pinch of nutmeg
1/2 cup finely chopped ham
1/2 cup buttered soft fresh bread crumbs

Preheat oven to 350°. Cook noodles until just tender and drain. Wilt spinach and chop finely. Add lemon juice. Sauté onion and garlic in butter. Add flour and gradually stir in cream or milk over gentle heat. Season with salt, pepper and nutmeg. Add spinach and stir well. Add noodles and ham and place in shallow, buttered baking dish. Top with crumbs and bake for 20 minutes or until lightly browned.

Popeye Burgers

2 lbs raw spinach, chopped
2 lbs ground beef
1/2 cup bread crumbs
1/2 cup shredded Cheddar cheese
2 Tb Worcestershire sauce
1 egg, slightly beaten
1 garlic clove, finely minced
salt and pepper to taste
2 Tb oil or margarine

Mix all ingredients well. Shape into 8 patties and cook in oil in large fry pan over medium heat until desired doneness. Turn only once. The patties may also be broiled. May be served on bread, hard rolls or just plain with mashed potatoes. Serves 4.

Easy Cream of Spinach Soup

1 lb (3 cups) chopped spinach or chard
¼ cup chopped onion
¼ cup margarine or butter
3 Tb flour
salt and pepper to taste
3 cups milk

Sauté onions in margarine or butter in heavy saucepan until translucent. Stir in flour, salt and pepper. Add milk gradually, stirring constantly. Cook over low heat to boiling. Simmer and stir for one minute.

Steam well-washed, chopped spinach or chard until it is just tender. Add to cream sauce base and serve.

Celery

Somewhere I heard that you burn more calories eating raw celery than you consume. That may be the reason celery is on almost every diet invented. But it also tastes good and has an appealing texture that helps you to think you are eating something far more substantial. Celery also has a wonderful flavor for soups, stews and salads that makes it an indispensable vegetable.

To prepare raw celery, wash it well, cut it into uniform strips, and eat it plain or serve it with a dip. It can also be filled with a mixture of bleu cheese and heavy cream.

To keep celery crisp, simply stick the stalks in ice water in the refrigerator, and they'll stay for days.

To boil celery, slice washed stalks crosswise

into 1-inch slices. Boil it gently in salted water until crispy-tender. It can be served plain with butter or in cream sauce or Hollandaise.

Braised Celery

Wash enough stalks to make 4 per person served. If they are very large, cut in half. Place in a lidded sauté pan and sauté in clarified butter for 2 minutes. Add salt and pepper and barely cover with hot chicken or veal stock. Cover and simmer until tender; remove the stalks to individual serving plates and keep warm in oven. Reduce the stock by at least half. Add again as much heavy cream and bring to a boil, stirring constantly. Add 1/4 to 1/2 cup shredded mild cheese and stir until thickened. Pour some sauce over each serving, and top with an ''X'' of pimiento.

Curried Celery

Cut one whole (large) bunch, or two small ones, into bite-sized pieces crossways. Pare, core and dice 1 large apple; peel and dice one medium onion. Melt chicken fat or lard (or substitute oil & butter) to the point of fragrance, and add the vegetables. Cook and stir until just barely beginning to brown. Turn down the heat and add 1 cup of stock (or bouillon) mixed with 1 Tb cornstarch, 1 tsp (or more) curry powder, 2 tsp capers, a pinch of ground ginger, salt and pepper. Cook over low heat, stirring regularly, until thickened and tender.

Greens

Collards and Mashed Potatoes

Cook the collards and potatoes in separate pans with water. Drain both. Chop the collards finely and mix with the mashed potatoes. Put in a baking dish in a 400° oven, dot with butter and bake until browned.

Endive Quiche

Quiche is nothing more, really, than scrambled egg pie with extras thrown in, but it tastes special.

    8"   partially baked pie shell
    4   cups raw, chopped Belgian endive (or spinach,
           chard or other cooked greens)
    2   Tb butter or margarine
    1/4   tsp salt
    2   Tb water
    1   tsp lemon juice
  1 1/2   cups whipping cream
    3   eggs
           pinch of mace
           freshly ground black pepper
    1/4   cup grated Swiss cheese
    1   Tb butter or margarine

Preheat oven to 325°. Place endive in 2-quart, buttered baking dish. Mix salt, water and lemon juice together and pour over endive. Cut a piece of brown paper the same size as the top of the baking dish, butter it and place it on top of the endive. Cover the dish and braise the endive in the oven for 20 to 30 minutes, or until tender.

While the endive is cooking, beat eggs until thick and beat in cream, mace and pepper. Remove endive from oven and drain. Turn oven up to 375°.

Fold endive into egg mixture, pour into pastry shell and sprinkle with cheese and dot with butter. Bake in upper part of oven for 25 to 30 minutes or until set. Serves 4 to 6.

Simple Watercress Soup

    1   lb peeled, diced potatoes
    1   lb peeled, sliced onions
  1 1/2   qts water or chicken stock or broth
    1   Tb salt
    1/4   lb watercress
    2   Tb butter
    2   Tb whipping cream
           salt and pepper to taste

Simmer the potatoes and onions together in water with salt until tender. Liquefy in blender or food processor. Chop watercress finely and add to soup. Simmer for 5 minutes. Add salt and pepper. Remove from heat and add butter and cream and serve. Decorate with chopped parsley or chives. May be served hot or cold. Serves 6 to 8.

One-Dish Supper

All greens are delicious cooked with salt pork.

    4   lbs greens (beets, chard, spinach, turnip, mustard)
    1/2   lb salt pork
    8   small potatoes

Slice salt pork down to the rind. Cover and simmer in sufficient water 1 1/2 hours. Wash greens in several changes of water. Add potatoes and well-washed greens to salt pork and cook until potatoes are tender — about 30 additional minutes.

Serves 4 to 6.

Egg Sauce

A nice accompaniment for hot cooked greens, especially beet greens, spinach, chard and kale.

    1   hard-boiled egg, chopped
    1/4   tsp salt
    2   slices bacon, cooked and crumbled
    2   Tb mayonnaise
    1/2   tsp grated onion

Mix all ingredients together and serve on hot greens.

Stir-Fried Kale

    8   cups fresh kale
    4   Tb vegetable oil
           salt and pepper to taste

Wash green part of kale leaves and drain.

Heat heavy skillet, electric fry pan or wok and add oil. When the oil is almost smoking, put in the kale. Toss and stir until it is wilted completely. Stir and cook another 5 minutes. Great served with chicken fricassee. Serves 4.

Dandelion Greens

Most people who eat dandelion greens don't plant them. They just pick them wild early in the spring in meadows and pastures — or on their own lawns.

Well-washed, young dandelion greens are very tasty served raw with sour cream.

If you want to serve cooked dandelion greens, wash them well in several changes of water. Put them in a large pot and cover with boiling water and simmer for 5 minutes. Drain and add fresh boiling water to them and cook until tender. Drain again and serve hot with butter or margarine or vinegar and salt and pepper to taste. If you like a more tangy flavor, cook them in just one water until tender.

Wilted Lettuce

6   slices of bacon
1/3 cup mild vinegar
     salt and pepper to taste
2   medium heads Boston lettuce or
1   medium head Cos or
     equivalent leaf lettuce

Wash lettuce well and tear into bite-size bits. Fry bacon until crisp. Remove bacon from pan and crumble. To fat in frying pan, add vinegar, salt and pepper. When the mixture boils, add the greens and stir until they are just wilted. Serve hot with bacon crumbles on top. Serves 4.

CANNING GREENS

Personally, I think greens should just barely be wilted for best taste. If they're cooked for much longer, I think they become bitter. Overcooking, I think, accounts for many people's — especially children's — dislike of greens.

To can greens safely, they must be cooked a long time. For that reason, I am not a great fan of canning them. However, they work well in soups and casseroles. So, if you want to do it — and I put up at least a few quarts every year — here's how:

1. For safety and health, it is important to be careful canning, and the first requirement is to use a pressure canner with an accurate gauge for canning all greens.

For complete instructions and precautions for pressure canning, please carefully read and follow the instruction booklets that accompany your canner and your jars. For additional canning information, write the U.S. Department of Agriculture, Washington, D.C. 20240 and ask them for *Home and Garden Bulletin* No. 8, *Home Canning of Fruits and Vegetables*. You have already paid for it with your tax dollars, so no additional money is required.

2. Assemble all utensils: Pressure canner, Mason jars, lids, bands, tongs or jar lifter, timer, cooling racks, wide-mouth funnel, slotted spoon, wooden or plastic spatula or "bubbler," colander.

Use only Mason jars for home canning. These self-sealing, air-tight jars are safe for canning, because the glass is heat-tempered, which is especially important for pressure canning.

3. Examine and clean all equipment. Check all bands for rust, dents or nicks and jars for chips and cracks.

Wash all equipment in hot, soapy water, but do not immerse top of pressure canner in water — just wipe it with a clean, damp cloth.

Keep clean jars and screw tops hot. Keep dome lids in hot water until ready to use.

4. Prepare freshest, cleanest greens possible. Use freshly picked, tender greens and remove stems and imperfect leaves. Wash greens thoroughly in several changes of water, lifting the greens out and letting the grit settle to the bottom.

5. Greens must be processed hot pack (pre-cooked). Steam (in just enough water to prevent sticking, or use steamer) about 2 1/2 pounds of greens until thoroughly wilted. To hasten wilting and prevent overcooking, turn greens over when steam begins to rise around edges of pan. Cut through greens with sharp knife, pack the greens in hot jars, leaving about one-inch headspace. Add salt, 1/2 tsp per pint or 1 tsp per quart. Cover with boiling water, retaining 1-inch headspace. Remove air bubbles by running non-metallic spatula around inside jar. Adjust jar lids.

6. Process in pressure canner. Pack only the number of jars your pressure canner can accommodate at one time. Put the canner on the burner, and put the jars on the rack in the canner. Add 2 inches of boiling water to the canner. Allow enough space between the jars and the sides of the pot so that the steam can flow freely. Clamp the lid securely.

Leave the valve or petcock open, and set the canner over high heat until steam has escaped for 10 minutes. Then close the petcock or put on the weighted gauge, and let the pressure rise to 10 pounds. Start timing and keep adjusting the heat so that the pressure remains constant. If the pressure drops below 10 pounds, the processing time must be started again.

Processing Time

Pints	70 minutes
Quarts	90 minutes

Your canner instructions may differ with the times given above. If so, follow your canner instructions.

Altitude affects pressure canners. You need to use more pressure and longer cooking time the higher you go.

Feet above sea level	Increase pressure	Increase cooking time
1,000		2 minutes
2,000	to 11 pounds	4 minutes
3,000		6 minutes
4,000	to 12 pounds	8 minutes
5,000		10 minutes

If using a weight control canner, increase pressure to 15 pounds at elevations higher than 2,000 feet.

Do not skimp on processing time!

7. After processing time is completed, turn off heat and wait until pressure has dropped to zero before opening canner. Using tongs or jar lifter, remove the jars and place them upright on a rack or thick towel in a draft-free area, allowing enough room between jars, so air may circulate freely. Do not tighten the rims on the dome lids; you may break the seals.

8. There are three tests for checking the seal on a dome lid.
1) As the vacuum forms, the lid pulls down into the jar and makes a kerplunking sound.
2) After cooling, the lid will be dished in the middle and should stay that way as long as the vacuum is present. You can feel it.
3) After cooling, press the top of the lid with your thumb. If it makes a clicking sound, the seal is *not* complete.

If you find some jars with incomplete seals, put the jars in the refrigerator, and use the food soon.

The greens are perfectly good to eat because they are so fresh and you have just cooked them. They just won't hold in storage with imperfect seals.

9. Wipe the jars with a clean, damp cloth and remove the screw bands for re-use. Label the produce clearly, including the date. Store in a cool, dark, dry area.

10. Before serving, reheat all greens by boiling them in an open kettle for 15 minutes. If they smell "off" or if the color or appearance doesn't look right, just dispose of them carefully.

FREEZING GREENS

Frozen greens can often be substituted with success in recipes calling for fresh greens. They aren't quite as good, but they sure are better than nothing or using commercially frozen or canned varieties.

As about two pounds of greens reduce to 10 ounces when wilted, it's easy to realize that you'll need a whole "mess o' greens" in order to have some to freeze plus enough to eat fresh. So if you like greens, just know that it's difficult to plant too much.

For best freezing results, follow these simple steps:

1. Select young, tender leaves. Remove tough stems and imperfect leaves. You may chop them into smaller pieces if you wish.

2. Wash greens thoroughly in several changes of water. Swish them around in a basin of water, and lift them out to drain. The grit will sink to the bottom.

3. Blanch greens in a kettle of boiling water. Almost all greens (beet, chard, kale, mustard, New Zealand and regular spinach and turnip) require 2 minutes blanching. The one exception is collards, and they should be blanched for 3 minutes. If the leaves are very tender, blanch for only 1 1/2 minutes.

4. Chill greens immediately in ice water to stop cooking process and to retain color. Chill for the same amount of time as they were cooked. Don't let them sit around in the water because they will lose flavor.

5. Drain greens well and pack in containers leaving 1/2-inch headspace. Seal, label with contents and date and freeze.

CHAPTER 10

Root Crops

Many people think of root crops as commonplace, uninteresting vegetables because they've been part of mankind's garden for so many thousands of years. We can appreciate them more when we consider they've been eaten by royalty, peasants, warriors and merchants at least since the beginning of recorded history.

Even before our ancestors learned how to grow their own food, they foraged for wild carrots and beets. As they began to garden, they cultivated these same crops, and gardening histories mention root crops being grown by the early civilizations of Mediterranean Europe, Asia, Africa and South America.

Just knowing that beets, carrots, turnips and parsnips have been popular for over 5,000 years should tell us something about them — root crops have survived because they are easy to grow and delicious to eat. Tastebuds haven't changed much over the years!

To give you an idea of the different characteristics of each, here are some brief descriptions, along with some facts and fables:

Beets — "Poor Man's Steak"

I've known many dedicated beet lovers over the years, and some swear that a juicy, deep red beet fresh from the garden is better than steak. I still like a good cut of meat, but I agree that beets make fine eating.

I always plant plenty of beets, so we can enjoy an early feast of beet greens, summer dishes of Harvard beets and cold beet salads, and an ample winter supply for the root cellar.

Although there are many more to choose from, here are some beet varieties to get you started. The first one is my best producer.

Detroit Dark Red — 59 days — Popular beet variety that is perfectly round; grows 2 1/2 to 3 inches in diameter; has deep red color; can be grown for both greens and roots; grows well in wide range of soil and temperature conditions.

Golden Beet — 55 days — These unusual carrot-colored roots take some getting used to, but they taste exactly like the red beets, and they don't "bleed." The greens are also delicious. If your kids don't like beets, try golden beets, and see if they don't change their minds.

Cylindra — 60 days — Long, cylinder-shaped beet; grows up to 8 inches long; perfect for uniform slices.

Lutz Green Leaf — 80 days — Unusual beet that grows up to four times the size of most beets, but tastes sweetest when harvested small; good winter keeper.

Carrots — Garden Gold

Carrots are such cheery vegetables! Kids go for them almost the same way they love creamsicles and jack-o-lanterns — it must be the bright orange color.

Most adults seem to feel the same way, too. I've seen both young and old folks turn up their noses at other vegetables, but for some reason they'll munch happily on carrot sticks. Our grandsons are real carrot fans — as soon as they see the feathery tops, they can hardly wait to start pulling up the roots. By the way, to keep your own carrot sticks full of vitamins, never peel away the skin. A good scrubbing with a vegetable brush is usually good enough, even for picky eaters.

Carrot varieties range from 3 1/2-inch **Little Fingers** that mature quickly in any kind of soil to 9-inch **Imperators** that need deep, well-worked soil. Of course, all carrots can be eaten when they are only two or three inches long — these "finger-lings" are delectable.

Each seed company has different names for their carrot varieties, but some characteristics stay the same.

Short 'n Sweets — 65 days — Grow well in heavy or shallow soil; sweet flavor in the 3 1/2 to 4-inch root; ideal for freezing or canning.

Chantenay — 70 days — Stocky carrot with broad shoulders and tapered root; 5 to 5 1/2 inches long; easy to pull; good tasting; best carrot for all soil types.

Nantes Half-Longs — 70 days — 6 to 7-inch root with nearly perfect cylinder shape; practically coreless; can be eaten raw, frozen or canned; my favorite.

Danvers Half-Longs — 75 days — 7 to 7 1/2-inch root; tapered to a blunt end; bright orange flesh with rich flavor and good texture.

Turnips — Backbone of the South

I often pull a young turnip on my way through the garden, to peel and eat just like an apple. My Southern friends don't even let the roots develop that much, they just grow the turnip for the greens — and serve them in more ways than you can imagine! Whether you're growing for the greens or the roots, you'll find that turnips are one of the best all-around vegetables.

If you ate a portion of turnip greens and roots daily, you could practically stop taking your daily vitamins. The roots contain vitamins A and C, and the greens are rich in calcium, iron, thiamine and other B vitamins. A daily diet of turnips would be boring, but it would be darned good for you.

Turnips germinate and grow quickly compared

to most of the other root crops, and they have definite temperature preferences for best production — they are not happy in hot weather. If the temperature is above 80°F for days at a time, it can cause turnips to mature before their time, giving them a strong, bitter flavor and spongy flesh.

I plant turnips in April here in Vermont and again around August 15. Like the rest of the root crops, turnips tolerate frosts well, so plant them both early and late. In the South, plant during the cool fall and winter months.

To stretch the turnip harvest over a two or three-month period, plant two or three different kinds of seeds in the first planting. You can harvest some very early as greens, and small roots for eating fresh. The turnips will be fully grown at different times instead of all at once.

Any turnip can be grown for its greens if harvested young, so you don't need to plant special "foliage" varieties, even if you want more greens than roots.

Purple-Top White Globe — 55 days — Most popular for home gardens; roots grow 4 to 5 inches across and look just like their name, with white bottoms and bright purplish-red upper portions; roots taste best if pulled at 2 or 3-inch size.

Tokyo Cross Hybrid — 35 days — Pure white, smooth shape; disease- and virus-resistant; grows up to 6 inches across; root won't get woody or fibrous if left in the ground after fully grown.

Shogoin or **Japanese** — 30 days for greens/ 70 days for roots — Grown mainly for greens, which grow lush, tender and mild; mature roots are 3 to 4 inches thick, and have delicate flavor when harvested small.

Radishes, Radishes, Radishes . .

I really am some kind of a radish nut! I plant radishes with practically everything in my garden — carrots, beets, onions, lettuce, parsnips, cucumbers — but never by themselves. It's not that I especially love to eat radishes, though I do enjoy them. It's just that in all my years of gardening I've discovered that radishes are the best, all-around, companion plants. And they also give me pleasure because they're among the very first vegetables to be harvested in the spring. Here's how radishes work for you in the garden:

Early radishes come up fast — in about 3 to 7 days — to mark rows. This allows you to cultivate early with confidence when you plant them with slow-growing vegetables.

Radishes act as natural cultivators, since their thick, round roots leave holes in the soil when harvested. These cavities provide "breathing space," so the remaining root crops can easily expand, moving the soil around them right into the cavities. Long, white icicle radishes are ideal for this, especially if you have heavy, clay soil or if you want to grow long carrots or parsnips. Let the radishes grow beyond the eating stage — until they are huge — and then pull them. The remaining plants will expand and thrive in the newly-created spaces.

Radishes are decoys for some garden insects. If there are hungry root maggots, leaf hoppers or flea beetles around, they'll usually go for the first plants they find. That's radishes in my garden. You may even find the radishes doing double duty with both their tops and bottoms acting as hosts for insects.

Radishes seem to repel some insects when planted as companions. Radishes may ward off cucumber beetles when sown with squash, melons and cukes and spider mites when sown around tomatoes. Although this seems to vary with soil and weather conditions, there seems to be an aroma given off by radishes that some insects dislike.

I guess you can plant radishes by themselves if you want, but it seems like a waste of space when they can be doing so much for your other crops planted right in with them. Although I never plant radishes alone, I always have a steady supply for eating — with plenty to spare, too.

Speaking of eating, the best-tasting radishes are small, about the diameter of a penny. Whether or not you plant radishes as a companion, harvest them for eating before they are fully mature — they'll taste better when they're young, and you'll beat the root maggots to them by pulling them early. By the way, even if the radish greens look chewed, the roots may still be okay to eat, so don't be fooled by their appearance.

Cherry Belle — 22 days — Extra early, favorite home variety; short tops; cherry-shaped, bright red-skinned root; white, crisp, firm flesh.

White Icicle — 27 days — Long, bright white radish that grows 5 to 8 inches long; pungent taste; grown for eating, companions and as natural cultivators.

Winter Radish — 55 days — Large radish that develops black, white or red skin with pungent, white flesh; needs cool weather at the end of its long growing season; good for winter storage; can be used in stir-fry recipes or boiled like a turnip.

Rutabagas

Rutabagas are a gardening wonder. They originated in the Middle Ages as a cross between cabbages and turnips, and they've developed into high-yielding, nutrition-rich, easy-to-grow vegetables.

Along with turnips and radishes, rutabagas belong to the same family as cabbages. Rutabagas look a lot like turnips, and they, too, can be grown for both their greens and their roots.

The rutabaga is called by many names — Swedish turnip, table turnip, mangel-wurzel, macomber or turnip-rooted cabbage, but they all refer to the same plant.

Rutabagas take longer to mature than turnips, but otherwise they grow the same way. The advantage of growing rutabagas is they don't get pithy if you leave them in the ground beyond their maturity date. They also have a longer storage life, their root flesh is firmer, and they contain more vitamin A than turnips.

Instead of sticking with the familiar turnip, give rutabagas a try.

American Purple Top — 90 days — Most common variety for home gardeners; firm flesh is light yellow surrounded by yellowish skin with purple shoulders; stores well for long periods of time.

Salsify — "Garden Oysters"

These unusual roots taste something like oysters, grow just like parsnips or carrots, and are members of the sunflower family. That may sound like an odd combination, I know, but it all adds up to one terrific vegetable!

Salsify takes its time to reach maturity — 120 to 150 days! Once you plant the seeds, tie a string around your finger so you don't forget they're out in your garden.

Even if you've never tried oysters, or if they are not your favorite food, try some salsify. The delicate flavor and crisp texture may surprise you.

The key to delicious salsify is to leave them in the ground until after a few frosts just as you would

parsnips. Better yet, wait until the ground thaws in the early spring to dig them up.

Mammoth Sandwich Island — 120 days — This is the standard seed type available in the United States; quality improves after a few frosts; roots are 8 to 9 inches long with creamy white flesh.

Parsnips — Worth Waiting For

This under-rated vegetable has been around since the times of the ancient Greeks and Romans, and it's been in America since the first colonists brought it over from Europe. It's hard for me to understand why more gardeners don't grow parsnips. They may tax your patience because they take so long to germinate, grow and reach maturity, but their flavor is well worth the wait.

My mother used to tell us that all you need for perfect soup is some water, a bay leaf and parsnips. But don't use these roots just for soups. They're good by themselves and in stews, too. I like them best dug up in the spring after a winter of in-ground storage, pan-fried in butter and served with fresh-caught trout.

Some gardeners say that if you can grow parsnips, carrots and beets, you can grow anything. But there's really no trick, other than planting them early in deep, well-worked soil, and leaving them in the ground until after a few frosts — or all winter long, for the best-tasting spring treat around!

Hollow Crown — 105 days — Fully developed roots are 12 inches long, tapered and relatively free of hairlike side roots.

All America — 120 days — Average length 12 inches; broad shoulders; white flesh with small core.

Harris Model — 120 days — Attractive roots, 10 to 12 inches long; smooth white flesh; very free of small branching roots.

Celeriac — Lazy Man's Celery

Are you looking for a way to get celery from the garden without worrying about blanching or stringiness? Interested in a new soup, stew and salad ingredient? How about a new vegetable dish? If you think it can't be done, consider growing celeriac.

The ball-shaped root tastes like celery and can be used the same ways in recipes. (Unless, of course, you plan to serve stuffed celery stalks at your next party!)

Growing celeriac is much easier than growing celery; as a root crop it needs very little attention as it grows. Just be sure to sow the seeds early, since it needs a long growing season (120 days) to reach maturity.

Because celeriac is relatively new in America, there aren't many varieties available.

Large Smooth Prague — 120 days — Common variety that grows a smooth, turnip-shaped root 4 to 5 inches in diameter; good winter keeper.

Alabaster, Apple, Snowball, and **Early Paris** are all similar varieties.

Seed Selection

When you open a seed catalog or make your first visit to the garden center each year, you may be boggled at the sight of all the different varieties for each root crop. As long as you get your seeds from a reputable seed company, you can choose according to your own soil condition and tastes.

For instance, if you have heavy clay soil, stick with short, stocky carrots rather than long, tapered varieties. If you have a very short or very long growing season, you can choose varieties that mature earlier or later than others. It's also a good idea to check with your local County Extension Agent or a gardening neighbor for advice as to seed varieties well adapted to your area.

Some seed companies indicate the traits of each variety right on the packet or in their catalogues. Keep this in mind if you're looking for good winter keepers, darker color, a short or long growing season, or ones that are especially good for freezing or canning. You'll develop preferences once you've tasted the results of each crop, but you're sure to have some success with any variety. So be adventurous and experiment a little.

GETTING STARTED

How Root Crops Grow

Root crops are cool season vegetables. Their tiny seeds germinate best in damp soil when the soil temperature is between 50° and 60°F. Early spring and fall are the best times to plant.

Germination is the sprouting action of seeds, and some root crops germinate more quickly than others. Radishes sprout in just two or three days; turnips and rutabagas, five to ten; the rest are slower, taking from seven days to twenty days to germinate. When they do, tiny seedlings push their way up through the shallow soil covering.

While the seedling develops into the greens above the ground, a large, edible taproot forms and grows downward. It's also the major storage organ of the plant, although it does form smaller branching side roots to help it gather food, oxygen and water. Some root crops have more of these hairlike roots than others, but you always scrub or wash them off before eating the vegetable.

As the root grows, it expands down, out and up, often showing its shoulders above ground. The sun discolors the exposed root, turning carrots green

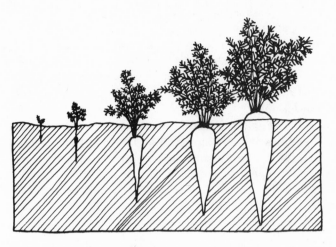

in soil temperatures between about 34° and 38°F. How's that for a gift from Mother Nature?

Planning on Paper

The gardening season catches some people by surprise every spring. I try to get ahead of the game by planning our garden on paper — a nice way to spend a snowy winter evening or two.

Your whole family can be involved in this part of gardening — it can be as important and as much fun as planning a family trip. Be realistic about how many beets, carrots or rutabagas your family will eat, and plan on planting only what you can use. If you're going to try a new vegetable, start off with only a few seeds until you see how you and your family like it. Remember, there's always next year.

As long as you're planning ahead, set up a planting and harvesting timetable so all your root crops won't be ready to eat at the same time. I plant fewer in the beginning of the summer than I do later on, because I just want that first crop to eat right away. My fall garden yields enough for us to freeze, can and store all winter.

And I know that the shorter the time span between harvesting, storage and eating, the tastier it will be. Therefore, I plan to store my root crops from my fall garden and use the summer ones for eating fresh.

When to Plant

Root crops are special to me because they mark the beginning and end of the gardening season. Treat yourself to some fresh air and fresh vegetables early by planting root crops early in the spring, as soon as the ground can be worked, and then plant again in midsummer for a fall garden that will extend your garden's production and give you lots of fresh produce for winter storage.

Depending on your appetite, you can plant once, twice or continuously for an all-season yield. I plant carrots three times during the season; beets, turnips and rutabagas twice; parsnips, celeriac and salsify just once, and radishes with just about everything every three weeks from April through September. The possibilities are endless, once you get going.

You really can't plant root crops too early or too late. In fact, gamble with them to get the longest possible harvest from your garden. The odds are in your favor, but even if you should lose some of that first or last planting, whatever crops do make it are a garden bonus.

and turnips purple. We try to avoid this with carrots by pulling them before they're big enough to show above ground. The green part gets hard and bitter in carrots, yet that colored top on turnips or rutabagas tastes fine, and we're glad to see it.

A cross-section of the roots shows that these plants are formed in three layers: a hard core, the edible fleshy part and the skin. The best-tasting roots have the least amount of that tough center, and quick, steady growth helps here.

All root crops need food, water and air. They also grow best if they meet no soil clumps or rocks to check their growth. Give them good growing conditions, and you'll enjoy straight, thick, good-tasting produce. Poor or improper soil preparation is usually to blame for crooked or forked roots. If you've ever bitten into a woody, fibrous carrot, you'll understand why I stress good growing conditions.

If root crops were to grow wild, some would have a two-year life cycle, forming the root in one season and producing a flowering seed stalk the next. In the garden we interrupt this natural process by harvesting the roots before they start the reproduction process. Once the roots send up the stem that bears flowers, they're beyond the eating stage.

These vegetables all vary in their growth rates, and so do the varieties of each one. Short, stocky carrots or beets mature fairly quickly while long, tapered vegetables take longer to fully develop. Since you can eat the roots as soon as they are finger or marble size, you have a lot of flexibility when it comes time to harvest — eat 'em early or leave 'em awhile — it's up to you.

Root crops could be called the "polar bears" of the garden, since both the seeds and the plants are well adapted to sudden drops in the mercury. Even severe frosts won't hurt them. In fact, parsnips and salsify need a few frosts to sweeten them. This is because the carbohydrates in the root change to sugars

Wide Rows — Less Work & More Food!

When you are drawing your garden plan, you can choose different ways to lay out the rows. I grow plenty of root crops with very little effort by planting the seeds in wide rows.

I adopted this method of denser planting after years of frustration at the wasted space between traditional single rows. I believe in using the soil for growing vegetables, not for walkways, and wide rows do this by creating more growing area with fewer paths. This method also cuts down on weed problems and lets you use a lot less mulch than is usually required.

Instead of planting my seeds in long, narrow rows, I broadcast them evenly over rows that are about fifteen inches wide — a rake's width. In the South they have been planting turnips in wide rows for years — I've seen blocks fifteen feet square sown solid with turnips in Georgia and Mississippi. Of course, this is an extremely wide row, mostly used for growing greens.

There are many advantages for growing root crops in wide rows:

You may get two to three times more produce per square foot than you can in single rows by having wider rows and fewer walkways.

Root crops planted in wide rows provide a continual harvest. By planting seeds closer together, some plants mature faster than others. Regularly pulling the largest vegetables leaves room for the others to grow.

Wide rows mean less weeding, since the greens grow thickly to shade the ground, creating a "living mulch" that smothers weeds before they can grow.

Soil stays cool and moist in wide rows, shaded by the living mulch. You never need to mulch within the rows.

Plants are protected from warm winds and hot sun, allowing cool weather crops to flourish even in the South.

Harvesting is easy, because you can reach many plants from one position. In a single row, you need to constantly bend and straighten as you move down the row.

Planting wide rows is child's play. You broadcast the seed over the seedbed without worrying too much about straight lines or spacing.

Multi-planting is easy in wide rows, whether you plant radishes with root crops or you make other combinations. As I said earlier, radishes make fine companions, and you only need to sprinkle some seeds sparsely after you broadcast the main crop.

Thinning is painless in wide rows, and even if you've planted more than you intended, I'll show you how to pull up those extras in no time with a garden rake.

The one consideration with wide rows is that all the plants are competing for soil nutrients and water. So, for the best results, it's important to make sure there's plenty to go around.

Single Rows

Fine root crops can be grown by planting them in single rows, too. But you'll need to have a larger garden or fewer plants because you'll need more rows and more walkways. You may want to try both single and wide-row methods with your root crops and compare the results as an experiment.

You can modify the single-row method by planting two rows side by side, creating double rows — or even three as triple rows. These make better use of garden space than single rows. If you do plant in multiple rows, leave four to five inches between them. This allows for easy cultivation.

SOIL PREPARATION

This part of gardening is the key to healthy root crops — you need to prepare a foundation for your plants just as you would for a house or a bridge. If your foundation is weak, your house falls down. Your plants can fail, too, but you won't have to worry if you get your soil into good shape before you plant. Here is the formula for success:

The Wonder of Organic Matter

Since we harvest root crops for what grows down, not up, they really need the best possible

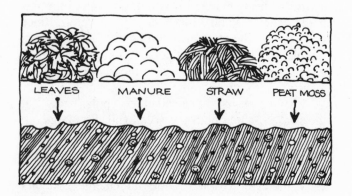

LEAVES   MANURE   STRAW   PEAT MOSS

growing quarters — the best is soil that is loose, rich and loamy.

The way to achieve this ideal soil condition is to work into the soil plenty of organic matter such as leaves, compost, grass clippings, garden residues or easy-to-grow cover crops — buckwheat, cowpeas or annual rye grass.

First . . .pH

You should check the pH of your garden soil at least every couple of years. The most accurate reading is taken in the fall. pH is the measure of soil acidity or alkalinity, with 7 indicating neutral on a scale from 1.0 to 14.0. Root crops and most vegetables prefer slightly acid soil, with a pH of 6.0 to 6.8.

Fertilizer

Root crops taste better if they grow at a steady pace, and they need certain nutrients for this smooth growth. These nutrients are available in commercial fertilizers, which you can broadcast over the planting area and mix into the top 2 or 3 inches of soil.

The best time to add fertilizer is on planting day. If you wait more than a few days between fertilizing and planting, some fertilizer is bound to leach away or lose its potency.

I apply fertilizer in this standard recommended amount: a 10 to 12 quart pail of a balanced fertilizer such as 5-10-10 for each 1,000 square feet, or 2 to 3 pounds for each 100 square feet. The numbers 5-10-10 or 10-10-10 refer to the percentages by weight of nitrogen (N), phosphorus (P) and potassium (K) in the bag of fertilizer, and they're always listed in the same order: N-P-K.

Of the three major plant nutrients, nitrogen aids in leaf and stem production, phosphorus promotes strong roots and potassium also helps in root development by conditioning the entire plant.

Seeds are sensitive, and they can get burned by any fertilizer that touches them. It's the nitrogen that burns them. By mixing the fertilizer thoroughly into the soil, you can prevent that kind of accident.

The easiest way to avoid fertilizing mistakes is to always mix it completely into the soil, and with root crops, to underfertilize rather than overdo it. Don't be tempted to add that extra handful of fertilizer. You may end up with no carrots at all — just lots of bushy tops!

However, you can aid root growth by adding a little extra phosphorus in the form of bone meal or

superphosphate (0-20-0). I sprinkle this directly onto the rows just before I plant the seeds, raking it into the top inch of soil, so it can be used by the young seedlings when they come up. There's no specific measure for this, but you can "guess-timate." A handful is about right for every four to six square feet.

Phosphorus won't burn the seeds, but the plants will only use as much as they need. So don't overdo it because excess will just go to waste.

You can also work a *light* coating of wood ashes into your soil before planting to ward off root maggots. Wood ashes can raise the soil pH because they are very alkaline, so don't overdo it. As with lime, the best time to add them is in the fall, but they may be added in the spring — they just won't have as much time to work. The right amount is 4 to 5 pounds per 100 square feet, mixed into the top 2 or 3 inches of soil.

PLANTING

Wide Row Planting

Once you've prepared the soil, follow these easy steps for wide row planting:

Mark the row by stretching a string close to the ground between two stakes spaced the length you want. You only need one string for a straight line — the width of your rake will determine the width of the row.

Hold one edge of an iron garden rake next to the string and drag the rake down the length of the row. This levels and smooths the seedbed while it marks off the area where you will broadcast the seeds. Garden rakes are usually 14 to 16 inches wide, and your wide row will be the same width as your rake.

Rake just the seedbed a few times to remove lumps and stones and get it really smooth before you plant. There is no need to rake your whole garden. And don't walk on the seed bed; you'll just pack it down again. A smooth, clod-free, loose seedbed is one of the most important elements for gardening success.

Add extra bonemeal or superphosphate now, raking it into the top inch of soil.

Sprinkle the seeds onto the planting area, trying to broadcast them thinly and evenly. Root crop seeds are small, and you'll have to find your own system to keep from sowing them too thickly. Beet seeds are larger than the others, and they're easier to control. But once you get the hang of it, the rest are no trouble, either. Since you'll be thinning the row when the seedlings first come up, don't worry if a few extra seeds slip out of your fingers as you go. In fact, more seeds will ensure not having any "skips" or bare spots within the row.

Lightly sprinkle radish seeds in with your main crop. When I say lightly, I mean only about 5 percent as much radish seed as the other vegetable.

Firm all the seeds into the soil with the back of a hoe. This anchors the seeds and gives them good contact with the soil, helping them germinate.

Cover the seeds with just a 1/4 to 1/2 inch of soil pulled from the side of the row with a rake, leveling the top of the seedbed as you go. The rule for all seeds is to cover them with fine, firm, moist soil to a depth 4 times their diameter. These small seeds don't need much soil over them. The only time you would cover them more would be in midsummer planting, when it's hot and dry. An extra 1/4 inch of soil would help.

Gently firm the soil again with the back of a hoe.

Single Row Planting

Stake out a single row just as you would a wide row, stretching a string along the ground between two stakes to mark off the length of the row.

Rake the seedbed smooth right over the string, then mark your planting line by drawing a furrow beside the string. Do this with the corner of a hoe, with the end of a rake handle or by laying the hoe or rake handle beside the string and pressing it lightly into the soil to make a shallow furrow.

Sprinkle the seeds thinly along the planting line, then sow radish seeds in the same line (again

about 5 percent). Firm the seeds into the soil, cover with 1/4 to 1/2 inch of soil, and firm again.

Whether you plant in wide rows, single rows or multiple rows, you should keep the soil around the seeds moist for the first week after you plant. Root crops won't germinate well in a dry seedbed. If the soil is dry, give the rows a light sprinkling of water right after planting. Because the soil is drier in the late summer, try this trick when planting for fall: wet the seeds for an hour or so before planting to give them a headstart on germination. Barely cover them with room temperature water on a saucer or plate, wait awhile, then plant. Once you've soaked the seeds you must plant them, since you've started the germination process. The wet seeds are a little harder to plant, but the results are worth it.

Keep an eye on the soil the first few days. If it rains, check it for a hard crusting when it dries. If the seedlings have to struggle through a crust, they'll suffer. Make it easy for them by carefully scratching the top 1/4 inch of soil in the row with an iron rake, a weeding tool or a piece of wire (a coat hanger works well).

Multi-Planting

I coined the phrase "multi-planting" after planting root crops with so many other vegetables to save space and take advantage of the benefits that occur. Besides radishes, you can plant all root crops with other vegetables with some terrific results. Beets and carrots do well together, carrots and lettuce are happy in the same row, and turnips can go in with spinach, chard or lettuce.

You can even grow three vegetables in one row — carrots, radishes and onions do fine in my garden.

Sowing Root Crop Seeds

The easiest way for me to sow root crop seeds is to sprinkle them from my hand, keeping it 2 to 3 feet above the row. This scatters the seeds more evenly than if your hand is down very close to the row. (If it's a very windy day, of course, move a little closer!)

Mix some fine soil or sand with the seeds to help even out the distribution.

You can also broadcast the seeds from a salt shaker if the holes are big enough, or right from the packet by tearing a tiny hole in one corner for the seeds to slip through. (Personally, I prefer to feel the seeds between my fingers as I plant.)

Every time you harvest one crop, you cultivate the row. The remaining roots benefit from the additional room you leave. Talk about growing a gourmet salad in one garden spot!

When you decide to combine your plants, choose partners that won't smother each other. For instance, the fast-growing, cool season crops such as lettuce and spinach will be ready to harvest before the slower growing root crops need the same sun and space. You should harvest or pull the first crop completely to guarantee the success of the second.

Multi-planting works especially well in wide rows. Just plant less of each crop than you normally would, and enjoy a much greater variety of vegetables in the same space you now have.

GROWING

Root Crop Care — Lazy Man's Delight

I call myself a lazy gardener because I like to find ways to save time and energy in the garden. This doesn't mean I don't love gardening; it just gives me more time for other things.

Root crops fit right in with my streamlining ideas by letting me take care of two or three jobs with one action. When you thin root crops, you cultivate the row at the same time by loosening the soil near the remaining plants. When you harvest, you are automatically thinning and cultivating. Just to keep each task clearly in your mind, I'll describe them separately. You'll see how these jobs overlap in your own garden.

The First Thinning

Thinning is a must with root crops. Starting when the seedlings are approximately a 1/4 to 1/2 inch tall, you can thin by hand or use my simple but effective iron rake method. Either way, you have to thin if you want roots that are big enough to eat. Crowded conditions cause them to become stunted or twisted around each other, and that's not good.

Thinning with a rake is a snap. Just pull an iron garden rake once across the row with its teeth going into the soil about a 1/4 inch. The teeth are spaced at intervals to catch just enough seedlings, pulling them from the row. Don't look down as you're doing this — it's a horrible sight. You may think you've destroyed the whole row of plants, but don't fret. The remaining ones will perk up in a day or so. You can thin a single row this way, too.

Raking also cultivates the soil, stirring up and killing "weedlings." Most young weeds have only had time to develop shallow roots with no deep taproot, so this initial thinning will pull them before they come up, exposing their roots and killing them. Some of the worst garden weeds have very strong taproots (pigweed, lambs quarters and many others), and the idea is to catch these weeds before they put down deep roots.

By thinning with a rake, you also break any crust on the surface, aerating the soil at the same time.

You can thin by hand if my technique seems a little too drastic. Simply pull up enough plants, so the remaining ones will stand 1 to 2 inches apart. You may not trust my method at first, but try it on at least part of a row. With the rake you can thin (and weed) all your root crops in just a minute or two, but thinning by hand seems to take me forever.

The best time to thin is a few hours after a rain or a thorough watering when the soil is damp but the plants have dried off completely. (You should never weed, thin or harvest around wet plants, because you can spread disease from your hands and clothing without knowing it.) Damp soil permits seedlings to be pulled without disturbing the roots of the remaining plants, and any weeds that start to germinate after a rain will be uprooted, too. If it's very dry on the day you decide to thin, water the surface of the soil, so you don't pull up more seedlings than you intend.

As I mentioned at the beginning, beet seeds will produce clusters of seedlings. The simplest way to thin these is with an iron rake. The rake teeth will uproot just the right amount of seedlings. If you thin by hand, don't try to remove any of the seedlings from within a single cluster. It's too easy to disturb the remaining ones. Instead, pull up whole clusters, leaving 2 to 3 inches between them. I sow the seeds a little thicker than is usually recommended on seed packages, since I use the later thinnings for beet greens and I love all the marble-sized beets this produces.

Thinning always seems more traumatic for the gardener than it is for the plants. People don't like to pull up those helpless seedlings that have just barely made it through the soil surface. Think of it as helping your whole crop, giving you more food to eat, and it will soon be a natural part of your garden routine!

Once your plants are up, you should stir up the soil within the rows every 4 or 5 days until the seedlings are well established. I've invented a tool for this called an In-Row Weeder that really does the trick. It has long, flexible tines that can be dragged right over the tops of young plants without harming them, scratching just the top 1/4 to 1/2 inch of soil, eliminating those weeds you can't even see!

I also save a lot of bending over by using a special tool called a Nar-Row Hoe for weeding. It has a strong, narrow blade with a curved goose neck that lets you pull weeds from even tight spots in the row without damaging the stems or roots of vegetables.

Once the plants get too tall to use a weeding tool, buckle down and hand pull every weed as soon as you see it. But by planting in wide rows, you'll have very little hand weeding to do. Keep in mind, though, that any weed that grows in your garden is a robber, stealing sun, water and food from your crops, and in the end, stealing food from you.

To keep down weeds between the rows, stir the soil surface there, too. Or, you can put a 2- to 3-inch layer of mulch (leaves, straw, lawn clippings or even newspapers) between the rows to do the work for you. Mulch has the added advantage of keeping the soil moist and at an even temperature. Your root crops will really appreciate this.

Naturally, the more weed prevention you can accomplish early, the easier it will be later on. But you're bound to get some weeds, so go out to your garden daily and keep 'em pulled!

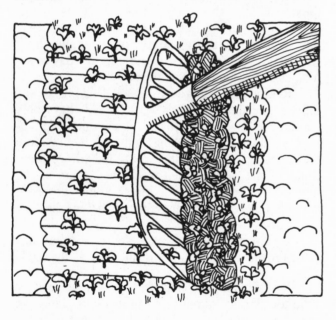

Weeding

Most root crops grow very slowly the first few weeks, and they cannot compete with weeds. But I have time-saving ways to stay ahead in the weeding game.

Try this trick in the early spring before you even plant a seed: Wait a week or so between the initial soil preparation and planting day. During this time, go out several times and till or stir the soil. This exposes and kills the first batches of tiny "weedlings" lurking near the surface that may try to overrun your young seedlings.

The First Harvest — The Second Thinning

This takes place when you harvest the radishes planted as companions. In heavy soil, leave white icicle radishes until they are quite large, then pull them to create that beneficial void in the soil. The beets, carrots, parsnips or turnips left in the row will push the soil around them into the gaps as they grow.

The third time you go out to thin, you'll be harvesting again, but more about that later. See how you kill a few birds with one stone, as each chore combines with the others?

Watering

Root crops need the same amount of water as most garden vegetables, about 1 inch per week. If you can supply this water evenly, with no long dry spells to inhibit the growth of the roots and greens, you'll encourage a healthy crop.

I know I told you to lightly sprinkle the seedbed when the seeds have first been planted, and that's bending the rules of watering a bit. Once the seedlings are up, return to these good watering habits:

Water when your garden needs it, not only by a calendar schedule. Don't be tempted to water your plants if the greens are drooping occasionally in the late afternoon sun — this is normal. But, if they look wilted before eleven o'clock in the morning, they need water.

Another mistake gardeners often make is to give their gardens many light waterings instead of a few thorough soakings. Once your seeds are sprouted, soak the soil when it needs it to a depth of 4 to 6 inches. By watering deeply you encourage the taproot to grow down seeking the moisture. Shallow waterings promote shallow root growth, which is exactly what you don't want, especially if you live in a drought-prone area.

How much does it take to water your garden to a depth of 4 to 6 inches? Well, if you're using a sprinkler, just put a pan in the area you're watering and when the water is an inch deep in the pan, the nearby soil will be sufficiently soaked — about 6 inches down. Dig down and check — it works!

Easy Raised Beds

Raised beds are nothing more than mounded-up garden soil that enhances vegetable growth. They're simple to make, even in the smallest garden, and they're helpful to all plants — especially the root crops.

Raised beds work because they make an ideal growing environment. Here's how:

The loose soil on raised beds has room on the sides to give with little or no resistance as the roots grow, even in hard-packed, wet soil. Roots develop easily, which makes them better-tasting, well-formed and healthy.

You can plant much earlier in the spring on raised beds since the soil warms up and dries out in the bed before it does in the rest of the garden. If you make some raised beds in the fall, you can plant on them very early the next spring. This way, you may be harvesting baby beets and carrots almost before your neighbors have planted a single seed.

If your garden stays waterlogged for a long time after each rain, raised beds solve that problem. On level beds, standing water cuts off the oxygen supply to the roots, and the weight of the water packs the soil so tightly it stifles root growth. On raised beds, water runs off and into the walkways in between. The soil in the bed dries out quicker, and the water seeps gradually back into the soil from the sides.

The added height makes the soil deep and loose, so you can grow longer carrots and parsnips than is possible on a level bed. In making raised beds, you place some of the valuable topsoil from the walkways onto them. This increases the total amount of topsoil on the seedbed.

Wide-row growing makes sense on raised beds to make the most efficient use of all of that growing space. If you're going to do the work making them, you might as well make it worthwhile by getting as much food from them as you can.

Raised beds are convenient and attractive. Your crops are five to ten inches closer to your hands, saving you some bending and kneeling. It's easier to keep children and pets from walking on the garden soil and packing it down or stepping on plants, since they can easily tell the walkways from the seedbeds.

Last, but not least, raised beds give your whole garden a neat, well-tended look that is very pleasing to the eye.

When I say raised beds are as easy as one-two-three, I mean it! Once you have the soil well-tilled or spaded to a depth of 6 to 8 inches, you can probably make a raised bed in less time than it takes to read this page. Here's how:

1. Determine the width and length of the bed and the walkways using stakes for guidelines. The dimensions will depend on whether you plant in wide rows or narrow.

2. Use a hoe to pull the loosely tilled soil from the walkways up onto the bed until its is 4 to 8 inches higher than the walkway.

3. Rake the top of the bed smooth, leveling the surface as you go. You're all set to plant.

You fertilize, plant, thin and harvest the same on raised beds as on level ground. You can add fer-

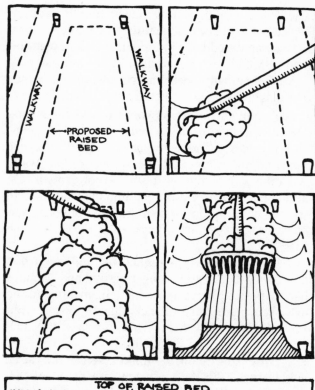

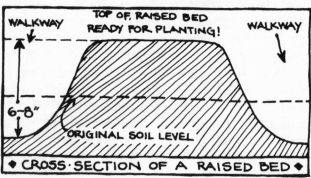

WALKWAY TOP OF RAISED BED READY FOR PLANTING! WALKWAY

6–8" ORIGINAL SOIL LEVEL

◆ CROSS·SECTION OF A RAISED BED ◆

tilizer to the whole plot before you make the beds, since the fertilized soil will end up on the beds anyway. You can also mulch between the beds to prevent weeds and keep the soil moist.

There's no need to brace the sides of beds 4 to 8 inches high unless you have the materials handy. For taller beds, railroad ties or planks give a neater appearance.

When I first experimented with raised beds, I was amazed. At test gardens in Georgia, I saw dramatic results. During a rainy spell there was an inch or two of standing water down in the furrows between some of the raised beds for days at a time. Yet, the carrots, beets and other crops growing on top of the beds were healthy and lush.

Raised beds work in every kind of soil, in just about any part of the country and with all of your garden vegetables. The only place I wouldn't recommend them is in very dry areas because they do dry out faster than normal beds.

You don't have to turn your whole garden into raised beds, but try growing a few root crops on some this year and you'll be convinced — raised beds make sense!

In the Trenches

If you want to grow terrific root crops in hard clay and packed soil, and you can get your hands on a lot of organic matter (leaves, grass clippings), give trenching a try. It's another way to create an ideal growing environment for those roots.

You dig an 8-inch trench, fill it with 5 or 6 inches of moist organic matter or compost, pull 2 or 3 inches of soil over the organic matter to fill the trench back to ground level, and plant your seeds in that.

The organic matter will decompose all summer, staying soft and moist. Your root crops will grow down into that loose, humus-rich material. You can grow tremendous, prize-winning roots this way, but remember the best-tasting ones are smaller, so pull them up before they get huge. Just for fun, leave one or two to mature past the eating stage, and get a snapshot for the family album. Your friends will never believe you grew them.

If the organic matter you use in the bottom of the furrow is mostly compost or well-rotted manure, there is no need to add fertilizer. If you're using old, chopped hay or leaves, sprinkle a small handful of 5-10-10 or 10-10-10 on every 2 to 3 feet of trenched organic matter to make up for the loss of nutrients that are used to break down those materials. Cover the fertilized organic matter with at least 2 inches of soil.

Trench composting works especially well in heavy, clay soil. It is also a wonderful way to spot improve your soil. If you rotate your root crops each year after a few years your whole garden will have benefited.

The main trick with trench composting is to moisten the organic matter you put in the trench, if it's dry. Plant the seeds just as you would on a regular seedbed. After that, it's practically just a matter of watching them grow.

PROBLEMS

Pests — Rodents and Other Root Crop Lovers

Mice, rabbits and other small animals like nothing better than fresh carrots or beets — both tops and bottoms — for a midnight snack. You can protect your entire garden with a fence, but just keeping the whole area around the garden mowed and weed-free also helps. If you use mulch anywhere in your garden, try to have it free of weed seeds, or you may be attracting seed-loving rodents to the garden without knowing it. Of course, nothing works better than a darned good cat, but good mousers are few and far between these days.

Diseases and Insects

Fortunately, root crops aren't bothered too much by insects or diseases, and the few that may strike can be prevented with a few good-gardening habits.

Rotate your root crops as well as all other vegetables in your garden from season to season and in your early and late plantings. This discourages insects and disease.

Make a daily visit to your garden, and pick off any harmful insects you see. Pull up and destroy any unhealthy or diseased plants. Or tear off the leaf or two that are infested and burn them. The rest of the plant may be fine.

Keep your soil healthy and productive by working in plenty of organic matter. Healthy soil means healthy and disease-resistant plants.

As soon as a crop is harvested, either till all the residues back into the soil or carry them off to the compost heap. By doing this, you don't furnish insects with a place to reproduce and live over the winter.

If, despite all your efforts, you do run into a problem with your root crops (root maggots, leaf miners, carrot rust flies or diseased roots) get help from your local Cooperative Extension Service Agent. Knowing the area, he or she will be able to diagnose the situation and give you specific advice about treatment.

Your soil test alone may indicate a nutrient deficiency that might cause disease, and the Extension Service can be helpful in this case, too. For instance, sometimes a lack of boron in the soil will cause a problem known as internal black spot in beets. Your Extension Agent can give you the right prescription for adding boron to the soil (in the form of Borax — a household product) to combat this.

If you're really plagued by root maggots, you might have to treat the soil with diazinon before planting. Follow the directions on the package carefully for the right amount to apply. A light application of wood ashes when worked into the soil will help deter maggots, wire worms and cutworms.

All in all, you shouldn't have much trouble keeping your root crops trouble-free, if you practice the basic steps I have outlined.

Harvesting

There are just a few pointers to keep in mind for the most bountiful and delicious harvest:

Start harvesting beets and turnips for their greens, and baby carrots the size of your little finger. This will give you a good start on a long harvesting period; the roots left in the row will have more room to grow; and you won't be faced with an entire row of vegetables ready to be pulled on the same day. Besides, the smaller the root, the better it tastes!

For a few extra meals of beet or turnip greens, just go out and snip off the leaves you want. As long as you leave some greens on the plant, it will continue to grow more — and a nice big root, too.

Pull the largest roots every time you harvest.

People are tempted to leave the biggest ones, so they'll grow even bigger. Don't do it! By always pulling the largest roots, you're sure to have them before they are so big they're all woody and bitter. Again, this encourages the remaining plants to fill in and grow bigger, giving you what seems like an inexhaustible supply of medium-sized, savory roots, and what more could a gardener ask?

Once some root crops get bigger, you may have to wiggle them back and forth (or use a trowel, pitchfork, or spade) to get them out. If a top breaks off in your hand, don't give up. Dig down into the soil and pull that root!

Harvest whenever you need fresh roots, picking just enough. You should be able to enjoy all your spring-planted root crops in this fresh, garden-to-table fashion.

Where's The Biggest Carrot?

If you want to find the biggest carrot in the row just by looking at the greens, remember this: the bigger the root, the darker the greens and the thicker the stem. With beets, radishes or turnips, the thickest stems of the greens will point the way to the biggest roots.

Ready, Set . . . Storage!

Here's how to have the produce from your fall garden last long and well in storage:

Have your fall garden of root crops mature as late as possible — by planting as late as possible. Cold weather sweetens the roots and you'll be putting the freshest produce into a cool root cellar, carport or back porch. Leave your last planting in the ground until the roots are fully mature; they'll store better, protected by a thicker skin.

Whether you are going to eat most of your vegetables fresh, or you intend to freeze, can and store them, a good rule of thumb is to harvest as close to the time you're going to eat them as possible. This gives you the best flavor and nutrition.

For a longer storage life, dig up the roots from your fall garden after 2 or 3 days of dry weather. Your root crops will be dry, and by leaving them out for a few hours in the sun right after you pull them, you'll kill the root hairs, making the plant dormant, and the soil on the roots will dry and fall off easily.

Never wash roots before you store them. Just "top" them right out in the garden. Leave about an inch of stem for beets, so they don't "bleed" in cooking. For other root crops, cut the tops close. Wash the roots when you're going to use them, not before.

Be careful not to bruise roots you want to store. Bruises are avenues of rotting that can spread to the other vegetables. (Yes, one bad apple can spoil a whole bunch!) If you should bruise any, eat them up. Also, don't ever clip off the bottom end of the root before you put it in storage; this, too, can open the plant to rot.

Winter Gardening

Whether your winter months are frozen and snow-bound like mine, or just cold and wet like those further south, you can store some of your root crops right out in the garden. Your winter garden can yield fresh vegetables all winter long and into the spring. If your soil freezes hard, you need to insulate the ground around your roots, so they don't freeze. Put a heavy layer of mulch (10 to 12 inches) over the rows. It's important to have this mulch extend out 18 inches on both sides of the rows. This will keep the soil all around the roots at an even 35° to 40°F — the ideal storage temperature. After this is done, you can go out anytime, move the mulch aside, and dig up some fresh roots. I've even dug carrots, beets and parsnips out from under 2 feet of snow!

Vegetables stored in the ground don't have good keeping power once you dig them, so be sure to eat them in a day or two.

Now, if you live in an area with mild winters or if you have no cool place available for winter keeping, you can really use in-ground storage. My Southern friends leave all their turnips, beets, carrots and radishes in the garden until they're ready to use them, letting nature be their root cellar. But, even in a warm climate, an 8 to 12-inch layer of mulch is needed to maintain an even soil temperature.

As I mentioned earlier, parsnips and salsify require a few frosts to sweeten their taste. I usually leave them out in the garden until the spring thaw, always digging them up before they start to put on new top growth. Those spring vegetables taste unbelievably sweet, perhaps because I'm harvesting them when I'm just planting everything else.

Storage — Plain and Fancy

You don't need an elaborate root cellar to store vegetables, even for months at a time. You can easily extend the fresh life of root crops using whatever storage space you now have. The length of storage time may vary according to your storage method, but with any of the methods I'm going to describe, you can be sure of at least a few extra months of fresh vegetables.

Root crops need just three things to stay crisp and fresh: cool, moist and dark surroundings. The ideal place would be about 34°F with high humidity. Usually we can only approximate these conditions. But whether you have a root cellar or just a spot under the back porch for storage, the most important element for long vegetable life is an *even*, cold temperature. Variations up or down even 5 degrees can cause new growth to sprout (which you don't want) or rotting. Here, insulaton is the key. There are many ways to give your roots the insulated low temperature they need.

If you have the space and the time to build one, a root cellar is wonderful. All you need is an unheated basement, and you can build a complete root cellar by partitioning one corner, installing some insulation and a good, sound door. You're actually making a refrigeration unit.

If your cellar is cool, but not insulated, a large sturdy cardboard or wooden box will do fine with 2 or 3 inches of some insulating material (obviously, not fiberglass or asbestos!) on the bottom and sides. I prefer freshly-cut sawdust, but moist peat moss and sand are okay, too. Place a layer of carrots on top of this leaving 2 or 3 inches near the sides. Cover the carrots lightly with sawdust — a quarter inch is fine. Alternate layers of carrots with sawdust, filling in all around the outsides with sawdust as well. Add a final 2 or 3 inches of sawdust on top, and store this "root box" in a cool basement area. In older homes, the cellar steps leading outside make handy storage areas.

Here are some other storage methods that work in a cool cellar: put the roots in a plastic trash bag, punch a few small holes in it, tie up the top and store the bag. Or, put your roots into a trash barrel with a plastic liner, put the lid on, and store the whole thing.

If you have no cellar, you can still use the insulated box method. But, you'll need a great, big box (supermarkets usually have some from deliveries of paper towels and napkins) lined bottom, sides and top with 4 to 5 inches of peat moss or sawdust. Store this in a cold place — your garage, carport, back porch or an unheated spare room. Whenever you need some vegetables, just take them out and repack the sawdust around the rest.

Roots can touch each other in storage, just don't pack them in tightly, like canned sardines. Some moist air must be able to circulate.

When you visit your storage area to get vegetables you want, check for any roots that may not be keeping well. Don't worry if a few are starting to deteriorate — some individual vegetables just don't keep as well as others. The rest will be alright.

If your vegetables freeze in storage, don't panic. You can still use them. But once they've thawed they won't keep for more than a day or so.

Your storage method can be as simple or complex as you like, but do be realistic about what your family will eat between gardening seasons. Just as in garden planning, a small, well-stocked area is better than a huge one in which food is wasted.

Of course, if you really want to keep it simple, your refrigerator crisper drawer will keep roots fresh for awhile, but you can only store a limited amount this way.

Horseradish — Some Like It Hot!

To some, horseradish is just too hot to handle. Not to us! Because we really like it, we don't mind that our four-year-old horseradish bed now occupies quite a large garden spot. You see, horseradish is a perennial root crop, planted from tuberous roots rather than seeds. Once you plant a few cuttings, they take hold quickly, spreading and multiplying year after year.

Since the plants reproduce so abundantly, plant only three to six roots at first. This should be enough for a household of four horseradish lovers. Also, be sure to plant them in an area that's away from the rest of your garden, so you don't have a horseradish takeover.

If you want to plant horseradish, get some root cuttings at a garden center, through the mail from a seed company or from a neighbor, who already has some growing. These straight, thin roots are really just the cuttings from a larger root than has been harvested to eat. If you buy them, they will be cut at a slant on one end, and that end should be planted downward. If a neighbor or friend gives you some, have him slant the end that was not attached to the stem, so you won't plant the root upside-down.

Horseradish should be planted in the early spring, at the same time you plant your first cool season crops. Prepare the soil just as you do for your other vegetables, tilling or spading the area to a depth of 6 to 8 inches.

Dig a hole or furrow about 4 to 6 inches deep, and put a handful of 10-10-10 or 5-10-10 fertilizer at the bottom. Cover this with another two inches of soil.

Lay the roots, slanted end pointed down, in the soil at a 45° angle rather than straight up and down. This way, the new roots that form along the entire length of each cutting can grow straight down themselves without becoming tangled up in one another. The top of the cutting should be about 2 inches below the soil surface.

Cover the top of the root with 2 inches of soil, and it should soon be growing like crazy. Keep the seedbed free of weeds, cultivating the soil regularly.

If you are starting a new bed wait until the next spring to harvest your first horseradish. Even with my established bed, I only harvest in the spring. That's when it's hottest. You can dig up some roots in the fall, and store them just as you would carrots or beets, or you can store it right out in the garden (year-round if you like), digging up a root anytime you're in the mood for fresh horseradish.

Hot Horseradish

1   cup horseradish roots
1/2 cup white vinegar
1/2 tsp salt

Wash and scrub roots well with a vegetable brush. Trim off the rough and dark spots, and with a vegetable peeler peel down to the white, meaty center.

Put horseradish, vinegar and salt in a blender or food processor and mince finely. If you are using a food chopper, grind the horseradish with the fine blade, and then add the vinegar and salt.

Pack in half-pint sterilized jars. Cover and seal tightly. It will keep indefinitely in the refrigerator.

Although you can get it fresh from the garden anytime of year, it's nice to have a good supply of the best quality from the hotter spring harvest, so we sometimes freeze spring horseradish — either in large pieces or packages of grated horseradish.

Garden to Kitchen

FREEZING

Beets

Baby beets freeze best. Remove tops, wash and cook until the skins slip off easily. Peel and cool quickly in cold water. Leave whole, quarter, slice or dice. Package in plastic freezer bags or boxes. Seal, label and freeze.

Carrots

Young, tender carrots are best. Scrub carrots and rinse them. Dice or slice lengthwise or crosswise. Baby carrots may be frozen whole. Scald cut carrots 3 minutes; whole carrots, 5. Cool quickly in cold water, drain and package. Seal, label and freeze.

Parsnips, Salsify, Celeriac

Cut off tops, wash thoroughly and peel. Drop into water that has lemon juice or vinegar in it (3 Tb per quart of water) to prevent darkening while preparing remaining vegetables. If the parsnips or salsify have woody cores, slice lengthwise and remove them. Scald in water containing juice of half a lemon for 5 minutes. Cool quickly in cold water, drain and pack. Seal, label and freeze.

Turnip, Rutabaga

Select young, firm vegetables. Remove tops, wash, peel, slice or dice. Scald 3 minutes. Cool quickly in cold water, drain and pack. Seal, label and freeze.

Sometimes I'll prepare twice the amount of rutabaga or turnip I'm going to serve and freeze half. It's good to have on hand to include in soups and stews, and with larger rutabaga, it eliminates waste.

CANNING

Carrots and beets are the only root crops that can be canned successfully. The others keep easily and well in a root cellar or frozen, so there's no problem. Carrots and beets, because of their low acid content, must be canned in a pressure canner and should be boiled for 15 minutes before serving.

For complete instructions and precautions for pressure canning, please carefully read and follow the instruction booklets that accompany your canner and jars. The United States Department of Agriculture offers additional, up-to-date information on canning, and the Ball *Blue Book* is regarded by many as the "canning bible."

Carrots

Hot pack. Scrub carrots and rinse. Slice, dice or leave whole. Boil in water for 3 minutes. Pack immediately in hot, clean jars, leaving 1-inch headspace. Salt, 1/2 tsp per pint, may be added. Cover with boiling water, retaining headspace. Remove air bubbles. Adjust lids and process: pints — 25 minutes; quarts — 30 minutes at 10 lbs pressure.

Raw pack. Scrub carrots and rinse. Slice, dice or leave whole. Pack firmly in hot jars, leaving 1-inch headspace. Salt, 1/2 tsp per pint, may be added. Cover with boiling water, retaining headspace. Remove air bubbles. Adjust lids and process: pints — 25 minutes; quarts — 30 minutes at 10 lbs pressure.

Beets

Wash beets well. Leave 2 inches of stem and entire root. Boil until skins slip off easily. Remove skins, trim roots. Leave whole, slice or dice. Pack into hot jars, leaving 1-inch headspace. Salt, 1/2 tsp per pint, may be added. Cover with boiling water, retaining headspace. Remove air bubbles. Adjust lids. Process: pints — 30 minutes; quarts 35 minutes at 10 lbs pressure.

Some people like to can them in vinegar (3 cups of vinegar to each cup of water), but I like to can them plain. Then when I serve them, Dick can add the amount of vinegar he likes, and I can eat mine just with salt, pepper and butter.

FAVORITE RECIPES

Cooked Carrot Accompaniments

Butter	Peas	Brown Sugar
Mint	Nutmeg	Cream sauce
Chervil	Stock	Cauliflower
Dill	Honey	Orange juice
Chives	Marmalade	Pearl onions
Ginger	Maple Syrup	Brussels sprouts

Freshly dug carrots take about half as long to cook as stored ones. Depending on their size and freshness, carrots take from 5 to 20 minutes to become fork tender.

To cook homegrown carrots, just wash them well and give them a good scrub with a vegetable brush. Especially if they're young, they don't have to be peeled. They may be left whole with just the ends trimmed or sliced into lengthwise strips, cubes or circles.

These carrot accompaniments are good individually and some are good in combination. It's fun to experiment to find the amounts and combinations that you like best.

Copper Penny Carrots

These are dangerous because they're so good. You may eat them all yourself at just one sitting.

2	lbs carrots
1	small green pepper, chopped
1	medium onion, chopped
1	can tomato soup
1/2	cup salad oil
1	cup sugar or honey
3/4	cup vinegar
1	tsp mustard
1	tsp Worcestershire sauce
1	tsp salt
	pepper to taste

Boil sliced carrots in salted water until fork tender. Cool. Place carrots, onions and green pepper in dish. Make marinade of remaining ingredients, making sure they are well blended. Pour mixture over vegetables and refrigerate. Serve cold. They can keep for weeks refrigerated, but at our house they don't get the chance.

Orange-Glazed Carrots

3	cups sliced, cooked carrots
2	Tb sugar
2	tsp cornstarch
1/2	tsp salt
1/2	tsp ground ginger
1/2	cup orange juice
1/4	cup margarine or butter

Combine sugar, cornstarch, salt and ginger in a saucepan. Add orange juice; cook over low heat, stirring constantly, until mixture thickens and bubbles. Boil gently for 1 minute. Stir in margarine or butter. Pour this mixture over hot, drained carrots. Mix lightly to cover with sauce. Serves 6. Excellent with duck.

Carrot Cake

A great dessert to make ahead for company because it can be frozen a week or two in advance and frosted once it's thawed.

       3   cups grated carrots
       2   cups flour
       2   cups sugar
       4   eggs
   1 1/2   cups vegetable oil
       8   ounces cream cheese, softened
       2   tsp baking soda
       1   tsp salt
     1/2   tsp nutmeg (optional)
       1   tsp vanilla
     1/2   tsp ground cloves (optional)
       1   cup chopped nuts
       1   cup raisins (optional)

Cream the sugar and cream cheese together. Add the eggs, oil, carrots and flour in that order. Then add remaining ingredients and mix well. Pour into greased, floured 9 x 13″ pan. Or for two thinner cakes use 8 x 12″ foil pans. Bake in preheated 350° oven for 55 minutes. Cool and frost with

Cream Cheese Icing

     1/4   cup butter
       8   ounces cream cheese
       1   lb confectioner's sugar
       2   Tb milk
       1   tsp vanilla

Cream butter and cream cheese together. Add sugar, milk and vanilla. Beat until smooth and spread on cool cake. Garnish top with carrot curls or grated carrot.

Carrot Casserole

       3   cups finely shredded, fresh carrots
     1/3   cup finely diced celery
       1   tsp finely chopped onion
     1/2   cup fine bread crumbs
       1   cup shredded cheese
   1 1/2   cup white sauce (recipe below)
     1/2   tsp salt
     1/8   tsp pepper (black)
       3   eggs, separated

Cook shredded carrots until tender. Combine all ingredients including white sauce, except eggs. Beat egg yolks, add to mixture and mix well. Beat egg whites until they stand in soft, stiff peaks and fold into mixture. Pour into a well-greased baking dish.

Bake 45 minutes. Serves 4 to 6. I like to serve buttered peas and tiny onions with this main dish.

Medium White Sauce

Melt 3 Tb margarine in saucepan. Blend in 3 Tb of flour, gradually stir in 1 1/2 cups of milk. Cook until fairly thick, stirring constantly.

Carrot Pickles

       4   cups sliced, uncooked carrots
       2   medium onions, sliced
     3/4   cup sugar
     3/4   tsp salt
     1/2   tsp cinnamon
     1/4   tsp cloves
     1/4   tsp celery seed
       1   Tb salad oil
       2   cups vinegar

Cook carrots and onion slices in 1 cup of water over low heat for 10 minutes. Drain, and add all remaining ingredients. Simmer gently for 15 minutes. Ladle into 4 sterilized pint jars and seal securely.

Beet and Onion Salad

       5   cooked, peeled medium beets
       1   red onion
     1/2   cup vinaigrette dressing
            lettuce leaves

Slice beets. Peel and thinly slice onion. Mix with vinaigrette and chill. Drain and serve on lettuce leaves. Serves 4.

Boiled Beets

Cut tops off but leave at least 1 inch of stem. Wash beets well, but do not peel before cooking. Put in pot with boiling water and depending on size, cook for 1/2 to 2 hours.

To save energy and substantially reduce cooking time, you may cook fresh beets in a pressure cooker. It only takes about 12 minutes for small beets and 18 minutes for larger ones.

When the beets are cooked, the skins slip off easily. Rinse each beet briefly under cold water before trying to peel it, so you don't burn your fingers.

Fresh beets are delicious plain with butter. A tasty addition is 3 Tb brown sugar and 2 tsp of orange rind. 1 lb beets serves 4.

Beet Greens

1   lb young beet greens
2   Tb butter
   lemon juice
   pepper and salt

Wash beet greens in several baths of cool water to make sure all grit or sand is gone.

Put greens in large, covered pot over medium heat. The moisture on the leaves is usually sufficient to steam them. Cook until they are just wilted. If there are small beets attached, add more water and cook until they are just tender. Serve with butter, lemon juice, salt and pepper. Serves 4.

Garnishes: cold with vinaigrette dressing; crumbled bacon; 1/2 cup sour cream, 1 Tb horseradish.

Pickled Beets

1   lb young, small, cooked, peeled beets
2   cups sugar
2   cups water
2   cups cider vinegar
1   tsp cloves
1   tsp whole allspice
1/2 lemon, thinly sliced
1/2 orange, thinly sliced
1   Tb cinnamon sticks

Pack cooked, peeled beets in hot, sterilized jars. Combine remaining ingredients in saucepan and bring to boil. Simmer for 15 minutes. Remove cinnamon. Pour over beets leaving 1/4-inch headspace. Adjust lids. Process in boiling water bath canner 30 minutes.

Red Flannel Hash

My grandmother used to make this old Vermont favorite. Although the origin in unknown, red flannel hash is thought to have been created by Ethan Allen or one of his Green Mountain Boys.

3   medium beets, cooked
1   large potato, cooked
1   lb ground chuck or ground leftover roast beef
    (leftover is better)
    salt
    pepper
1/4 lb butter
1   medium onion, chopped
1   Tb cream

Chop beets, potato and onion and combine with meat. Melt half the butter in skillet. Add meat and vegetable mixture and cook over low heat for 10 minutes. Do not stir if you want a bottom crust to form. Top with cream and dot with remaining butter. Place under pre-heated broiler for 5 minutes or until it has a rich, brown crust. May be topped with poached eggs. Serves 4.

Harvard Beets

1   Tb cornstarch
1/2 tsp salt
1/2 cup sugar
1/4 cup cider vinegar
1/4 cup reserved cooking liquid
2   whole cloves
2   Tb butter
3   cups cooked whole, diced or sliced beets.

Combine cornstarch, salt and sugar in saucepan. Add vinegar and cooking liquid. Cook over medium heat stirring constantly until the sauce is clear, smooth and beginning to thicken. Add cooked beets and butter and serve hot. Serves 4 to 6.

Variations: substitute orange juice for vinegar; substitute 3 Tb honey for sugar; add 1 tsp ground ginger.

Best-Ever Beets

3 cups cooked, sliced beets
1/2 cup sour cream
1 Tb grated horseradish
1 Tb chopped chives
1 tsp grated onion

Heat ingredients in double boiler. Serves 4.

Borscht
(Peasant Beet Soup)

1 bay leaf
1 garlic clove
1 lb lean beef, cubed
   soup bone (optional)
1 1/2 quarts water
1 tsp salt
3 sprigs parsley
1 medium onion or 2 leeks
2 coarsely chopped carrots
2 cups coarsely chopped beets
2 cups coarsely chopped potatoes
1/2 red cabbage, shredded
2 Tb tomato puree
   freshly ground black pepper
2 tsp lemon juice

Boil meat and soup bone in salted water with bay leaf, garlic, parsley, carrots and onion for 1 hour.

In a covered pot simmer beets, potatoes and cabbage for 20 minutes. Add contents of other pot and remaining ingredients and simmer for an additional hour.

The soup may or may not be strained or sieved, as you prefer, and served either hot or cold. Good garnished with sour cream and grated cucumber and served with pumpernickel bread.

Pennsylvania Dutch Red Eggs

1 tsp dried mustard
2 Tb sugar
1 tsp salt
1/2 cup cider vinegar
1 lb cooked, peeled baby beets
4 shelled, hard-boiled eggs

Boil mustard, sugar, salt and vinegar together. Pour over beets and let cool. Add eggs and refrigerate overnight in closed container. Shake container occasionally, so that the eggs are evenly colored. Serve beets cold in salad. Eggs may be served separately or with the beets as a garnish. Serves 4.

Turnips and Rutabagas

These two vegetables may be used interchangeably. If you want to know the difference between them, the smaller, white ones are the turnips, and the larger, yellow ones are the rutabagas. Both go wonderfully with game and are often served with turkey.

Turnip Soufflé

This isn't a light, fluffy soufflé, but it is lighter than mashed turnip. Even people who don't think they like turnip come back for seconds.

3 cups turnip
3 Tb butter
4 tsp sugar
1 1/2 tsp salt
1/8 tsp fresh ground pepper
3/4 cup soft bread crumbs
2 eggs, separated
1 Tb melted butter

Preheat oven to 350°. In food processor, finely chop raw turnip. Or cook turnip and mash it. (Using the food processor gives sweeter results.) Combine with remaining ingredients except egg whites and butter. Whip egg whites until they form peaks. Grease straight-sided baking dish with melted butter and add turnip mixture. Fold in egg whites and bake for about 35 minutes, until top is slightly brown.

Wonderful served with turkey or wild game. Serves 4 to 6.

Turnip Greens

6   cups of leaves
      salt to taste
1/4 cup butter

Wash greens well. Put in large, covered pot over medium heat until greens wilt. Add butter, salt, toss and serve.

Turnip Greens — Southern Style

1   lb salt pork or fatback
1   lb turnip greens (or turnip and mustard greens)
4   white turnips, peeled and coarsely chopped

Boil salt pork or fatback in lightly salted water until tender, adding water if necessary. Wash greens thoroughly. Add greens and turnip to meat and cook over low heat 45 minutes. Serve with cornbread. Serves 4.

Mashed Turnip or Rutabaga

1 1/2 lb turnip or rutabaga
2   large potatoes (optional)
       salt and pepper
6   Tb butter
1/2   cup heavy cream

Wash and peel the turnip or rutabaga and cut it into slices or cube. Peel and prepare potatoes in same manner. (Some people, who feel that turnips or rutabagas are bitter, find that the potatoes take away the bitter flavor.) Put in pot and barely cover with water. Add 1 tsp salt and bring to boil. Cook until tender (about 15 minutes). Drain and mash with potato masher, or put through ricer. Season to taste and add butter and cream — generously. Serve hot. Serves 4. Good sprinkled with bacon bits.

Twice-Fried Rutabaga

Cut peeled rutabaga into very thin strips — not more than 3/16 inch thick.

Preheat fat or oil in deep fryer to 200° to 330°. When fat is heated, drop in about 1 cup of rutabaga slices at a time and cook for about 2 minutes. Remove rutabaga and let cool for at least 5 minutes.

Then heat oil to 375°. Place slices in a basket and finish frying them — about 3 minutes. They should be golden brown and crisp. Serve at once.

Vegetable Crisp Dippers

Sliced turnips and rutabagas are great (and low calorie) for dips — along with kohlrabi, cauliflower, radishes and carrots.

Turnips in Sour Cream

6   white turnips
     boiling salted water
1   Tb caraway seeds
1/4 cup sour cream
1/2 tsp dried basil
     paprika
     lemon juice

Preheat oven to 350°. Cook turnip in boiling water with caraway seed for 10 minutes. Drain and cool. Peel and slice turnip and place in buttered casserole. Add sour cream and basil, cover and bake until tender, about 15 minutes.

Sprinkle with paprika and a little lemon juice and serve hot. Serves 6 to 8.

Radishes

There are some vegetables best left alone, and I believe radishes are among them. Well washed with the tops cut off and chilled — a terrific way to eat radishes! They're nice to munch on, good sliced thinly in salads and colorful as a garnish.

I've found recipes in cookbooks for radish relishes and cooked radishes, radishes in sour cream, but why bother when they're so good plain? But, then again, maybe I'm missing out on a good thing.

Salsify and Parsnips

Salsify and parsnips discolor when exposed to the air. A few easy precautions prevent it, however. Just prepare a bowl of water with lemon juice or vinegar in it (3 Tb to each quart of water) before peeling a root. After you scrape or peel one, put it immediately in the water.

Take out one salsify or parsnip at a time and cut it into 3-inch sticks. Drop them into a heavy pot containing salted water and the juice of half a lemon. Cover and cook for about 7 minutes or until almost fork tender. Drain, and they are ready for further preparation.

Braised Parsnips

1   lb parsnips
3   Tb butter

Prepare parsnips so they do not discolor and parboil them. Put them in shallow pan and add butter. Place in 300° oven until tender and golden, basting occasionally. Excellent if braised in the juices of roasting beef or leg of lamb.

Glazed Parsnips

6   medium parsnips
3   Tb melted butter
1/4 cup maple syrup or brown sugar
1/2 cup apple cider
1   tsp salt

Prepare parsnips so they do not discolor and parboil them. Drain thoroughly. Arrange parsnips in shallow baking dish. Mix remaining ingredients together and spoon mixture over parsnips. Bake for 20 minutes in pre-heated 400° oven. Baste occasionally. Serves 4.

Salsify in Butter

2   lb salsify
6   Tb butter
     salt
     freshly ground white pepper

Prepare salsify so they do not discolor. In a heavy casserole heat half the butter and add salsify. Season with salt and pepper and simmer over low heat for about 10 minutes. Dot with remaining butter and serve very hot. Serves 4 to 6.

Additions: fresh tarragon, parsley, chives, garlic or nutmeg.

Celeriac

Good in soups and stews, celeriac is also good as a vegetable dish. Although the plant has a crown of leaves, you only eat the dark root.

Celeriac, like parsnips and salsify, darkens when exposed to the air, so follow the basic preparation outlined under salsify before proceeding with any recipe.

If you have never eaten celeriac raw, give it a try. It's wonderful grated and mixed with garlic mayonnaise.

Braised Celeriac

2   lb celeriac (about 4 medium-sized roots)
6   Tb butter
     salt
     freshly ground white pepper
1   Tb parsley

Cut celeriac into slices 1/4-inch thick. In heavy saucepan, sauté slices in butter over low heat for 5 minutes. Season with salt, pepper and parsley.

After braising in butter, it can be topped with grated Swiss cheese and placed under the broiler for a few minutes until the cheese melts and browns.

CHAPTER 11

Potatoes

The history of the potato dates back more than 2,000 years to the time when the Inca Indians of the South American highlands were bringing wild varieties under cultivation.

The early European explorers of South America brought the first potatoes home to Europe, probably between 1530 and 1550, and Ireland became the first country to adopt them wholeheartedly, in part because the cool climate of Ireland is so well-suited to growing them. Many people still refer to the crop as "Irish" potatoes today.

By the 1660's the potato was firmly established in Ireland, and for the next 250 years the people of Ireland (and of some other countries, too) came to depend on it.

A colony of Presbyterian Irish introduced the potato to America in the early 1700's when they settled in New Hampshire. Potatoes eventually became America's most important vegetable. As in other countries, they were the mainstay of the winter food supply for many years. They're an all-year-round crop now.

The terrible famines in Ireland in the 1840's resulted partly from the country's dependence on one crop — the potato — and partly in the way the farmland was then distributed.

By the early 1800's, much of the Irish countryside was owned by absentee landlords, and the average Irish family did not have much farmland left. On the land they had, many families grew grains to pay the rent. They had scant space for growing their own food. Thus, their food supply came to be based entirely on the dependable, nutritional, storable potato. As one historian put it, "It was either eat potatoes or starve."

Late blight fungus was noticed in the Irish crop as early as the 1820's, but it wasn't a serious problem until 1845. That year the blight wiped out the crop nationwide — about 900,000 acres altogether. Diseased seed potatoes that were used the following seasons resulted in two more crop failures, and that caused the tragic starvation which claimed nearly half of Ireland's population and sent a million Irish to new homes around the world.

The Irish still grow potatoes — but only about ten percent of what was grown in the 1800's.

Worldwide, the potato is still a major crop, of course. In the U.S., we eat plenty of them, but unfortunately home growing of potatoes has slipped in recent years. People are eating them increasingly in processed forms: chips, fast-food fries, etc.

HOW POTATOES GROW

Potatoes grow from other potatoes. You always plant a whole, small potato, or a piece of a larger one for a new plant. The whole potato or cut piece has several slightly recessed, dormant buds or "eyes" on the surface. When conditions are right, these buds will sprout, whether the potatoes are in the ground or in a kitchen cupboard. The sprouts then develop into independent plants.

The cut potato piece or "seed piece" provides the new sprout or seedling with nourishment from its supply of stored starch.

After you've planted a seed piece, it usually takes about one to two weeks for the main stem and first leaves to appear above ground. The root system develops quickly and begins to absorb nutrients as the food supply in the seed piece is used up.

The top, leafy part of the plant puts on a lot of growth in the first four or five weeks after planting. The main stem of the plant will stop growing or terminate and produce a flower bud. When that happens, the plant will have as many leaves as it will ever have.

With proper sunshine, the leaves eventually produce more food than the plant needs, and the excess energy is channeled downward to be stored. This storage system is what makes a potato a potato. The energy is stored in the "tubers" — thick, short, underground stems — which we simply call potatoes. White potato tubers develop above the original seed piece, rather than below it like many other underground vegetables.

In my experience, the storage process starts five to seven weeks after planting, often when the plants have flowered. Some varieties will produce great potatoes with no flowering at all, but for me, flowering is a sign that something is definitely happening under ground, and that I'll have something to eat very soon.

Incidentally, potato flowers don't produce any nectar, so they're not visited much by bees or insects. The flowers are self-fertilized, and many potato plants produce small green seed balls about one inch in diameter, which contain up to 300 seeds. These seeds are mostly used by potato breeders.

When the tubers start forming, cooler temperatures are a blessing. Years ago, research showed that fewer and fewer tubers were formed on the plants as the temperature went from 68° to 84°F. In fact, none formed at 84°F. (This helps to explain while potatoes may be a summer crop up North, they are a late winter, spring or fall crop in the South.)

The best crops are produced when the daytime temperature is in the 60°-65°F range, and when night temperatures are below 57°F. When the weather is hot, the top part of the plant respires heavily, reducing the amount of food material that can otherwise be put into storage in the tubers below ground.

In a big potato-producing state like Idaho, for example, cool summer days and nights keep energy losses to a minimum. Plenty of starch is stored in the tubers, helping to make the Idaho potatoes big, mealy and great bakers.

As potatoes enlarge underground, the outside layer of the tuber gets tougher and tougher, keeping moisture within the potato and protecting it from outside attacks by organisms that can cause rot.

This toughening of the skin continues even as the plant tops die, the signal to the gardener that the harvest is at hand. Potatoes can remain underground for a little while after the tops die, so that the last energy in the tops can be transferred to the tubers. After the potatoes are dug, if the outer skins can't be rubbed off, they will store well.

GETTING STARTED

Since home gardeners start potatoes by cutting and planting last season's tubers, common sense says you should use the healthiest tubers possible.

How do you get disease-free potatoes for planting? Simple. Go to a good garden store in the spring and **buy certified potatoes for your "seed."**

Certified seed potatoes are grown under carefully

monitored conditions where state agricultural inspectors enforce high standards of disease and pest control, plant health and quality of harvested tubers. Most certified seed potatoes are grown in northern states where there are fewer disease-spreading insects than in the south. However, the cooler temperatures of the north favor the development of some diseases. This is good in a way, because plants that do become infected at the breeding ground can be spotted and eliminated, leaving only the strong, disease-free plants.

Gardeners who save some of their own crop to use for seed potatoes the next season are taking a chance. While the tubers may look fine and be perfectly okay for eating, certain virus diseases may be present. If these potatoes were planted, the disease would likely pass from the seed piece to the new plant.

When I was growing up on the farm, we couldn't afford to buy certified seed potatoes for our entire crop each season. Each year, though, we bought some certified potatoes, planted them in a special area, and saved some of the potatoes they produced for the bulk of our seed requirements the next year.

Potatoes from the market usually don't make good seed potatoes. They may have diseases and usually are treated with a growth-stopping chemical, so they don't sprout in the stores or in storage. But for seeds that are unavailable, for instance certain Idaho varieties, supermarkets may be your only source.

Where I live, the garden stores buy certified seed potatoes in 100-pound bags and break them down into smaller packages for gardeners. How much should you buy? Well, about eight to ten pounds of seed potatoes should plant about 100 feet of row, and from that length of row you could harvest three to four bushels of potatoes if you let them grow to maturity. If you harvest some when they're small for mid-summer eating, then the total yield will be less.

If you get your seed potatoes and can't plant them right away, simply store them in your root cellar or a cool, dark, well-ventilated place.

IRISH POTATO VARIETIES

Only about ten potato varieties are widely available to home gardeners in the U.S. Because some of them do better in some parts of the country than others, there are often as few as four or five varieties of potatoes we can buy at planting time to cut up for our seed. That's okay,

	Variety	Resistant to	Shape	Skin Color
EARLY	Cherokee	Late blight, common scab	round	creamy white
	Early Gem	Common scab	long, elliptical	light russet
	Irish Cobbler	Mild mosaic	roundish	creamy
	Red Lasoda	Common scab	long, elliptical	red
	Norland		oblong, thick	red
MID-SEASON	Chippewa	Mild mosaic	long-oval flat	white
	Superior	Common scab	round	white
	White Rose		long, flattened	white
LATE	Katahdin	Mild mosaic, brown rot, wart	oval	white
	Kennebec	Mild mosaic, late blight	elliptical	creamy buff
	Red Pontiac		oval, round	dark red
	Russet Burbank	Common scab	long, roundish	russet
	Sebago	Yellow dwarf	oval-round	white

though. Once you find a couple of winners, varieties that taste good and yield well year after year, you usually stick with them.

To find out which potatoes do best in your area, ask around — quiz gardeners, your local Cooperative Extension Service office or the people at a good garden store. Ask about early-maturing varieties (so you'll have some tasty, mid-season eating) and late varieties (for your main crop and winter storage).

I discovered my favorites after gardening for many years in Vermont. To me **Norland** is the best-tasting, early, red-skinned potato. Many gardeners prefer the white, round **Irish Cobbler** for an early potato, but I'm disappointed in the size of the Cobbler — I like them a little bigger.

Katahdin is a good white mid- or late-season potato (depending on when I plant). Katahdins are roundish and are good multi-use potatoes.

Kennebec is my "old reliable." I plant six or eight long rows of them each season and store quite a number of large, smooth, well-shaped potatoes from our big harvest. Most years the outstanding size of my Kennebecs seems too good to be true.

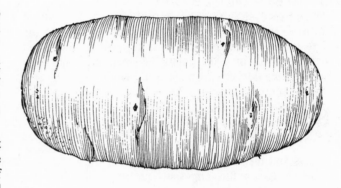

Former U.S. Senator George Aiken of Vermont stopped by one fall and took a look in my root cellar. He cast a cool, thoughtful eye on my bins of potatoes, one of which was filled with extra-large one- and two-pound Kennebec potatoes. "Yup," he reflected, "you grow Norlands for early eating, Katahdins to cook with, and Kennebecs to show off."

The **Russet Burbank** is probably the most widely grown variety in the U.S. The Russet or "Idaho" types are famous for their superb baking quality, though they can be fussy. They like the Western growing conditions and are not ordinarily available to gardeners in the East at planting time. If they're not at your garden store, you can experiment with Idaho potatoes from the grocery. See page 276. In the South, **Red LaSoda** is a popular early variety and **Sebago** is a favorite late type.

If you want to devote only a little of your garden space to potatoes, try an early variety. You can start harvesting early varieties about ten weeks after planting, so most gardeners still have time to clear out or till in the potato vines after the harvest is over and plant something else. Fall crops such as lettuce, cabbage or kale will do well when the weather cools off.

There's an early, white, novelty potato available from several mail-order seed companies. It's called the **Fingerling Potato,** so named because the tubers are small, only a couple of inches thick and shaped like fingers. They're good sliced for home fries or potato salad.

Soil Preparation

Potatoes will grow in just about any soil that is well-drained. They won't do anything in soil that is soggy all the time. Since potatoes do all their growing underground, they'll have an easier time expanding in loose, loamy soil than in heavy, clay soil that compacts and keeps plant roots from having the air and water they need.

Heavy soils can dampen your potato-growing enthusiasm, but if you add organic matter (leaves, hay, peat-moss, etc.) to the soil, especially at planting time, you'll be able to ease the hardship of tough soils.

Organic matter, when worked into heavy soils with a shovel and rake or tiller, wedges itself between the tiny soil particles. It works to open up the soil, letting air and water circulate. If you have light, sandy soil that can't hold water, organic matter will also work to help the soil hold moisture better.

Work organic matter into the soil whenever you don't have a crop growing: before the season gets underway, between crops, or after the harvest. Stockpile compost, leaves and grass clippings for these opportunities.

Another good way to build up organic matter in the soil is to grow a crop especially for tilling right back into the soil. We call these "green manure" or "cover crops." At my place I sow green manure or cover crops, such as quick-growing annual ryegrass, in late summer after harvesting my crops. I simply work the crop residues into the soil, sow the annual ryegrass seeds and let them grow until frost kills them. By planting time the next spring when I till the rye into the soil, the grass has decomposed fairly well, so it can supply the crops with moisture-holding organic matter and nutrients they need.

If you can't grow a cover crop, try to spread four or five bushels of compost onto each 100 square feet of potato growing area, and work it into the soil well before planting.

Gardeners who must work with heavy clay soil often incorporate very large amounts of organic matter right in the rows where they plant. For example, covering the seed pieces at planting time with a lot of leaves mixed with soil will give the plants the breathing room they need but couldn't get if planted in plain soil.

Rotate Each Season

Crop rotation is a must with potatoes. Troublesome insects and diseases can build up in the soil when you plant potatoes in the same spot year after year. So move the potato patch each season to a new, sunny location. If possible, don't go back to the same area until three seasons have passed.

Since potatoes, tomatoes, peppers, and eggplants are all members of the same family, consider them together. Don't put potatoes where tomatoes, peppers or eggplant were grown the previous year and vice versa.

Nearly everyone who gives advice about growing potatoes mentions soil pH — the measure of soil acidity or alkalinity — as an important factor. Commercial, large-scale potato growers monitor their soil pH quite carefully and try to keep it in the range of 4.8 to 5.4, which is an acid soil condition. (7.0 on the pH scale is neutral; higher figures indicate an alkaline condition.)

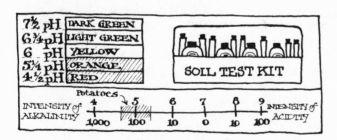

The 4.8 to 5.4 range is important to commercial growers because the common scab fungus, **streptomyces scabies,** which causes raised, scabby marks on potato skins, is not active in the soil in that pH range.

Most gardeners don't have to be that particular about the soil pH of their potato rows. You can raise good potatoes with soil pH ranging from 6.0 to 6.5, the slightly acid condition that is still suitable for many vegetable crops. However, lower pH is preferred for greater yields and less disease.

If scab disfigures too much of your crop, then you should try to keep the soil pH down. Avoid adding lime or wood ashes, which raise soil pH, to the soil where your potatoes will grow. Rather than tinkering with my soil pH, I'm willing to accept a little scab on some potatoes. Scab doesn't cause rotting or decaying of potatoes, it just doesn't look great. It's okay to eat scabby potatoes; simply peel and cook them normally.

Timing

Potatoes can be planted very early in the season — almost as soon as the frost is out of the ground and you're able to work the soil. I plant my first crop of early-maturing potatoes in April, usually about six to eight weeks before the last frost here in Vermont.

But for many of you, especially in the South, the planting dates will be quite different. Down South, planting times range from September to February. Where winters are relatively mild, you can plant a fall crop in September. In central Florida gardeners plant potatoes in January; and February is potato planting time in Georgia.

Don't be afraid to start early with potatoes. I visited gardeners in Oklahoma in mid-February once, and they told me their potatoes had been planted that week but were not up yet. The next day a storm dumped six inches of snow over most of the state. The potatoes survived very well.

The soil, and not the calendar, will tell you when it's time to plant. The soil should not be so wet that it sticks together and is hard to work. Let it dry out a bit first. Potato seed pieces, like other seeds, can rot if planted in ground that is too wet.

Food for Potatoes—Fertilizer

For a rewarding potato crop, the plants must make a rapid, healthy start.

There are a couple of good ways to add the extra nutrients at planting time to supplement the natural fertility of your soil. First choose either a balanced commercial fertilizer, such as 5-10-10 or 10-10-10, compost or organic fertilizer.

Broadcasting is one easy way to spread the fertilizer over the entire planting area. Use about a 12 quart pail of 5-10-10 per 1,000 square feet of garden soil. Walk over the area, scatter the fertilizer uniformly by hand, then work it into the top 3 to 4 inches of soil with a rake or tiller.

However, I fertilize the potato crop a little differently. I think my method works better, and I do it right at planting time.

Each cut seed piece will be planted about 10 to 12 inches from the next in the row. Before I place the seed pieces in the row, I put down a small handful or two of compost every 10 or 12 inches, along with a small handful of superphosphate (0-20-0), a fertilizer high in phosphorus. Phosphorus helps potato roots develop quickly. My compost includes a balance of nitrogen, phosphorus and potassium, the major plant nutrients, and other elements, too.

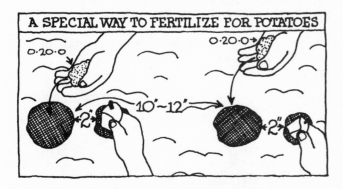

Then I cover the fertilizer with a couple of inches of soil. Looking down the row after this step I see small mounds every foot or so. When I plant each piece I'll put it at the edge of the fertilizer, but not directly over it. Research for commercial growers has shown that the best placement for fertilizer is 2 inches to the side and slightly below the seed piece. We home gardeners don't have to be as precise, but it is vital to keep the seed piece from coming into contact with any commercial fertilizer, such as superphosphate or 10-10-10 if you use it, as that will injure it.

Fresh manure should not be used on the potato patch as a fertilizer because it often contains scab-causing organisms. Old, thoroughly composted or decomposed barnyard manures are usually okay, though.

Potato Eyes

Small seed potatoes can be planted whole, but larger ones should be first cut into pieces that have at least one "eye" or recessed dormant bud. The pieces should be blocky, about the size of a large ice cube. Cut to that size, each piece weighs about 1½ to 2 ounces, which researchers say is the ideal size for a seed piece.

Seed pieces can have more than one eye. In fact, I cut my seed potatoes to get three or four eyes on each piece, which is just my own way of getting a seed piece about the right size.

Larger or smaller seed pieces will work. Larger seed pieces produce plants which yield a high number of medium to small size potatoes. Planting pieces that are smaller than recommended may give you fewer, but larger, potatoes.

It may be tempting to plant smaller pieces in the hope of getting big potatoes, but stick to middle-size pieces. You see, small pieces obviously have less starch stored up to nourish the developing plant. Their food supply is quickly exhausted. A larger piece has more energy to offer, and this can help a young plant recover from an early-season injury.

For example, if you plant very early in the season, a late frost could injure the plants after they've come up. Plants from a good-sized seed piece can continue to draw on the stored energy of the piece to recover more rapidly and resume normal growth.

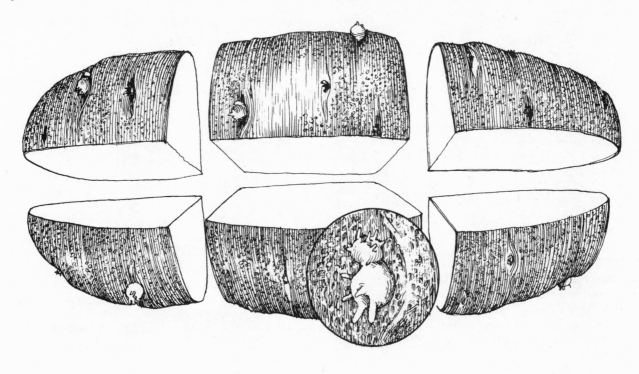

The Wait Debate

At planting time there's always talk around the neighborhood about whether to cut seed potatoes and plant them right away or whether to cut them and store them until the cut pieces "heal over."

I've planted potatoes both ways, and I prefer to cure the seeds after cutting them. I've had fewer failures than when I cut and planted on the same day.

Many researchers and growers feel you should cut the seed pieces and give them time to heal to develop a protective covering over their exposed surfaces. They suggest that you store or "cure" the cut seeds at least two or three days at around 70°F and high humidity. This will promote fast healing of the surface and keep the seed pieces from drying out. When you plant them, the protective covering will retain moisture and energy and serve as a barrier against rot organisms.

Others feel you should plant the seed immediately after cutting. In a recent book for home gardeners, the U.S. Dept. of Agriculture urged cutting and planting right away, saying, "Otherwise, viability will be lowered by loss of moisture and entrance of rot organisms." I think this is good advice when the soil is relatively warm, for instance when you're planting late in the spring. In early spring, though, the soil is cooler and more moist — conditions favorable for rot organisms in the soil. I think it's wiser to heal the pieces if you're planting early in cool soil.

There are a couple of other ways to protect cut seed potatoes, too. Sulfur powder is a natural, inexpensive, seed protectant. You can get it at most drugstores. A couple of ounces protects approximately 10 pounds of seed potatoes. Simply put some seed pieces in a paper bag, add a tablespoon or two of sulfur and shake the bag. The powder sticks to the pieces and protects them from rot organisms in the ground.

You can also treat the seed with a fungicide dust such as captan. It will protect against rot in the ground and help give you a better stand. Be sure to follow directions carefully when using fungicides or any other chemical.

Sprouting Tip for Earlier Harvest

If you look forward to early potatoes, you can hurry the harvest along by forcing the eyes to sprout a few weeks before planting. By planting potato pieces that have already sprouted, you shorten the time it takes a plant to come out of the ground and develop the leaves which will eventually provide energy to be stored in the potatoes.

To sprout seed potatoes two to three weeks before planting, spread them out in a single layer on an enclosed porch or in a warm room where they will get some sun and where the temperature will stay near 60°F or warmer. The potatoes will develop short, green sprouts, rather than the long white sprouts they produce in the dark.

Because the potatoes become green, this sprouting process is often called "greening." Green potatoes aren't good to eat, but when you plant them the crop will be fine. When planting time comes, cut the potatoes as you would normally and plant the seed pieces as usual without breaking the tiny sprouts.

This past summer I presprouted a number of Idaho potatoes from the grocery store this way. (I plant Idahoes strictly for fun, since Vermont weather isn't supposed to suit them, and I wouldn't want to depend on them.) Sprouting them indoors assures me that chemicals to keep them from sprouting have worn off.

Seed Potatoes for Fall

There's usually plenty of certified seed available for spring planting across the country, but often, as fall planting time rolls around down South, good seed potatoes may not be available.

What's the solution? The best bet is to provide your own, even though there's a small risk of planting diseased potatoes.

Take some potatoes from the harvest of your earliest crop and use them as seed potatoes for your fall planting. But it's not as easy as it sounds. You must do it *carefully*.

Immediately after harvest potatoes go dormant, and they won't sprout or produce plants when they're resting. If you plant your own seed potatoes from your spring crop and they are still in this rest period, you won't have much of a fall crop.

There are two ways to avoid this:

1. Plant part of your spring crop as early as you can, as much as 1 to 6 weeks before the last frost — to give the crop plenty of time to mature. Mature potatoes have shorter dormant periods than immature ones.

2. Store the seed potatoes at a high temperature (around 75°F) for three or four weeks before planting. For many varieties, this brings them out of the dormant phase.

Fall planting in the South is usually done in hot weather. To reduce the losses from seed pieces rotting in the ground, plant the smallest of the mature seed potatoes you've saved. It's not advisable to use your large seed potatoes and cut them because cut seed loses more of its energy when it's hot.

PLANTING

The first step in planting is to work the soil, tilling or spading it to turn in any old organic matter and to smooth out clods of earth to form a loose, deep seedbed. If the seedbed is loose, potato roots will be able to grow easily and search food and water deep in the soil.

Instead of planting at level ground as I do for most other vegetable seeds, I plant potato seed pieces in 4 to 6 inch-deep furrows or trenches. I dig the furrows about 36 inches apart with a hoe or tiller. The length of the row isn't important, make it as long as you need. But be sure to plant the seed pieces 4 to 6 inches deep.

After creating the furrows, I put down a handful of compost or fertilizer every 10 to 12 inches and cover it with an inch or two of soil, forming a small mound. Then I plant the seed pieces, cut side down, at the edge of each little mound. When seed pieces are planted too close, the yields tend to drop. So if your potatoes are consistently small, try giving them a few extra inches of growing space.

Though the seed pieces are deep in the ground, I

Dig trenches 4 to 6 inches deep, 36 inches apart.

Put a handful of compost or fertilizer in furrow every 10 to 12 inches.

Cover fertilizer with inch or two of soil and plant seed pieces, cut side down, a few inches away from each mound.

cover them with only three or four inches of soil, and then firm the soil with the back of a hoe. Because the potatoes form above the seed piece, I help them by mounding soil around the plants — a process called hilling — after the plants are up and growing. That gives the tubers room to expand.

Lazy-Bed Planting

Planting potatoes under mulch (heavy layers of organic matter over the soil) is becoming increasingly popular — especially for folks who don't have much land for spudding or much inclination for weeding.

The technique is simple, and that's what people like. Start by tilling or spading a small area of garden soil, say 10 feet by 10 feet, or more if you want. Work some compost or a light application of 5-10-10 fertilizer

into the top inch or two of soil. Then plant seed pieces about 10 inches apart in all directions. Put the cut surface face down and push each piece in until the top of the piece is at ground level.

Then cover the area with about 18 inches of mulch, such as old or spoiled hay, leaves, chopped corn stalks, etc. If you decide to use hay, try to find some that is fairly weed free because seeds attract mice, who may eat the potatoes when they run out of seeds.

Once the mulch is on, your work is almost over. You may have to water once in a while, or add some extra mulch in case some tubers start to show through.

I've noticed over the years that potato bugs don't bother the plants under mulch as often as they do regular rows of potatoes. In fact, in mulched plantings, potato bugs usually stay on the perimeter and don't bother the plants in the middle. A scientist told me that this might be due to the fact that potato bugs prefer not to travel over mulch, that perhaps mulch is somehow unsettling or too different from solid ground.

As with potatoes planted normally, you can reach in to harvest some new potatoes any time there's something to pick and eat. Just push the mulch aside, harvest what you want and replace the mulch. The "new" potatoes grown under mulch are great — smooth, almost skinless, and delicious.

Spuds in a Basket

Ever think of growing a few potato plants in bushel baskets? Well, you can — it's easy and fun. You can be a potato grower in the smallest yard or just on the back porch or patio.

Line a bushel basket with plastic, punch a few holes in the bottom and put in a layer of stones for drainage. Stir a few tablespoons of house plant food or fertilizer

into a bucket of moist soil. Put a four or five inch layer of soil in the basket and lay a few seed pieces six to eight inches apart, then top with three or four more inches of soil.

Keep the basket in a warm, sunny place. As the plants grow, add more soil around the stems to give the tubers room to expand, and keep the soil well-watered.

POTATO CARE

Cultivation

Stirring up the soil on the surface keeps it loose so that the plants' roots can get water and air. They have to drink and breathe as we do. Whenever the soil becomes too packed or crusty, raking the top inch of soil lightly can help.

If you hill your potatoes during the first four to eight weeks after planting, you shouldn't have any problems with weeds. Hilling buries weeds near the plants, and it usually takes care of most walkway weeds, too.

Once the hills are made, though, don't disturb them with a hoe or any other tool. If you want to get rid of some weeds, pull them by hand.

Hilling

There are several reasons why you must pull soil up around the stems of your potato plants, or 'hill' them, once or twice during the season:

1. The additional loose soil allows the developing tubers to expand easily.

2. Hilling helps keep the potatoes from poking through the soil and becoming "green" from the sun. ("Greening" gives them an unpleasant "off" flavor.)

3. Hilling buries and kills weeds around the plants before they become a serious and time-consuming problem.

4. Since rain collects in gardens with heavy soils, blocking the flow of air to the plant roots, a hilled row of potatoes will shed water. Hilling keeps them better drained and more productive because the earth will not pack around the plants.

5. Pulling soil from between the rows up around the plants creates a natural irrigation ditch.

I hill the plants for the first time about a week or so after they poke through the soil. Do the job with a hoe or a tiller with a hilling attachment and pull up as much soil as you can around the stems. If you cover some, or even *all,* of the leaves of the plants, don't worry about it. They'll push back through in a few days. In fact, when my early-planted potatoes are up and there's a chance of a late frost, I cover the plants entirely to protect them from injury. Potatoes can take a light frost; burying them is just added insurance.

My second, and usually *last,* hilling is three or four weeks later, before the potato vines spill out into the walkways.

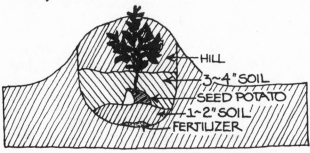

Water

Potatoes need a steady, season-long supply of water, but water is most important when the plants start to develop their tubers, which is about 6 or 10 weeks after planting.

An uneven water supply will often cause knobs or growth cracks in your potatoes. If the plants don't get enough water, the potatoes underground grow very little and their cells start to mature. Then, when a sudden increase in water does occur, the potatoes start a second, new growth. They'll show cracks or develop into odd shapes.

Over the years I have found that potatoes can take some periods of dry weather. However, if it's been very dry and the potatoes are beginning to develop underground, I water them.

If you must water, do a thorough job. Continue applying water until the soil is moist eight to ten inches below ground. Deep watering is the only way to go. University of Nebraska potato researchers report that irrigated potatoes obtained 57 percent of their water from the top foot of soil, 24 percent from the second foot of soil and as much as 13 percent from the third foot of soil. Though the potato plant is mostly shallow-rooted, some roots do indeed go deep for water.

Diseases

You may have a disease problem in the potato patch one year, and none at all the next. The weather plays a big part in the health of a potato crop. Moisture and temperature conditions may trigger certain diseases, which will spread rapidly through the potato rows. But don't simply sit back and let the environment determine the fate of your crop.

Here's how you can help protect your crop. Rotate the potato plot each year. Plant healthy, certified seed. And consider using a standard potato dust or spray regularly through the season. The potato dust or spray is a chemical mixture which prevents some diseases such as late blight. It thwarts some pests, too, such as the Colorado potato beetle. If you do use a potato dust or spray, read the directions carefully and follow them. To be effective, most standard dusts must be applied to the potato foliage every seven to ten days, beginning when the plants emerge from the ground.

If you have questions about diseases or pests, your local Cooperative Extension Service can probably help you.

Here are brief descriptions of some common potato diseases.

Aphids can spread the viruses that cause **mosaic**. The potato leaves become curled and almost two-toned (light and dark green). It occurs throughout the U.S. and cuts down on the harvest, but it won't kill the plants. Kennebec, Katahdin and Sebago varieties have some resistance to certain kinds of mosaic.

The fungus that causes **common scab** lives in the soil for many years. It's not active, though, when the soil pH is below 5.4, so if you have a serious scab problem, take a soil pH test. You may want to lower the pH by *not* liming or adding wood ashes to the potato section of the garden.

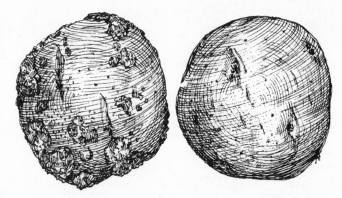

Early blight injures foliage and reduces overall yields. The affected leaves develop small, dark brown spots which often get bigger. Gardens in Central, Southern and Eastern states are most susceptible. Planting certified seed and using a standard potato dust or spray can prevent this disease.

Late blight is caused by the downy mildew fungus, *phytophthora infestans,* that triggered the Irish crop failures of 1845-'48. You'll notice the disease first by water-soaked areas on the leaves which turn brown and black as the leaf dies. The disease strikes often during cool, wet weather and may spread rapidly if the weather warms up. Plants may die in a severe case, and potatoes can be seriously affected, especially in storage. Again, plant certified seed and use a potato dust to guard against late blight.

Pests

Don't ignore your potatoes during the season because they look okay tucked off in a corner of the garden. Damaging pests can work quickly in a potato patch.

Stroll through the patch regularly looking for pests and damage they cause. It's a lot easier to deal with a pest before it becomes a disaster.

Remember, if you choose to use sprays or dusts to prevent or control a pest problem, please take care. Read directions with all substances and follow them carefully.

Colorado Potato Beetle. You can't be a potato grower for long without meeting this beetle. They're present and working in just about every state. I spent a lot of time as a youngster going through the family potato patch picking off these potato bugs and checking the underside of leaves to rub out their orange egg masses. Both the adults, which are yellowish with black stripes, and the larvae, which are dark red or orange with black spots, will feed on potato foliage. Pick them off or use a standard potato dust regularly.

Flea beetles. Flea beetles are tiny, black or brown, and pesky. They chew small holes in the leaves of plants. They can really do damage fast if they get working on young plants. Spraying with malathion can control them.

Aphids. These tiny insects can transmit virus diseases and also suck juice from leaves and stems of potato plants, injuring them badly. Again, a spray of malathion is effective.

Wireworms. Wireworms are the larvae of the click beetle. They are a problem when potatoes are planted in a section of garden that was recently sodded. When fully grown, wireworms are from one-half to one and one-half inches in length. They're slender, brownish or yellowish white and tunnel into plant roots and tubers to spoil them. If your soil is heavily infested, contact your Extension Service Agent for advice on solving the problem.

HARVEST TIME

New Potatoes

The earliest or "new" potatoes of the season brought me many customers in my market-garden days. I'm not selling them now, but I still am impatient for the first new potatoes of the year — the small, round, smooth ones that go so well with peas, beans, milk and a little fatback. So when I think there's an early potato big enough to eat, I look for it. I reach into my early hills and feel for the best-sized spuds and haul them out. The plant keeps right on growing and producing more.

During seasons when the soil has been quite moist (which makes hunting by hand tougher), I dig up *entire* plants, harvest all the baby potatoes I can find and put the plants back in the earth. They survive this rude transplant and produce quite a few more potatoes.

When there are a lot of rows to dig, a few family members or neighborhood volunteers help dig. Working fast is important; freshly-dug potatoes shouldn't stay in the sun very long.

I find that the best tool for digging is a 5 or 6-pronged fork. You dig under a hill and lift up. The dirt falls between the prongs, and you're left with a forkful of potatoes. There's less bending this way.

Later Harvest

My main storage crop is ready to harvest in September, when the days are getting cool and frost is not far

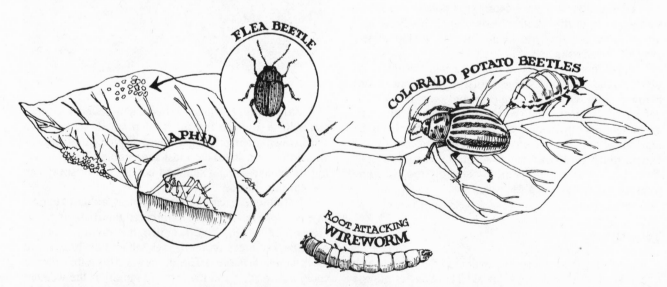

off. That's when the tops of the plants are dying and sending the last of the vine energy down to the tubers.

Since we'll store most of the late potatoes, I try to wait for the best time possible to dig them up — a warm, dry day after a period of little or no rain. Cloudy days are all the better, since too much light will green newly dug potatoes and change their flavor if they're left in the sun too long.

After you dig a few hills, you'll realize that all the potatoes in a hill are at pretty much the same level, so once you discover how deep to dig your fork, you won't injure as many potatoes. Of course, if you've got some beginners on the work crew, there'll be a few spiked spuds. Put them aside for the evening meal; they won't keep.

A pointed shovel does a good job, too. You can dig deep enough next to a hill to raise the entire hill at one time.

Be gentle. Try not to rough up or bump the potatoes around. Each bruise lowers the storage quality and appearance of the potato.

AFTER THE HARVEST

Leave the potatoes outdoors for an hour or so to dry. In that time they'll dry off, and most of the soil stuck on the potatoes should drop off. There's no real need to brush the potatoes, although some people use a very soft brush gently to take off clumps of dirt. Don't wash the potatoes because it's tough to get them totally dry afterward.

Put the potatoes in the dark after they've dried in the open for a short time. Don't leave them in burlap bags or other containers where light can penetrate and start them greening.

If possible, storage potatoes should have a short drying or "curing" period of one to two weeks after the harvest. Keep them in a dark place with temperatures around 55° to 60°F with high humidity, up to 85 to 95 percent.

Curing allows for rapid healing of any slight cuts or bruises on the potatoes. Occasionally, I have skipped this curing period, placing the potatoes directly into cooler storage, with no harmful effects.

After a curing period, potatoes belong in a much cooler, dark place for winter storage. Experts recommend 35° to 40°F with moderate humidity and ventilation. If these standards are met in your basement or root cellar, you can expect mature potatoes to store for up to eight months. Higher temperatures, however, will mean quicker sprouting and shrivelling.

A root cellar needs good circulation of air because potatoes have to breathe in storage. They are still carrying on normal life processes. Potatoes use oxygen to heal bruises and cracks and give off carbon dioxide, heat and moisture. Good air circulation in the storage room helps this continuing process. That's why I store potatoes in bins with *slatted* sides and bottoms and never pile them higher than six to eight inches.

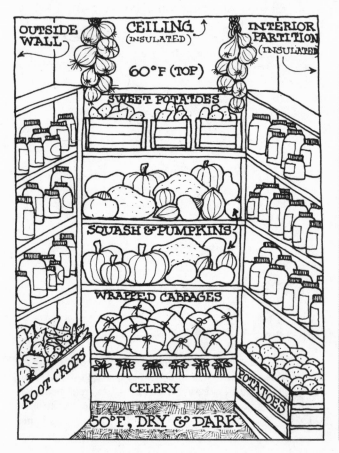

Perhaps you've heard of potatoes becoming "sweet" during storage. Inside a potato a certain amount of starch is converted to sugar. The sugar is used up in the living process. When potatoes are stored in cool root cellars, though, the breathing slows down, and all the sugar the potato produces is not used up. The extra sugar in potatoes sometimes gives them a sweet taste if taken directly from cool storage and cooked. This has never been a problem for me, but it's easy to restore full potato flavor; just bring a week's supply of potatoes out of storage at one time and keep them in a warmer spot. The extra sugar will revert to starch — a process experts call "reconditioning."

SWEET POTATOES

Sweet potatoes are a long-season, tropical vegetable, so it's no surprise that they are grown mostly in southern states. There the plants can get plenty of heat and the four or five months' growing time they need to develop sweet, chunky roots. When the extreme summer heat makes the garden too hot for most vegetables (and many gardeners), the sweet potato is thriving.

It's possible for even Northern gardeners to grow good sweet potatoes (sweet potatoes are a cash crop for many New Jersey farms), but it's often a real challenge. The plants are very tender; they can't take frost and refuse to grow in cool soil. Plants yield best if night temperatures average around 72°F. Some of our clear August nights in Vermont are so cool that I'm sure sweet potatoes here stop growing in protest.

A Note on Greening

When potatoes are exposed to light, their skins start to turn green, a sign that a toxic substance, solanine, is developing. Potatoes that stick out of the soil while they're growing will develop deep green spots. If you keep potatoes in the sun after the harvest for too long, they'll start to turn green, too. Even potatoes stored indoors at the supermarket will slowly turn green if they are in the light.

Because solanine is slightly toxic, it's possible to get sick if you have a big helping of greened potatoes. Peeling or cutting away green sections before cooking usually eliminates the problem, as most of the solanine is located in the skin.

I've never had much trouble storing potatoes in all my 40 years of growing them. In fact, even in those years when my family had to depend on potatoes for the winter's supply of food, I only remember one year when the crop didn't keep well. We replaced the lost potatoes with turnips we had raised to feed our pigs. I recall a lot of different ways to eat turnip from that winter!

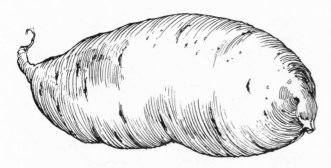

At my home garden, the frost-free period is often shorter than the 150 days required for good sweet potatoes, but we still have pretty fair crops. The sandy soil warms up early in the summer, so I can put my sweet potato plants in the ground in late May (would you believe that's the time of our average last frost date?) and keep my fingers crossed.

Travelling in Southern states, I've taken a close look at how gardeners grow and store sweet potatoes. I've also tasted some of the hundreds of ways of cooking them — every dedicated grower has a special recipe it seems, from sweet potato pies and casseroles to salads and custards. In the South, many people call sweet potatoes simply "potatoes," and refer to the white and red cool-weather potatoes as "Irish" potatoes.

Like Irish potatoes, sweet potatoes furnish us energy, supplying sugars and other carbohydrates, some protein, calcium, iron and other minerals. They're high in Vitamin A and C, too. Sweet potatoes used to be more popular. In the 1920's, when many farm families grew sweet potatoes for winter food, the average consumption per person in the country was about 30 pounds per year. Now with fewer families "growing their own," average yearly consumption is about five pounds. Some people think of the sweet potatoes only as a traditional holiday vegetable, but if you grow them and store them, you can furnish your family good nutrition many months of the year.

GETTING STARTED

To grow sweet potatoes you have to start with young sweet potato plants. These are simply tall sprouts that grow from sweet potatoes kept from the previous crop. You can call these sprout-producing sweet potatoes "seed potatoes." Each potato will produce many sprouts or plants. They have been given various names: slips, draws, poles, transplants.

You can grow your own plants, or buy them from a local garden or feed store, or send away to one of several companies that ship plants all over the country.

Most home gardeners purchase plants locally. Shop for "certified" plants because these are grown under carefully controlled conditions and are virtually free of diseases and pests. Good slips will be stocky, six to nine inches long, having at least five leaves, tough stems and healthy root systems.

If you order certified plants through the mail (an easy way for a Northern gardener to start sweet potato growing), be sure to specify the date you want to receive them — when your soil has warmed up and the danger of frost is just about past.

When you receive the plants, unpack them. Damaging heat can build up in a tight package of plants. The slips may look off-color, but they'll usually be okay. Sweet potato plants are tough. Even ones that smell a bit off can come back and give good results. To revive them before planting, stick the roots in water for a day or so, and they'll perk up. You can easily keep the plants a week or so if you must wait for some reason before planting them. Pack the roots in moist peat moss or soil and keep them moist.

Varieties

There are basically two types of sweet potatoes. One type features flesh that is dry and mealy when cooked. Varieties of this type such as **Jersey Orange** or **Big Stem Jersey** are often referred to as a group: the Jersey types. They're said to grow a little better in northern gardens than the second kind of sweet potato, the more moist, sweet and soft varieties. Studies show that during cooking, more of the starch is converted to sugars in moist-fleshed varieties such as **Porto Rico, Centennial** and **Nemagold.**

In the past I've sent away for Centennial and Porto Rico slips, and the Centennial plants do much better in my northern garden.

The term "yam" is often mistakenly used by grocers and shoppers when talking about moist-flesh sweet potatoes. The true yam is an entirely different plant, and is rarely grown in the U.S.

Growing Your Own Seed Stock

No matter where you live, you can easily grow your own transplants or slips. In the North where springtime weather is cool, it's better to grow them indoors. In many areas down South, you can start them outside.

What do you need to start? Good sweet potato seed stock — which simply means sweet potatoes that are as free from disease as possible. A good local sweet potato grower might have seed stock to spare in the spring.

By planning ahead, home gardeners can produce their own seed stock. Here's a brief rundown on the process: buy certified plants, plant them in the best section of your garden, keep them free of pests and diseases through the season, and after harvesting and curing them, store the best roots carefully. These top-grade potatoes from certified plants will be the ones for your own slips the next spring.

Since Northern gardeners don't usually store sweet potatoes over the winter, it's necessary to start plants in March or April using large, bruise-free sweet potatoes from the grocery. Most years the plants are quite healthy. Occasionally, some plants are diseased, but if you start enough plants in the spring, you can avoid using questionable transplants.

Indoor Slips

Start your plants indoors or in a cold frame seven to eight weeks before the average last frost date in your area. For a small garden, place about a dozen or so sweet potatoes close together without touching in grow boxes or flats. Potatoes 1½ to 2 inches in diameter are good. You don't have to cut them at all. Lay them in the flat and cover them with two to three inches of moist, commercial soil mix. Cover the flats with plastic to retain moisture until shoots appear. Then remove the plastic, and put the

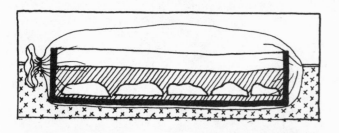

flats in a cold frame or near a sunny window or under fluorescent lights.

After a couple of weeks, add a little plant food to the water you give them. If the temperature in the room is about 70°F, it'll usually take six or seven weeks for the plants to reach six to eight inches in height.

Before they are planted in the garden, the seedlings have to be hardened off just like tomato and pepper seedlings. Put the flats in a well-protected spot outdoors for a few hours the first day of this hardening process. Then gradually increase the time they spend outside, exposing them to more and more direct sun and wind.

Growing Slips Outside

If you live where late winter and early spring weather is mild and often warm, you can grow sweet potato transplants outside. But you always have to be alert for a late snap of cold weather that could hurt the plants.

Southern gardeners bed their seed potatoes in cold frames or hot beds — outdoor growing houses that protect the slips from cool weather damage. In hot beds, it's common to use fresh barnyard manure under a heavy layer of soil to heat up the bed. There's no heat source in cold frames, but they are usually glassed in to trap heat during the day and protect the plants on cold nights.

Gardeners I know in Florida grow their transplants in mid-February when daytime temperatures average 70° to 80°F and the nights are quite mild. They don't use cold frames or anything — they don't have to.

As with the indoor method, start six weeks or so before you expect to put the slips in their permanent place in the garden. Whether you're bedding the sweet potatoes at the edge of the garden or in a cold frame or hot bed, lay the seed potatoes close together, cover with two to three inches of soil and water them gently if the soil is dry. One Alabama gardener I met covers his potatoes in a hot bed with three inches of soil that is mixed with cottonseed meal and a little rotted manure. He told me each sweet potato grows so many slips they look "as thick as hair on a dog's back."

Each season you should change the location of the slip-starting area because sweet potato diseases can build up there. Soil from permanent hot beds and cold frames should be dug out and replaced with disease-free commercial soil mix or with garden soil from an area where sweet potatoes have not been grown for four or five years.

Kitchen Counter Slips

Kids love to grow a few sweet potato plant slips on the kitchen windowsill. Just submerge a seed potato or two halfway in a pan of water. Keep them next to a window and maintain the water level. The plants will get

pretty big in about a month and in time will grow handsome vines.

Soil Preparation

Because the roots of sweet potatoes need to swell and expand easily, the slips are usually planted in raised rows, ranging from six to ten inches high and from two to three feet wide. Raising the soil up in hills or "ridges" is especially important with clay soil. Heavy soils tend to compact and restrict the growth of the roots underground, sometimes resulting in rough and odd-shaped potatoes. They also tend to drain poorly.

Just as with white potatoes, you can improve heavy problem soils for better sweet potatoes by mixing in plenty of organic matter such as leaves, grass clippings, hay, compost, or peanut hulls whenever and wherever you can.

You can prepare your ridges a week or so before planting, while the indoor-grown slips are hardening off or when your bedded slips reach 6 to 9 inches in height. Till or spade the soil first, working crop residues into the soil, making the soil as loose as possible. The soil pH should be in the 5.6 to 6.5 range, slightly on the acid side. As soil pH nears 7.0 (neutral), sweet potato plants become more susceptible to certain diseases.

Stake out where you want your sweet potato rows, allowing enough space between them, usually three feet, to walk through to weed or cultivate. Use a hoe to draw up the tilled, loose soil and form a fairly level planting bed. You can easily smooth out the ridges with a rake before planting the slips.

Fertilizer

Sweet potato plants gobble up a lot of nutrients from the soil to feed their burgeoning roots and extensive vines, which for some varieties may reach fifteen to twenty feet in a long growing season.

Fertilizing, though, is a delicate matter as too much plant food — especially nitrogen — will produce skinny potatoes. With too much nitrogen, the vine portion of the plant dominates the growth, and root formation is delayed. With too little fertilizer, the harvest won't meet your expectations.

When using commercial fertilizer, the basic guideline is about four to five pounds of 5-10-10 for each 100 feet of row. If your soil is quite fertile, though, you can cut this recommendation to two or three pounds for each 100 feet of row.

The simplest way to apply the fertilizer is to broadcast it before making your ridges. Spread it uniformly over the row and include some of the soil area you will use for building your ridge.

Ready to Plant

Follow this rule of thumb on planting slips — wait two or three weeks after the average last frost date because for good growth, air and soil temperature should be over 60°F. The *planting* season in central Florida, for example, ranges from March to July.

Up where I live, though, we have to gamble. If the weather is warm enough, we set plants out close to the average last frost date because we just can't wait any longer. We're never sure how long (or short) our frost-free season will be, but even so I always get some sweet potatoes.

If you're using your own slips, pull them out of the ground or their flats with a twisting motion. This will easily free them from the seed potato under the soil and all other slips, yet retain many of their tiny roots. Some people recommend cutting the stem of the slips one inch above the soil to reduce the chance of spreading soil-borne diseases from the bedding area to the sweet potato rows. These rootless slips must be kept well-watered after transplanting, so they'll root quickly.

Set the slips twelve to fifteen inches apart in the row, and about five to six inches deep. Just make a little hole for them, set them in and give them a gentle watering after firming the soil around them. If you have some short slips, that's okay. Put them into the soil with just one leaf showing above ground. They'll do fine.

If you have a long growing season, you can take slips or "cuttings" from young sweet potato plants after they've been growing a few weeks. It's a good way to avoid the work of raising and caring for slips, and this "second crop" is a simple way to extend the season. Take the cuttings from anywhere on the vine — they can

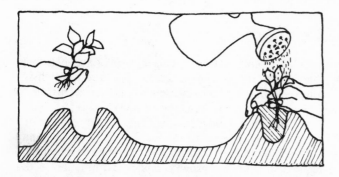

be up to twelve to fifteen inches long. Plant them right away — again, twelve to fifteen inches apart and five to six inches deep on ridges. Keep them shaded from bright sun, and be sure to water them several days in a row; they'll root quickly.

SWEET POTATO CARE

Cultivation

It's important to take care of any weeds that pop up soon after planting, because they'll steal water, nutrients and sunlight your sweet potatoes need. If you delay cultivating, the quick-growing potato vines could sprawl and make it difficult to walk between the rows to get the weeds.

So before the plants have begun to produce runners, gently stir up the soil around the plants and in the rows to get rid of weeds. This also aerates the soil, letting the roots breathe easily.

After a while the many large sweet potato leaves tend to block out new weed growth. After the vines spill out into the walkways, your weeding is all but finished.

Water

Watering is very important in the few days following planting. Be sure to keep the soil around the slips wet, so the roots can start to expand quickly.

Once the roots have anchored the plant well, sweet potatoes can be considered drought-hardy; they'll take some dry weather and still yield quite well. If you can steer around any dry spells with proper watering, great! The plants need about 3/4-inch of water weekly at the beginning of the season, but they need more — about two inches weekly — when they're in the heat of mid-summer.

As with the Irish potato, if the potato plants must endure a severely fluctuating moisture supply, they'll develop growth cracks. These will heal in time and not damage the cooking quality, but the appearance will definitely suffer.

Mulch can be important for holding moisture and providing the even supply the plants need for best growth. Recently, I heard from a Pennsylvania gardener who puts black plastic over his ridges before planting. He puts the mulch down after a rain, when the soil is moist and plants his slips soon after. The plastic holds in the moisture and traps heat, helping to give the plants the "tropical" atmosphere they love.

Other mulch possibilities are layers of newspaper, leaves, grass clippings, compost or any other organic material that will conserve soil moisture and choke out weeds.

Sidedressing a Must

After the plants take hold but before their vines really start to run along the ground, you should give them more fertilizer as a sidedressing. Try one cup of 5-10-10 per ten to twelve feet of row, applying it thinly on both sides of the ridge. Bonemeal, high in phosphorus, is also good sidedressing fertilizer. Apply one cup for each 20 feet of row.

Extra sidedressings every four or five weeks are important, too, especially if it rains often, because that will wash nutrients down through the soil.

Sweet Potato Rx

The most serious diseases can be avoided by home gardeners by just following sound, sanitary garden practices:

• Use the best quality seed or slips possible. Look for "certified" slips and seed potatoes.

• Try to obtain plants of disease-resistant varieties if possible.

• If you store your own seed stock, keep it away from your kitchen potatoes, so any diseases that strike them won't reach the seed potatoes.

• Consider treating seed stock with a seed protectant or fungicide before bedding them.

• Use clean, pasteurized soil in hotbeds and cold frames if you can. At least change the soil each season, replacing the old soil with soil from a section of garden that hasn't grown sweet potatoes for several years.

• Rotate the crop. Wait three years before planting sweet potatoes back in the same place.

• Till or spade in all crop residues after the harvest to remove breeding grounds for diseases and pests.

• Never use "volunteer" slips that sprout from roots left in the ground after the season.

Diseases

Fusarium (also known as stem rot, yellow blight or blue stem) is one disease common to many gardens. It's caused by a fungus that can live for several years in the soil on decaying vegetation. It can pass from diseased seed stock to the plants. The youngest leaves on the plant lose their vibrant color and turn yellow between the veins. The vines will wilt, and the stems will darken inside, too. Unfortunately, there is no known control. Pull out infected plants to prevent spreading.

Soft Rot or **Rhizopus Rot** attacks the sweet potatoes after harvest. The decay begins in wounds or bruises that haven't healed and quickly claims the whole potato. It shows first as a white, whiskery mold. To avoid, be very careful not to bump or injure sweet potatoes while harvesting. Good curing is necessary, too, to prevent this disease.

Nematode Infection can be a problem in Southern gardens. There are several species of nematodes, microscopic aquatic worms, that can stunt plant growth, kill root systems and cut down on your yield. It's very hard to deal with a bad problem of nematode infestation. Specific rotations of cover crops and vegetable crops and chemicals that fumigate the soil have been used as control measures. But if you are having difficulty with nematode-caused problems, you should ask your local Cooperative Extension Service for advice about handling the situation.

Pests

Several kinds of insects and soil grubs can damage the sweet potato crop, but home gardeners don't usually have any serious problems. In my Vermont garden, for example, **flea beetles** may bother the plants just after I set them out, but that's usually the only trouble I have.

In the southern part of the country, the **sweet potato weevil** and the **sweet potato beetle** are two more common pests. The larvae of the weevils, also known as root borers, eat down through the plant from the stems, tunneling into the roots. Sometimes they'll emerge from sweet potatoes in storage and that's not pleasant. Damaged potatoes have a very bitter taste. Throw them away.

The weevils do not hibernate. To keep them in check, you have to remove their food supply, and the only way to do this is by tilling in or disposing of crop residues after the harvest.

The larvae of the sweet potato beetle feed on the leaves of the plant. Sometimes they eat entire leaves, causing the plants to wilt and die.

Some other pests may damage vines and leaves, but

sweet potato plants grow so fast that for many home gardeners the bugs can't keep up with the leaves.

HARVESTING

Sweet potato plants will grow and grow as long as the weather stays warm. Their vines don't die and signal the harvest time like Irish potatoes. If you have a long growing season, you must keep checking the hills and harvest the roots at the best cooking stage.

A friend of mine in the Deep South remarked that seven-and eight-pound sweet potatoes often show up at the county fair, "They're just roots past the cooking stage that are left in the ground to grow and grow. They get as big as footballs." I guess you could cook those footballs, but who wants to keep the oven on for two or three days?

Gardeners in North Carolina, the biggest sweet potato-producing state, time their plantings so the roots will be good-sized by late September and early October.

This gives them time to harvest before the first frost, so the potatoes are in storage as the weather turns cool.

Frost and cold weather can hurt sweet potatoes at harvest time even though you might think they're insulated underground. When frost kills and blackens the vines above ground, decay can start in on the dead vines and pass down to the roots. A friend from Virginia said that whenever a freeze hits his sweet potato plants, his first chore in the morning is to cut the vines off right above the soil. He says this allows him to leave the potatoes in the ground for a few days longer without injury.

Try to dig the sweet potatoes on a dry, overcast day. Leaving sweet potatoes in direct sun for long can open pathways of infection that will damage the crop in storage. Dig gently around the hills, starting from a few feet away, so as not to slash any wandering roots with your shovel or fork.

Let the potatoes dry on the ground for just a couple of hours. If you dig late in the day, don't leave the roots out overnight; you risk damage from cold weather and moisture, too. Don't wash the potatoes after the harvest.

Sort any badly cut or bruised potatoes to eat first; they won't keep well. Sort the rest according to size in boxes or baskets to cure before storage.

Curing, which is important for sweet potatoes, can be done in about ten to fourteen days simply by keeping them in a warm, dark place with some ventilation. The temperature should be 80 to 85°F if possible, and the humidity should be high, too. Under these conditions, bruises and wounds will heal quickly, sealing out rot organisms.

After curing, put the containers of sweet potatoes in a dry, well-ventilated area at 55 to 60°F with a relative humidity of 75 or 80 percent. If you achieve these ideal conditions, it's possible to keep a mature crop through to the next early harvest.

My root cellar in Vermont is quite cool — it stays well below 55° most of the time, a temperature great for most vegetables, but definitely not sweet potatoes. They will spoil in a short time in cool storage. My wife, Jan, and I prefer to cook our sweet potato harvest and freeze it. We find that's easiest.

Sweet potatoes bruise easily and can suffer quickly when manhandled in storage. I know a gardener who enforces a household rule that once any sweet potato in storage is touched, it must be cooked and eaten. "Never turn or pick over the potatoes," she says. The less you handle the crop, the better off you'll be.

POTATO MOUNDS

A gardener in the South showed me how he builds old-time mounds to store his crop. Mounds are small, outdoor storage houses which used to be a backyard feature of many small farms. These are his directions:

Choose a well-drained spot in or near the garden. If it has some protection from wind, say a nearby fence or barn, that is excellent. Lay down eight to ten inches of wheat straw and then carefully pile the cured sweet potatoes in a cone or pyramid. In the old days, mounds were often quite tall, but three to four feet is a good height for your first one. Then cover the pile of potatoes

with a very heavy coat of wheat straw. Then, as best you can, cover the whole thing with about two to three inches of dirt. Then stack some boards around it and fasten them at the top so they won't blow down. The boards will keep rain from washing the dirt off and ruining the insulation.

Usually you can dig into a mound for a weeklong supply of potatoes without harming the remaining ones. Because of the variable weather, you will probably lose some potatoes to rot, but if you start with a large supply, that needn't be a worry.

Garden
to
Kitchen

Potatoes, both Irish and sweet, are versatile year-round vegetables that deserve lots more eating. Potatoes are lower in calories and better for you than rice, pasta or bread. So, even if you're watching your weight, you can still enjoy potatoes.

Since potatoes store so well, we have always considered them a staple. They can be served very simply or with lots of embellishment at nearly every meal. The recipes are unlimited.

I've included basic cooking techniques, some classics, my own specialties and some new potato recipes I've discovered that I think you'll enjoy. I've also listed ingredients that are tasty accompaniments for potatoes, and know you'll be inspired to create your own special dishes.

Many of the recipes call for white potatoes. But, often sweet potatoes can be substituted with delicious results. When you see (***SP),** you'll know that the recipe is also good substituting sweet potatoes. Happy cooking and good eating to you!

Freezing and Canning

White Potatoes: We don't freeze or can white potatoes because our root cellar keeps them in perfect condition all winter with no work! We have tried canning potatoes, but it really seems like too much time and effort, and the results are seldom up to par.

Home freezers aren't equipped to adequately process raw potatoes the way commerical freezing operations do, and some people feel that frozen, cooked white potatoes are watery.

Sweet Potatoes: Here in Vermont, sweet potatoes don't keep especially well in our cool root cellar, although they do fine further south. So, we peel, cube and boil our sweet potatoes until tender for freezing. To keep sweet potatoes from darkening, dip sliced or cubed potatoes in a solution of 1/2 cup lemon juice and one quart water; or for mashed sweet potatoes, mix 2 tablespoons of orange or lemon juice in each quart of potatoes. Pack in rigid containers leaving 1/2-inch headspace, label, date and freeze.

Potato Cooking Basics

Although there are many potato varieties, there are really only three types you need to consider when it's time for cooking. Sweet, new white (Irish), and mature white. If you have a choice, use small, waxy, new potatoes for boiling and salads, because they hold their shape when cooked.

Use mature white potatoes for baking, mashing and French frying to take advantage of their dry, mealy texture.

Although there is a difference between "boiling" and "baking" potatoes, don't let it prevent you from trying certain recipes if you have the "wrong" potato on hand. Either will be fine for most recipes.

Whether you bake, boil, mash or fry your potatoes, here are some secrets that will make every dish better. Always sort potatoes according to size, and use similar-sized potatoes in each recipe, so they'll cook uniformly. Scrub potatoes carefully just before you cook them. Whenever possible, include the skins as part of the eating. Potato skins are high in vitamins and as long as they're well-scrubbed, they're delicious.

Most of all, use your imagination! Potatoes go well with many foods, and it's fun to try new combinations. Here are just a few good Irish potato partners. . .

Bacon bits	Curry powder	Mint
Basil	Dill weed	Mustard
Bread crumbs	French dressing	Olive oil
Broccoli	Freshly ground pepper	Onions
Butter	Garlic	Paprika
Carrots	Grated cheese	Parsley
Catsup	Horseradish	Peas
Celery seed	Leeks	Salt pork
Chives	Lemon juice	Sour cream
Cottage cheese	Margarine	Tarragon
Cream	Mayonnaise	Yogurt

FAVORITE RECIPES

Boiled New Potatoes

Allow 4 to 6 new potatoes per person. Scrub well and place in enough boiling, salted water to just cover potatoes. Boil until fork tender, about 20 minutes. Drain well. To dry potatoes after draining, shake them in a pan over low heat for a minute or two.

Place potatoes in a serving dish and toss lightly with butter or margarine, parsley, or your own special topping.

Note: When boiling larger potatoes (*SP), allow more cooking time, about 30 to 35 minutes. If you're in a hurry, cut big potatoes in halves or quarters and boil for 15 to 20 minutes.

Perfect Baked Potatoes

Select mature, well-shaped, firm potatoes (*SP) for baking and allow one medium potato per person. Wash potatoes well, scrubbing off dirt and any sprouts on the skin. Dry.

Some cooks wrap potatoes in foil before baking. This is a good idea if you want to roast potatoes over hot coals for a barbeque or clam bake, or if you want to keep oven-baked potatoes hot for some time before serving. The foil keeps in heat and moisture, which is why restaurants often cook their potatoes in foil. Foil-wrapped potatoes, however, tend to become soggy because the foil holds in most of the steam that builds up during cooking. For flaky, crisp-skinned potatoes, don't use foil.

Grease the skins lightly with vegetable oil, butter or bacon fat and pierce the potato once or twice with a fork allowing the steam to escape.

Set potatoes on the middle rack of a preheated 375° oven and bake 60 to 75 minutes, depending on the size. Potatoes are done when they are fork-tender or soft to the touch.

French Fried Potatoes

6   medium potatoes (*SP)
1 to 2   pints salad oil, lard or shortening
Salt to taste

Pare potatoes, cut into lengthwise strips 1/4 to 3/8 inch wide. Dry on paper towels.

Fill deep fat fryer or large saucepan 1/2 full with oil. Heat to 375°F. Fill basket 1/4 full with potatoes. Slowly set in hot fat. If fat bubbles excessively, raise and lower basket several times. Keep potatoes separated with a slotted spoon.

Fry 5 to 7 minutes or until potatoes are golden brown. Drain on paper towels or absorbent paper bags. Sprinkle with salt and keep hot while you continue frying rest of potatoes. Serves 4 to 6.

* Also good using sweet potatoes.

Double French Fries

These potatoes retain their crispness longer.

Place cut strips in pan of ice water. Preblanch strips (drained and free of most moisture) at 375°F in good cooking oil (pure beef fat is best for superior taste) until strips feel spongy when pinched but are still white in color.

Spread on paper towels in pan and allow to cool completely. You can even refrigerate well in advance of using them.

Drop blanched strips into frying basket and cook at 375°F until they rise to surface and take on a golden brown color. Sprinkle with salt and serve.

Potatoes McManus

8 medium potatoes, peeled
8 medium onions
1/2 lb butter
2-3 cups cream/milk mixture
    salt
    freshly ground black pepper

Chop the onions and potatoes together. It's important to chop rather than slice them; it gives them a different flavor and better texture. Place chopped potatoes and onions in heavy, deep casserole. Add butter, plus milk/cream mixture almost to cover potatoes. The more cream you use, the richer the dish. Add salt to taste.

Here's the key. Add more pepper than you dare: either until your arm gets tired from grinding the pepper mill, or until black pepper specks turn up in each spoonful of potatoes.

Bake uncovered in 350°F oven for an hour or more, until the top is bubbly and brown and the potatoes are tender. If you need to keep them cooking, simply turn down the heat. If they start to dry out, just add more milk.

Serves 8.

Scalloped Potatoes

4 cups potatoes, peeled and thinly sliced (*SP)
1/4 cup chopped onion
1/4 cup flour
    salt and pepper
1/4 cup margarine
2 1/2 cups milk
    cracker or bread crumbs
1 1/2 cup cooked ham, chopped (optional)

Arrange a layer of potatoes in greased 2-quart casserole dish. Sprinkle with 1 Tb each of onion, flour, and margarine plus a dash of salt and pepper. Continue layering potatoes and remaining ingredients until you have about four layers. Heat milk to scalding and pour over potato layers. Sprinkle crumbs on top. Bake in 350°F oven for 1 1/2 hours. Let stand 10 minutes before serving. Serves 4 to 6.

Tomatoed Potatoes: For a colorful variation, substitute canned tomatoes for milk in the recipe above.

* Also good using sweet potatoes.

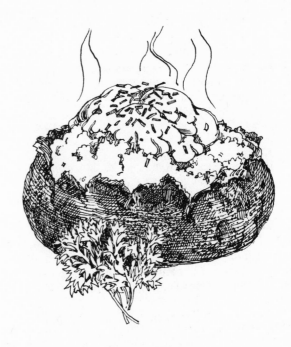

Baked Potatoes Sublime

6 hot baked potatoes
2 (4 1/2 -ounce) cans tiny shrimp
2 Tb butter or margarine
2 egg yolks, beaten
1/2 cup heavy cream
1/2 tsp salt
1/2 cup sour cream
1/8 tsp ground ginger
6 drops Tabasco sauce
1 Tb fresh parsley, crumbled

Drain shrimp, saving liquid. Set shrimp aside. Combine 1/4 cup reserved liquid and butter in a small saucepan over low heat. Stir in egg yolks and cream and cook, stirring constantly, until slightly thickened.

Remove from heat and stir in salt, sour cream, ginger, Tabasco and parsley. Cook over low heat 5 minutes. Stir in shrimp.

Split potatoes open and spoon a heaping tablespoon of sauce over each potato. Serve immediately. Serves 6.

One-Pot Potato Supper

6 to 8 small new potatoes
1/2 to 1 lb. salt pork — sliced to the rind (or use ham)
1 to 2 pints vegetables: peas, beans or greens

Cook salt pork 1 to 1 1/2 hours in large pan with water to cover. Do not drain. To this add washed potatoes. Cook until tender. Add fresh or frozen vegetables, cover and simmer until the vegetables are cooked through.

Place meat and vegetables on a serving platter. Sprinkle with chopped parsley. Serves 4 to 6.

Potato Salad

5 or 6   medium boiling potatoes
3 to 5   hard-cooked eggs, chopped
1/2   cup minced onion
1/2   cup celery, chopped
1/2 to 3/4   cup mayonnaise
    salt and pepper to taste
    paprika

Boil potatoes until tender, drain and peel while they're still hot. Hold hot potatoes on a fork for easy, painless peeling. Cut into cubes and toss all the salad ingredients together except paprika.

Chill salad for at least 1 hour to allow flavors to blend. Sprinkle with paprika and serve. Serves 4 to 6.

For lively color and texture, add assorted chopped vegetables: carrots, cucumbers, green peppers, corn, radishes, dill pickles, olives, tomatoes, peas or green beans.

For extra zip spice up your favorite potato salad dressing with a little grated horseradish, prepared or dried mustard, cayenne pepper, Tabasco sauce or pickle juice.

Just for fun, leave the skins on the potatoes. The appearance takes a little getting used to, but the skins add a great taste!

Variations:

French Potato Salad — Marinate cooked potatoes, raw celery, onions and eggs in 1/2 cup warm French dressing for 1 hour. Serve as is, or stir in 1/2 cup mayonnaise.

German Potato Salad — Use 1/2 to 3/4 cup sour cream instead of mayonnaise. Or, combine sour cream and mayonnaise.

Hot German Potato Salad

6   medium potatoes
5 or 6   slices bacon
1/2   cup chopped onion
1 to 2   Tb flour
2   Tb sugar
1   tsp salt
1/2   tsp celery seed
    Dash pepper
2/3   cup water
1/3   cup vinegar

Wash, peel and cook potatoes in salted, boiling water for 30 to 35 minutes, or until tender. Drain and set aside.

Fry bacon in skillet until crisp. Drain on paper towel. Cook and stir onion in bacon drippings until tender. Stir in flour, sugar, salt, celery seed and pepper. Cook over low heat until smooth and bubbly. Gradually stir in water and vinegar, being careful not to let mixture burn. Stirring constantly, bring mixture to a boil. Boil for 1 minute. Crumble bacon and stir into hot mixture. Slice potatoes thin or cut in cubes. Pour hot dressing over potatoes and toss until lightly coated and heated through. Serves 4 to 6.

George's Potatoes

This is a specialty of a bachelor friend of ours who says, "It's quite easy, but when you take it out of the oven, it looks like it took a lot of work."

6   large potatoes
2   cups large-curd cottage cheese
1   cup sour cream
1   clove garlic, mashed
1   tsp salt
3   to 4 scallions, finely chopped
1   cup grated Cheddar cheese
    paprika and parsley flakes

Boil potatoes until slightly tender, about 10 minutes. Drain, cube and place in buttered casserole dish. Combine cottage cheese, sour cream, garlic, salt and scallions. Toss cheese mixture with potatoes until well mixed. Top with grated Cheddar cheese. Lightly sprinkle paprika and parsley on top. Bake at 350° for 30 minutes. Serves 6 to 8.

Duchess Potatoes

These are delicious and decorative mashed potatoes for garnishing meat and fish dishes.

6   medium potatoes
1/4   cup butter
3   egg yolks, beaten
3 to 4   Tb milk or cream
    Salt and pepper to taste
Optional seasoning: pinch of nutmeg, chives or dry mustard

Peel, boil, drain, dry, and whip potatoes until absolutely smooth. Add remaining ingredients and season to taste. Mound potatoes around edge of a heat-proof serving dish and brown in the oven or under a broiler. Sprinkle mixture with grated cheese, melted butter or beaten egg yolk for a rich glaze, if desired.

If you have a pastry bag, use a fluted nozzle to shape ruffles, rosettes or wavy scallops. Potatoes must be warm to do this. To keep them warm until you're ready to use the mixture, partially cover the potato pan and set it in a pan of hot water. Stir frequently with a wooden spoon. Serves 4 or 5.

Potato Nest

Use Duchess potatoes to turn every-day hamburger into something special.

- 1 lb. ground beef
- 1/4 cup chopped onion
- 1 Tb Worcestershire sauce
- salt and pepper to taste
- 3 Tb flour
- 1 1/2 cups water
- 4 cups hot Duchess potatoes, arranged around serving platter

Combine meat, onion, Worcestershire sauce, salt and pepper in a large skillet and cook until meat is browned and onion is tender. Mix flour with water and stir into meat mixture. Simmer, stirring occasionally, until gravy is thickened.

Spoon meat mixture into the potato nest. Serves 6.

Potato Bread

- 4 medium potatoes
- 1 quart water
- 3 Tb sugar
- 2 packages active dry yeast
- 7 to 8 cups flour
- 1 Tb margarine, melted
- 2 tsp salt

Wash, peel and cut potatoes in 1-inch cubes. Boil in 1 quart water with salt in a covered pot until potatoes are tender, about 15 minutes. While potatoes and water cool, combine sugar and yeast in measuring cup. Place lukewarm potatoes and water in blender or through a sieve until blended smooth. Add yeast mixture and 4 cups flour. Let stand a few minutes to let the dough rest.

Add remaining flour. Turn out onto floured board and knead until dough is light and elastic, about 10 minutes.

Place dough in a greased bowl, turning over once to grease top. Cover and let rise in a warm place until doubled in bulk, about 1 1/2 hours.

Knead dough slightly and shape into loaves. Place in greased loaf pans. Cover and let rise until double, about 40 minutes. Bake in preheated 400°F oven for 10 minutes, then lower heat to 350°F and continue baking for 50 minutes. Makes 3 medium loaves.

Potato Rolls: After first rising, shape dough into rolls. Arrange rolls in greased 9 × 9-inch baking pans, cover and let rise until doubled in bulk. Bake at 425° for 12 to 15 minutes. Brush tops of rolls with melted butter, turn onto wire racks and cool. Makes 2 1/2 dozen rolls.

Soup Stock

When you peel potatoes, save the skins to make soup stock. Simmer peels alone, with other vegetable scraps, beef or chicken bones, or with herbs and spices. The result will be your own delicately flavored, golden brown broth.

Peels from 6 to 8 medium potatoes, well-washed
- 1 1/2 quarts water
- 1 onion
- salt and pepper
- 1 bay leaf (Use dill weed, basil or other spices according to your tastes.)

Simmer all ingredients in covered pot over low heat at least 1 1/2 hours.

Tips: If you don't have time to make soup when you have the ingredients available, start a "stock pile" in your freezer. When you have vegetable or meat parts you'd like to save for stock, put them in a plastic freezer bag. Keep adding to the bag until you're ready to put the stock pot on the stove. Don't thaw the ingredients, just drop them into the pot of water and simmer.

To create your own bouillon cubes, pour cooled, strained stock into ice cube trays and freeze. Pop the cubes into freezer bags or containers and use whenever a recipe calls for broth. Don't dilute with water or you'll reduce flavor.

Another convenience in making soup stock is a slow-cooking crock pot. Follow the manufacturer's directions for use in making soups.

I use potato peel soup stock instead of water in all my favorite soup recipes. It's especially good in Easy Vichyssoise (see chapter on onions) and as the base for stormy day chowders.

Potato Pizza

- 2 cups mashed potatoes, still warm or reheated
- 3/4 cup flour
- salt and pepper to taste
- 6 Tb vegetable oil
- 2 cups tomato sauce
- 1/2 lb mozzarella cheese, sliced thin
- 1/3 cup grated Parmesan cheese
- 1 Tb chopped, fresh basil

Preheat oven to 350°F. Combine potatoes, salt, pepper, flour and 2 TB oil. Work mixture to a smooth, spreadable dough. Pat dough to 1/2-inch thickness and place in a greased 9-inch pie pan. Spread 2 Tb oil over potato shell. Cover with tomato sauce, mozzarella and Parmesan cheese, in that order.

Sprinkle with basil and remaining 2 Tb oil. Bake for 20 minutes or until cheese has melted. Brown cheese under broiler for 1 minute, if desired. Serves 6.

Spring Garden Supper

As soon as our first peas and new tiny red potatoes are ready, I invite a few friends for this chicken supper to celebrate the early harvest.

    6   Tb margarine
    1   cut up broiler-fryer chicken (2-2 1/2 lbs.)
    1   lb small new potatoes
        salt and pepper to taste
    2   Tb lemon juice
    3   green top onions, chopped
    2   cups fresh peas, shelled
  1/4   cup chopped fresh parsley
    1   cup sour cream
    1   tsp thyme leaves, crushed
  1/2   tsp salt
  1/4   tsp pepper
        parsley for garnish

Scrub potatoes and peel a strip around the centers for a special look. Melt margarine in large pan. Add chicken and potatoes and brown slowly on all sides. Season with salt and pepper. Sprinkle chicken with lemon juice. Reduce heat, cover and simmer for 30 minutes.

Move chicken and potatoes aside and stir in onions. Sprinkle peas and parsley over chicken and potatoes, cover again, and simmer 10 minutes or until chicken and potatoes are tender.

Remove chicken and vegetables to serving platter and keep warm. Remove pan from heat, and add sour cream, thyme, salt and pepper.

Stir and mix well to loosen drippings. Pour over chicken or serve as gravy. Garnish with parsley and serve immediately. Serves 4.

Potato Stuffing

This recipe came from Dick's mother, and it's a must for all bird and pork dishes at our house.

    4   cups mashed potatoes
    3   cups crumbled, dry bread crumbs and 1 Tb poultry
        seasoning/or 3 cups Bell's Stuffing Mix
  1/2   cup margarine
    1   cup minced onion
  1/2   cup chopped celery
    2   eggs
        salt and pepper to taste
    1   cup milk or water

Mix potato, stuffing mix, milk and eggs. Hold back on the salt if you use ready-made stuffing; they often have plenty. Sauté onion and celery in margarine until tender. Add to the potato mixture. Use this mixture to stuff chicken or turkey. I often bake it separately. To do this, place the stuffing in a greased casserole dish and bake at 350°F for 30 minutes.

Hash Browns

    4   medium potatoes (*SP)
    2   Tb chopped onion
  1/2   tsp salt
  1/8   tsp pepper
    2   Tb margarine or butter
    2   Tb bacon drippings or oil

Wash and cook potatoes in salted boiling water. Cool slightly and shred to make 4 cups.

Toss potatoes lightly with onion, salt and pepper. Melt margarine or butter and oil in skillet. Pack potato mixture firmly in skillet leaving a space around edge for turning.

Cook over low heat 10 to 15 minutes or until bottom is browned. Cut in fourths and turn each section. Add a little oil if necessary. Cook until brown. Serve hot with eggs or sausage for breakfast. Serves 4.

If you want the hash browns to be in one piece, loosen around the edges with a spatula and invert onto a plate. Slide potatoes back into skillet and brown other side.

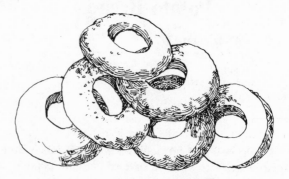

Quick Mashed Potato Doughnuts

An overnight guest would be really surprised to have these for breakfast. They're wonderful.

  3/4   cup hot mashed potatoes
  3/4   cup sugar
  3/4   cup milk
    1   egg plus 1 egg yolk
2 1/2   cups flour
    1   tsp baking powder
  1/2   tsp salt
  1/4   tsp nutmeg

Dissolve sugar in hot mashed potatoes. Add other ingredients and mix until thoroughly blended. Roll out and flatten to 1/2-inch thickness. Cut with floured doughnut cutter and fry at 375°F until golden brown. Drain on absorbent paper and cool on wire rack. Makes about 1 dozen doughnuts.

If possible, serve these doughnuts warm. Sprinkle with cinnamon sugar, top with a scoop of vanilla ice cream or dip in a sugar glaze or chocolate frosting.

Vermont Potato Pancakes

4   large potatoes, peeled and grated (*SP)
1/4   lb. Cheddar cheese
1   medium onion, grated
2   eggs
3   oz cream cheese, softened
3   Tb flour
1/4   cup milk
1   tsp salt
1/8   tsp pepper
    oil for frying

Wrap potatoes in a clean dish towel and wring the towel to remove excess moisture. Toss potatoes with Cheddar cheese and onion in a large bowl.

Beat eggs and cream cheese until smooth. Stir into potato mixture. Add flour, milk, salt and pepper and mix thoroughly.

Heat oil in large skillet. Spoon mixture into pan to form 3-inch pancakes, 1/4-inch thick. Cook a few minutes until brown on the bottom. Turn and brown on the other side. Serve with maple syrup, applesauce or fruit preserves. Makes about 20 pancakes.

* Also goes with sweet potatoes.

Sweet Potatoes Go with . . .

Allspice	Cream sherry	Nutmeg
Almonds	Ginger	Orange juice
Apples	Green peppers	Pecans
Brown sugar	Honey	Pineapple
Butter	Ice cream	'Possum (of course!)
Cinnamon	Maple syrup	Raisins
Cloves	Margarine	Rum
Coconut	Marshmallows	Walnuts
Cranberry sauce	Molasses	Whipped cream

Sweet Potato Bake

This is always a special treat at our house on our holiday dinner table.

3   cups sweet potatoes, peeled, cooked and sliced
1/2   cup flour
1/2   cup brown sugar
1/2   cup quick oats
1/4   cup margarine
1 1/2   cups miniature marshmallows
1   tsp cinnamon

Combine flour, brown sugar, oats, cinnamon and margarine. Mix until it resembles coarse crumbs. Combine one-half of the sugar mixture with the sweet potatoes. Place in 1 1/2-quart casserole dish. Top with remaining sugar mixture. Bake in 350° over for 30 minutes.

Sprinkle marshmallows over casserole. Broil until marshmallows are partially melted and lightly browned. Serves 6.

Sweet Potato Kabobs

2   large sweet potatoes
2   apples, cored and cubed
1   green pepper, cut in 1-inch pieces
1/4   cup vegetable oil
3/4   cup pineapple chunks
1   cup cooked ham, lamb or chicken, cubed
1/4   cup maple syrup or molasses

Peel and parboil potatoes seven to ten minutes. Drain and cool slightly. Cut in 1-inch cubes. Arrange on metal skewers with cubes of raw apples and green pepper. Brush with oil and place skewers on oiled baking sheets. Broil 5 minutes, keeping skewers at least 5 inches from flame to keep pepper from scorching.

Thread pineapple chunks and meat cubes on ends of skewers and continue broiling under low heat until potatoes are tender and meat is heated through, about 10 minutes. During last minute of cooking, brush with maple syrup or molasses for a sweet, brown glaze. Serve on a bed or rice. Serves 4 to 6.

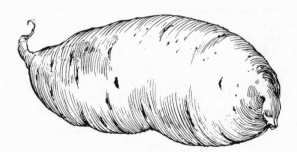

Scalloped
Sweet Potatoes & Apples

This is a harvest favorite at our house.

  6   medium sweet potatoes, cooked, peeled and sliced
1/2   cup brown sugar
1 1/2 cups sliced apples
1/2   tsp salt
1/2   tsp mace
  2   Tb butter or margarine

Combine sugar, salt and mace. In greased casserole dish, alternate layers of potatoes and apples. Sprinkle each layer with sugar mixture. Finish with a layer of apples and the sugar mixture. Dot with butter, cover and bake in 350°F oven about 50 minutes. Serves 6.

Variation: Substitute 1 cup pineapple chunks for apples. Pour 3/4 cup pineapple juice over all the layers, dot with butter, cover and bake.

Deluxe Sweet Potato Pie

The coconut and cream make this Southern dish into a prize-winning dessert!

  2   cups cooked, mashed sweet potatoes
  3   eggs
1/3   cup honey
1/4   cup brown sugar
  1   tsp salt
  1   tsp cinnamon
1/2   tsp nutmeg
1/4   tsp ginger
1/8   tsp cloves
  1   cup light cream or evaporated milk
1 1/2 cups flaked coconut
  1   unbaked 9-inch pie crust

In large bowl, beat eggs with honey, sugar, salt and spices. Add sweet potatoes and cream and mix well. Fold in coconut and turn mixture into unbaked pie crust. Bake in 350° oven for 50 minutes or until pie is thoroughly set. Serve with whipped cream.

Index

OTHER GARDEN WAY BOOKS
YOU WILL ENJOY